Building Search Applications

Lucene, LingPipe, and Gate

Manu Konchady

Mustru Publishing,
Oakton, Virginia.

Building Search Applications: Lucene, LingPipe and Gate
by Manu Konchady

 Mustru Publishing,
3112 Bradford Wood Court,
Oakton, VA 22124.
http://mustru.sf.net

Cover design: Renuka Konchady

Copyright © 2008 by Manu Konchady
First Edition, ISBN: 978-0-61520-425-3
Printed in the United States of America

Library of Congress Catalog Card No.: 2008927106

Contents

iv

Preface

The need for better search applications has become more urgent with the rapid growth of online information. New content is created and old content is rarely deleted. The result is that information (email, Web pages, and online documents) accumulates over time and it is not unusual for even a medium sized organization to have several terabytes of stored content.

Search applications not only have to find useful information in a massive data collection, but also perform the search in a reasonably short time. The term *Search 2.0* has been used to described a new generation of high performance search applications that go beyond a simple list of results. We will explain the use of open source tools in this book to build these types of search applications.

The expectations of most users of the Web has risen following the use of large scale Web search engines and the ability to search for information in a fraction of a second is taken for granted. Unfortunately, not all organizations can achieve this level of performance and frequently users are left wondering why it is so much easier to find information on the Web and not on a relatively smaller intranet or even the desktop.

High performance hardware alone is not the answer to this problem. There is a need to build a search application that will search, suggest, visualize, and combine the results from many information sources to present an easy to use and coherent view of available online information. This book covers several open source tools to build search applications including search engines, classifiers, and Web crawlers. The first four chapters cover the tools needed to build a search engine. The standard search engine features including spelling correction, a term highlighter, and links to related information are implemented. The remaining six chapters implement functions such as extractors and classifiers to supplement a list of search results. The final chapter illustrates ways to combine the results from many sources to present a potentially more useful view of information than just a plain list of hits.

Audience

This book is primarily for readers who need to build search applications. It is also for anyone who wants to learn about some of the popular open source tools to manage information. The code examples are written in Java and at least a beginner's knowledge of Java is needed to understand the code. The Java source code for the examples in the book will be distributed along with third party `jar` files. All the `jar` files used in the book are taken from open source projects. We will cover the APIs of the high performance tools such as Lucene and LingPipe and explain the use of multiple tools to build a search application.

You do not need a strong background in mathematics or natural language processing to use the tools mentioned in the book. But, it does help to have some knowledge of probability to understand the results from these tools. The mathematics behind LingPipe includes topics from probability, statistics, and information theory. This book does not cover the theory behind these tools and several references are included in the Appendix. A brief description of Bayes classifiers is included in Appendix B, since it has been mentioned often in the book. Most of the equations used in the book are fairly simple.

The book focuses less on the theory and more on how tools can be used to build applications. The code examples although basic, can be easily extended to build useful applications. In many examples, the performance of tools is evaluated, but the evaluation of large scale search applications is beyond the scope of this book.

Organization

The first chapter begins with a description of the information overload problem and a set of sample search applications. The second chapter starts at the lowest level of text processing - tokenization. Several methods of tokenizing text are shown and some of the problems of identifying tokens are identified.

In the third chapter, the first part of building a search engine, indexing is described. The Lucene search engine API is used to implement an index from a collection of documents. This chapter also covers the maintenance, performance, and use of a search engine index. The use of a database in association with the index to build a more efficient search application is included.

The fourth chapter covers the second part of building a search engine, the search interface. This interface is the visible part of the search engine and provides simple ways to find information. The query syntax in Lucene is broad to build a large range of queries, many of which will be covered. Further ranking, an important issue in search engines will also be explained in some detail.

Search engines build indexes by tokenizing the text extracted from documents. However, usually no meaning is assigned to any of the tokens. The meaning of a noun could be a place name, a person, an organization, or any other type of entity. This type of information extraction is time consuming and not performed by all search engines. However, the use of entity extraction can lead to more precise results from a search engine.

Two methods of extracting entities will be implemented in Chapter 5 and a method to find key phrases in a document will also be shown. A part of speech (POS) tagger assigns a POS to individual words in a text chunk. This is useful when we would like to identify the nouns or adjectives in a sentence.

The sixth and seventh chapters explain methods to organize a collection of documents. The two well-known methods of organizing documents are clustering and categorization. The first method, clustering, assumes no prior knowledge of the contents of the document collection and builds a set of groups by finding documents that are more similar to each other in the group, than with all other documents. The second method uses a pre-defined taxonomy of categories to which documents are assigned. A document can be assigned to one or more categories based on the degree of closeness between the document and the category.

In Chapter 8, the link structure and social networks on Web is described. Although the Web appears to be a disorganized collection of information, there is a well-defined structure in the billions of links embedded in Web pages. These links provide an underlying graph structure to identify authoritative sources. We will examine the Web as a graph and look at the use of a popular open source crawler, Nutch, to build a search engine for an Intranet or a Desktop.

Information from some Web pages, such as blogs or news sites is in constant flux. Monitoring these pages is of importance to companies and individuals, since the news published on such pages may have a substantial impact on a company's product or services. Chapter 9 explains methods to detect the sentiment in text and detect plagiarism.

The final chapter concludes with some of the recent developments in building more usable search applications. Future Web applications should be able to answer simple and complex questions that may involve compiling lists, information analysis, and ranking that are currently being performed manually. However, the reasons why this task is difficult will be explained and the implementation of a meta search engine will be shown.

Conventions

The following typographical conventions are used in the book.

`Constant Width:` Indicates file names, variable names, classes, objects, command line statements, and any other code fragment.

Italics: Indicates proper names such as the names of persons, books, titles, or quoted sentence fragments.

`ConstantWidthBold:` Indicates an URL, email address, or a directory name.

Bold: Indicates header or title text such as the column names of a table.

Math : Indicates an inline math formula or a numbered math equation.

Getting Started

This book assumes a beginner's knowledge of Java. All of the code examples in this book are written in Java and use third party open source code to build search applications. The Eclipse IDE (`http://www.eclipse.org`) was used in the development of the code, but is not necessary to run the code. Some familiarity with Ant (`http://ant.apache.org`) and JUnit (`http://www.junit.org`) is also assumed. The sample code for each chapter is saved in a separate package. Import statements and exception code is not included for the sake of brevity. You can run the sample code included in this book on a machine with 128 megabytes of memory and a small hard disk. However, if you plan on building applications that will process many gigabytes of text, you will need a reasonably fast machine with at least 256 megabytes of memory. The sample code used in all chapters of this book can be downloaded from `http://mustru.sf.net`.

You will need to download the Java Runtime (JRE) that includes the core Java Virtual Machine (JVM) classes and supporting files (from `http://java.sun.com`) to run the sample code. The `jar` files that are needed to run the examples are included with the sample code. New versions of the `jar` files may be available by the time you run the sample code and may have features to achieve the same functions in different ways or more efficiently. Sample data files used in this book are provided for experimental purposes and any other use of this data may be allowed depending on the software license. In some cases, large datasets that were used to test the code will not be included. Instead, links to sites from where these and other datasets can be downloaded will be mentioned.

If you are not familiar with Java, you can run the examples in this book to get a feel for the types of search applications that can be built and evaluate the performance of such applications. Java also provides support to build a mixed programming language application. You can call Java methods from a C or C++ program using the Java Native Interface (JNI). Other methods, include protocols to connect a scripting language like PHP with a JVM using a Java bridge. This allows you to use PHP to build a Web application with a Java-based search engine API like Lucene (see Chapters 3 and 4).

Support

Visit `http://mustru.sf.net` to download the sample code used in this book. The sample code is written in Java and is organized in packages by chapter. A cross reference table of the listings and the classes is included in Appendix A. Please report bugs, errors, and questions to `mkonchady@yahoo.com`. Bugs in the code will be corrected and posted in a new version of the sample code. Your feedback is valuable and will be incorporated into subsequent versions of the book. Please contact the author, if you would like more information on some topics that have not been covered or explained in sufficient detail. I have attempted to make the contents of the book comprehensible and correct. Any errors or omissions in the book are mine alone. The accompanying code is for demonstrative purposes.

Acknowledgements

First, I would like to thank the developers of the open source tools Lucene, LingPipe, and Gate who have made this book possible. It goes without saying that open source code has made life a lot easier for software developers.

I particularly would like to express my gratitude to Bob Carpenter for his valuable and detailed comments. I am also indebted to Steven Rowe and Tyler Ortman for their feedback on the manuscript. I also thank Linda Lee of Oracle Corporation for her comments on the Berkeley DB.

Finally, I thank my wife Renuka and children Tarini and Jatin who supported and encouraged me to finish this project.

1 Information Overload

The growing capacities of hard disks have made it possible to store terabytes of information on a single PC. Add the seemingly infinite information available on the Web, and it is easy to feel overwhelmed with information. In 1983, Gerald Salton, the father of information retrieval (IR), predicted a time when people would be forced to use information that was easily available and ignore the rest.

Long before the ubiquitous Web search engine, there were information retrieval systems that ran on large mainframes, and as a result, access to information was expensive and limited to a privileged few. Salton's prediction has come true today; the costly IR systems of the past have been replaced by Google and other modern search engines that provide worldwide access to several terabytes of information in seconds. The analysis of large search engine logs has shown that most searchers do not view more than one page of results and use fairly simple queries. Still, there is little doubt of the benefits of having almost freely available, instant access to such huge volumes of information.

However, search engines do have limitations. The user interface for a search engine has not changed significantly since the 1970s. The standard interface, a boolean query[1] is not intuitive for the casual user. It is somewhat unnatural to specify a request for information in the form of a set of keywords and operators. An expert user, who knows the correct keywords and operators to use when creating a query can interactively fine tune a query to precisely find the right information source. But the casual user is left to infer which keywords best state a request for information and how they should be combined with operators to form the most appropriate query. A beginner researching a topic is unlikely to know the relevant terminology to use as keywords and will most likely not immediately find the best information source. The use of very common English keywords in a query, such as *run* and *line* that have over 30 different meanings in a dictionary, will return a wide range of results.

---

[1]A boolean query consists of the terms and operators entered in a search box.

Many queries are requests for information on a person, topic, or company. These requests are easy to state in the form of a set of keywords and current Web search engines do return relevant results for such queries. For example, the question *What is the capital of Iceland?* is easily translated to a boolean query *capital AND Iceland*. The question *What are the effects of DDT in South Asia?* is more complex and could be translated to the query *("DDT's effects" OR "effects of DDT") AND "South Asia"* which may give different results from a query formed by simply listing the content words – *effects DDT South Asia*. Finally, the question *Which companies manufacture Ethanol and where are they located?* may require more than one boolean query. It still takes some human effort to manually scan document lists, collect, organize, and analyze information. Search engines also control the view of the Web seen by the searcher by ranking some documents higher than others.

The keyword-directed approach to find information is based strictly on the appearance of the identical query keywords in the text of matching documents. The wrong keywords can quickly lead searchers astray, possibly causing them to give up the search. On average, an English word has two or more synonyms, while slang words may have ten or more synonyms. There is a need to match documents in a collection not just by keywords, but also by metadata that defines the meaning of the document in terms known to the user. In addition, documents usually do not exist in isolation, and in a large collection there will be many implicit and explicit links between documents. Incoming and outgoing hyperlinks, as well as bibliographies, end notes, and works cited can be exploited to find information sources more precisely related to the query at hand.

A natural interface to access the information in a collection of documents is to simply ask questions. There are innumerable ways to ask a question and the methods to extract the correct answer from a mass of information are not well-defined; making computers understand natural language questions is a difficult task indeed. Metadata that supplements the source's contents, as well as methods to accurately translate questions to search engine queries, are needed to find answers. For example, the most likely sentence to contain an answer for the question - *How many calories are there in a Big Mac?* should contain a numeric value and match one or more phrases from the question. The metadata created to answer such questions will identify numeric values, person names, and places.

Such factoid questions can be answered in a single word or a short phrase, but definition or list questions are harder to answer. The answers to questions such as - *List the Textile companies in South Carolina* or *What is the golden parachute?* are complex and require more than one sentence. The search engine must find the potential answer sentences and compile the list into a single coherent answer.

1.1 Information Sources

We collect information from all types of sources including the Web, personal digital assistants, cell phones, and other media (such as CD-ROMs or DVDs). A study published by the University of California Berkeley (`http://www2.sims.berkeley.edu/research/projects/how-much-info-2003/`) estimated that 4.6 million terabytes of new information was produced in 2002 in magnetic media(includes text and multimedia data). A small fraction of the information in magnetic media is text-based. Imagine if every person wrote a book that was converted to a file of about 2.5 megabytes, we would have generated 15,000 terabytes of information (assuming a population of six billion people). Other interesting statistics include the estimated size of the visible or surface Web, the size of the deep or dynamic Web, the volume of instant messages generated in a year, and the annual volume of email (see Table 1.1).

Table 1.1: Information Sources in 2002

Medium	Terabytes
Surface Web	167
Instant Messaging	274
Deep Web	91,850
Email	440,606

The current figures for the storage of electronic media will be undoubtedly much higher, and continue to grow as the Web expands. A more recent estimate by the technology firm IDC estimates that we generated 161 million terabytes in 2006. While storing information on ever-growing hard disks is not difficult, it is harder to manage and make sense of our information.

Figure 1.1: Subset of Email Traffic from the Enron Dataset displayed using the Pajek [Pajek] Network Analysis Tool

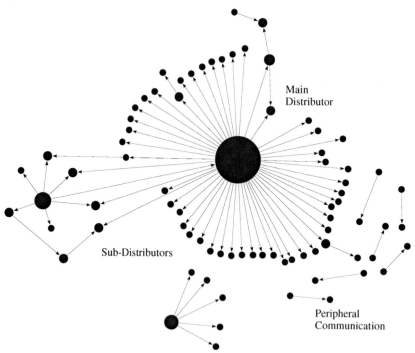

Take email for instance. It represents an unending stream of information that tends to accumulate over time. Individuals who receive a hundred or more emails a day will find it necessary to use some type of tool to manage this volume of information, or risk spending hours poring over one email after another. Looking at individual emails alone is a short-sighted view of this valuable information source. A tool which indexes, categorizes, or shows trends and patterns in email is very useful. A visual representation of email traffic gives users a global view of the main participants in a particular email network (see Figure 1.1)

The Enron email dataset (`http://cs.cmu.edu/~enron`) consists of email from about 150 employees at Enron Corporation. The U.S. Federal Energy Regulatory Commission made this document collection public during its investigation of the company. This email dataset has been analyzed and filtered to remove email unrelated to the investigation. Figure 1.1 shows a subset of that filtered email collection. The figure shows the links between participants in this email network. For simplicity, links between two nodes are shown when the number of messages between the two nodes exceeded three. Notice, the central hub node in this network, two smaller hub nodes, and a collection of independent node pairs on the periphery of the network.

Email is still the most popular form of online communication and is the primary medium for business transactions, personal communications, and advertisements. Other communication forms such as newsgroups, blogs, and instant messaging are less popular than email, and are ultimately unlikely to overtake the email as the most popular form of communication. The high volume of email makes it difficult to manage without specialized tools. In addition, the storage requirements for email will grow endlessly unless emails are deleted or archived on a regular basis.

Companies in the U.S. have regulatory requirements that provide guidelines for information discovery and disclosure that may be needed during litigation. A single request to a company to provide information on emails exchanged a year ago can result in many hours of work unless a process for email management has been implemented. In Table 1.1, we saw that email is easily the largest information source and without storage procedures, search tools, and hardware it can be tedious and expensive to respond to information discovery requests during litigation.

Apart from email messages, we also collect Web pages, formatted documents, letters, reports, etc. All of this data is stored in different formats and often on a network with no single interface to find useful information. Fortunately, we have available a number of tools that can be assembled to build practical text management applications. Some of the tools to build applications are described below.

1.2 Information Management Tools

The most popular tool to manage a collection of documents is the search engine. The size of Web search engines has scaled beyond most expectations and millions of queries are processed daily by current search engines. Its simplicity and almost instant response is appealing and one of the main reasons for its popularity.

1.2.1 Search Engines

The typical search engine has three parts - a crawler, an indexer and a search interface (see Chapters 3 and 4 for more information on these technologies). For most users, the crawler and indexer are invisible. The crawler locates documents that can be indexed on a local machine or over a network. A desktop crawler will search directories on a local file system for files that can be indexed. Any text based file such as a Web page created with hypertext markup language (*html*), a Microsoft Word document (*doc*), or a portable document format (*pdf*) file will be fetched and passed to the indexer. The text contained in these files is then extracted and associated with the document.

A distributed Web crawler starts with an initial set of Web page addresses (uniform resource locators or URLs) from which the network is scanned for more Web pages. An unconstrained Web crawler can quickly get bogged down, fetching millions of pages, and disrupt traffic on a network. There are several ways to control a crawler (also called a *spider* or *bot*) –

- Set a time limit for the spider to complete a crawl

- Specify a set of domains that the spider must crawl and exclude all other domains

- Use a set of terms, one or more of which must occur in the text of a fetched document

- Specify a numeric limit for the number of Web pages from any single site

In Chapter 9, we will look at the structure of the Web and identify the best initial pages for a crawl. The importance of the initial set cannot be understated, since the rest of the crawl depends completely on these core URLs. Site owners typically do not welcome visits from crawlers for several reasons. One, a crawler does not represent a person actually visiting the site using a browser. Two, crawlers can submit far more queries to a site than an individual can from a browser and finally crawlers can harvest large quantities of information, which can then be re-distributed. For example, online book libraries (such as O'Reilly's Safari) are the frequent target of unwanted spidering. Informal protocols to deny or allow a crawler to visit a site do exist; however, it is left to the crawler's author to observe a site's crawler directives.

The indexer performs the important task of building the index that will be used to locate relevant documents. The text of a document retrieved by a crawler is first extracted using a filter and passed to a tokenizer (see Chapter 2). The indexer uses the set of tokens from the text to create an inverted index (see Chapter 3). Since the early 90s when the Web became popular, search engine indexes have grown from handling millions to billions of documents. It is remarkable that despite the exponential growth of the index, query response times are still relatively short. Most large Web search engines are also optimized to handle the small percentage of queries that form the majority of all queries. In Chapter 3, we will build an index using the popular Lucene API from the Apache Software Foundation.

The third and most visible part of the search engine is the search interface (see Chapter 4). Simple search interfaces have been shown to be highly effective and the plain hit list with a summary and associated information is easy to use. Most search engines handle the boolean query syntax that was originally developed for IR systems. However, some Web search engines do have proprietary syntax to build precise queries that can quickly lead to relevant results. Unfortunately, the average user does not exploit all the features of a search engine and usually provides a handful or fewer keywords in a query.

In Chapter 4, we will look at various query forms that can be constructed in Lucene. Word patterns, date ranges, and field specific querying are some of the features included to generate precise queries. A sample interface will be implemented with spelling correction, links to similar documents, query expansion, paging, and document specific links.

1.2.2 Entity Extraction

Most search engines match documents and queries based on keywords alone. Tools that perform semantic analysis of text can provide more precise results. Metadata may or may not be included with a document, and on the Web, the accuracy of the metadata cannot be taken at face value. Information extraction is the task of automatically extracting structured information from unstructured text. Entity extraction is a sub-task of information extraction to find the names of people and organizations, place names, temporal expressions, numeric values, names of products, gene names, URLs, and email addresses in unstructured text.

Compare this with structured text stored in a database table. Every column has an associated attribute and the text in a cell has an explicit meaning. For example, a numeric column titled *price* represents the cost of some item. Extracting the same information from unstructured text is harder, since numeric values can represent any attribute.

The extraction of entities from text complements the set of tokens normally generated from a text segment. An entity in this context is the name of a person, place, organization, a dimension, date/time, or any other term that explains the type of noun. The simplest entity extractor is just a collection of lists for each entity type. A dictionary lookup is all that is needed to identity an entity in text.

There are of course problems with this approach. One, the dictionary has to be periodically updated with new terms that describe the entity. Two, it is not feasible to include the name of every known person or organization in a list. Three, the precise detection of an entity that either partially matches or overlaps a dictionary entry, may need additional information. It may be reasonable to use this method to extract entities when the lists of entities are well-defined and easy to maintain. In Chapter 5, we will look at two methods to extract entities using LingPipe (`http://www.alias-i.com`) and Gate (`http://gate.ac.uk`). LingPipe uses a language model that has been trained to find entities in text. It will extract a set of predefined entity types using the model. The model is created using training text that is tagged with entity types.

Gate uses an alternate method to find entities. A gazetteer, or a dictionary of entities for a specific entity type such as a place name, along with a regular expression-like language, is used to spot entities in text. The use of the gazetteer along with a pattern matching language offers more flexibility to define new entity types than a model based entity extractor. For example, the name of a person — *Fred Jones* can be mentioned in several ways –

- "Fred Jones", "Mr. F. Jones", "F.W. Jones", "Jones, F.W.", "Jones, Fred", or "Fred".

We can create patterns to match all possible ways of specifying a name using the gazetteer and regular expressions. New entity types can be added by creating a list and specifying a pattern for the entity type. For example, a pattern to spot prices in text can be defined to extract the cost of items in a Web page.

1.2.3 Organizing Information

Search engines find documents based on the occurrence of keywords in text. Although this is often sufficient to satisfy an information need, the entire contents of a document and its relationships with other documents are not known. We can organize a collection of documents using all or most of the keywords in the text.

Two common methods of organizing documents are *clustering* and *categorization*. The former method assumes no knowledge of the collection and attempts to build structure by comparing pairs of documents. A clustering algorithm creates groups of documents that have similar content from a similarity matrix. It is simpler and quicker to view a list of clusters than a long list of documents to find relevant information. Further, a cluster of relevant documents makes it easy to spot all documents that have similar content without browsing a list.

Text categorization assumes that the categories to which the documents belong are known beforehand. The categorization problem appears to be simpler than clustering since we merely have to find the category that has the highest similarity to any document. Every category has a representative collection of words or other features that best describe the documents in the category.

Documents are transformed from unstructured text into a set of words, phrases, and features. The similarity between any pair of documents or a document and a category can be computed using standard methods for comparing two vectors (see Chapter 6). A document is assigned to a category, when its similarity with the category description exceeds a threshold. Some documents may not belong to any category and can be assigned to a *miscellaneous* category.

1.2.4 Tracking Information

Dynamic sources of information such as blogs, news Web sites, and chat groups generate information that is difficult to manually monitor. But crawlers can periodically visit such Web sites and collect information for analysis. This information can be scanned to identify the sentiment expressed in the text. For example, a positive message will contain adjectives that express confidence or high quality. However, a negative message contains adjectives that are pessimistic or unfavorable. A neutral message will be a mix of the two types of adjectives.

The easy availability of information on the Web makes it difficult to identify original from plagiarized information. There are too many sources to check and manually compare to spot copies of documents. Automated tools can detect plagiarism in it's various forms. Some documents may be partially plagiarized or subtly altered to appear original.

Modified source code is the perfect example of this kind of alteration. It is relatively simple to change variable names and add a few comments to make code appear original, and thereby avoid licensing issues. In Chapter 9, we will look at some tools to detect plagiarism in source code and text.

1.3 Visualization

The term *visualization* was coined in the 1980s when computer simulations and laboratory experiments generated large quantities of numeric data that was difficult to understand in its raw form. A visual or an animation presents the same data in a concise, form that is easier to interpret and understand than a series of symbols. While graphs and plots are not new, interactive visualizations on a computer can show large quantities of information that would otherwise have been difficult to analyze.

In the 90s, users of text faced a similar problem with the huge quantities of online information that was easily available. It was tedious to browse and find information in a large collection. A search engine alone was not sufficient to observe patterns or trends and identify links between groups or individuals. The results of many queries needed to be collected, analyzed, and presented to make informed decisions.

The methods that were used in scientific visualizations contained mostly numeric data with fewer dimensions. However, text has far more dimensions (each word or entity being a dimension) than numeric data. Therefore, methods used for scientific visualization could not be directly applied for text or information visualization.

The new visualizations created for text were extensions of existing tools with modifications to handle a large number of dimensions. Among the popular methods were displaying a large graph with features to zoom and examine sub-graphs, a navigable landscape, 3D images of files and text, treemaps, plots of trends, and many other creative visual ways of showing word frequency, time, and links.

1.3.1 Social Network Visualization

A visualization developed at the University of California Berkeley was used to analyze the Enron email dataset (`http://jheer.org/enron/v1`). This type of visualization examines a huge social network with hundreds of nodes and thousands of links. While the network is initially overwhelming, sub-networks can be examined in detail with an accompanying window to show the text of the email. In information visualization, it is often necessary to switch from the visual to textual display and back again to examine a text dataset.

Figure 1.2 shows a smaller network with links between the two key players in the Enron scandal and words that appear in context. This visual is taken from a sample of about 1700 emails. The words on the right hand side of the visual co-occurred with the words on the left hand side. The thickness of the link is roughly proportional to the frequency of co-occurrence. Vince Kaminski was a risk management official at Enron in the late 90s who warned top executives of partnerships that were fraudulent. The U.S. Federal Energy Regulatory Commission (FERC) is an agency monitoring inter- state electricity sales, electric rates, natural gas pricing, and oil pipeline rates.

Such plots can also be used to examine consumer complaints to identify key components that are most often defective. The problems from more than one model of a product can be simultaneously viewed to observe relationships between models.

1.3.2 Stock Price and News Visualization

Figure 1.3 is a plot of the occurrence of words in email over time compared with a stock price. The movement of the stock price of a company is mostly based on news that is publicly available. Bad news is inevitably followed by a drop in the stock price and this plot shows how the frequency of occurrence of two words in internal emails compares with the stock price. During the first half of 2001, internal communications reveal a higher interest in *investigations* that were ongoing at that time. By the second half of 2001, there is much less discussion and the change of CEO could not stop the slide in the stock price and the eventual declaration of bankruptcy at the end of the year.

Such timelines are very useful to examine a long running story such as a court case or a political scandal. The terms used to describe the events of the story differ

Figure 1.2: Links between two participants in an email network based on frequency of term co-occurrence

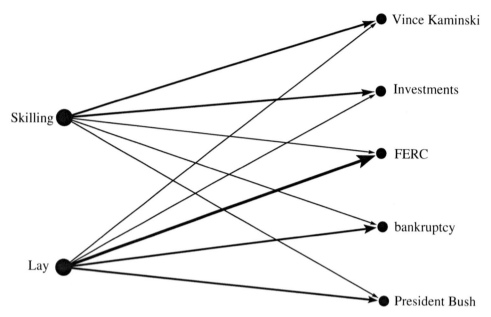

over time and reveal a growing or shrinking interest in a person or topic. We can quickly find the key terms or phrases that affected the course of the story.

1.3.3 Tag Clouds

A tag cloud is a simple, but effective way of showing the frequency and currency of words. Figure 1.4 shows a tag cloud generated from a State of the Union speech given by President George W. Bush (used with permission of Chirag Mehta, `http: //chir.ag`). A list of 100 words that occurred frequently in the speech are shown in alphabetic order. The font size is proportional to the frequency. So, terms like *Iraq* and *Terrorist* appeared more frequently than terms such as *Africa* or *Lebanon*. The cloud excludes stop words such as *and*, *of*, and *the* that appear in most documents. The *log* of the frequency of words is often used to smooth the large differences in raw frequency counts of words.

Figure 1.3: Plot of stock price and word occurrences in email

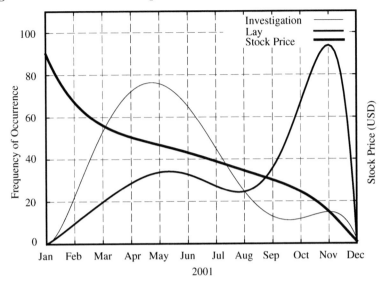

The list of words in the tag cloud is mostly nouns, verbs, or adjectives. Words derived from a common root form (lemma) are collapsed into a single word. For example, words like *promised* and *promises* are generated from the lemma *promise*. The word *Baghdad* was used in more recent speeches than the word *Africa* and therefore appears brighter. This particular tag cloud simultaneously uses brightness to compare the text from multiple State of the Union addresses and font size to compare words from the current State of the Union address with prior State of the Union addresses.

1.4 Applications

The main goals of text applications are to find documents, reveal patterns, and provide answers in response to an information need. We view text in many different forms including short messages, Web pages, email, e-books, and articles. No single application exists that can handle all types of text and the following is a sample list of text applications.

Figure 1.4: A Tag Cloud Generated from a State of the Union Address

abandon accountable affordable afghanistan africa aided ally anbar armed army baghdad bless challenges chamber chaos choices civilians coalition commanders commitment confident confront congressman constitution corps debates deduction deficit deliver democratic deploy dikembe diplomacy disruptions earmarks economy einstein elections eliminates expand extremists failing faithful families freedom fuel funding god haven ideology immigration impose insurgents iran iraq islam julie lebanon love madam marine math medicare moderation neighborhoods nuclear offensive palestinian payroll province pursuing qaeda radical regimes resolve retreat rieman sacrifices science sectarian senate september shia stays strength students succeed sunni tax territories terrorists threats uphold victory violence violent war washington weapons wesley

1.4.1 Spam Detection

Currently, spam email continues to be a major problem for Internet users and service providers. The volume of spam has dramatically increased; some estimate that about 75% of all email is spam. It costs time and money for individual users to filter email while the cost to send spam continues to fall. A spammer may also use a collection of compromised machines (bots) in a botnet to avoid detection and transmit spam at almost zero cost.

Efforts to curtail and accurately categorize email are not consistently successful. The problem of spam detection is difficult since the relationship between spammers and spam detectors is adversarial. Spammers know the techniques used to categorize email, and look for ways to embed their message in a seemingly innocent message. Simplistic detection methods fail to detect these types of spam. Over time, detection methods have become more sophisticated and can detect a high percentage of spam. However, spammers have also evolved too, by including images and irrelevant text. Words that flag a potential spam message are altered by adding a space or some other character making it difficult for the simple word matcher to spot.

Textual images in a message involve more work for the spam detector. The text from the image must be scraped to generate an accurate representation of the message. Text embedded in images is not easily extracted and is often mixed with unrelated text to confuse the extractor. Embedded HTML messages are also potentially confusing for a detector. An HTML extractor will identify the text in the message; however, HTML encodings will not be seen by the extractor.

The HTML enabled email client will display readable character strings, while the detector will extract encoded characters that will not match a spam token. For example, the HTML encoding Viagra represents the common spam word, *Viagra*. There are several other methods employed by spammers to foil spam detectors. Some of these methods will be discussed in Chapter 6.

1.4.2 Email Usage and Management

Despite the annoyance of spam, email is invaluable, and is the most popular means of communication. Corporations rely heavily on email to communicate with employees and it is often preferred over other forms of communications. Email is very reliable and does not require the receiver to respond immediately. Its convenience has been exploited for communication, but it can be used for other purposes as well.

The contents of emails are presumed to be private and not shared with all employees of an organization. In a large organization where employees are physically distributed, there is a likelihood of employees not being aware of others in the organization with similar skills. Implicit groups of employees can be generated from the most frequent keywords used in emails. Individuals who work with the same technology tend to use similar terms and can be grouped together even though they may belong to separate divisions within a larger organization.

A profile for every employee that describes individual interests and skills will increase the precision of the application. This profile can be customized and adapted to reflect new skills or interests. The group is created implicitly and is used when a member needs specific information that can be answered by one or more members of the group. Building such communities fosters knowledge sharing that benefits the whole organization.

For example, an employee who needs to find a person who has previously set up an office in another country may send an email to a dynamic group created based on a search with the country name and other keywords. A person may opt-out of receiving such emails if needed. But, if used properly, such an application can put employees in touch with other employees without a great deal of effort. In a large organization, it is often difficult to find specialized expertise unless such information is well-known or publicized.

A separate application is the management of email. In Table 1.1, we saw that email is the largest information source and several billion emails are generated daily worldwide. Even though email may be distributed on several servers, it quickly accumulates and can begin to occupy large volumes of disk space. Due to regulatory requirements, it may not be possible to delete old emails and a search engine to retrieve emails is needed.

The legal costs of not archiving and maintaining email can be high. Most investigations begin with the collection of past email in search of evidence. For example, the investigation of the Enron scandal involved the collection of over half a million emails excluding attachments from 151 users. Email is also *legally discoverable*, which simply means that in a lawsuit a litigant could ask for all emails exchanged over a year or longer. Collecting this information and providing it can be expensive unless there was an email management system in place. In some cases, permanently deleting emails may not be viable since copies may exist in the recipient's server. It may also imply a potential cover up of evidence.

The benefits of email are universally accepted, but like any other application, it can be used for malicious purposes. For example, an employee may threaten or send hate mail using a corporate mail server. The management of an organization will be held responsible for monitoring this type of behavior. Email that matches a "hate profile" can be flagged and monitored to detect the source and intended recipient. Similarly, email that contains pornography will match a "porn profile".

Companies rely on email for more than just communication; many transactions such as purchases and contracts are processed via email. Emails document the history of a transaction from its initiation to termination. Many transactions will generate a large collection of email that needs to be made searchable and maintained for a reasonable period of time.

1.4.3 Customer Service

Providing good customer support for products and services is no longer seen as an afterthought. A service provider or manufacturer needs to track customer complaints to stay in business for the long term. Complaints can come in various forms including audio, email, and letters. Together, this collection of text can be analyzed to find the products with the most complaints and components that are prone to fail. The collected information needs to be concisely summarized for developers to build a better version of the product.

Manual scanning of complaints does not always reveal a hidden pattern in the text. These patterns can only be seen when the entire collection of the text is summarized and presented in some visual form. It is tedious (and impractical) for an individual to scan a large volume of text looking for particular terms or phrases to build a global view of the set of complaints.

In this particular application, a plot or visual chart that accompanies the text analysis will quickly reveal the reasons for most complaints. The first step in processing a complaint is to identify which product or service is referred to in the complaint. This is a text categorization problem that is covered in Chapter 6, Organizing Information. The next step is to collect all complaints related to a common product and extract key phrases and terms that appear frequently. For example, complaints about a washing machine may mention a particular fan or motor. A link analysis plot (Figure 1.2) can show links between one or more models and terms in complaints. A thicker line will indicate a higher frequency of complaints and the plot also serves to differentiate problems between two or more models of the same product.

1.4.4 Employee Surveys

Many companies periodically conduct employee surveys, which come in the form of a questionnaire where some of the questions are multiple choice and others are free form. Questions where employees can enter text are harder to tabulate and load into a database for summarization. In addition, most of the surveys are scanned individually and it is hard to infer a summary when results are viewed individually. However, it is relatively easy to glean the main problems or issues from a summary.

The unstructured text from responses to open questions needs to be categorized and key terms such as *workspace, environment,* or *noise* extracted. We can define a set of such terms that characterize an employee's domain and form the basis of a complaint. More often than not, the respondents to employee surveys who submit a text answer have a negative experience to relate and the extractor focuses on finding terms from such answers. A simple ranked term list in descending order of frequency will show the top reasons for a complaint. A sentence extractor (see Chapter 5) can display the list of sentences that contain a particular term. For example, sentences that contain the term *noise* can be viewed in a set to find out why employees are unhappy with the noise level.

1.4.5 Other Applications

There are many other text applications including automatic essay grading, case analysis, competitive intelligence, political surveys, analysis of legislation and floor debates, and monitoring tools. There is still some debate as to whether a computer can accurately identify a good essay from a bad one. If we treat this problem as a text categorization problem like spam detection, we would look for features that distinguish a good essay and use those features to categorize an unknown essay. Statistical features would include the length of the essay, the size of the vocabulary, and length of sentences. Linguistic features include coverage of the topic and organization of the essay. The US-based Educational Testing Service (ETS) has developed several tools to evaluate and score the writing abilities of test takers [Burstein].

The information associated with a lawsuit may consist of court transcripts, statements, affidavits, verdicts, written motions, and other documents. All this information can be analyzed with the help of tools that can find names of people, create links between documents, and show a timeline.

Intelligence

A set of similar tools is needed in competitive intelligence to monitor activities in an industry. The list of patents filed by a company are one indication of a company's research areas. Tracking the Web site of a competitor may also be useful to find out new products and announcements. Text applications can also search a large collection of patents to identify possible infringement.

Umbria (`http://www.umbrialistens.com`) is a marketing intelligence company that monitors blogs, Usenet groups, message boards, and product review sites to track issues and the discussions of products. Nielsen BuzzMetrics (`http://www.nielsenbuzzmetrics.com`) is another organization that measures consumer generated media to identify product related opinions, preferences, issues and trends.

Medical Information

Online medical systems were among the earliest users of search engines and the volume of medical information generated is comparable to the size of some of the largest legal document collections. The Medline system of the U.S. National Library of Medicine contains many terabytes of medical information that is accessible through a search engine. The types of medical documents include patient reports, drug trials, journal papers, books, and technical reports.

Although this information is digitized in most cases, there is a need to organize and summarize this information. One particular problem is the categorization of a patient report into a medical code that is reported to an insurance organization. A patient report that is automatically categorized into the wrong category code may indicate that the medical provider is not treating the type of patients as claimed. Another related problem is the summarization of a large number of notes collected from hospital emergency rooms to identify new syndromes or trends that is of interest to government agencies.

The Mitre text and audio processing system was developed to monitor infectious disease outbreaks and other global events (`http://www.encyclopedia.com/doc/1G1-96126591.html`). The information from multiple sources was captured, categorized, and summarized for individuals involved in humanitarian assistance and relief work.

2 Tokenizing Text

We begin at the lowest level of text processing with the raw data. This data is stored in files without any tags or formatting information and is readable with a typical text editor (vi, Emacs, Kwrite, or WordPad). There are huge collections of text available on the Web. The Gutenberg project (`http://www.gutenberg.org`) hosts a library of several thousand multi-lingual e-books available in different formats including plain text. The Linguistic Data Consortium (`http://ldc.upenn.edu`) publishes a number of large collections for researchers and developers. The European Language Resources Association (`http://www.elra.info`) distributes numerous multilingual document collections for academic research.

2.1 Character Sets

This book deals primarily with English text, but the tools (Lucene, LingPipe, and Gate) described in the book to process text do handle other languages as well. The first encoding schemes, EBCDIC and ASCII, represented keyboard text characters in 7 bits, with extensions for accents and other diacritical marks. These encoding schemes were not sufficient for languages such as Chinese, Japanese, Arabic, and Hebrew. The Unicode standard (`http://unicode.org`) was created to accommodate languages with a large number of characters.

Unicode assigns unique integer ids (code points) to characters. For example, the uppercase characters 'A' through 'Z' can be mapped to the 16 bit hexadecimal sequences '\u0041' through '\u005a'. The leading '\u' is an Unicode escape character to indicate that the following four hexadecimal characters should be converted to the corresponding Unicode character. A complete set of characters and the corresponding integer ids is called the character set (charset).

A character encoding translates a sequence of bytes into a sequence of characters and vice versa. For example, the variable length character encoding scheme UTF-8, uses one byte to encode the 128 ASCII characters (Unicode range \u0000 to \u007F) and more than one byte for other Unicode characters. The UTF-8 encoding scheme is a backward compatible Unicode encoding to handle ASCII files and is the assumed encoding scheme for the data files in this book. All the tools described in this book use characters at the lowest level. Java classes like the `InputStreamReader` class use a character encoding to convert the raw bytes of a file into a stream of characters. Although, the remainder of the book deals with English text alone, software such as the International Components for Unicode (ICU) libraries from `http://www.icu-project.org` enable a single program to work with text written in any language. The library code hides the cultural nuances and technical details to customize software for a locale.

Text that will be processed by a computer may have some markup to ascribe meaning or interpretation to certain text chunks. Such documents are formatted using a plain text editor or using a word processor like OpenOffice.org or Microsoft Word. The *Text Extraction* section later in this chapter (see section 2.6) explains how the contents of such formatted files can be extracted. In the following sections we will look at three approaches to extract tokens from plain text and to create your own customized tokenizer.

2.1.1 Tokens

Individual characters from text without context are not useful and must be assembled into text units called *tokens*. Typically, a token is a single word or term, but can also be a character sequence, a phrase, an emoticon, email address, URL, or acronym. Tokenization is a bottom up approach to process text, where the smallest chunk of text considered is a token. Other methods include breaking text into sentences and parsing each sentence. We will emphasize the bottom up method for several reasons. The text from some sources such as Web pages is very difficult to parse and often cannot be divided into sentences. Secondly, the sentences that are extracted may have many different parses, and it is hard to decide which parse is best suited for the author's intended meaning. Thirdly, it takes much less time to tokenize text than to parse text. The task of extracting the meaning and attempting to understand the text is left to higher level modules that work with larger chunks of text.

A list of tokens is useful to build several types of text-based applications. The most well-known application is the search engine, which finds text that matches query terms in documents. The query terms are defined by the list of tokens entered in a search box on a Web page or in an application. Other examples of applications include finding the best text chunk that may answer a question. The sentiment expressed in a document can also be detected based on the type of adjectives used in the text. Different text samples can be compared to evaluate similarity or to detect plagiarism. We can also find the most popular phrases (see Chapter 5) mentioned in the text of a document-these may indicate the subject or theme of the document. Finally, a list of tokens is sufficient to assign a document to a category with reasonable accuracy.

Lucene uses `Analyzers` to tokenize text. An `Analyzer` breaks up a stream of characters into tokens that can be used to build a search engine index. The term "analyzer" is derived from the analysis of text to find the most likely boundary for any token. English is one of the easier languages to tokenize because of the use of whitespace characters to delimit tokens. Languages such as Chinese are written without whitespace characters to separate tokens, and it takes a fairly intelligent analyzer to tokenize such languages. Lucene includes analyzers for several languages including French, German, Greek, and Russian.

LingPipe uses the term *"tokenizer"* to refer to the same function performed by a Lucene `Analyzer`. A LingPipe `TokenizerFactory` accepts a text stream and returns a `Tokenizer`. The `Tokenizer` provides an `Iterable` stream or array of tokens. The text stream is passed to the `tokenizer` method of the `TokenizerFactory` in the form of a character sequence with offsets for the start and end positions. The tokens from a Lucene analyzer include information such as *position* and *type*, which are of use in a search engine. Gate uses a more complex and slower method to build tokens and can identify a variety of token types including emoticons, URLs, emails, and short phrases. LingPipe tokenizers are lightweight classes to extract tokens compared to similar classes in Gate and Lucene. A `Token` in Lucene can optionally include metadata (`Payload`) in the form of a variable length byte array. This is an experimental feature as of version 2.2 and is useful to assign greater importance to specific terms in a document based on their location or font size or even to store ids and term positions.

2.2 Lucene Analyzers

The Lucene (`http://lucene.apache.org`) search engine API provides a number of built-in analyzers to tokenize text. Each analyzer is tuned for a particular purpose or language, and you can choose any one of the analyzers included in the distribution, or create your own. Consider the following text chunk taken from Lewis Carroll's "Alice in Wonderland".

> *Alice was beginning to get very tired of sitting by her sister on the bank, and of having nothing to do: once or twice she had peeped into the book her sister was reading, but it had no pictures or conversations in it, 'and what is the use of a book,' thought Alice 'without pictures or conversation?'*

We will use several analyzers to tokenize this text starting with the simple white space analyzer and build more complex custom analyzers. Each analyzer uses a custom method to detect the boundary of a token. In some cases, more than one token may be detected at the same text position. A token in Lucene consists of the text that makes up the token, the start and end character positions, a token type, and optionally any other type of information such as the part of speech. Multiple tokens such as synonyms or spelling corrections, may begin at the same character position. A single token may be comprised of multiple words, including the spaces between the words.

2.2.1 WhitespaceAnalyzer

The sample text contains alphabetic characters and punctuation characters such as question marks, apostrophes and colons. Most search engines ignore characters such as commas, quotation marks and colons, both in queries and in documents. These characters are punctuation characters that are in most cases not needed in a search engine. The exceptions are characters like apostrophes and hyphens (see section 2.5, Tokenizing Problems). Consider the code in Listing 2.1 to generate a list of tokens from the text chunk. The `LuceneTools` package (line 14) is included in the software distribution that accompanies the book.

Listing 2.1: Extract tokens from test using a Lucene Analyzer

```
1   public class LuceneTokens {
```

```
 2    private Analyzer analyzer;
 3
 4    public static void main(String[] args) {
 5      analyzer = new WhitespaceAnalyzer();
 6      String text = "Alice was beginning .... ";
 7      displayTokens(analyzer, text);
 8    }
 9
10    private static void displayTokens(
11      Analyzer analyzer, String text) {
12      // get the list of tokens using the passed analyzer
13      // with org.btext.utils.LuceneTools
14      Token[] tokens = LuceneTools.tokensFromAnalysis(
15          analyzer, text);
16      int position = 0;
17      for (String token: tokens) {
18        position += token.getPositionIncrement();
19        System.out.println(position + ": "
20        + new String(token.termBuffer(),0,token.termLength())
21        + ": " + token.type() + " " + token.startOffset()
22        + ":" + token.endOffset());
23      }
24    }
25  }
```

The WhitespaceAnalyzer (line 5) is one of several analyzers include in Lucene. It is the most simple analyzer and merely breaks the text into chunks whenever a whitespace is seen in the text stream. A whitespace character includes the newline or tab characters and consecutive whitespace characters are collapsed into a single character. Punctuation characters are not removed and are included with the text of a token unless there is an intervening white space character. For the given text string, we would get the following list of tokens —

```
1:  Alice:  word 0:5
2:  was:  word 6:9
3:  beginning:  word 10:19

    .   .   .

54:  'without:  word 266:274
55:  pictures:  word 275:283
56:  or:  word 284:286
```

```
57:  conversation?':  word 287:301
```
There are a total of 57 tokens in the text string. Every Token has a type and start/end character positions (offsets) in the text string. In this case, all the tokens are of type *word*. The positions of the token are the positions in the string and take into account all whitespace characters. It is easier to show matching text strings when the exact start and end positions of the token are known. Notice, some of the tokens have non-alphanumeric characters such as *?* or *'*. A query would need the trailing *?* character in the query "conversation?" to find a matching hit.

2.2.2 SimpleAnalyzer

The alternative `SimpleAnalyzer` uses a letter tokenizer and a lower case filter to extract tokens from text. A letter tokenizer defines token boundaries at non-letter characters and generates tokens from consecutive letters in the text stream. Numeric characters are dropped and the identification of a letter character is defined by the `isLetter` method from the core `java.lang.Character` class. This works reasonably well for languages that separate words with spaces, but is not suitable for languages such as Chinese where there is no equivalent character delimiter to separate words. We replace the call to instantiate an analyzer (line 5) in Listing 2.1 with

```
analyzer = new SimpleAnalyzer();
```
The same number (57) of tokens is returned with a `SimpleAnalyzer`. The differences between the analyzers can be seen in the list of generated tokens.

```
1:  alice:  word 0:5

 .    .    .

54:  without:  word 267:274
55:  pictures:  word 275:283
56:  or:  word 284:286
57:  conversation:  word 287:299
```
The first token is converted to lower case and the 54th and final tokens do not have any punctuation characters. The other types of analyzers include the `StandardAnalyzer`, the `KeywordAnalyzer`, and a number of language-specific analyzers. The differences between these analyzers lies mainly in the types of tokenizers used and the combinations of filters that transform tokens.

2.2.3 Analyzer Design

The design of an analyzer in Lucene is shown in Figure 2.1. The input text stream is provided to the analyzer using a `Reader` instance. The abstract `Reader` class provides methods to read single characters, a group of characters, or a set of characters located at an offset in the text stream. The initial tokenizer generates a list of tokens based on a set of rules. Some tokenizers such as the `LetterTokenizer` or `CharTokenizer` are simple and merely build groups of characters that belong to a class of acceptable characters and ignore all other characters. Other tokenizers such as the `StandardTokenizer` follow a set of rules to build different types of tokens.

Figure 2.1: Design of a Lucene Analyzer

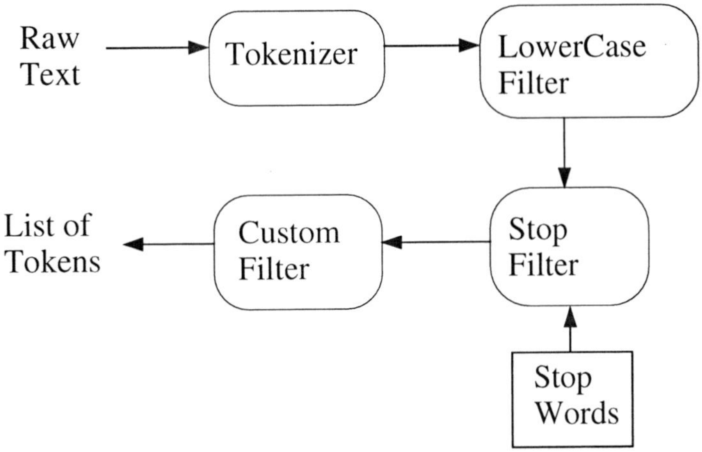

For example, in the following text stream - "*AT&T and I.B.M. today announced a series of strategic agreements (contact@ibm.com)*" the token *AT&T* would be a COMPANY token, *I.B.M.* an ACRONYM token, and *contact@ibm.com* an EMAIL token. The remaining tokens such as *today* and *announced* are of type ALPHANUM. The rules to build such token types will work when the individual characters of the token do not have intervening characters. The pattern rule for a company token type is a leading alphanumeric token followed by either the ampersand or at sign characters and a trailing alphanumeric token. Extra spaces ("AT & T") or omitted periods (IBM) break the rules for definitions of the company or acronym token types and are not recognized. In Chapter 5, we will look at more robust ways of tagging such tokens that can be specified in more than one way.

A `TokenFilter` class transforms a stream of input tokens into another stream of tokens. The `LowerCaseFilter` transforms each token in the input stream to lower case and returns the list of transformed tokens. Multiple filters based on the `TokenFilter` class can be chained in a sequence to perform a particular type of analysis. For example, the following code builds the chain of filters in Figure 2.1

```
return new CustomFilter(
  new StopFilter (
    new LowerCaseFilter(
      new StandardTokenizer(reader)),
    StopAnalyzer.ENGLISH_STOP_WORDS));
```

The innermost filter (`LowerCaseFilter`) is first applied to the stream of tokens generated by the `StandardTokenizer` followed by the `StopFilter` and `CustomFilter` in order. The `StopFilter` uses a default set of English stop words in the `StopAnalyzer`. A filter can also add or drop tokens from the list. For example, the `LengthFilter` can include only those tokens in a particular range of lengths, while the `StopFilter` will remove a set of stop words from the list of tokens. The `LowerCaseFilter` follows the tokenizer step in Figure 2.1 since the following filters may compare the token text strings with a list of pre-defined words in lower case.

2.2.4 StandardAnalyzer

The `StandardAnalyzer` is a fairly popular analyzer for English text that uses a grammar-based `StandardTokenizer`. Tokens are built using a set of rules and a set of stop words. The rules govern how tokens are generated from a character stream. A rule specifies if a new token should be generated or if the current character should be appended to a token based on the context of the character. For example, the rule for the stream of characters *another.dot.com* would generate a single token of type HOST unlike the `SimpleAnalyzer` that would have generated three separate tokens – *another*, *dot*, and *com*.

Some words (called *stop words*) are filtered out of the list of tokens, based on the number of times they appear in a text stream. Words that appear very often in the text stream and in many documents are in most cases not useful in a search engine index. The following 33 words are the standard stop words for English in Lucene (version 2.3).

> *a an and are as at be but by for if in into is it no not of on or such that the their then there these they this to was will with*

These words appear too frequently in most English text to have much value in a search engine index. You can customize this list depending on your requirements. For example, if you have a large patent database, then terms such as - *invention*, *claim*, and *herein* may be additional stop words that are added to the standard stop word list. These stop words can be provided to the analyzer using a file or a list of words. Stop words are selected based on the utility of such words in a query. Words that appear in practically every document in a collection will have little value in a search engine index. The call to instantiate an analyzer in Listing 2.1 is replaced with

```
private static final String[] STOP_WORDS = {
  "a", "and", "are", "as", ...
};
analyzer = new StandardAnalyzer(STOP_WORDS);
```

The tokenizing process precedes the creation of an index for a search engine (see Chapter 3). Dropping stop words from a search engine index reduces the size of the index, but makes queries that contain stop words difficult to process. A search for the phrase *"BBC on the Internet"*, may find matches that do not contain the phrase, if the StandardAnalyzer was used, since the words *on* and *the* would not be indexed. Instead, matches for just the words *BBC* and *Internet* would be returned, and these matches may not include the search phrase. Rare queries such as *"to be or not to be"* would not match any document since all the words in the query are stop words. Stop words also appear in names like *"Lord of the Rings"*, *"The New York Times"*, and even as part of a name *"Will Smith"*. The StandardBgramAnalyzer (see Section 2.2.6) described later in this chapter can handle stop words in phrases.

2.2.5 PorterAnalyzer

Words such as *beginning, began,* or *begun* all have the same root word — *begin*. Most dictionaries provide the root word (lemma) as the main entry and cite the associated set of inflected words (lexemes). There are several reasons why we are interested in finding root words. The meanings of the different inflections are usually the same and represent variations in the tense, number, or person. A stem is often the same as the root of a inflected word, but can also be a token that does not exist in the dictionary. For example, the stems of *running* and *stabilize* are *run* and *stabil* respectively.

We may get better performance from a search engine if stems of words are matched, instead of the words themselves. A query with a stemmed word will match a larger number of words than the original token (see Wildcard Query in section 4.4.2). At the same time, the accuracy of the matches based on word stems may be poorer than matches based on the original words. For example, the words *political* and *polite* share the same stem *polit* (using the Porter stemming algorithm), even though both words have distinct meanings. Document matches based on the stem alone will have some irrelevant hits. The size of a search engine index will be smaller, if we store just the root forms of words alone.

The main argument for using the stems of words is to build an index using the canonical form of words such that various inflections of a word will still match the root word. Theoretically, this should improve performance, since a search engine will no longer rely on an exact match of words and instead use a higher level word stem match. But in practice, no conclusive evidence was found to justify using word stems and most Web search engines do not use stemming. The errors introduced by stemming algorithms offset some of the gains from matches at the root word level, leading to lower accuracy. It is difficult to generate a set of stemming rules that can be uniformly applied to all words.

While the use of word stems in a search engine is optional, they are needed to find if a word exists in the dictionary. All inflections of a word are not always included in a dictionary. An inflection can be as simple as adding the character *s* to the root word to form a plural (*cat* to *cats*) or adding a suffix string (*child* to *children*). Some words such as *modern*, *modernize*, and *modernization* share the same word stem but belong to different syntactic categories. These derivations do not always share the same meaning and differ from word inflections that add grammatical information to a common word stem. Some derivations are formed with a suffix, but there are a few that can be generated with a prefix (*do* to *undo*).

A stemming algorithm returns the word stem for any given inflected or derived word form. The simple algorithms apply a set of rules, while other algorithms may selectively apply rules based on usage. The main purpose of a stemming algorithm is to find the root meaning of a word such that searches using any one of the morphological variants of a stem with the same meaning will return the same set of documents. First, we will look at a simple stemming algorithm and describe a more complex version in the WordNet section.

Martin Porter [Porter] wrote the most well-known stemming algorithm in 1980 and an implementation of the algorithm is included in Lucene. We can build a custom stemming analyzer (see Listing 2.2) and use it to tokenize a passage.

Listing 2.2: A Lucene Analyzer using the Porter Stemmer

```
1  public class PorterAnalyzer extends Analyzer {
2    public TokenStream tokenStream (
3        String fieldName, Reader reader) {
4      return new PorterStemFilter(
5        new StopFilter(
6          new LowerCaseTokenizer(reader),
7          StopAnalyzer.ENGLISH_STOP_WORDS));
8    }
9  }
```

The list of stemmed tokens extracted for the Alice passage include words such as *begin* (from *beginning*) and *tire* (from *tired*). However, note that nonsense stems have been created as well: "words" such as *onc* (from *once*) and *noth* (from *nothing*). The reason behind these strange forms is that the Porter stemmer uses a sequence of rules to remove suffixes without a supporting dictionary. The use of word stems in a search engine index that do not exist in the language may not matter, since the purpose of these stems is only to fetch documents from the search engine, and they are usually not returned in a search response.

The letters of a word are categorized into consonants and vowels. Rules are expressed using the letters V and C for vowels and consonants respectively with regular expression metacharacters * and + to represent quantities. A * by itself represents zero or more characters and a + represents one or more characters. For example, the rules to form *begin* from *beginning* and *tire* from *tired* are —

```
if (*V*ed) then ed --> null;
if (*V*ing) then ing --> null;
```

Notice, the application of these rules alone does not complete the stemming process. Additional rules are needed to add the character *e* to *tir* and the extra *n* is removed from *beginn*. If the * metacharacter follows a parentheses as in (C)*, then it represents a sequence of zero or more consonants. These rules are applied in five steps in sequence and follow logically. A suffix is removed when a rule's conditions are satisfied and control moves to the next step. However, if the word does not match the rule's conditions, then the following rules in the step are tested in order until either a match is found or there are no more rules in the step. Control is passed to the next step and the algorithm terminates when all five steps have been completed. The Porter stemmer is still popular since it does not require a dictionary and can be relatively easily implemented.

2.2.6 StandardBgramAnalyzer

The term *ngram* is used to refer to a subsequence of *n* characters from a string of characters. The 3-grams (trigrams) generated from the word *guide* are *gui*, *uid*, and *ide*. A bigram (2-gram) can also be generated using tokens instead of characters. We discuss character-based ngrams later in this chapter and the use of ngram models in chapters 6 and 7. Here we introduce a word-based bigram to handle the problem with stop words. Queries for stop words like *the* are not very meaningful since there is no context to limit the number of matched documents. A more specific query, with a stop word and another word such as a noun in a phrase, will match fewer documents.

There are three possible ways to handle query phrases that contain stop words. One, all stop words can be dropped from the index. This makes it difficult to find hits without a secondary search for such phrases in matching documents (a slow process). Stop words can be included in the index, increasing the size of the index, but allowing for phrase matches. The third possibility is to create a bigram (two word token) that will appear in the index at the same position in the text. So, the search for "*BBC on the Internet*" would consist of the following five tokens

bbc: <ALPHANUM> 0:3

bbc_on: <BIGRAM> 0:6

on_the: <BIGRAM> 4:10

the_internet: <BIGRAM> 7:19

internet: <ALPHANUM> 11:19

The first word *bbc* is combined with the stop word *on* and an underscore character to form a bigram *bbc_on*. Two consecutive stop words *on* and *the* are combined to form the bigram *on_the* and finally the last word *internet* is prefixed with the stop word *the* to make the bigram *the_internet*. The formation of these bigrams can be described by a finite state machine shown in Figure 2.2. Notice, the number (5) of indexed words and bigrams is higher than the number (2) of indexed words without stop words. In general, the size of an index with bigrams may be 25% or more larger than an index without stop words.

The benefits of the larger index are that matches for phrases with stop words will be precise. Queries with embedded stop words will match the bigram tokens in order. While the use of these bigrams does increase the size of the index, this procedure is more efficient than storing all the stop words in a search engine index. Words such as *the* would be associated with almost every single document and queries with a stop word alone would generate a long but mostly irrelevant hit list. The combination of a stop word and a non-stop word or two stop words occurs less often than a single stop word and can be saved in the index without the associated problems mentioned earlier.

The Nutch project (see Chapter 8) uses a similar analyzer to handle stop words in phrases. The **Start** and **End** states represent the beginning and the end of the text stream respectively while the **Stop** and **Word** states indicate the occurrence of a stop and a non-stop word respectively. The arcs indicate a transition from one state to another with the optional emission of one or more tokens. The numbers on the arcs correspond to the cases mentioned in the code.

The eight links in the figure represent all pairs of combinations of a word, stop word, and the null value. The first link is the appearance of a stop word alone that is not indexed by itself and therefore no token is emitted. The third and fifth links combine the stop word with either another stop word or a word to form a bigram that is added to the list of tokens. The second and sixth links represent the appearance of a word that would be indexed as before. A bigram is created from a stop word that appears after a word in the fourth link. Finally, the seventh and eight link are

Figure 2.2: Creation of Words and Bigrams from a Text Stream

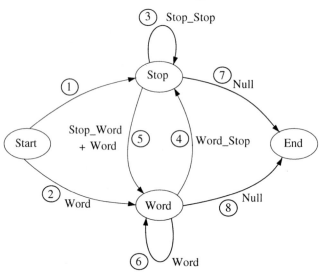

transitions at the end of text stream. Listing 2.3 contains the code to build a custom analyzer to generate bigrams and words from a text stream.

Listing 2.3: A Custom Analyzer to Handle Stop Words

```
1   public class StandardBgramAnalyzer extends Analyzer {
2
3     public StandardBgramAnalyzer() { }
4     public TokenStream tokenStream (
5       String fieldName , Reader reader) {
6       return new StandardBgramFilter(
7         new LowerCaseFilter(
8           new StandardFilter(
9             new StandardTokenizer(reader) ) ) );
10    }
11  }
```

The StandardTokenizer (line 9) returns a list of tokens that have been parsed using a set of rules that works well for most European languages. It splits tokens at most punctuation characters including hyphens, but excluding the apostrophe and a period followed immediately by an alphabetic character. This will return possessive forms (the *cat's* meow) and acronyms (*U.S.A.*) as a single token. The `StandardFilter` (line 8) that follows makes some corrections to remove plurals from tokens with apostrophes and periods from an acronym.

The `StandardBgramFilter` (line 6) class creates the final list of tokens returned to the caller, from the list of tokens passed to the constructor. The set of stop words can be customized as needed. In this example, a list of 33 stop words has been used. The current, previous, and saved tokens and types are tracked since we need to build bigrams using more than one token.

The `next` method of the `StandardBgramFilter` class (not shown in the listing, but included in the distribution under the `ch2` directory) contains most of the code to generate token bigrams and returns the next `Token` in the stream. Tokens that start at the same position in the stream will be returned in ascending order by length. There are three types of tokens that can be seen in a text stream – a word, a stop word, and a null. The eight possible sequences in which these three types of tokens can occur in a stream are shown in Figure 2.2. The start position of a bigram token is the initial character position of the first token and the end position of the bigram is the final character position of the second token. The underscore character joins the two tokens to form the single bigram token of type BIGRAM.

2.2.7 Other Analyzers

Lucene includes a number of analyzers (in the `contrib` directory) to tokenize languages such as Chinese, German, and Russian. You can also use different analyzers for different parts of a document. For example, the contents of a book can be tokenized using the bigram analyzer while the title may be tokenized with a `WhitespaceAnalyzer` and the ISBN number using a `KeywordAnalyzer`. An ISBN number may consist of a sequence of digits or letters separated by a dash character. However, a partial ISBN number is generally not useful and the `KeywordAnalyzer` creates a single token from a text stream. In the next chapter, we will build a search engine index and set specific analyzers for parts (fields) of a document.

2.3 LingPipe Tokenizers

LingPipe (`http://www.alias-i.com`) has a set of tokenizer factories that are analogous to the Lucene analyzers. Each tokenizer factory uses a specific set of rules to generate tokens. However, in LingPipe a token is merely a string and does not contain any additional metadata such as the type, start, or end positions.

2.3.1 IndoEuropeanTokenizer

We can run the same sample text to generate a list of tokens using a LingPipe `IndoEuropeanTokenizerFactory` (see line 6 in Listing 2.4). A token is built using a set of rules that define a token boundary and with character sets for letters, numbers, and punctuation.

Listing 2.4: A LingPipe Tokenizer using the `IndoEuropeanTokenizerFactory`

```
1  public class LingpipeTokens {
2    public static void main(String[] args) {
3      String sentence = "Alice was ...";
4      char[] cs = sentence.toCharArray();
5      TokenizerFactory tokenizer_Factory =
6        new IndoEuropeanTokenizerFactory();
7      Tokenizer tokenizer = tokenizer_Factory.tokenizer(
8                          cs, 0, cs.length);
9      String[] tokens = tokenizer.tokenize();
10     for (int i = 0; i < tokens.length; i++)
11       System.out.println(i + "-->" + tokens[i] + "<--");
12   }
13 }
```

A list of the tokens is returned by the `tokenize` (line 9) method of the `Tokenizer` created from the tokenizer factory. The results from this tokenizer are similar to the list of tokens generated using the Lucene `SimpleAnalyzer`. LingPipe includes punctuation characters such as ? and , in separate tokens that are not extracted in the `SimpleAnalyzer`. The rules to generate a token in this tokenizer are fairly similar.

- A sequence of alphanumeric characters as defined by the `isDigit` or `isLetter` functions from the core `java.lang.Character` class.

36

- A sequence of digits, periods, or commas.

- A sequence of periods, dashes, equal signs, single or back quotes.

The list of tokens returned by the `tokenize` method is usually filtered to either remove stop words, generate word stems, or convert tokens to lower case.

2.3.2 Filtered Tokenizers

LingPipe provides tokenizers that perform functions similar to the Lucene filters. Notice, that none of the standard stop words have been removed and capitalization is preserved. If we replace the tokenizer statement in Listing 2.4 with the following statement, the list of tokens will exclude stop words and all returned tokens will be in lower case.

```
Tokenizer tokenizer = new LowerCaseFilterTokenizer(
  new EnglishStopListFilterTokenizer(
    tokenizer_Factory.tokenizer(cs, 0, cs.length)));
```

The English stop list filter class in LingPipe uses a set of 76 stop words (compared to Lucene's 33). There is no standard set of stop words; the most appropriate set of stop words will depend on the type of text being analyzed. The set of stop words are typically words that are seen in most documents and unlikely to be useful in a query. The stop list filter tokenizer allows the use of a custom stop word list.

```
HashSet<String> stoplist = new HashSet<String>();
stoplist.add("a"); stoplist.add("and"); . . .
Tokenizer tokenizer =
  new StopListFilterTokenizer(
    new LowerCaseFilterTokenizer(
      tokenizer_Factory.tokenizer(
      cs, 0, cs.length), stoplist));
```

LingPipe also includes a `PorterStemmerFilterTokenizer` class that implements the same stemming algorithm found in Lucene. It is the last filter applied in a chain after the stop list and lower case filters.

```
Tokenizer tokenizer =
  new PorterStemmerFilterTokenizer(
    new StopListFilterTokenizer(
      new LowerCaseFilterTokenizer(
        tokenizer_Factory.tokenizer(
        cs,0,cs.length), stoplist)));
```

Notice, Lucene uses a similar set of filters in the same order to construct a `PorterAnalyzer`. There are two other tokenizers in LingPipe used to extract tokens that match a regular expression and to build a list of character-based ngrams.

2.3.3 Regular Expression Tokenizer

Consider a text stream from which you need to extract a list of email addresses. You can build a custom regular expression tokenizer by defining the regular expression that must be matched for any token to be included in the list of tokens returned to the caller.

```
String regex =
  "\\b[\\w.%-]+@[\\w.-]+\\.[a-zA-Z]{2,4}\\b";
tokenizer_Factory = new RegExTokenizerFactory(regex);
Tokenizer tokenizer = tokenizer_Factory.tokenizer(
                      cs, 0, cs.length);
```

The list of tokens returned will include just the email addresses found in a text stream. You can build similar regular expression tokenizers to extract the list of URLs from a Web page. The `Pattern` class of the core `java.util.regex` package is used to check for matches and you can use the standard Java regular expression character sets, quantifiers, and boundary matchers to build a custom regular expression tokenizer.

2.3.4 Character-based Ngram Tokenizer

The ngram tokenizer in LingPipe is a character-based tokenizer that will generate ngrams from the input stream of characters. An ngram is a window of consecutive characters of a fixed length. Consider the sentence fragment - "*Alice was*". The ngrams of length five that can be generated from this text string are — "*Alice*", "*lice*", "*ice w*", "*ce wa*", and "*e was*". You can visualize the creation of ngrams as a sliding window of size five characters that moves from left to right till the last character of the text string. The size of ngrams can also be specified in a range.

```
tokenizer_Factory = new NGramTokenizerFactory(5, 7);
Tokenizer tokenizer = tokenizer_Factory.tokenizer(
                 cs, 0, cs.length);
```

The first parameter passed to the ngram tokenizer factory is the minimum size of ngrams and the second parameter is the maximum size of ngrams. In addition to the five ngrams of length 5, four ngrams of length 6 ("*Alice* ", "*lice w*", "*ice wa*", and "*ce was*") and three ngrams of length 7 ("*Alice w*", "*lice wa*", and "*ice was*") are included in the list of tokens. Consecutive space characters will not be collapsed into a single space character.

At first, generating character ngrams does not appear to be very useful, since most of the generated tokens do not represent words in a dictionary and the number of generated tokens is much higher than from other tokenizers. Yet, character ngrams play an important role in text processing tasks such as search engines (Chapter 4), categorization (Chapter 6), clustering (Chapter 7), and plagiarism detection (Chapter 9).

2.3.5 A LingPipe Tokenizer in a Lucene Analyzer

The task of plagiarism detection involves a fine grained comparison of test documents with a list of registered documents. The text from the list of original (registered) documents is tokenized and saved in a Lucene index. An analyzer is needed to create a Lucene index and we can generate a custom analyzer using the LingPipe ngram tokenizer (see Listing 2.5). Note, Lucene does include a `NGramTokenFilter` and a `NGramTokenizer` to build a ngram analyzer without LingPipe. This example illustrates how `Tokenizers` from LingPipe can be embedded in a Lucene `Analyzer`. The `StringTools` package (line 24) is included in the software distribution that accompanies the book.

Listing 2.5: A LingPipe Tokenizer Wrapped in a Lucene Analyzer

```
1  public final class NGramAnalyzer extends Analyzer {
```

```
2     public int minNgramLen , maxNgramLen ;
3
4     public NGramAnalyzer(int minNgramLen , int maxNgramLen) {
5       this.minNgramLen = minNgramLen ;
6       this.maxNgramLen = maxNgramLen ;
7     }
8
9     public TokenStream tokenStream(
10            String fieldName , Reader reader) {
11      return new NGramTokenizer(
12             reader , minNgramLen , maxNgramLen);
13    }
14
15    class NGramTokenizer extends Tokenizer {
16      String[] tokens ;
17      int currentToken = 0;
18      int currentPos = 0;
19      int tokenLen = 0;
20
21      public NGramTokenizer(Reader input ,
22             int minNgramLen , int maxNgramLen) {
23        super(input);
24        String text = StringTools.readerToString(input);
25        TokenizerFactory tokenizer_Factory = new
26          NGramTokenizerFactory(minNgramLen , maxNgramLen);
27        char[] cs = text.toCharArray ();
28        com.aliasi.tokenizer.Tokenizer tokenizer =
29         tokenizer_Factory.tokenizer(cs, 0, cs.length);
30        tokens = tokenizer.tokenize ();
31      }
32
33      public final Token next() {
34        if (currentToken >= tokens.length) return null;
35        int tlen = tokens[currentToken].length();
36        if (tlen != tokenLen) {
37          currentPos = 0;
38          tokenLen = tlen; // reset current position to zero
39        }                  // to start ngrams of a new length
40        Token token = new Token(tokens[currentToken],
41              currentPos , currentPos + tlen , "NGRAM");
42        currentToken ++;
```

```
43          currentPos++;
44          return token;
45      }
46    }
47  }
```

The `minNgramLen` and `maxNgramLen` (line 4) parameters passed to the analyzer correspond to the minimum and maximum lengths of ngrams. The inner `NGramTokenizer` (line 15) class extends the Lucene `Tokenizer` class. The constructor creates a string from the passed `Reader` (line 21) object and passes the text string to the LingPipe ngram tokenizer with the specified minimum and maximum ngram sizes (line 25). The `tokenize` (line 30) method of the LingPipe tokenizer class returns a list of token strings.

The `next` (line 33) method returns a Lucene token generated from the list of LingPipe tokens. In addition to the token text string, the start/end positions, and the type of token is needed to generate a Lucene token. When the size of an ngram changes, the current position in the text stream is reset and new tokens are built as before. The Lucene `TokenStream` (line 9) is analogous to the LingPipe `Tokenizer`. However, a Lucene `Analyzer` is more general and uses `Tokens` with position and type attributes in addition to the token text returned from the LingPipe tokenizer. Lucene version 2.1 includes an `NgramTokenizer` that has a similar signature and generates an identical set of ngrams.

2.3.6 A Lucene Analyzer in a LingPipe Tokenizer

A typo in a query submitted to a modern search engine will usually return a link - "Did you mean X ?" in an attempt to correct a spelling error. LingPipe's spell checker can be used to implement the "did you mean" link in a search interface. We need a LingPipe tokenizer that generates the same tokens as a Lucene analyzer to create a precise spell checker. In Listing 2.6, the `StandardBgramAnalyzer` is wrapped in a LingPipe `TokenizerFactory`.

Listing 2.6: A Lucene Analyzer Wrapped in a LingPipe Tokenizer

```
1  public class StandardBgramTokenizerFactory
2     implements TokenizerFactory {
3
4     public Tokenizer tokenizer(char[] ch,
```

```
5        int start, int length) {
6        return new StandardBgramTokenizer(ch, start, length);
7    }
8
9    class StandardBgramTokenizer extends Tokenizer {
10      private StandardBgramAnalyzer analyzer = null;
11      private TokenStream stream;
12
13      public StandardBgramTokenizer(char[] ch,
14         int offset, int length) {
15         analyzer = new StandardBgramAnalyzer();
16         String text = new String(ch);
17         if ( (offset != 0) || (length != ch.length) ) {
18            text = text.substring(offset, length);
19         }
20         stream = analyzer.tokenStream("contents",
21               new StringReader(text));
22      }
23
24      public String nextToken() {
25        Token token = stream.next();
26        return (token != null) ?
27           new String (token.termBuffer(),
28              0, token.termLength()):
29           null;
30      }
31    }
32 }
```

A LingPipe TokenizerFactory (line 2) class contains a tokenizer (line 4) method that returns a Tokenizer reference. The corresponding Tokenizer is used to build a list of tokens that are returned in order to the caller. The StandardBgramTokenizer (line 9) class uses the corresponding Lucene analyzer to generate a set of tokens. The tokens in this case are just strings alone, and do not include type or position information. The tokenStream method of the analyzer returns a stream from which individual tokens are extracted.

The abstract nextToken (line 24) method of the Tokenizer class is implemented to return the next token from the list of tokens. The tokenizers, filters, and analyzers in Lucene and LingPipe provide many ways to extract tokens from a text stream; you can see by this example, the power of combining tools from the two projects. For the most part, the extracted tokens are reasonable and work well in analyzing news articles or reports. However, extracting tokens from other types of unstructured text can be messy.

2.4 Gate Tokenizer

Gate [GATE] from the University of Sheffield is a general architecture to build text applications. We can build a more intelligent tokenizer using tools from Gate to extract some of the more complex tokens such as emoticons and collocations. Consider the following sentence from a news article.

> *A five billion USD credit facility being arranged for two units of British Petroleum Co Plc attracted over 15 billion dlrs in syndication but will not be increased, Morgan Guaranty Ltd said on behalf of Morgan Guaranty Trust Co of New York, the arranger.*

Notice, the currency figures are spelled out in more than one way and the abbreviation for dollars does not end in a period. The currency amounts can be given in words or in digits and there are many ways to specify US dollars (USD, US $, $, Dollars, or dlrs.). Numbers may be specified with or without commas and periods, and may use abbreviations such as *bln* and *mln* to represent billion and million respectively. Newswire text is mostly well formatted and such abbreviations are used fairly consistently, but blogs and other text genres are harder to predict and may use a format unknown to the tokenizer.

There is no guarantee that any tokenizer will always find composite tokens such as currency figures, dates, collocations, or emoticons. We can build dictionaries and rules for constructing such composite tokens and identify most of the composite tokens in a text stream. The Gate tokenizer uses this model to find tokens. For example, to identify a currency token, the dictionary for currencies and numbers is combined with a simple rule to tag a token. The rule to tag currencies is —

```
( {Lookup.majorType == currency_prefix} )?
    (NUMBER)
( {Lookup.majorType == currency_unit} )
```

A collection of dictionaries can be found in the `gazetteer` directory under the `plugins/ANNIE/resources` directory of the `data/gate` directory of the software distribution that accompanies this book. A dictionary is simply a list of terms in a plain text file. The name of the dictionary for currencies is `currency_unit.lst` and it contains a list of several hundred currency phrases such as *Deutsch Mark*, *USD*, and *Pounds Sterling*. All possible spellings for currencies to handle plurals and known abbreviations are included. A list has a major type and a minor type. For example, a list of city names will have a major type of *location* and a minor type of *city*. Similarly, a list of state names will have a major type of *location* and a minor type of *province* or *state*.

The `lookup` command in the rule describes a search for a major or minor type and the dictionary. Each dictionary has an associated major type and optional minor type. The major and minor types are specified in the `lists.def` file in the `gazetteer` directory. This file contains the table of dictionaries in the gazetteer and includes lines in the following format —

```
currency_prefix.lst:currency_prefix:pre_amount
currency_unit.lst:currency_unit:post_amount
```

Each line may have two or three fields. The first field is the file name, followed by the major type, and the optional minor type. In our rule to extract currency amounts, the major types of `currency_prefix` and `currency_unit` have been used. The currency prefix is an optional country code. You can specify phrases in a dictionary file and Gate will take care of finding a sequence of tokens to exactly match the phrase. This greatly simplifies the problem of finding multi-word currency tokens such as the "*Asian Currency Unit*".

Gate rules use a combination of lookups to find string matches and regular expression metacharacters to specify quantities. The question mark following the first pattern match for a currency prefix stands for 0 or 1 occurrences. Similarly, the metacharacters * and + can be used to represent 0 or more and 1 or more occurrences respectively. The rules to tag tokens are defined in the **NE** directory under the `plugins/ANNIE/resources` directory of the `data/gate` directory. This architecture (see Figure 2.3) for finding tokens offers more flexibility to extract and tag tokens than the Lucene analyzers or LingPipe tokenizers, but takes longer to run due to the additional dictionary lookups and semantic tagging. The Figure 2.3 is a simplified version of the Gate semantic tagging process.

Figure 2.3: Tokenizing a Text Stream using Gate

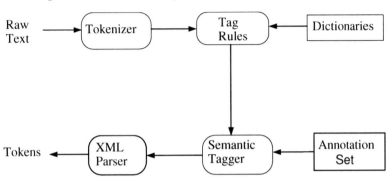

Raw text is fed to a tokenizer as before and the set of extracted tokens is passed to the tag rules to identify potential composite tokens. The initial tokenizer is simple and splits tokens on whitespaces and non-alphabetic characters with the exception of the hyphen character. The list of tag rules are validated using the gazetteer and composite tokens that match a rule are tagged in the text stream. The semantic tagger builds an XML tagged text stream using the list of annotations specified in the application. Finally, an XML tagged string is passed to a parser that builds tokens of specific types and returns a data structure containing lists of tokens for each particular entity type specified in the annotation set. Listing 2.7 is a tokenizer using the Gate architecture with a **GateTools** package (included in the software distribution that accompanies the book) to simplify the task.

Listing 2.7: A Gate Tokenizer using GateTools

```
1  public class GateTokens {
2    private static GateTools gt;
3    private static final String[] ANNOTATION_LIST = {
4      "Collocation", "Emoticon", "urlAddress",
5      "Number", "Token"
6    };
7
8    public static void main(String[] args) {
9      String sentence =
10       "Alice was beginning to get tired of ...";
11     gt = new GateTools();
```

45

```
12      gt.setforTokens(ANNOTATION_LIST);
13      String xmlOutput = gt.buildTokens(sentence);
14      gt.releaseResources();
15      ParseTokens parseTokens = new ParseTokens(
16         ANNOTATION_LIST);
17      parseTokens.runParse(xmlOutput);
18      // dump the tokens by type
19      Map<String, List<String>> allTokens =
20         parseTokens.getTokens();
21      for (int i = 0; i < ANNOTATION_LIST.length; i++) {
22        String etype = ANNOTATION_LIST[i];
23        List<String> eList = allTokens.get(etype);
24        System.out.println("Type: " + etype);
25        for (int j = 0; j < eList.size(); j++)
26          System.out.println(" " + eList.get(j));
27      }
28    }
29 }
```

The annotation set (line 3) is the list of token types that we would like to extract from the text stream. There are several other token types that are not shown in the listing and the annotation set can be truncated to extract a limited set of token types.

An instance of the GateTools (line 11) package is first created. The GateTools package contains methods to simplify the extraction of tagged tokens from a text stream. The buildTokens (line 13) method returns an XML tagged string containing a tagged text stream. So, the string returned from buildTokens for the sentence fragment shown in Listing 2.7 would look like —

```
<Start> <Token>Alice</Token> <Token>was</Token>
<Token>beginning</Token> <Token>to</Token> <Token>get</Token>
<Collocation> <Token>tired</Token> <Token>of</Token></Collocation> .
.   .
```

ParseTokens (line 15), an inner class not shown in the listing, implements an XML parser. The runParse (line 17) method accepts a tagged XML string and returns a HashMap containing token types and associated lists of tokens. Chapter 5 contains more information on Gate and how you can use it to extract currency amounts, names of people, places, organizations, dimensions, and Internet addresses.

2.4.1 A Gate Tokenizer in a Lucene Analyzer

The Gate tokenizer's unique features can be wrapped in a Lucene analyzer and used in a search engine. We may be interested in finding out how many smiley emoticons co-occur with a description of a product using a search engine. In Chapter 9, we will evaluate the sentiment of a text passage using a categorizer, and extracting emoticons will help to accurately predict sentiment. Similarly, identifying the collocations and their meanings will be useful to build an accurate semantic representation of a document. The Gate dictionaries and rules can be extended to add new terms or token types as needed.

The Gate analyzer works exactly like the Lucene analyzers we saw earlier, except that we pass the constructor a list of token types that should be tokenized. In the following example, three different token types are extracted.

```
String[] etypes = {"Token", "Emoticon",
  "Collocation"};
analyzer = new GateAnalyzer(etypes);
str = "Its a big project to lay on the line, "
  + " but it won't be long now. :-)";
displayTokensWithDetails(analyzer, str);
```

The list of extracted tokens have a start / end positions, a token type, and the contents of the token. The plain token types are similar to the tokens extracted using the `SimpleAnalyzer` with the exception of the punctuation tokens that are not included.

```
1:  Its:  Token 0:3
2:  a:  Token 4:5
3:  big:  Token 6:9
4:  project:  Token 10:17
5:  to:  Token 18:20
6:  lay:  Token 21:24
 .   .   .
10:  lay on the line:  Collocation 21:36
 .   .   .
14:  wo:  Token 45:47
15:  n't:  Token 47:50
16:  wo n't:  Collocation 44:50
```

. . .

24:   :-):   Emoticon 65:68

The `GateAnalyzer` in Listing 2.8 is similar to the earlier custom Lucene analyzers. The `GateTools` (line 21) class is used to extract tokens with the specified token types listed in the annotation set.

Listing 2.8: A Lucene Analyzer with a Gate Tokenizer

```
1   public final class GateAnalyzer extends Analyzer {
2     private String[] ANNOTATION_LIST = {"Token"};
3     public GateAnalyzer() { }
4     public GateAnalyzer(String[] annotationSet) {
5       this.ANNOTATION_LIST = annotationSet;
6     }
7     public TokenStream tokenStream(
8         String fieldName, Reader reader) {
9       return new GateTokenizer(reader);
10    }
11
12    class GateTokenizer extends Tokenizer {
13      private ArrayList<Token> luceneTokens =
14            new ArrayList<Token>();
15      private int currentToken = 0;
16      public GateTokenizer(Reader input) {
17        super(input);
18        // extract the text string from the reader
19        String text = StringTools.readerToString(input);
20        // Use Gate to tokenize the test
21        GateTools gt = new GateTools();
22        gt.setforTokens(ANNOTATION_LIST);
23        String xmlOutput = gt.buildTokens(text);
24        gt.releaseResources();
25        // Parse the tokenized string and build
26        // Lucene Tokens
27        ParseTokens parseTokens = new ParseTokens(
28              ANNOTATION_LIST, luceneTokens);
29        parseTokens.runParse(xmlOutput);
30      }
31    public Token next() {
32      if (currentToken == luceneTokens.size()) return null;
33      Token token = luceneTokens.get(currentToken);
34      currentToken++;
```

```
35      return (token);
36   }
37 }
```

A list of Lucene tokens is kept in an array and returned in order to the caller. If a list of token types is provided, then it is passed to the `GateAnalyzer` which then passes it to the `GateTokenizer` and finally to the `GateTools` class. The default is the plain `Token` type. The tagged text is built using the `buildTokens` (line 23) method of the `GateTools` class. Finally, the tagged text is parsed using the `ParseTokens` (line 27) class (not shown) and the list of tokens is returned in the array `luceneTokens`. Collocations and emoticons are not useful unless their meanings can be extracted and used to support search or other text applications. Fortunately, a widely used open source dictionary (see section 2.7 WordNet) is available and has a fairly comprehensive list of words, meanings, and a variety of relationships.

2.5 Tokenizing Problems

It is difficult to build a tokenizer for all genres of text without a universally accepted definition of a token. The basic definition of a token is a string of contiguous alphanumeric characters that may include hyphens and single quotes with a space character on either side. This definition excludes the start and end tokens in a text stream that may have a space character on just one side.

Unfortunately, text is not generated uniformly and may include abbreviations, missing spaces, missing punctuation, and interpreted numeric data, among a host of other possibilities that do not follow the strict definition of a token. For example consider the string "*$23.50*"; should the dollar sign be part of the numeric token or be excluded? There is no rule for the generation of such tokens and it probably depends on your application. If your application needs to capture currencies as part of a price, then it makes sense to include the dollar sign, otherwise the numeric value is sufficient to indicate a price. An alternative would be to index both the numeric value and the entire string with the dollar sign, providing more flexibility in query generation. In Chapter 4, we will look at the use of various query types and queries to match a range of numeric values.

Hyphens

The basic definition of a token includes a hyphen as one of the accepted characters to form a token. So, the text string "one-on-one" will be treated as a single token. However, sometime hyphens do appear at the end of a line when a word is broken to align the lines. Because of the ambiguity of these hyphens, which could either be introduced for alignment purposes or exist as part of an ordinarily hyphenated token, they cannot be arbitrarily removed to build a whole token.

Roughly four percent of the words in a dictionary (See section 2.7 WordNet in this chapter) contain a hyphen. The 7200 hyphenated words in the dictionary include words such as — *.22-caliber*, *able-bodied*, *African-American*, *x-ray*, *e-mail*, and *Al-quaida*. However, hyphenation is often inconsistently implemented in text, even for these words; the hyphen may be replaced with a space or even omitted (*email*). We need to collapse the various spellings of these words to identify a canonical form to find the corresponding dictionary word. In a formal publication, inconsistent usage of the same term would be corrected during the editing process, but in a Web page or a blog there is no defined usage convention. In Chapter 5, we will look at ways of extracting specific token types using pattern matching with Gate. Hyphenated words are rare. In a sample newswire text of 20K words, only about 0.5% of the total number of words were hyphenated.

A hyphenated word is often used as a modifier for a noun and occurs *before* the noun. For example, the modifier *armor-clad* in the sentence - "*The armor-clad vehicle was used to hunt for roadside bombs*" occurs before the modified noun *vehicle*. A modifier *following* a noun and well-known modifiers may not be hyphenated.

Some words are modified with a prefix and hyphen to form a compound word. For example, the modifier *non* is added to the words *member* and *food* to form the compound words *non-member* and *non-food* respectively. Neither of these compound words exists in the dictionary, and separating the compound words would not retain the meaning of the word. Other examples of such words include *pick-up*, *down-time*, *April-March*, *end-December*, and so on. Some of the common prefixes are a number, *un*, *non*, and *pre* while common suffixes include *member*, *based* and *term*. In general, a hyphenated word made up of more than three words should probably be split into individual words. There are a few rare cases that can be found in a dictionary such as *jack-in-the-pulpit* and *up-to-date*.

The en-dash (–) and em-dash(—) are longer forms of the hyphen character. The en-dash is used to represent a range as in the set of digits 0–9. The even longer em-dash is typically used in a long sentence to indicate a break in the structure of the sentence or thought expressed in the sentence.

Apostrophes

There are other characters such as the apostrophe (') that are usually not part of the token character set. The apostrophe is found in proper nouns such as the name *O'Reilly* and the country *Côte d'Ivoire* . The most common method of extracting such tokens is to use a Gazetteer containing the list of known entries with apostrophes. It is easier to make words containing an apostrophe the exception and then check if any can be found in the gazetteer. A small percentage (0.8%) of the words in the WordNet dictionary contain apostrophes. Examples include - *rock'n'roll, t'ai chi,* and *Ohm's law.*

Many of the dictionary words containing apostrophes indicate the possessive form of a noun. An apostrophe and the letter *s* are added to a common noun such as *owner* to form *owner's*. The Lucene standard analyzer generates these tokens with type APOSTROPHE and strips the trailing *s* character. In LingPipe, the `isLetter` method (`IndoEuropeanTokenizer` class) can be modified to include the apostrophe as a legitimate token character.

Another use of the apostrophe is to indicate the omission of letters in words (called *contractions*) such as *wouldn't, he'll,* or *I'm*. Keeping contractions as they appear or expanding them to their full form depends on the application. Specifically, it will be easier to identify pronouns that refer to a noun elsewhere in the text when the expanded form of the text is used. The apostrophe (') is distinguished from opening quotes ("), closing quotes ("), and typewriter quotes ("). Additionally, apostrophes can indicate a plural as in - "*mind your p's and q's*" or *1980's*. A few English words that have foreign origins such as *maitre d'* and *coup d'etat* also use the apostrophe.

Diacritic Letters

Words with diacritic letters like *Les Misérables* or *naïve* are handled using the character's category defined in the core `java.lang.Character` package. Tokenizers will include any legitimate character in a token belonging to a *letter* or *digit* category.

The `StandardAnalyzer` does not modify such letters and the generated tokens will include these letters. You can filter these letters to their unaccented form using the `ISOLatin1AccentFilter`.

```
public class DiacriticAnalyzer
    extends StandardAnalyzer {
  public TokenStream tokenStream(
      String fieldName, Reader reader) {
    return new ISOLatin1AccentFilter(
      super.tokenStream(fieldName, reader));
  }
}
```

The `DiacriticAnalyzer` is similar to the custom analyzers we saw earlier such as the `PorterAnalyzer` and `StandardBgramAnalyzer`. A token stream returned by the parent `StandardAnalyzer` is filtered to remove diacritics and returned to the caller. Removing diacritics may improve the recall (see section 4.5) of a search engine. The same analyzer is used during indexing and search.

Other Characters

Some of the other characters that can be found in a token include the period, one or more digits, and the slash character. The period is found in several other types of tokens.

- Honorifics such as *Mr.*, *St.* or *Dr.*

- Words like *.com*, *.Net*, and *.22 caliber*

- Abbreviations *a.k.a.*, *o.k.*, and *p.m.*

In most cases honorifics are followed by a person name and should be considered a single token. Abbreviations are somewhat harder to handle since the period is not always provided. There is also the problem of detecting the period in a sentence that ends with an abbreviation. The period serves as a punctuation mark ending the sentence, as well as indicating an abbreviation. Some honorifics such *St.* and *Dr.* can also be abbreviations for *street* and *drive* respectively and the meaning of such tokens depends on the context. Finally, there is a miscellaneous collection of tokens that contain dashes, digits, and slashes — *carbon-14, 22-karat, 9/11, y2k, 1980s, 401-k, 4-1/2,* and *20/20.* In general, numbers that are spelled out should be detected as numeric tokens; methods to detect such tokens will be described in Chapter 5.

Collocations

Till now, we have mostly considered tokens that consist of a single word. However, there is a large number (41% in WordNet) of entries in a dictionary that consist of more than one word. These words are very often seen together in order and have a distinct meaning. For example, the words *"take on", "close in"*, and *"pay out"* have unique meanings that are not easily discernible, if the constituent words are not shown in order. Such composite words or collocations are selected by lexicographers for inclusion in a dictionary, if the individual words tend to co-occur more often than just by chance and whose meaning is not easily gleaned from the component words.

Idioms tend to be a little longer than the earlier examples and use a symbol or an image to convey a meaning more clearly. The individual words alone do not express the meaning and idioms become popular through frequent usage. Some examples include - *"once in a blue moon"*, *"rule of thumb"*, and *"walk the plank"*. A tokenizer that breaks up such words will clearly lose the intended meaning. We can identify such tokens using a rule-based tokenizer (see section 2.4 Gate Tokenizer).

Special Tokens

Other types of tokens such as URLs and phone numbers can be extracted using the tokenizers we have seen so far. An *emoticon* is a string of special characters used in text messages to indicate emotions or attitudes that would normally be conveyed using body language in face-to-face communication. Such tokens are difficult to extract using a simple set of rules since almost any character can be used to build an emoticon and the list of emoticons continues to grow. One way to detect emoticons is to compare extracted tokens against a dictionary of all known emoticons (see section 2.4 Gate Tokenizer). Other special tokens use non-alphanumeric characters to form abbreviations such as *$$$* for *expensive* or *Micro$oft* to disparage a company.

URLs and other Internet addresses are special cases of tokens, and rules can be built to detect such tokens. For example, an URL will have a prefix from a known set of protocols such as `http`, `ftp`, or `file` followed by a colon and two slashes and an Internet host name and optional file name. These rules can be built using regular expressions to extract a complete Internet address. In chapter 5, we will look at how to build such regular expressions using Gate. Note that these regular expressions will simply verify a pattern against a text string and do not check the semantics. For example, a text stream that ends a sentence with a period and no leading space for the next sentence (end.In ...) may falsely indicate an Internet host name.

A simple numeric token is a string of digits with optional commas and periods. More complex numeric tokens can be expressed in a scientific notation and include characters such as $+$, $-$, and the letter E. Other numeric tokens that match a pattern may indicate a phone number, a social security number, or a credit card number. These numeric tokens include characters such as $($, $)$, and $-$. The number of digits and format for a phone number is not universal and each country may follow a unique format. In some cases, the leading part of the phone number that indicates a country or city code may be optional. Despite these differences, it is not very difficult to construct a regular expression to extract phone numbers, provided all the occurrences in the text follow the rules for phone numbers. However, regular expressions are brittle and a slight change in the format may lead to a pattern mismatch. Credit card and social security numbers are similarly extracted with hand crafted regular expressions to match all possible ways of expressing these numbers.

Not all numbers are stated using digits alone. A text representation of a number such as "*twenty one*" is not converted to a number in most tokenizers. The two words *twenty* and *one* are simply added to a list of tokens and the intended meaning is lost. A tokenizer should convert the text description into a numeric description and optionally keep both descriptions. Some text descriptions of numbers can be more than five words in length and can include fractions. The numeric description makes it much easier to perform arithmetic computations such as addition or comparisons. The Gate tokenizer (see Section 2.4) can identify most of these text descriptions of numbers.

2.6 Text Extraction

All the examples we have seen so far have used plain text files or hard coded text strings. Nonetheless, it is more common to find formatted text files than plain text files. Text extraction is not related to tokenization, but is a necessary precursor to extract tokens from a formatted file. Formatted text files can be made to look like printed documents with colors, fonts, and styles. A text filter created for a particular type of formatted document in most cases extracts the text contents alone, ignoring any metadata. Unfortunately, there is some loss of information in this process since an author who highlights or enlarges the font of text intended to assign greater importance to a chunk of text. In general, text filters do not retain this information; header text will be given the same importance as the body text.

We select the text filter for a document using a simple look-up in a table (see Figure 2.4). If files are named using a standard file naming convention, then the suffix is a key to the text filter table. For example, a file with a `pdf` suffix would use the `PdfHandler` class of the `org.btext.bdb` package. You can download a collection of open source filters from `http://mustru.sf.net`. These filters are based on third party libraries which have independent open source licenses. Of course on the Web, the suffix of a file cannot be trusted and it may be necessary to verify the format of a file before using a filter. The filters described in this section are not comprehensive and many commercial alternatives exist to handle a larger number of formats.

MS Word

Microsoft Office is still the dominant desktop office suite; many documents on the Internet are formatted using proprietary Microsoft formats such as .DOC and .PPT. The Apache Jakarta Poor Obfuscation Implementation (POI) project was initiated to build a set of Java APIs to read and write MS Office files. In our examples, we are mainly interested in extracting text from these files and less with manipulating the contents. The POI APIs are fairly easy to use and work well most of the time, but it can be useful to have a backup program to handle those cases where the POI API fails to extract any text. Listing 2.9 shows a simple MS Word text filter using the POI API.

Figure 2.4: Text Extraction from Formatted Files

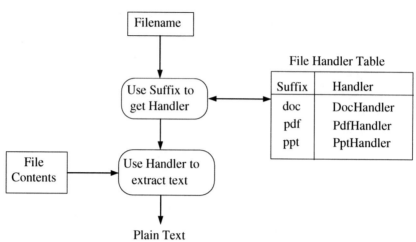

Listing 2.9: Extracting Text from a MS Word Document using the POI API

```
1  public class DocFilter {
2
3     public static void main(String[] args) {
4        String textFile = "sample.doc";
5        System.out.println("Extracted Text: "
6           + getDocument(textFile));
7     }
8
9     public static String getDocument(String ifile) {
10       WordDocument wd = new WordDocument(
11          new FileInputStream( new File(ifile) ) );
12       StringWriter docTextWriter = new StringWriter();
13       wd.writeAllText(docTextWriter);
14       docTextWriter.close();
15       return(docTextWriter.toString());
16    }
17 }
```

The name of the file is passed to the `getDocument` (line 6) method which returns the plain text contents from the file. A `WordDocument` (line 10) is instantiated using an `inputStream` created from the file name. The `writeAllText` (line 13) method dumps the text to a `StringWriter` that collects the output in a `StringBuffer` and finally returns a string to the caller. If no text was extracted, you can either try an alternative POI API or a program like Antiword (`http://www.winfield.demon.nl`).

PDF

Files formatted using the Portable Document Format (PDF) format from Adobe are as popular as MS Word files and text from these files can be extracted using the PDFBox library (`http://www.pdfbox.org`). This Java open source library includes features to extract text and manipulate PDF files. An encrypted PDF file will not be read unless the correct password is passed to a decrypt document method. PDF documents also may include other metadata information such as the title, author, keywords, and summary. The PDFBox library contains methods to extract this optional metadata. An example of the code to extract text from PDF files is shown in the `PdfHandler` class of the `org.btext.bdb` package.

HTML

There are many different ways of extracting text from HTML files and we will look at one method using the HtmlParser (`http://htmlparser.sourceforge.net`) project. At first, the text extraction task appears to be simple since HTML files are already in plain text, all that remains is to remove tags. However, HTML documents can be very messy and a simple regular expression to remove all tags will work on only the most simple HTML pages. A more robust solution is to use a parser that will tolerate errors and not drop text that is formatted with broken HTML tags.

The `HtmlHandler` class in the `org.sf.mustru.filters` package uses the Html-Parser API to extract text from a HTML document. The parse methods are powerful and specific portions of the HTML document such as the title or metadata alone can be extracted. You can also extract finer grain metadata information such as the author and keywords. HtmlParser has other uses as well including extraction of HTML links, collecting form data, and monitoring sites.

PPT

Microsoft PowerPoint is the presentation tool in the MS Office suite and is also quite popular. The Apache POI API that we used to extract text from MS Word documents can be used for MS PowerPoint files as well. The API includes methods to extract the text and notes from slides. Notice, the text from the title and the body are treated equivalently. Although the API is simple to use, there will be occasions where no text is extracted and as a backup a simpler class (called the quick but cruddy text extractor) may work. Example code is shown in the `PptHandler` class of the `org.sf.mustru.filters` package.

PS

The PostScript (PS) format was once the de facto standard for documents published online. The PS format has since been superseded by PDF, which combined part of the PostScript description language with fonts and graphics that could be bundled into a single file. There are several Postscript converters that extract text from a PS file - ps2a, ps2ascii, ps2txt, and ps2ascii. The example code in the `PsHandler` class in the `org.sf.mustru.filters` package, creates a batch script to run the `ps2txt` executable program. The output of the script is saved in a buffer and returned to the caller. You will need to compile the **ps2txt** C program to run on your platform.

OpenOffice.org

The OpenOffice.org suite of tools is the multi-platform open source alternative to MS Office and supports over 60 different languages. It includes a word processor, spreadsheet, presentation manager, and a drawing program. While separate programs were created (reverse engineered) to handle proprietary MS Office formats, extracting text from OpenOffice.org files is much simpler.

Files are published using the OpenDocument file Format (ODF) unless the user specifically requests a different format. The ODF format is an XML based format that is distributed freely. All OpenOffice.org files with the exception of Math documents use the ODF format. The actual files are compressed using the ZIP archiving tool, originally developed by PKWARE, Inc. ODF has become an open format that can be implemented by both open source and proprietary software.

The extraction of text from OpenOffice.org files requires two steps. In the first step, we uncompress the file to generate the XML tagged file and other associated files. Any XML parser can then be used to extract the data from the XML tagged file. The example code in the `SxwHandler` class of the `org.sf.mustru.filters` package uses the Simple API for XML (SAX) parser (`http://xml.apache.org`). The core `java.util` package contains methods to extract files from a ZIP archive. We are interested in a particular file called `content.xml`. This file is the XML tagged version of the text contents of the OpenOffice.org file. However, we need the Document Type Definitions (DTD) to utilize the data. The DTD files are freely available and included with the sample code. In our example, we are merely extracting the text in a buffer to pass on the file contents to another application. There are a few default suffixes for OpenOffice.org files, but many other suffixes are used as well.

RTF

The Rich Text Format (RTF) is a proprietary document format developed by Microsoft to allow cross-platform document interchange. You can view and edit RTF files using several word processors. The specification for the RTF format is distributed freely by Microsoft and this allows vendors of output devices and other word processors to support RTF files. The example code in the `RtfHandler` class of the `org.sf.mustru.filters` package uses the `RTFEditorKit` class available in the `javax.swing` package to extract text from a RTF formatted file.

LaTeX

LaTeX and TeX are document preparation tools, popular in the scientific and technical communities to publish articles and books. It is a markup based language, but unlike XML, it is compiled to a device independent format which is translated to an output device format. The example code in the `TexHandler` class of the `org.sf.mustru.filters` package uses third party software (DeTeX) to extract text from a LaTeX or TeX source file. Note that mathematical formulas will be extracted to plain text and will not be very useful to identify equations.

XLS

Most files created using the Microsoft Excel spreadsheet program use the xls suffix. The earlier versions of Excel used a proprietary binary format and the later versions use an XML based format. You may have to use different tools to extract text from an Excel file depending on the version of Excel used to produce the file. The example code in the `XlsHandler` class of the `org.sf.mustru.filters` package uses the Horrible Spreadsheet Format (HSSF) package of the Apache POI project. The HSSF classes provide methods to iterate over all cells in the spreadsheet. The example code loops through all rows and for every row, the text from each column is appended to a buffer. Finally, the buffer is dumped to a string and returned to the caller.

Other Sources

There are several other text sources that may contain useful information. Audio and video transcripts are distributed by information providers to make the text searchable as well as accessible to those who cannot view or hear the contents. Public media organizations usually make available the transcripts of interviews and documentaries. These text files are harder to manage than well formatted newswire articles. Typically, the conversion to text is made automatically using speech recognition software. Voicemail and phone conversations can also be similarly converted to transcripts for future reference.

The transcripts may not clearly indicate punctuation or sentences, and includes pauses and errors in the conversion. Since the transcript is a recording of an audio presentation, there may be broken sentences, intermittent pauses, corrections, and noises such as applause or laughter to contend with. An oral correction that follows an error is not indicated in the transcript.

Speech recognition software has become more accurate over the years and the number of transcript errors are fewer. Occasionally, accents do cause problems in the conversion process, for example *"Iraq"* to *"I Rock"* and *"pool"* to *"Paul"* or the harder to detect *"their"* to *"they're"*. Abbreviations for time such as *a.m.* and *p.m.* may appear as individual letters without any periods. These errors cannot easily be automatically detected and corrected.

Several large scale digital library projects are underway to convert the thousands of printed books and journals in libraries to a digital form. The Million Book project at Carnegie Mellon University is an attempt to make available the vast quantity of information that lies unused in physical libraries. Most students and faculty tend to rely on online information that is easily accessible. The speed and convenience of information access with a Web search engine is hard to match in a traditional library system. When the project is complete, the contents of a million or more useful books and journals will be accessible online. An added benefit of these projects will be the availability of this information to anyone who has access to the Web.

Multimedia files have little or no text that can be extracted from the file contents itself. Most image, audio, and video files have little or no metadata that is suitable for indexing. It is still very hard to automatically create a description of an image from binary image data alone. Features such as mountains, faces, and other objects can be automatically recognized, but a manually generated description is almost always of higher precision.

2.7 WordNet

A traditional dictionary lists words and their meanings in alphabetical order with little additional information about the various relationships between the words and their meanings. Each word may have the meaning, pronunciation, part of speech, and optionally a brief description of the origin of the word. WordNet (`http://wordnet.princeton.edu`), a freely available resource from the Princeton University's cognitive science department, contains the meanings of words, the senses, and a number of relationships betweens words and meanings. Every word belongs to a set of synonyms (or *synset*) that defines the meaning of the word. The words in a synset express the same meaning. For example, one of the meanings of the noun *subject* is described by the synset – *subject*, *topic*, and *theme*. The synset consisting of *national* and *subject* is another meaning. Words that have more than one meaning will be part of multiple synsets, each representing a sense of the word.

The dictionaries for content words in WordNet come from four parts of speech – nouns, verbs, adjectives, and adverbs. The software distributed with the book contains the same files in a format that can be loaded into a database made up of five tables (see Table 2.1).

Table 2.1: WordNet Database Tables and Descriptions

Name	Description
Words	The word, a part of speech and all synsets that include the word
Synsets	The synset, all member words of the synset, and an example sentence fragment
Word Relationships	A word, a related word, and a description of the type of relationship
Synset Relationships	A synset, a related synset, and a description of the type of relationship
Excluded Words	A word, a part of speech, and a word stem

The first two tables, the *Words* and *Synsets* tables, describe the many-to-many relationship between words and synsets. The next two relationship tables describe a collection of word relationships and synset relationships. The last table is used to build word stems for words that are not explicitly included in the dictionary.

Words from the four parts of speech make up over 95% of the words in a traditional dictionary. There are over 20 different types of word relationships used in WordNet, including synonyms, antonyms, hypernyms, hyponyms, meronyms. and derivations. Some of the common relationships are shown in Table 2.2.

Table 2.2: Common Relationship Types

Relationship	Type	Paired Relationship
Holonym (whole)	Synset	Meronym (part)
Hypernym (general)	Synset	Hyponym (specific)
Antonym (opposite)	Word	Synonym (similar)

A meronym represents a part relationship and a holonym the whole relationship — a *finger* is a meronym of *hand* and the *hand* is a holonym of *finger*, *palm*, and *metacarpus*. In WordNet both holonyms and meronyms are specialized into member, part, or substance categories. A hypernym is a more general meaning of a word and a hyponym is a specialized meaning — the hypernym of *athlete* is *contestant* and some of the hyponyms of *contestant* include *athlete, rival, challenger, competitor,* and *opponent.* The first four relationships in Table 2.2 are synset relationships, which implies that the meanings of the words and the associated synonyms are related. The remaining two relationships, antonyms and synonyms, describe relationships between individual words.

Part of the raw data for the WordNet dictionary is distributed in the form of index and data files. A data file and an index file is included for each of the four parts of speech. The index files for nouns contains a list of all nouns in alphabetic order with the associated relationships and synsets. A single noun may be part of several synsets. For example, the word *son* is part of two synsets (see Figure 2.5). Each synset is a numeric offset into a data file for the part of speech. So, the synsets for the word *son* are located at the offsets *10624074* and *09537144* in the *data.noun* file. The synset, associated relationships and synsets, and examples of usage are found at the offsets. Figure 2.5 shows four different synsets and relationships between words within synsets and the synsets themselves.

Figure 2.5: Synset and Word Relationships

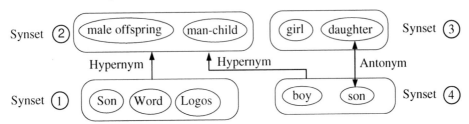

There is a many-to-many relationship between synsets and words. The word *son* occurs in more than one synset and a synset may contain more than one word. A hypernym is a semantic relationship between two synsets and represents a more general meaning of a specific synset. An antonym is a lexical relationship between two words in two separate synsets. All relationships in WordNet are either semantic or lexical relationships.

A word that occurs in more than one synset is said to have multiple senses. The word *son* has more than one sense — the meaning in synset 4 and the religious meaning in synset 1. In this case both synsets are noun synsets, but a word such as *equal* has a total of six senses (two adjective, one noun, and three verb senses). In a lexical relationship, a word from one sense is related to a word in another sense. However, the word itself may participate in more than one lexical relationship. The word *equal* has an antonym in the verb sense (*differ*) and another antonym in the adjective sense (*unequal*).

The raw dictionary files from WordNet are hard to extend, since the location of synsets is identified with hard-coded byte offsets. Instead, the source files can be translated into a set of tables that can be loaded into a database. At least four types of tables are needed — words, synsets, word relationships, and synset relationships. The word table (see Table 2.3) has three columns, the word, a part of speech and the associated synsets.

Table 2.3: Sample Rows from the Words Table

Word	POS	Synsets
son	noun	n10624074, n09537144
equal	adjective	a00889831, a00051045
equal	noun	n09626238
equal	verb	v02664769, v02672187, v00417001

The list of words (155K) in the *Words* table is maintained in lower case, making it easier to search. Since all WordNet synsets are kept in a single table, the offsets have been prefixed with the first letter of the part of speech, to insure uniqueness. The unique key to this table is the combination of the word and part of speech. The next table is the table of synsets (see Table 2.4).

Table 2.4: Sample Rows from the Synsets Table

Synset	Words	Examples
n10624074	son, boy	a male human offspring ...
a00051045	adequate, equal	having the requisite qualities ...
n09626238	peer, equal, match, compeer	a person who is of equal ...
v02672187	equal, touch, rival, match	be equal to in quality ...

Each synset is a unique key in this table of about 117K rows. The words are members of the synset and the examples illustrate the usage of some of the words in text fragments. The third table is a list (42K) of the relationships between words (see Table 2.5).

Table 2.5: Sample Rows from the Word Relationships Table

Word1	Relationship	POS	Word2
son	antonym	noun	daughter
equal	antonym	adjective	unequal
equal	antonym	verb	differ

The key to the word relationship table is the combination of the word, relationship and part of speech and the associated row contains a single related word. Notice, a word such as *equal* can have more than one antonym. The word relationships shown in Table 2.5 are reflexive, i.e. a corresponding row exists for each of the three rows with the words in columns **Word1** and **Word2** swapped. The last table (see Table 2.6) is the synset relationship table, which also happens to be the largest table, with over 163K entries.

Table 2.6: Sample Rows from the Synset Relationships Table

Synset	Relationship	Synset
n10624074	hypernym	n10285938
n10285938	hyponym	n10624074

The hypernym of synset n10624074 (*son, boy*) is the synset n10285938 (*man-child, male_offspring*) and the paired or hyponym relationship is shown in the second row. The source for these tables can be found in the `data/wordnet` directory of the software distribution. The `LoadTables` class (`org.btext.bdb` package) loads four database tables from the source data. The open source Berkeley DB Java Edition (from Oracle) is used to load and access the tables. A relational database such as MySQL or PostgreSQL can also be used, but the embedded Berkeley DB has little overhead, is scalable, and works well for a read-only database.

The `WordnetTools` class in the `org.btext.wordnet` package contains methods to access the WordNet tables. The source data for the WordNet tables should be loaded before using any of these methods. Listing 2.10 shows the code to find word and synset relationships.

Listing 2.10: Finding Relationships of Words using WordNetTools

```
1  public class TestWord {
2    public static void main(String[] args) {
3      WordnetTools wnetTools = new WordnetTools();
4      wnetTools.openBDB();
5      System.out.println("The antonyms of equal are " +
6        wnetTools.relatedWords("equal", "antonym", true));
7      System.out.println("The hypernym of athlete is " +
8        wnetTools.relatedWords("athlete", "hypernym"));
9      System.out.println("The hyponyms of mustang are " +
10       wnetTools.relatedWords("mustang", "hyponym", true));
11     wnetTools.closeBDB();
12   }
13 }
```

This program will generate the following output:
```
The antonyms of equal are differ, unequal
The hypernym of athlete is contestant
The hyponyms of mustang are bronco, bronc, broncho
```
The `relatedWords` (line 6) method returns a string of words for synset and word relationships. The first parameter is the word, followed by the relationship, and an optional boolean flag to find all possible relationships. If the flag is set to true, then related words from all parts of speech will be returned. The `relatedWords` method is also overloaded to accept a part of speech as well, so you could find only the noun hyponyms of the word *mustang*.

Word and synset relationships are handled differently. The related words for a word relationship can be extracted directly from Table 2.5. It takes three steps to find the related words for a synset relationship. In the first step, the associated synsets of a word are extracted from Table 2.3. Next, the related synsets for parts of speech are found from Table 2.6, and finally the list of words from the related synsets are returned using the Table 2.4. Synonym relationships are an exception since only two Table lookups (2.3 and 2.4) are needed to find related words.

2.7.1 Word Stems and WordNet

Earlier in this chapter, we used the Porter stemmer algorithm to build a custom Lucene analyzer. The main reason for using a stemmer was to reduce the size of the index, by collapsing word inflections to root words, and also possibly to improve performance (see section 2.2.5 PorterAnalyzer earlier in this chapter). Words such as *taller* and *tallest* would be reduced to the single stem word *tall*. However, the Porter algorithm is strictly rule-based and cannot collapse words such as *said* to *say* or *were* to *be*. As we also saw, some of the root words created with the Porter algorithm do not exist in the dictionary.

WordNet takes a slightly different approach to find a root word. First, a dictionary of exclusion words is checked for a match. The table of exclusion words (see Table 2.7) contains the inflected words, part of speech, and the associated root word.

Table 2.7: Sample Rows from the Excluded Words

Inflected Word	POS	Root Word
stirring	verb	stir
jumped off	verb	jump off
worst	adjective	bad

The table of about 6K rows contains words whose stems cannot be easily constructed by applying a set of rules — so-called irregular forms. Notice, WordNet also uses the part of speech to define a root word in the table. If the table lookup fails, a rule based suffix algorithm is used. If the word *instructs* is not found in both the words (Table 2.3) and exclusion words (Table 2.7) tables, then a suffix rule is invoked to generate the root word *instruct*. The suffix rules in WordNet are shown in Table 2.8.

The hybrid approach of combining a table lookup and suffix rules makes it easier to handle the many exceptions to a suffix removal rule. A root word is found by first checking the exclusion table before applying the suffix removal rule. The `baseWord` method of the `WordnetTools` class in the `org.btest.wordnet` package uses an `inDictionary` method to find if a word exists in the dictionary (see Listing 2.11). A root form of the word is generated from the exclusion table (Table 2.7) and suffix removal rules (Table 2.8).

Table 2.8: WordNet Rules to Remove Suffixes

Noun Rules	Verb Rules	Adjective Rules
s→null	s→null	er→e or null
ses → s	ies → y	est→e or null
xes→x	es→e or null	
zes→z	ed→e or null	
ches→ch	ing→e or null	
shes→sh		

Listing 2.11: Searching the Dictionary for Words or Root Words

```
1  public class WordNetExamples {
2    static WordnetTools wnetTools;
3    public static void main(String[] args) {
4      wnetTools = new WordnetTools();
5      wnetTools.openBDB();
6      System.out.println("Boy in dictionary: " +
7        wnetTools.inDictionary("boy"));
8      System.out.println("Mark up in dictionary: " +
9        wnetTools.inDictionary("mark up"));
10     System.out.println("Marked up NOT in dictionary: " +
11       wnetTools.inDictionary("marked up"));
12     System.out.println("Base word of marked up: " +
13       wnetTools.baseWord("marked up"));
14     System.out.println("Base word of granulomata: " +
15       wnetTools.baseWord("granulomata"));
16     wnetTools.closeBDB();
17   }
18 }
```

The inDictionary (line 7) method checks the Words table (Table 2.3) for the existence of an entry with an associated part of speech. If no part of speech is passed, then all four parts of speech will be used to search the dictionary. Words such as *boy* and *mark up* exist in the table while the inflected word *marked up* is not present. It is harder to find the root word of collocations since the removal of the suffix of the last word may not be sufficient to extract the root word. For example, the suffix of the first word in the collocation *marked up* should be removed to obtain the root word.

2.8 Summary

In this chapter we looked at a number of tokenizers / analyzers to extract a list of tokens from a text stream. Some of the tokenizers used a simple list of rules to define the characters that make up a token and a token boundary. Other tokenizers used a dictionary and a set of rules to find tokens made up of more than one word or a set of symbols.

There is no single tokenizer that is ideal for all applications and the best analyzer depends on the type of text and usage in an application. A complex tokenizer may be better suited for an application that uses semantic tools to understand the meaning of text. A simpler tokenizer may be appropriate for a ngram-based application. A tokenizer that performs many dictionary look-ups will also be slower than a tokenizer that breaks up text using a set of rules.

Finally, you can create a custom tokenizer for a specific application. Both LingPipe and Lucene include base classes that can be extended to build custom tokenizers. Our discussion in this chapter has been limited to the tokenization of English alone, but Lucene includes analyzers for several other languages including German, French, and Russian. Tokenizing text in languages like Chinese and German is harder than tokenizing English text. There are no whitespace characters to separate tokens in Chinese, and German uses compound words that should be broken to make up more than one token. Tokenizers are not limited to processing text alone, and can be used to handle source code as well. A Lucene analyzer for source code would perform the same function as a lexical analyzer in a compiler for the programming language in which the source code is written. In Chapter 3, Indexing Text, we will look at building an index from a set of documents using the Lucene API.

3 Indexing Text with Lucene

This chapter introduces indexing, a crucial part of the most common tool to manage a large collection of documents: the search engine. This chapter assumes that you have an existing collection of documents to index. It is challenging to build a high performance index for a collection of documents from scratch. Fortunately, there are several open source options available and this chapter will introduce the Lucene API to build an index.

> *Note: In Chapter 8, we will look at the collection of information from an Intranet or the Web using a spider. Chapter 4 will include the development of a search interface for the indexed documents.*

3.1 Databases and Search Engines

The initial computer applications in the early 1950s were primarily developed to solve computationally intensive problems such as weather prediction and ballistic trajectories. The data processing applications that followed were viewed as efficient solutions to store and retrieve a large number of records. Later, it became possible to store small amounts of text, typically bibliographic data that could be searched. The vast improvements in hardware and storage capacities have made it possible to store the entire text of documents including metadata. Today, the major computer-based information systems are database systems, search engines, and question-answer systems.

A search engine is used to store, retrieve, and manage unstructured text data. This is in contrast to a database that processes structured data and question-answer systems that are designed to answer questions in a particular domain. Both databases and search engines are concerned with similar functions to store, access, and manage information.

The ubiquitous relational database makes managing data much easier than with simple file organizations. The database in its most basic form is a centralized system to organize information that can be viewed, added, updated, and deleted. Information is managed in a structured collection of rows or records with a *schema* or a *catalog* that contains metadata describing the contents of each data item or column. The development of the relational database provides a very organized and fast method to access data using the Structured Query Language (SQL) (see Figure 3.1).

Figure 3.1: Information Access using Search Engines and Databases

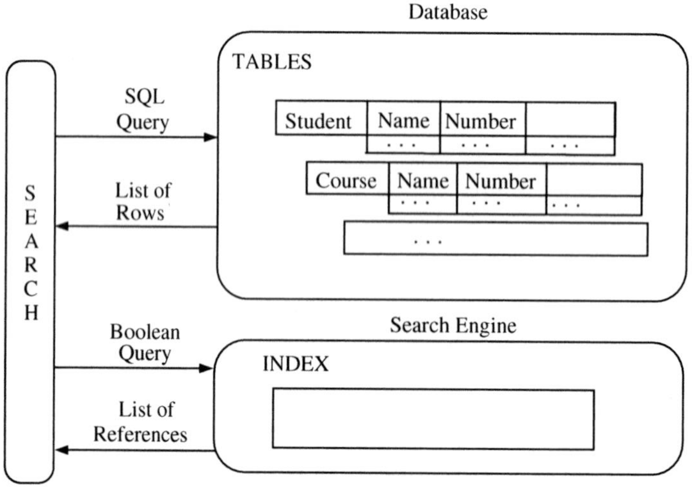

In contrast, a search engine is more loosely organized than a database, with no schema that defines attributes for data. The Lucene API uses field names to assign text segments to different attributes of a document, but does not restrict the type of text (integer, floating point, date, time, or a list of allowed text values) that can be stored in the field. The term *data* here means both text and numeric information and an *index* refers to a search engine index, which is distinct from the index data structure for a relational database. However, the purpose of the index in both a search engine and a database is to speed up access to information.

The lack of standard methods to assign meaning to data maintained in a search engine and the absence of a powerful query language like SQL makes the job of fetching precise information much harder in a search engine. The tasks of creating, updating, deleting, and retrieving information is common to both databases and search engines. A search engine on an Intranet runs in a more controlled environment than the Web with specific information sources and a limited number of content providers. Verifying the integrity of the data in a Web search engine is more difficult, since there is little control over the contents of a document added to the search engine. Even on an Intranet, there are few controls to check the validity of numeric or date information found in the text of indexed documents. For example in a database, alphabetic data cannot be entered in a numeric field, and the schema limits the size and type of data that can be loaded in a table. A database is also organized into a collection of tables to separate different types of information. These controls are absent in a search engine and all types of data are combined in a single repository.

A hybrid approach is to use information from a database to complement the results of a search engine. In this chapter, we will describe a combination of the Berkeley Database and the Lucene search engine API to build a robust search engine index. A Database Administrator (DBA) is typically responsible for maintaining the integrity of database tables and performing other tasks such as backup and recovery. A Search Engine Administrator has similar tasks and we will study the creation, modification, and maintenance of a search engine index in the following sections.

3.2 Early Search Engines

The first search engines were created in the late 60s to manage proprietary document collections, such as legal, medical, and academic articles. As with most computers during that era, access was limited, and the hardware (mostly IBM Mainframes) to run these systems was expensive. Their main purpose was to provide access to large collections of documents containing unstructured text that was difficult to search with simple tools.

The high performance index and access methods designed for relational databases were created to manage structured data alone. Information retrieval (IR) systems did not have the equivalent of a standard Structured Query Language (SQL) to store, update, and retrieve information. The vendors of IR systems developed proprietary query languages based on the popular boolean query model. A search engine returns a list of documents in response to a query, in contrast to a list of rows returned by a database given an SQL query.

The term *search engine* was coined by the developers of the first IR systems for the Web in the early 90s. The first Web search engines used the same technology as contemporary IR systems to handle a much larger volume of information. Current Web search engines have evolved to handle billions of documents with many safeguards to prevent manipulation of the ranking order of documents in response to queries.

3.2.1 Web Search Engines and IR Systems

The early IR systems did not become popular due to their high costs and limited availability. The first adopters of this technology were the medical and legal industries, two industries that have historically generated large volumes of information. The modern Web-based Medline search engine was built in the early 70s and today contains links and citations to over 15 million articles in several languages. Search on Medline was founded on an inverted file organization that is still in use today by most search engines. In fact, several of the features developed for MedLine are still used by Web search engines today. The query language in Medline was based on a simplified boolean query language to iteratively direct a query to the most likely relevant documents. However, in Medline, successive queries could use the results of the previous query to reduce the number of hits to a manageable figure, unlike most current Web search engines where every query is an independent transaction. Some search engines do cache the results of previous queries and the use of hidden fields in a query can utilize these results to narrow a search.

The simple but highly effective inverted index file system design from the 70s has been scaled to handle billions of documents on a modern Web search engine. Most of the IR systems prior to Web search engines used some form of an inverted index and a boolean query model. Lucene uses a fairly popular (TF/IDF) indexing method based on the frequency of words in a document and across the collection to build an inverted index. A matching document may have one or more query terms and is ranked based on the frequency of term occurrence and number of query terms present in the document. Most Web search engines also use the social network (see PageRank algorithm, section 8.2.3) based on embedded hyperlinks to rank documents. Lucene includes many different types of query forms (see Chapter 4) to generate a broad range of queries.

The other tools developed for proprietary IR systems, such as document ranking and the vocabulary for the index, were modified for Web search engines. The information stored in a mainframe IR system was in most cases controlled by the equivalent of a database administrator. The type of documents and the contents were carefully monitored. For example, articles from journals for the Medline collection were selected by a Literature Technical Review Committee. Medline also included a controlled vocabulary thesaurus called the Medical Subject Headings (MeSH) that organized index terms in a hierarchy. At the top level were broad terms such as *Anatomy*, *Diseases* or *Health Care*. Over 20 types of diseases such as *virus diseases*, *parasitic diseases*, and *eye diseases* were categorized under the broad term *Diseases*. In turn *virus diseases* were sub-categorized into 20 types and so on. This hierarchy is somewhat analogous to the WordNet (see Section 2.7) hierarchy based on hypernym / hyponym relationships. We use the word *term* here to mean the smallest unit of text processed by a search engine which is sometimes also referred to as a *token*.

Unfortunately, the Web is not organized like any of the early IR systems, and the developers of Web search engines have had to cope with some of the unique problems in a distributed and uncontrollable domain. In Chapter 8, we will look at how Web search engines have addressed these problems, as well as at the ranking algorithms for Web pages.

3.3 Generating an Index

Metadata tags give clues to indicate the type of content, but the majority of the text is found in the body of a document. This text is extracted, indexed, and optionally saved by the indexer of the search engine. Our goal is to automatically build an accurate index that is comparable to a manually generated index. Many published books use a manual or semi-automated method to create an index. If you look at the index of a book, you will find that the index terms often consist of more than one word. In a book about astronomy, you may find terms made up of one word like — *Ganymede*, *Rigel*, and *Jupiter*, and multi-word terms like — *Galilean satellites*, *rings of Saturn*, or *NGC 281*.

A multi-word term is similar to the collocations we saw in Chapter 2. These are two or more word sequences that are seen in order more often than not. It is not very difficult to automatically capture such phrases from a text stream. A tokenizer from Chapter 2 will return a list of tokens from which a set of ngram words can be generated. We would get $(n-1)$ bigram tokens and $(n-2)$ trigram tokens from a sequence of n tokens in a stream. If these lists of tokens are sorted in descending order of frequency, we can set a frequency threshold based on n and return the top ranking bigrams and trigrams for inclusion in the index. The discriminating capability of the ngram words is another component that must be considered before adding these words to the index.

Manually generated indexes also include cross references. So, an index entry *aircraft* would be cross referenced to the more standard *airplanes* index entry. A cross reference may refer to a term that is similar to the current term (a synonym), to a term that is more broad (a hypernym), or to a term that is more specific (a hyponym). WordNet contains an "*also see*" relationship between words; for example the word *scrimpy* is cross referenced to the words — *insufficient*, *deficient*, *minimal*, *minimum*, and *scarce*. It is extremely difficult to automatically find these relationships without a dictionary like WordNet. While WordNet is suitable for English words in common usage, you will need separate dictionaries to handle technical terminology and text written in other languages.

Index terms in manually generated indexes may also be arranged in a hierarchy. For example, the root term *Moon* may include branches such as *phases*, *eclipses of*, or *named features*. These hierarchies are shown in a tree-like structure with indentation to denote the generic level of the term.

Moon,

    phases,

    eclipses of,

    named features

A reference may be repeated with a different lead term to make it easy to find in the index. For example, *phases* may be a lead term in the root of another hierarchy, with *Moon* one of the branches, along with other branches such as *Venus*. A more specific index term will in general lead to more relevant results and higher precision.

A search engine built for documents about astronomy may have some single word index terms such as – *Cepheids*, *epicycles*, and *redshift* that are sufficient to generate relevant hits. However, a majority of the index terms that lead to specific references will be multi-word terms.

Therefore, a domain-specific search engine will have much to gain by using a customized indexing module compared to a simple tokenizer that lacks cross references and uses single words alone. It will be difficult to generate such an index without the help of a dictionary like WordNet, which may not be available for some specialized topics.

An alternative is to use a simple indexing method, but add smarter methods to filter and organize the results. This is the post retrieval method that first fetches the documents for a query and then looks for ways to organize the results for higher precision. The post retrieval method is somewhat constrained by the limited time available to perform the filtering and organization of the results. Users expect short response times from a search engine and may not look favorably on a long post retrieval process. However, when the volume of text from the initial query is small, it may not take a substantial amount of time to process the results.

3.3.1 Term Weighting

The list of tokens generated from the text stream of a document is the basis for the index terms that will represent the document. We use the word *term* here to mean a word or phrase that is considered as a unit. The order of terms in the list may not resemble the order in which they were seen in the text. At first, this may appear to be a mistake since the meaning of a document is not just a *bag of words* arbitrarily strung together. However, the purpose of a search engine is not to find the meaning of text in documents, but instead to find the most relevant documents for queries. Ideally, the best index terms are the ones that discriminate one document from another.

First, lets consider a single document in isolation. In the following example, the text from the book — *"Producing Open Source Software"* by Karl Fogel is used to illustrate the generation of index terms. We begin with the observation that when a particular term or phrase is repeated often in the text, it has an implied higher importance compared to other words that occur less often. It is known that words do not occur randomly in a document and their frequency of occurrence is uneven[Salton]. We can observe a pattern if we arrange words in descending order of their frequency of occurrence. In Table 3.1, we show a subset of words and their associated frequencies in the text.

Table 3.1: List of Words and Frequencies

Rank (R)	Word	Frequency (F)	R × F / N	Cumulative F(%)
1	the	6931	0.059	5.98
2	to	4005	0.069	9.43
4	of	2681	0.092	14.34
6	is	2064	0.106	18.12
8	that	1818	0.125	21.37
10	for	1229	0.106	23.72
20	but	682	0.117	30.11
30	will	482	0.124	35.90
40	when	354	0.122	39.30
50	work	305	0.131	42.08

From Table 3.1, we can make several inferences. One, the most frequent words are function words like prepositions, determiners, and conjunctions. The first noun, *project* was found at rank 19 in the list. The high frequency of occurrence of function words like *and*, *the*, and *for* is seen in all genres of text and is the basis for the creation of the stop word list we saw in Chapter 2. You can create a custom stop word list by running sample text through a tokenizer and building a list of words similar to the ones shown in Table 3.1.

Two, the frequency of occurrence of the vocabulary can be characterized by the constant rank-frequency law of Zipf. The law states that the product of the rank (R) of a word and its frequency (F) is roughly constant. In other words, a small percentage of the unique words in a text account for the majority of the words employed. This observation follows the general "*principle of least effort*" in which a person tends to use the same words often and rarely coins new or different words. A plot of the cumulative percentage of words vs. the fraction of unique words in Figure 3.2 makes this observation more clear.

Figure 3.2: Word Usage Statistics

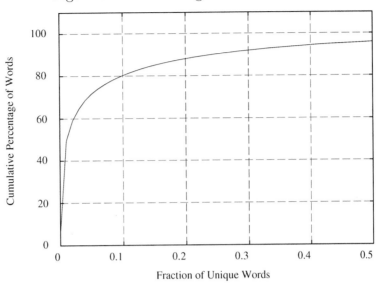

The unique words are sorted in descending order of their frequency. The plot shows that 20% of the most frequently occurring words accounts for over 80% of all words in the text. We can use this observation as the basis to identify the best index terms to represent a document. An initial idea would be to use the words that occur mainly in the center of Figure 3.2. These are words that do not occur too frequently and at the same time are not very rare. The words that occur too frequently will also occur in other documents and therefore will not be able to discriminate between documents. Words that occur very rarely in the document may not be appropriate to accurately describe the contents. So, it would seem like the best index words for a document are those words that occur in medium frequencies.

There are a few drawbacks to this proposal. First, setting a threshold for high frequency terms may eliminate some terms that are broad and occur often in the text, but are still useful in fetching relevant documents. Second, removal of all low frequency terms will reduce precision, since these terms are possibly very specific. These problems illustrate that any index term must fulfill two roles. The term must be related to the content of the document, but at the same time must be sufficiently unique such that it discriminates the document from other documents.

TF / IDF Indexing

The individual values of the two components for an index term are combined to create a weight that defines the overall value of an index term for a document. The first component measures the term frequency (TF) in a document and represents the value of the term in defining the content of the document. A second component is the inverse document frequency (IDF) which represents the inverse of the number of documents in the collection in which the term occurs at least once. Together the TF and IDF components are combined to create a term weight. The TF of a term for a document is simply the number of times the term occurs in the document. Lucene also uses a damping function (square root) for the term frequency to limit the influence of a large number of term occurrences in a single document, that may bias the weight. The IDF for a term is the *log* of the inverse of the fraction of the number of documents in which the term appears. We have used the natural logarithm (base *e*) to measure the information content of a term from the inverse of the probability of the term occurring in a document. If the number of documents in which the term occurs is n and the number of documents in the collection is N, then the IDF value of the term is

$$log(\frac{N}{n}) + 1 \qquad (3.1)$$

We add 1 to handle cases where n and N are equal, which would make the IDF value zero. Notice when n is 1, the IDF value is maximum indicating that the term is a very strong discriminator. The minimum value of n is 1, since if the term does not exist in any document, it will not be part of any description for a document. The default IDF implementation in Lucene adds 1 to the denominator to avoid a floating point exception, if the value of n is accidentally set to zero. The final indexing weight for a term in a document is the product of TF and IDF values.

This indexing scheme is possibly the most popular and commonly called the *TF/IDF* indexing or term vector method. The IDF value is a global value and does not depend upon individual document sizes. However, TF can be manipulated by repeating a term many times to effectively raise the index weight of the term for the document. Increasing the index weight of a term i for a document implies that the document is more relevant for a query with the term i and therefore should be ranked higher than other documents. Alternatives to using the raw frequency count are to simply use a density or even a binary measure. The density measure gives the fraction of terms in the entire document containing a term i. The binary measure ignores the number of occurrences in the document and merely indicates the presence or absence of a term in the document. Lucene uses the square root of TF in the default implementation and later applies a length normalization factor to minimize the natural advantage of long documents.

Other Indexing Methods

There have been many other indexing methods since the TF/IDF method, including the *Okapi BM25* and *Latent Semantic Indexing* (LSI) methods. The Okapi indexing method is based on a probabilistic model for document retrieval. If we know beforehand that a term i occurs in n documents within a collection of size N, then the probability of any random document containing the term i is $\frac{n}{N}$. The *log* of this probability gives the information content of the word. Given accurate relevance information for terms, the probability model has a strong theoretical basis for finding the most likely relevant documents. In reality, the occurrence of terms in documents is bursty, i.e. if a term occurs in a document, a second occurrence is more probable than the value predicted by the uniform distribution $\frac{n}{N}$. The implementation of the TF/IDF and BM25 indexing methods are similar, with differences in how term weights are computed.

The LSI indexing method uses a linear algebra model to capture index weights. A document-term matrix is constructed where the terms and documents are represented by the rows and columns of the matrix respectively. A single element in the matrix defines the frequency of occurrence of a term in a document. This matrix is transformed using a complex mathematical technique called the *Singular Value Decomposition* (SVD) to create three separate matrices. One of the matrices is a square matrix containing singular values sorted in descending order. Each of the singular values represents a "composite dimension" made up of multiple terms that tend to co-occur in documents. The original matrix can be approximated by using a few of these composite dimensions.

The idea behind decomposing the original matrix and using the approximation is that the use of a few dimensions will reduce the *noise* that is typically present in the original matrix leading to a more accurate representation of documents. Unfortunately, the SVD method is not scalable and applying the LSI indexing method to a collection with a million or more documents is computationally demanding. The benefits of LSI are that documents that are similar but do not use the same terms will be retrieved in response to a query that uses any one of the related terms. The LSI method does more than just handle synonyms, it also uses inherent document-document, term-term, and document-term relationships in the index. The Apache Lucene software does not currently implement Okapi BM25 or LSI, but you can adapt Lucene to implement a custom index method. We will cover the TF/IDF indexing method alone in the rest of this chapter.

3.3.2 Term Vector Model

An indexing method translates a document from its original form into a collection of words and associated weights. The weight of each term represents the relative importance of the term in the document. The expression *term vector* is frequently used to describe this representation of a document. If each term in the document representation represents a *direction* (or dimension), then the weight can be assumed to be a *magnitude* and each individual term is a vector. A document becomes a collection of term vectors and this model of representing documents is called the *vector space model* or *term vector model*. The collection of individual term vectors is also called the *document vector*. This document representation model was first introduced by G. Salton [Salton] in the SMART information retrieval system. Consider two documents i and j made up of just two terms *project* and *software* (see Figure 3.3).

The terms *software* and *project* each represent a dimension that is present in both documents i and j. The term vector for document i is the line from (0,0) to (0.4, 0.8) and for document j it is the line from (0,0) to (0.8, 0.6). The weight of the term *project* is higher in document j than document i while the weight of the term *software* is higher in document i than document j. The term vector model for representing documents makes it relatively easy to compare two documents based on the degree of co-occurrence of terms in documents (see Chapter 6).

3.3.3 Inverted Index

The inverted index is a compact data structure used to store the vector representations of documents, and is widely used in search engines. It is also referred to

Figure 3.3: Term Vector Model for Documents in Two Dimensions

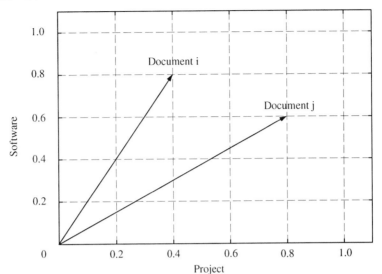

as the *postings* file or an *index* file. The inverted index was first developed for the early IR systems of the 70s, but is still popular, since it is one of the fastest ways to find matching documents given a set of terms. Consider the following set of three documents (see Table 3.2).

Table 3.2: A List of Documents and Associated Text

Doc ID	Text
1	Tom sat on Matt.
2	Matt saw Tom.
3	Tom got a cat.

There are a total of six words – *Tom, sat, Matt, saw, got,* and *cat,* excluding the stop words *on* and *a*. In an inverted index, each word would have a posting for every document in which it occurred. For example in Table 3.3, the word *Matt* occurs in two documents 1 and 2.

Table 3.3: Index File for Documents in Table 3.2

Word	Documents
Tom	1, 2, 3
sat	1
Matt	1, 2
got	3
cat	3

A postings entry in Table 3.3 contains just a document reference. A more descriptive posting would include other information such as the position in the text as well as the weight of the term. If a word occurs multiple times in the document, then the positions of each occurrence will also be included in the postings. Consider an HTML document containing text in the title, metadata, and the body that will all be included in the index. In the present form of the index file, there is no difference between a word occurring in the title or the body. A practical index would assign more importance to a word that occurs in the title or metadata.

Web search engines like Google differentiate between a word occurring in the text (a *plain hit*) and a word occurring in the title or the anchor text (a *fancy hit*). A higher score is assigned to documents that match words from fancy hits than plain hits. Google also assigns higher weights to words that occur in a larger font relative to the font size of the page, words that start with an upper case letter, and also based on the position of the occurrence in the text. Higher ranking documents can be quickly retrieved if the postings for a term are sorted in descending order of weight. These simple but effective changes to handle HTML pages lead to higher search engine precision.

3.4 Creating an Index with Lucene

Building an index in Lucene is relatively simple. In Listing 3.1, a collection of PDF files stored in a directory are indexed individually. The text from the PDF files is extracted using a `PdfHandler` (line 13) and passed to a `PdfDoc` (line 17) object. In this example, the text for the index is extracted from the local file system, but text can also be extracted from documents or Web pages on a remote server. The `DirTools` package is included in the software distribution that accompanies the book.

Listing 3.1: Building an Index for PDF Files

```
1  public class CreatePDFIndex {
2
3    public static void main(String[] args) {
4      Directory dir = null; // index directory
5      IndexWriter writer = null;
6
7      dir = FSDirectory.getDirectory(SE_INDEX_DIR);
8      writer = new IndexWriter(dir,
9        new StandardAnalyzer(), true);
10     String pdfDir = TESTING_DIR + FS + "pdf";
11     DirTools dirTools = new DirTools();
12     List<String> flist = dirTools.dirScan(pdfDir, true);
13     PdfHandler pdfHandler = new PdfHandler();
14     for (String filename : flist) {
15       PdfDoc pdfDoc = new PdfDoc(filename);
16       pdfDoc.setId(System.currentTimeMillis() + "");
17       pdfHandler.getDocument(filename, pdfDoc);
18       Document doc = new Document();
19       doc.add(new Field("id", pdfDoc.getId(),
20         Field.Store.YES, Field.Index.NO));
21       doc.add(new Field("filename", filename,
22         Field.Store.YES, Field.Index.UN_TOKENIZED));
23       doc.add(new Field("body",
24         pdfDoc.getContents().toString(),
25         Field.Store.NO, Field.Index.TOKENIZED,
26         Field.TermVector.YES));
27       writer.addDocument(doc);
28     }
29     writer.optimize();
30     writer.close();
31   }
32 }
```

The first step in creating an index is to specify the name of the directory which is passed to the `getDirectory` (line 7) method of the static `FSDirectory` class. The `IndexWriter` constructor (line 8) takes three parameters - a directory, a default analyzer for all `Fields` of an indexed document, and a boolean flag to indicate if a new index is being created or an existing index will be modified. When a new index is created, the existing files in the directory are deleted. If the index directory does not exist, a new directory will be created and old lock files will be deleted.

The setid method (line 16) uses the current timestamp as an unique identifier. Notice, the id is stored, but not indexed (line 20) since the purpose of the id is to find a corresponding row in a database table. The filename is stored and indexed (line 22), but not tokenized since we need to search the index using a complete file name. The body is indexed since we need to search the index using terms found in the body (line 25), but not stored since the contents of the file may be large. The addDocument method (line 27) adds the document to the index using the default analyzer specified in line 9. These additions to the index are initially generated in memory and periodically written to the index directory. The optimize method (line 29) is usually the last method called before completing all changes to the index and closing all index files. The purpose of this method is to speed up the time to search and typically involves a memory intensive merge of index files into a single file.

A lock file is a Lucene security mechanism to control read/write access to the index directory. The directory for the lock files can be found in the system property org.apache.lucene.lockDir and can be set through the Java system property java.io.tmpdir. By default this property is set to /tmp in Linux and C:\TEMP in the Windows platform. A lock file will look something like -

lucene-405c959f639106033b4af5eea1f6f59b-write.lock

Notice, this is a write lock file which prevents two concurrent modifications to an index in the same directory. In Lucene version 2.1, the name of the lock file was changed to write.lock and is found in the index directory. You can check this directory for old lock files that were not removed during normal cleanup, if you have problems creating or modifying an index due to the failure of a prior indexing operation. You will get "Lock obtain timed out:" errors depending on the setting of the boolean flags passed to the IndexWriter constructor. Earlier versions of Lucene also used a commit lock to control modifications to an index that was replaced in version 2.1 with a write lock. You can disable the use of locks when the FSDirectory is created, if you know that your index will be used in a read only environment alone. This may speed up search performance since repeated checks for lock files are not necessary.

Choosing the best analyzer (see Chapter 2) for your application is important, since the generated terms are the only way by which documents can be retrieved. It is not necessary that a single analyzer be used for all fields of a document. In Listing 3.1, the indexed PDF file has three fields — *id*, *filename*, and *body* (lines 19-23). The first field (*id*) is stored but not indexed and the remaining two fields (*filename* and *body)* are indexed. The `StandardAnalyzer` that was specified in the constructor for the `IndexWriter` is used to tokenize the text of the *body* field. Consider the *title* field in a PDF document for which the `StandardAnalyzer` is not suitable, since it drops stopwords. In this case, we can create an analyzer wrapper that uses separate analyzers for individual fields.

```
PerFieldAnalyzerWrapper pfAnalyzer =
  new PerFieldAnalyzerWrapper(new StandardAnalyzer());
pfAnalyzer.addAnalyzer("title",
  new KeywordAnalyzer());
```

The `StandardAnalyzer` is the default analyzer and the `title` field uses a different analyzer. The `add` (line 18) method of the `Document` class is used to generate the index for different parts of the document. For example, if we were indexing an HTML document, the list of fields may include – *title, author, keywords, links, images,* and *body*. Each of these fields can be searched independently of the other fields (see Chapter 4). The per field analyzer wrapper or one of the other analyzers is passed to the IndexWriter constructor. The `add` method of the `Document` class accepts a `Field` and appends it to a vector that contains a list of document fields.

You can also pass an optional analyzer to the `add` method that would be used exclusively for a particular document. Every field in the document has a name and a value that is mandatory in the `Field` constructor. The name is a string passed in the first parameter to the constructor of a `Field` constructor. The value of the field is usually a text string, but can also be a binary value or a `Reader` object. A binary field can only be stored and not indexed.

3.4.1 Field Attributes

The text contents of stored fields are saved as-is in index files, adding to the overall size of the index. The decision to store a field is based on the need to return the text contents of the field in response to a query. The advantage of storing the value of a field is that its contents can be fetched using the `get` method of the `Document` class and returned in a hit list. This make sense for descriptive fields like the *title*, *author*, or *date*. The more pressing question is whether to store the complete body of an article as a field.

One disadvantage of not storing the body of an article or a book is that the context of a hit cannot be shown. In response to a query, the typical search engine shows a snippet of text that contains the query term in context (see Chapter 4) — the context cannot be shown unless the value of the field is available. The advantage of not storing the complete text of an article is a smaller index that may have better retrieval performance. However, the `Field.Store.Compress` option that will compress the text can be used to reduce the size of the stored field.

The stored and indexed attributes for a `Field` can be combined in several ways shown in Table 3.4. The default is to index and not store the contents of a field. When a `Reader` object is passed to the `Field` constructor, the default option alone is available and the rest of the entries in the table are valid for text or binary values. The three possible actions for any `Field` are stored, indexed, or stored and indexed.

Table 3.4: List of Actions for Field.Store and Field.Index Attributes

Stored	Indexed	Action
Not specified	Not specified	Indexed and not stored (default)
Yes	Not specified	Stored (valid for binary values alone)
Yes	Yes	Indexed and stored
Yes	No	Not indexed and stored
No	Yes	Indexed and not stored
No	No	- Invalid -

In Lucene version 2.0, a `Compress` field was added to the `Field.Store` class to optionally reduce space for the contents of fields that were stored. Two other fields were added to the `Field.Index` class — `UN_TOKENIZED` and `NO_NORMS`. Both field options specify that the contents of the `Field` should not be tokenized, but rather kept as-is. This is appropriate for short text chunks such as a part number or an ISBN number that will be part of a search key. The `NO_NORMS` will not store individual `Field` normalization information that is used to rank documents (see Chapter 4).

The last optional attribute is the `TermVector` flag, which can be passed to a `Field` constructor with a `Reader` or a `String` value. In Figure 3.2, we saw the term vectors for two documents i and j. Each term vector is a set of terms that occur in the document, along with the associated frequencies. A term vector can be stored in the index for a particular `Field` of a document. By default, term vectors are not stored since they require additional space in the index. You can construct a term vector at run time, if you have the entire contents of the field available. The term vector is a list of terms, a corresponding list of term frequencies, and optional offset and position information. An offset is the character position where the term was located and the position is the index of the term in the list of all terms. With a term vector, you can make comparisons to other term vectors (see Chapter 6) and find other groups of documents that are similar. It is also possible to assign documents to categories based on similarity computations, when every category has an associated term vector. Every document that has a term vector must be indexed as well.

The same content can also be indexed twice under different `Field` names. For example, the text contents may be stemmed and lower cased in a `Field` x to allow more matches and indexed without any filtering in a `Field` y. Text from a document that matches the content in `Field` y would be ranked higher than the text from a document that matches the content of `Field` x alone (see Table 3.5). Fields x and y contain the stemmed and original terms of a common text string. The stemmed terms will match a larger set of query words than the original terms.

Table 3.5: Terms with and without Stemming

Field Name	Terms
x	lucen, full, featur, text, search, engin, written, entir, java
y	Lucene, is, a, full, featured, text, search, engine, written, entirely, in, Java

3.4.2 Boosting

In any collection of documents, there will be a few documents that are considered more important or relevant than others. These documents are assigned a higher weight compared to the rest of documents and returned to searchers more often. For example, a site that periodically collects information from the Web can boost the weight of documents that were collected more recently than older documents. Sorting by the date of a document may not be the most appropriate ranking for a hit list and boosting documents by date gives a solution that can combine other ranking attributes to find relevant documents. You can boost the weight of a document with the `setBoost` method of the `Document` class which will effectively boost the weight of every `Field` in the document.

The code below to boost all documents that are less than a month old by 2.0, compares the current time in milliseconds with last modified timestamp. While we have arbitrarily chosen a boost value of 2.0, you could use another value, which may be more effective. The ideal boost value for a document may require some experiments with search results and feedback to improve precision.

```
if (pdfDoc.getMdate() > (
    System.currentTimeMillis() - (30 * 24 * 3600)))
  doc.setBoost((float) 2.0);
```

Boosting individual fields is more fine grained boosting, appropriate when certain parts of a document are more important than others. For example in an HTML page, the *title* text should be weighted higher than the *body* text and similarly in an email, the *subject* text should also be given more weight than the text in the *body* of the email. The `Field` class has a `setBoost` method with an identical signature as the `setBoost` method in the `Document` class.

Finally, individual terms can be boosted in a query (see Chapter 4). Unfortunately, individual terms in the document text of a `Field` cannot be boosted. You can manually boost the weight of a term by repeating it in the text passed to the constructor of the `Field`. The default similarity measure uses the square root of the term frequency to compute the ranking of a document and you can create your own similarity measure that uses a different function for the term frequency. A binary measure would set TF to 1, if the term was found in the document and 0 otherwise.

3.5 Modifying an Index with Lucene

One of the nice features of Lucene is ability to perform incremental indexing. Once an index is created, you will need to modify it when new documents are added to

the collection, an existing document is modified, or if a document is deleted. If a
new document is added to the collection, the code (see Listing 3.2) to index the
document is quite similar to the code in Listing 3.1. A document that exists can
be modified in a single atomic operation using the **updateDocument** method of the
IndexSearcher. The **IndexTools** package is included in the software distribution
that accompanies the book.

Listing 3.2: Adding a New Document to an Existing Index

```
1  public class ModifyPDFIndex {
2
3    public static void main(String[] args) {
4      Directory dir = null;
5      IndexWriter modifier = null;
6      IndexSearcher searcher = null;
7
8      dir = FSDirectory.getDirectory(SE_INDEX_DIR, false);
9      modifier = new IndexWriter(
10       dir, new StandardAnalyzer(), false);
11     String filename = TESTING_DIR + FS + "pdf"
12       + FS + "producingoss.pdf";
13     PdfDoc pdfDoc = new PdfDoc(filename);
14     pdfHandler.getDocument(filename, pdfDoc);
15     pdfDoc.setId(System.currentTimeMillis() + "");
16     Document doc = new Document();
17     doc.add(new Field(
18       "id", "" + pdfDoc.getId(),
19       Field.Store.YES, Field.Index.NO));
20     doc.add(new Field(
21       "filename", filename,
22       Field.Store.YES, Field.Index.UN_TOKENIZED));
23     doc.add(new Field(
24       "contents", pdfDoc.getContents().toString(),
25       Field.Store.NO, Field.Index.TOKENIZED);
26
27     if (IndexTools.existsDoc(searcher,"filename",filename)) {
28       modifier.updateDocument(
29         new Term("filename", filename), doc);
30     } else {
31       modifier.addDocument(doc);
32     }
```

```
33        modifier.optimize();
34        modifier.close();
35    }
36 }
```

First, the directory object is created as before, but this time the contents are not cleared out (line 8). We have used an `IndexWriter` class to add the new document to the collection. If an identical document currently exists in the index, the new duplicate document will be silently added without any warning or exception. During a search, two copies of the document will appear in the hit list. In general, it is better to remove duplicate documents from the index before they are added, than to filter a search list to remove duplicates.

In Listing 3.2, we have used the file name to check for an existing document in the index. An indexed document with the same file name is replaced with the current document. The `existsDoc` method (line 27) of the `IndexTools` class uses the file name parameter and an `IndexSearcher` (see chapter 4) to check for an existing document. The `docFreq` method (not shown in the listing) of the `IndexSearcher` returns the number of matching documents containing the file name. The `updateDocument` method (line 28) replaces a document, if an existing document with the same file name was found in the index, otherwise the `addDocument` method (line 31) creates a new document in the index.

There are several other ways to track duplicate documents in an index. One is to save a unique key such as an id or URL in a stored field of the document. When a new document is being added, we first check if a document exists with the same key in the index using a query (see Chapter 4). If a document does exist, then the current document is skipped, otherwise it is indexed like a new document. The other option is to store a compact message digest representation of the contents of the document in a database. When a document with identical contents is indexed, a duplicate *message digest* will be detected in the database. There are several algorithms included in the `MessageDigest` class of the `java.security` package, that use the MD5 and SHA [Digest] cryptographic hash functions to create a message digest from a text string. The `shaDigest` function in the `StringTools` package will accept a text string and return a 40 character signature generated from the string.

```
String signatureKey = StringTools.shaDigest(
    pdfDoc.getContents().toString()):
```

A signature looks like `aa9bdf7519c4147f25b357796b0d50e243238085` and is generated from the text string. In general, we can assume that this signature is unique and will not be generated by a different text string. This signature is a key in the database table that contains the metadata for files indexed by the search engine. Two files that have identical content will have matching signatures, and therefore will not be stored twice in the search index and database.

3.6 A Database Backed Index

Consider a search engine database table (see Table 3.6) with rows for every indexed document and fields representing metadata values. This table contains useful information to identify duplicate documents and check if a document has changed since the last index timestamp, as well as a collection of metadata that is useful to show in a search hit list. The use of a database table like the one shown in Table 3.6 to support a search engine index is valuable and may improve the retrieval performance of the index. Document fields that are relatively short in length and that are not indexed can be stored in a database instead of the index.

Table 3.6: Database Table to Complement a Search Engine Index

Name	Description
Id	A unique identifier for the document
Title	The title of the document
Author	Author of the document
Mdate	Last Modified timestamp
Idate	Last Indexed timestamp
Summary	Summary of document contents
Name	File name or URL of document
Length	Length of file
Language	Contents language
Signature	Message digest of document contents
Contents	Complete (or subset of) contents

A document may be an article, a Web page, or any other unit of text that can be considered a single entity in the search engine. Table 3.6 contains a list of some of the common features of documents that are typically tracked in a search engine. The example code in Listing 3.1 builds a search engine index for a collection of *pdf* documents alone, but can be extended to handle other types as well.

The DbTools class in the org.btext.utils package (in the software distribution accompanying the book) has a number of methods to manage a Berkeley Database. The Java Edition (JE) of the Berkeley DB can be downloaded from (http://www.oracle.com/database). The code in Listing 3.3 creates an index from a collection of pdf documents and is similar to the code in Listing 3.1, with the addition of database code to complement the search engine index.

Note: We have used the Berkeley DB for demonstration purposes, other relational databases such as MySQL can be substituted.

Listing 3.3: Building an Index for PDF files with a Metadata Database Table

```
1   public class CreateIndex {
2     private static Directory dir;
3     private static IndexWriter writer;
4
5     public static void main(String[] args) {
6       dir = FSDirectory.getDirectory(SE_INDEX_DIR, true);
7       writer = new IndexWriter(dir,
8         new StandardBgramAnalyzer(), true);
9       // open the database environment
10      boolean readOnly = false;
11      DbTools dbt = new DbTools();
12      dbt.openEnv(BDB_DIR, readOnly);
13      // create the databases
14      boolean createFlag = true;
15      dbt.dropDB(SE_DOCS); dbt.dropSecDB(SE_SEC_DOCS);
16      dbt.createDB(SE_DOCS, createFlag);
17      dbt.createSecDB(SE_SEC_DOCS, readOnly,
18        new SecKeyDoc( new PdfBinding() ));
19   . . .
20       for (String filename : flist) {
```

```
21        // check if the document is a duplicate document,
22        if (IndexTools.dupDoc(dbt, pdfDoc)) {
23          logger.info("Found a duplicate doc: " +
24            pdfDoc.getFileName() + " in the database");
25          continue;
26        }
27        // add the document to the database
28        else if (!IndexTools.addDoc(dbt, pdfDoc)) {
29          logger.error("Could not add doc: " +
30            pdfDoc.getFileName() + " to the database ");
31          continue;
32        }
33        // add the document to the index
34  . . .
35        try {
36          writer.addDocument(doc);
37        } catch (IOException ie) {
38          IndexTools.delDoc(dbt, pdfDoc);
39        }
40      }
41      dbt.closeEnv(); // close the database environment
42      writer.optimize();
43      writer.close(); // close the index writer
44    }
45  }
```

We first create a handle for the database convenience methods (line 11). Next, the DB environment is created in a directory named in the BDB_DIR variable (line 12). The Berkeley DB directory contains a list of log and data files that are appended, when tables are modified or created. Periodically, the files in the database directory are compacted to remove obsolete entries.

Every table that is created has a unique name with a set of associated parameters to describe the environment for the table. The parameters describe if a new table should replace an existing table, if duplicate keys should be allowed, or whether transactions should be implemented. By default, duplicate keys are not allowed and transactions are not implemented. Two tables are created – the first table SE_DOCS (line 16) is the primary table and the second table SE_SEC_DOCS (line 17) is the secondary table. The primary table contains the fields listed in Table 3.6 and the secondary table provides an alternate key to search the primary table. Notice, there is no schema for the DB and the description of individual fields is maintained in the `PdfDoc` class with a `PdfBinding` binding class to fetch and store individual records.

We loop through the list of files in the source directory as before, but now check for duplicate documents. Since duplicates are not allowed, every indexed document must have a unique filename and signature. The `dupDoc` (line 22) method of the `IndexTools` package creates a signature for the contents of the passed document and checks for a matching entry in the `SE_SEC_DOCS` table. If a matching entry is found with the same file signature, then the document is a duplicate.

The `addDoc` (line 28) method of the `IndexTools` package loads the document into the `SE_DOCS` table. The value of the fields for the document are set when the `PdfHandler` extracts the text from the document. If the size of the contents is beyond a limit set in the `org.btext.utils.Constants` class, then a truncated version of the body of the document will be stored. Finally, the document is added to the search engine index as before (line 36). If for some reason the document is not added to the index, then the entry in the database table must be removed to maintain the integrity of the search engine index.

The addition of database tables to backup a search engine index can improve retrieval performance of documents that contains several fields that are not searched, but also adds maintenance overhead. The search engine administrator has to manage a database as well as a search engine index. Both the index and database must be synchronized to accurately reflect the state of the document collection. If the database contains obsolete or corrupt entries, then the metadata generated for a document will be inaccurate. A document found in the index may not have a matching entry in the database. Periodically, the index should be scanned to identify and repair such errors (see section 3.7 Maintaining an Index).

3.6.1 Deleting a Document

Removing a document from the index is a two step process. First, the document is removed from the database table and then from the index. The `delDoc` method of the `IndexTools` package takes a `PdfDoc` object and deletes it from the `SE_DOCS` table and in the secondary index table `SE_SEC_DOCS`. There are two ways to remove a document from an index — one way is to provide the unique Lucene document `id` associated with the document. You can fetch this id by submitting a query to the search engine and then use the `id` method of the returned `Hits` object. A simpler way of deleting the document is to call the `deleteDocuments` method with a field that contains a unique value for every document. In our example code, this field is the named `id`.

When a document is added to the index, the `id` `Field` is set to the current time in milliseconds and also stored in the table entry for the document. We can extract the `id` from the table and use it to delete the document from the index.

```
FSDirectory fsd = FSDirectory.getDirectory(
  new File(SE_INDEX_DIR));
IndexReader ir = IndexReader.open(fsd);
ir.deleteDocuments(
  new Term( "id", "1177924890201") );
ir.close();
```

The `deleteDocuments` method of the `IndexReader` will delete all documents that contain the value *1177924890201* in the `id` Field. A single document will be deleted since only one document in the index matches this condition. Two or more documents will have the same `id`, if more than 1K documents are indexed per second. The core Java `nanoTime` method gives the current time in nanoseconds and is an alternate unique identifier for documents.

Note, we use the ***IndexReader*** *class to delete* ***Documents*** *and not the* ***IndexWriter*** *class. The name* ***IndexReader****, does not aptly describe the range of index functions the class provides, which include methods to read and modify the index.*

The `close` method of the `IndexReader` writes the changes to disk. Typically, one or more documents will be deleted at a time and it is more effective to delete a set of documents in batch. A list of all of the `ids` of documents that will be deleted is created first, and then deleted in sequence. When delete operations are performed in batch, the total time that the index is locked for modification is minimized.

3.6.2 Updating a Document

A new document is created when a document with the same `id` is added to the index. Lucene does not automatically check for duplicates and will simply add duplicate documents to the index. You can construct a method that does an update operation in three steps. First, we check for the existence of a document in the database with the same `id` or content. Next, if a document does exist, then it is deleted from the database and index. Finally, a new document is added to the index and database.

A duplicate document can either have the same `id` or content. We saw earlier that the message digests of the contents of documents can be compared to find documents with identical contents. Typically, an index with multiple copies of the same document has little value, but mirrored versions of a document may be made available. Any document with the same filename or URL is also a candidate duplicate document. However, if a file has been modified since the last index timestamp, then its contents are likely to be different and the index should be updated to reflect the new contents.

Lucene does have a convenience `update` method in the `IndexWriter` class that accepts a `Term`, `Document`, and an optional `Analyzer`. This method will first delete all documents that contain the `Term` and add the new document in a single transaction. A single document will be deleted if you pass a `Term` that uniquely identifies a document in the index. The `update` method is useful since it handles cases where the delete or add operations were not successful. The failure of either the delete or add operations will not corrupt the index. If you write your own update method, then you will need to rollback the delete if the add operation fails. Two or more updates of the same document will be processed in sequence.

3.7 Maintaining an Index

An index is a dynamic data structure like the tables of a database that may change over time. However, the index is merely a compressed representation of the contents of a document collection. In a dynamic collection, new documents are added, old documents are removed, and existing documents may be modified. These changes should be reflected in the index such that it represents the most current view of the document collection. Consider the types of changes that can be made to an indexed file system (see Table 3.7)

Table 3.7: Changes to a File System and Associated Effect on the Index

File Action	Index Effect
New file added	Not available
Existing file renamed	Dead link
Existing file modified	Possible incorrect link
Existing file moved	Dead link
Existing file deleted	Dead link

These actions are only pertinent for the file system that contains the directories being indexed. A typical index is not notified when a new file is added to a directory. Some operating systems may include a kernel feature to automatically notify registered applications when there is any change in the file system. An index application that runs in the background can index files in real time as the changes occur, thereby keeping the index current at all times.

An indexed file that has been renamed, moved, or deleted will refer to an invalid filename that causes a dead link in a search. The third file system change in Table 3.7 is a modification to the file contents, which may be a minor modification or which may completely replace the original contents. In either case, the file needs to be re-indexed to reflect the new contents. Listing 3.4 scans the entire index and checks if every index entry has a corresponding filename that exists in the file system.

Listing 3.4: Scan the Index and Check if Files Exist

```
1  FSDirectory fsd = FSDirectory.getDirectory(
2    new File(SE_INDEX_DIR));
3  IndexReader ir = IndexReader.open(fsd);
4  List<String> delFiles = new ArrayList<String>();
5  synchronized (this) {
6    for (int i = 0; i < ir.maxDoc(); i++) {
7      Document doc = ir.document(i);
8      if ( ( doc != null)
9          && (!new File(doc.get("filename")).exists() )
10       delFiles.add(doc.get("filename"));
11   }
```

```
12   for (String delFile: delFiles)
13     ir.deleteDocuments(new Term("filename", delFile));
14 }
```

The maxDoc (line 6) method of the IndexReader class returns one greater than the largest possible document number and the document (line 7) method returns the ith document in the index. An IndexReader is an interface for accessing and modifying the index using an unique number to fetch a Document. However, this number is unique only for the duration that the index is locked and may change if new documents are added or old documents are deleted. A series of files are deleted in a single thread using the synchronized Java directive. A file system-based write lock is created before the index is altered to prevent other threads running on the same JVM or even remote threads from simultaneously modifying the index. The filename (line 9) is a Field in the Document that contains the full path name of the file and is used to verify if the file is valid. Invalid file names are added to the delFiles list and finally removed from the index. We can similarly scan the database and check if the filenames in the table are valid (see Listing 3.5).

Listing 3.5: Scan the Database and Check if Files Exist

```
1  boolean createFlag = false;
2  boolean dupFlag = false;
3  dbt.openDB(SE_DOCS, createFlag, dupFlag);
4  ArrayList<String> delFiles = new ArrayList<String>();
5  PdfDoc idoc = new PdfDoc();
6  Cursor cursor = dbt.getCurrentDB().openCursor(null, null);
7  DatabaseEntry key = new DatabaseEntry();
8  DatabaseEntry data = new DatabaseEntry();
9  while (cursor.getNext(key, data, LockMode.DEFAULT) ==
10    OperationStatus.SUCCESS) {
11    PdfDoc pdfDoc = (PdfDoc)
12      new PdfBinding().entryToObject(data);
13    if (!new File(pdfDoc.getFileName()).exists()) {
14      delFiles.add(doc.get("filename"));
15      IndexTools.delDoc(dbt, pdfDoc);
16    }
17 }
18 FSDirectory fsd = FSDirectory.getDirectory(
19    new File(SE_INDEX_DIR));
20 IndexReader ir = IndexReader.open(fsd);
```

```
21  for (String delFile: delFiles)
22    ir.deleteDocuments(new Term("filename", delFile));
23  ir.close();
24  dbt.closeDb();
```

The openCursor (line 6) method of the database handle returns a cursor to scan the database table in sequence. A file name is extracted from each entry in the database and verified against the file system. Any file that does not exist is deleted from the database and added to a list of files to be removed from the index (line 14). The final step is to remove the list of files that do not exist from the index in a batch. In this example, we have illustrated the maintenance of a list of indexed files, but the same ideas apply to URLs as well. A link to an invalid URL is equivalent to a file that does not exist.

A popular search engine has a tendency to grow in size over time as more information is supplied by larger numbers of publishers. Documents are rarely deleted in a search engine index unlike a database where individual table rows may be deleted by an application. This leads to a situation where the search engine index may become too large and outdated. An alternative may be to remove documents from the index that have never been fetched in the last n months. This may result in a more manageable index and periodically cleaning up obsolete documents may maintain the size of the index within the hardware limits of the server.

3.7.1 Logs

The logs of a search engine track the types of submitted queries and the most frequent queries. A number of statistics can be accumulated over a period of time to evaluate how users interact with the search engine. One source of user frustration is the absence of any hits for a query that is expected to return a hit list. These types of queries with zero hits can be detected from a Web log and verified through an index browser. Other statistics include the most popular documents returned for all queries and the popular query topics. A search engine administrator can proactively use this information to suggest documents for "*hot topics*". The analysis of the list of submitted queries is useful to suggest alternate queries that are either more general or specialized. The edit distance (see Chapter 4), a measure of the distance between two text strings, is one way of finding alternate queries for zero-hit queries.

3.7.2 Transactions

The main reason to use transactions in an index or database is to maintain the integrity of the data up to some point in time. In Lucene, the `IndexWriter` constructor includes an `autocommit` parameter to specify if the modifications made to the index should be written to disk automatically, when the `flush` method of the `IndexWriter` is called. The call to flush the index is either triggered by usage of memory or specific calls that are made periodically during the index process. An automatic call to `flush` is triggered when memory usage exceeds a buffered RAM limit, that can be set for a specific `IndexWriter`. A modification to the index includes the addition or deletion of documents. An `IndexReader` does not immediately detect the changes made to the index upon an `IndexWriter` flush call. The `IndexReader` must be reopened to view the index since the last commit or flush.

The Berkeley DB provides transaction support to maintain the integrity of the database. The main reason to use transactions is to protect the database from application or system failures. There is little possibility of corrupting a database, once data modifications have been committed to disk. However, data loss due to hardware problems or physical destruction can only be recovered from a backup. Fortunately, it is relatively simple to make a backup of a Berkeley DB by simply copying the data and log files from the database directory to the backup location when the database is not being updated.

3.7.3 Database Index Synchronization

The concurrent maintenance of a database and a search engine index does offer flexibility in storing and managing different types of information. In general, there is no need to store information in an index that will not be indexed and consequently will not be used in a query. The exception is a *key* or *identifier* that uniquely identifies the stored document. Information that is used to describe and not search for documents is best maintained in a database. The added complexity of maintaining both an index and a database is an additional chore for the administrator (see Table 3.8).

A discrepancy between the database, index, and file system leads to an incorrect index entry that may end up in a hit list for a query. For example, if the index contains an entry for a file that is no longer present, then the index must be corrected. In a large index with millions of files, this is a significant issue since maintenance is

Table 3.8: Index and Database Maintenance for Files

Database	Index	File	Action
No entry	Entry exists	Exists	Add to DB
No entry	Entry exists	Does not exist	Remove from Index
Entry exists	No entry	Exists	Add to Index
Entry exists	No entry	Does not exist	Remove from DB
Entry exists	Entry exists	Exists	OK
Entry exists	Entry exists	Does not exist	Remove from DB and Index

time consuming and a thorough search of the index for dead links or missing files may not be possible. One alternative is to check the existence of just a subset of the indexed files that are returned most often. This reduces the size of the maintenance problem and is also a satisfactory solution for a majority of queries.

3.7.4 Lucene Index Files

A lot of thought and prior experience went into the design of the Lucene index. The original Lucene index conceived by Doug Cutting has grown into a highly scalable structure to manage thousands and even millions of documents. The primary requirements for an inverted index are

- The list of documents that contain any term should be easily accessible.

- The description of the occurrence of a term in a document should optionally include frequency, offset in the document, font size, and the type (body, title, or author) of text in which the occurrence was found

We assume that the most frequent operation in a search engine will be a *query* to find documents that contain a term. So, the design of the index should support quick access to lists of documents for a set of query terms. Modifications to the index such as an *add*, *delete*, or *update* operation occur much less frequently than a query. Most index modifications are performed in batch to minimize the time that the index is locked. Multiple threads that concurrently modify or delete index entries should be synchronized to execute in serial order.

One of the main reasons for the popularity of Lucene is its scalability and performance. It works well with small collections of a few thousand documents and large collections with millions of documents. Additionally, the index files are organized to provide quick access to documents for queries. Finally, a large index can be distributed across multiple directories and searched concurrently (see section 3.8.5 Index Scalability). The Lucene index has a logical and disk structure shown in Figure 3.4.

Figure 3.4: Logical and Disk Structure of the Lucene Index

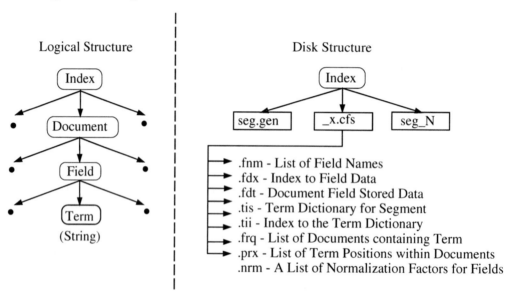

An index is made up of many Documents, each of which has one or more Fields, and each Field has a set of Terms. Every Field has a name that describes the type of information and a value stored in the set of Terms. Most Document types have more than one Field. The physical structure of the index is more complex and is made up of a number of files organized in segments. Each segment is a sub-index that can be searched independently and segments are created when new documents are added to the index. The segments (pre-2.1) file contains information such as the name of the prefix for all index files that make up this segment, the number of documents in the segment, and a flag to indicate if a compound file is used in the segment. A compound file is simply a composite file constructed from the individual segment index files. The purpose of using a compound file in an index was to limit the number of open files during the creation of an index. The compound file contains the list of segment files with offsets to the start locations of the files in the compound file itself. The use of compound files may have a minor impact on performance and can be set when the `IndexWriter` is created.

In version 2.1, the `segments` file has been replaced with a `segments.gen` file and a `segments_N` file. The `segments.gen` file points to the current `segments_N` file, where the value of `N` is a base 36 number that is incremented as index segments are created. All index files that belong to a segment have the same prefix and different extensions. An `IndexWriter` in version 2.1 dynamically tracks the files that are deletable, earlier versions of Lucene created a separate file called deletable in the index directory to monitor obsolete segment files. In Figure 3.4, the extensions of eight index files is shown.

Every segment has three `Field` files – a file (with suffix `.fnm`) with a list of the `Field` names sorted in alphabetic order from all the indexed documents in the segment and two files to manage stored `Field`s. The first file with a `.fdt` suffix contains a list of stored `Field` values with attributes to specify the number, type of data (binary or text), and the value of the `Field`. The second index file (with suffix `.fdx`) keeps track of the location of stored `Field` data by document number.

We saw earlier that fast access to terms was a primary requirement for an inverted index and the Lucene index uses a series of term files to satisfy this requirement. A term dictionary file contains a list of all the terms that occur in the segment sorted in lexicographic order. A term index file speeds up access to the term dictionary file and is usually small enough to be saved in memory. The remaining three files maintain the frequencies of terms in documents, the position of each term in the document, and a normalization value (see Chapter 4) for every `Field` in a document.

The use of term vectors is optional and specified when the `Field` of a `Document` is created. Three additional index files (`.tvx`, `.tvd`, and `.tvf`) not shown in Figure 3.4, are created to handle term vectors. Recall, a term vector is a list of the terms and associated frequencies in a document that is useful to compare documents with each other or even a query vector. The term vector may also include the position of the term occurrence in the document. The format of the index files is described in more detail at the Lucene Web site, (`http://lucene.apache.org`). The Luke index browser written by Andrzej Bialecki for the Lucene index is an excellent tool to browse the index from a GUI (`http://www.getopt.org/luke`).

3.8 Performance

In general, the size of a document collection is much larger than the size of the memory on an average PC. A large document collection may consist of several terabytes of data while a PC may have just a few Gigabytes or less of memory. A rough estimate of the size of the index files is approximately 30% of the size of the original collection. This estimate assumes that large text fields are not stored in the index and stop words are removed. The index alone may not completely fit in the memory of a single PC. The techniques in this section are mainly about efficiently managing memory when creating and searching the index.

Parts of the index are saved on disk, since an entire index will not fit in memory. The time to read and write from disk may be a thousand times or more slower than from memory due to the latency and access times. The performance tuning parameters in Lucene deal with controlling the number of writes to disk and the size of the memory buffer. Increasing the size of the memory buffer will reduce the time to index, but may increase the time to search. The performance gap between memory and hard disks may be narrowed with the introduction of solid state (flash) disks.

3.8.1 Index Tuning Parameters

Lucene builds an index made up of segments from individual documents (see Figure 3.5). Consider a collection of 10K documents that will be indexed. Each document is first indexed in memory and then a set of documents are merged into a segment. The number of documents that are buffered in memory before forming a segment on disk is controlled by the `maxBufferedDocs` parameter. The `maxBufferedDocs` parameter is set to five in Figure 3.5, which means that for every five documents indexed in memory, a new segment is created on disk. Internally, a dynamic segment is created in memory for every document and therefore the total number of segments created during the index will be higher than the number of segments shown in Figure 3.5. Temporary segments are also created when a segment is being merged to handle cases where the merge fails and the index is restored to its original state before the merge. The creation of segments and rollback in case of failure is handled transparently by Lucene and the application developer has to merely manage three performance tuning parameters – `maxBufferedDocs`, `mergeFactor`, and `maxMergeDocs`.

Figure 3.5: Creating Index Segments from Documents

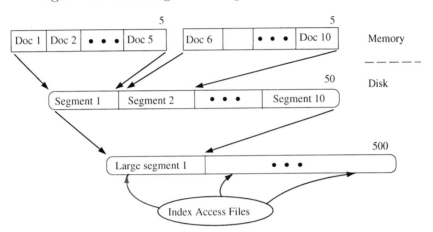

In Figure 3.5, the `mergeFactor` is set to 10, meaning that when 10 segments have been created, a new large merged segment composed of the 10 smaller segments is created in disk. All segments that have been merged can be removed from memory or disk to free up space. This process continues in a hierarchy and works for large collections of documents, where the sizes of all segments will be a product of 50. The default value for the mergeFactor is set to 10 and a small value (minimum of two) will use less memory during the merge process compared to a larger value. A large value (> 10) is preferable for batch indexing and a smaller value (< 10) for online indexing.

Notice in the segment hierarchy, there will be more frequent merges at the lower levels than at the higher levels (see Table 3.9). A larger mergeFactor means a flatter segment hierarchy with many more segments that can slow down a search, but will reduce the time to index the collection. You will also need more memory to handle the merges of the large higher level segments. The amount of memory required during a merge may exceed twice the size of the segments being merged.

Table 3.9: Number of Segment Merges for Merge Factors and Max. Buffered Documents

Indexed Documents	Merge Factor	Max. Buffered Docs	No. of Merges
10K	10	5	222
100K	10	5	2222
1M	100	50	202
10M	100	50	2020
100M	100	100	10101

When the merge factor is large, the number of generated index files grows rapidly. The number of open files can exceed 5K, even for a small collection of 10K documents, if the `IndexWriter` does not use compound files. In Table 3.9, 90% or more of the merges occur at the lowest level for all merge factors. At higher merge factors, 99% of the merges occur at the lowest level, with a few large merges at the higher levels. Increasing the number of maximum buffered documents will reduce the number of segment merges but will require more memory. Each segment will contain a larger number of documents in memory before flushing to the disk. Figure 3.6 illustrates the time to index a collection of 10K documents using various combinations of values for merge factor and maximum buffered documents.

3.8.2 Evaluation of Parameters

A sample collection of 10K Reuters news articles was created to test index performance. Each article contained an average of 1 kilobytes in a plain text file with a range of sizes from a minimum of 0.25 kilobytes to a maximum of 13 kilobytes. The performance curves show an initial decrease in the index time when the maximum number of buffered documents was increased to about 100 for all merge factors. Higher values of maximum buffered documents did not have a corresponding reduction in the time to index the collection. A higher merge factor is similarly initially beneficial but did not generate substantial gains with larger values. The time to merge segments is a time consuming operation taking up to 75 % of the total index time and the added memory for larger buffers minimally reduces the index time on the right side of the curves in Figure 3.6.

Figure 3.6: Performance Curves for mergeFactor and maxBufferedDocs for a 10K Collection

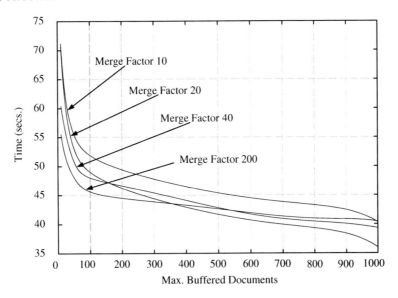

Each segment merge combines all `Fields`, `Terms`, `TermVectors`, and field normalization information of all memory segments into a single disk segment. First the merged segment files are created on disk followed by the creation of the next generation segment file. A new single segment index file with the suffix `cfs` will be created, if the index uses compound files. The old segments created in memory for the indexed documents and the old segment index files on disk will be deleted. This is a fairly complex operation and Lucene takes care of rolling back the merge, if there is a failure in the merge transaction. The two main reasons for failure are insufficient disk space or memory and an excessive number of open files.

Note:Java currently does not allow the size of allocated memory to be changed dynamically in a program. If you need to use more memory, then you will

> *need to specify the initial (-Xms) and maximum (-Xmx) heap memory runtime parameters, before running the program.*

The third parameter to tune index performance is the `maxMergeDocs`. This parameter limits the number of documents in a single segment file. The index hierarchy in Figure 3.5 does not limit the size of the large segments at higher levels and in a huge document collection, the size of a single segment file may be excessive. The default value for this parameter is the largest `Integer` value. In effect, the `maxMergeDocs` parameter nullifies the `mergeFactor` and creates new segments when the maximum number of permissible documents in a segment is reached. The main purpose of this parameter is to overcome problems due to limits on file sizes in a platform.

In addition to adequate memory, you will need sufficient disk space for index operations such as the `optimize` method of the `IndexWriter` class. The `optimize` method is a time consuming and space intensive operation to generate a compact index that can be searched quickly. The time to complete the index optimization may take up to 15% or more of the total index time. Fortunately, disk space is relatively cheap and it is preferable to use a large disk several times the size of the index to avoid any problems due to a lack of space. An index will be partially optimized, if the disk space is insufficient, but should still be usable. In other words, the index will not become corrupted, if an exception occurs during the `optimize` operation.

3.8.3 Memory-Based Index

The three parameters we have seen so far are reasonably sufficient to tune the performance of the creation of the index. Another method is to manually create index segments in memory and periodically merge the segments to disk. Lucene uses a memory-based `RAMDirectory` that behaves almost identically to its disk-based counterpart, the `FSDirectory`. A `RAMDirectory` exists in memory within a process and has separate methods for locking and initialization. On a multi-processor machine, multiple processes can concurrently build memory-based indexes that are periodically merged. Listing 3.6 illustrates a method to create a `RAMDirectory` that is merged onto disk based on a tuning parameter.

Listing 3.6: Use of RAMDirectory to Speed Up Indexing

```
1  public class MemoryIndex {
2    private static long intDocs = 0;
3    private static RAMDirectory ramDir = null;
4    private static FSDirectory fsDir = null;
5    private static IndexWriter ramIw = null;
6    private static IndexWriter fsIw = null;
7    private static int DOC_LIMIT = 10000;
8    private static int MERGE_LIMIT = 2000;
9
10   public static void main(String[] args) {
11     fsDir = FSDirectory.getDirectory(SE_INDEX_DIR);
12     fsIw = new IndexWriter(fsDir,
13         new StandardBgramAnalyzer(), true);
14     ramDir = new RAMDirectory();
15     ramIw = new IndexWriter(ramDir,
16         new StandardBgramAnalyzer(), true);
17     ramIw.setMaxBufferedDocs(Integer.MAX_VALUE);
18     ramIw.setMergeFactor(Integer.MAX_VALUE);
19     String txtDir = TESTING_DIR + FS + "txt";
20     DirTools dirTools = new DirTools();
21     ArrayList<String>flist = dirTools.dirScan(txtDir,true);
22     TxtHandler txtHandler = new TxtHandler();
23     intDocs = 0;
24     for (String filename : flist) {
25       if (!(filename.endsWith(".txt")))
26         continue;
27       TxtDoc txtDoc = new TxtDoc(filename);
28       txtHandler.getDocument(filename, txtDoc);
29       txtDoc.setId(System.currentTimeMillis() + "");
30       Document doc = new Document();
31       doc.add(new Field("id", "" + txtDoc.getId(),
32         Field.Store.YES, Field.Index.NO));
33       doc.add(new Field("filename", filename,
34         Field.Store.YES, Field.Index.NO));
35       doc.add(new Field("contents",
36         txtDoc.getContents().toString(), Field.Store.NO,
37         Field.Index.TOKENIZED, Field.TermVector.YES) );
38       ramIw.addDocument(doc);
39       if ((++intDocs % MERGE_LIMIT) == 0) copyIndex(false);
40       if (intDocs == DOC_LIMIT) break LOOP;
```

```
41       }
42       copyIndex(true);
43     }
44     public static void copyIndex(boolean last) {
45       Directory[] dirs = { ramDir };
46       ramIw.close();
47       fsIw.addIndexes(dirs);
48       if (last) {
49         fsIw.close();
50       } else {
51         ramIw = new IndexWriter(ramDir,
52           new StandardBgramAnalyzer(), true);
53       }
54     }
55   }
```

A RAMDirectory is created without specifying any directory name. Next, we create an IndexWriter as before, using the memory-based directory. A disk-based file system directory and index writer is also created (lines 11 and 14). Documents are added to the memory-based index in the same manner as the disk-based index. A persistent index will eventually be written to disk. Periodically the partially generated memory-based index is copied to disk (line 39). The MERGE_LIMIT parameter controls how often the index is copied from memory to disk. A low value will mean frequent copies that may diminish the value of creating a memory-based index, while a high value will give better performance but will require more memory. In this example, the partial memory-based index will be copied five times to disk to create the complete index.

The copyIndex (line 44) function first closes the IndexWriter created from the RAMDirectory. Next, the addIndexes (line 47) method of the disk-based IndexWriter is used to merge the index. In this case, a single directory is merged; a more appropriate use of this method is to merge multiple indexes into a single index (see Figure 3.7). Consider a very large document collection with millions of documents. Indexing one document at a time would take an excessively long time. In most document collections, each document is a separate entity and can be indexed independently of other documents. The task of indexing a huge number of documents can be distributed evenly on a multi-processor machine.

Figure 3.7: Indexing Documents in Parallel

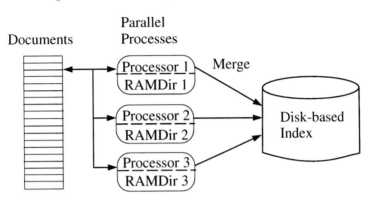

Two or more processes can concurrently access a list of documents and uniquely select a subset of documents to index. Each process creates a separate memory-based directory to temporarily hold the index. Periodically, the indexes created in memory are merged with a disk based index using the `addIndexes` (line 47) method we saw in Listing 3-6. During the merge, there are several possibilities for exceptions such as a disk error or a time out while waiting for a merge to complete. The `addIndexes` method is synchronized and also uses transactions to rollback any errors that occur during a merge.

We can create an `IndexSearcher` (see Chapter 4) from a `RAMDirectory` to reduce the response time for queries. The constructor for a `RAMDirectory` accepts a `File` that points to the location of the disk-based index. For example, if we know that the index created for a document collection is small and will fit in memory, we can create and use a memory-based `IndexSearcher`. Of course, any changes made to the index on disk will not be seen and changes may to the `RAMDirectory` will not persist unless they are written to disk. This is an efficient method to provide a fast search interface to a small collection of documents that are updated infrequently.

3.8.4 Index Performance with a Database

The Lucene API makes it simple to imitate the schema of database tables where a column roughly corresponds to a `Field` of a `Document`. An indexed document may contain the same information as a row of a database table. Given the flexibility of adding documents to an index and the absence of a schema, it may appear as if a database is not necessary to supplement an index. For a small collection of 10K-100K documents, the overhead of creating and using database tables may overcome any performance benefits.

The overheads occur during indexing and searching. A row is inserted in a table for every document added to the index. The time to insert a row in a database table is added to the time to index a document increasing the total time to scan a document collection. The results of a query will require a database lookup in addition to a search of the index. These delays exclude the time needed to acquire or release a database connection and load the database structures.

The benefits of using a database to back up an index are more apparent in a large document collection. One, the size of the index is smaller since long `Fields` are saved in a table instead of the index. The size of a database backed index could be less than 50% the size of the original index. For example, storing the contents of short news articles in a 10K document collection increased the size of the index from 7.7 Mbytes to 17.9 Mbytes.

Two, it takes less memory and time to optimize a smaller than a larger index with stored `Fields`. Optimizing an index is a memory and time consuming process that does improve query performance. The time to optimize a database backed index was almost half the time to optimize a fully contained index for a sample 10K document collection. Finally, a larger document collection can be indexed and searched without investing in a larger machine to manage the additional memory requirements.

3.8.5 Index Scalability

In a growing enterprise, the volume of the collected documents will increase and a scalable solution is needed to meet the increased demands of the user community. Typically, as the size of a collection grows, the number of submitted queries also increases, leading to a situation where the load on a single search index becomes excessive. Segmenting the index and distributing the workload across a cluster of machines is one solution to this problem. Smaller indexes on multiple machines may also lead to higher performance, since a larger portion of the index may fit in the memory of an individual machine.

There are at least two ways to divide an index. One way is to build separate indexes of a common document collection on multiple machines and the other way is to partition the index by terms that are within an alphabetic range. In the former method, indexes are built in parallel on individual machines (see Figure 3.7) from separate subsets of the large document collection. A single merged index is not created and queries are submitted to all indexes. The results are compiled into a single list of hits returned to the user. The index to search is selected based on the query terms in the second method and is based on a table lookup to identify the index associated with a query term.

There is far more to this simple explanation of a scalable index. The Apache *Nutch* (see Chapter 8) project is an effort to build a scalable Web search engine. The resources needed for a Web search engine are substantial and a distributed architecture is the most economical method of achieving the high performance necessary for such a search engine. The *Nutch* project uses the *Hadoop* distributed file system to create the segmented index and the *MapReduce* software framework to implement parallel programming constructs.

A search engine for a large document collection becomes a critical resource and solutions to limit downtime should be implemented. The most common solution is to replicate the index across multiple search servers. Search queries can be routed to an alternate search server, if any one of the servers does fail. Replication can also be accomplished on a single machine by using redundant hard disks that can be swapped or re-configured.

3.8.6 Index Vocabulary

The final parameter for tuning an index is the `maxFieldLength`. This parameter limits the number of terms that will be indexed for any `Field`. The default value of `maxFieldLength` is 10K. The `IndexWriter` will stop building an index segment when the number of terms in a text string for the `Field` exceeds 10K. The limit is defined for the `IndexWriter` and should be set to an appropriate value depending on the type of documents in the collection. For example, consider the 181 page book - "Producing Open Source Software" by Karl Fogel. The first 10K tokens from the Lucene `StandardAnalyzer` covers only about 25 pages of the book, where each page contains roughly 400 words. In other words, the `maxFieldLength` will need to be increased substantially in order to accurately index the entire book. The number of words in a page depends on the font size, size of the pages, and number of graphics or tables. The plot in Figure 3.8 shows the percentage of vocabulary covered for different Field length limits for this particular book.

Figure 3.8: Vocabulary Coverage for Field Length Limits

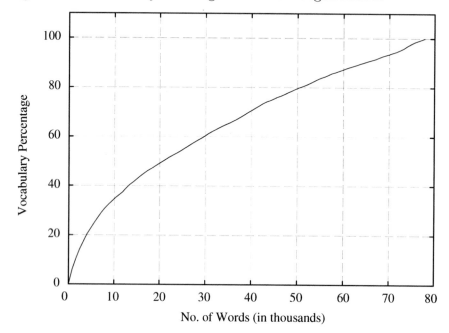

The first 25% of the words covers about 50% of the vocabulary. The next 25% makes up another 25% of the vocabulary and the last half of the words cover the remaining 25% of the vocabulary. The plot shows that the growth in vocabulary is high initially and then gradually tapers off. This phenomenon in natural language text is described with *Heap's Law* (http://encyclopedia.thefreedictionary.com/Heaps' +law). The law makes predictions of the growth in vocabulary as the number of words increases. The vocabulary growth in Figure 3.8 would have been slower had stop words not been removed. Most Web search engines do limit the indexed size of a Web page to about 100 kilobytes or less to avoid problems with excessively long pages that will consume more resources and may add little value. A good value for `maxFieldLength` is the estimated number of terms in the largest indexed document. The price for increasing this limit is a larger index and a longer time to build or update the index.

3.9 Date Fields

A `Field` in Lucene is a part of a document that has a name and a value. The name is a description of the value such as *Date, URL, ISBN,* or *Contents.* The value is the associated text or binary value of the `Field`. It may be tempting to make an analogy with the columns (`Fields`) of a database table (Lucene Document). A document is made up of one or more `Fields`, each of which has a distinct value and meaning. However, the analogy breaks down when we consider the type of data that can be loaded in a column and a `Field`. The database schema specifies the type of data that is legal for every column of every table. The format of the data entered in the database table is controlled by specifying a type such as numeric, date, or text. These controls are absent in a search engine index and any legitimate text data can be entered.

The `Date` field is a common `Field` in most indexed documents. All Web pages have a creation date or the last modification date that is usually included in the index. Similarly, documents such as books, articles, and emails all have associated dates. Storing the date in a separate field makes it relatively simple to sort a list of documents by date or to search for documents in a date range. Unfortunately, many of the core Java date functions cannot be used for lexicographic sorting.

Consider a set of three numeric strings – 2, 12, and 6. A lexicographic sort in ascending order would generate the list – 12, 2, and 6. This is not what is normally expected and one solution to this problem is to prefix leading zeroes such that all strings are of equal length. The list – 02, 06, and 12 is sorted numerically as well as lexicographically. We use the same idea to sort dates by specifying a date in a standard format in the index. The highest date resolution that you can use in Lucene is a 17 character timestamp yyyyMMddHHmmssSSS that includes a four digit year, month, date, hour, minutes, seconds, and milliseconds.

The `DateTools` package in Lucene makes it simple to create such timestamps that are prefixed with leading zeroes (see Listing 3.7). The main purpose of the package is to convert between Java `Dates` and `Strings` such that a lexicographic sorting order is preserved, and to handle a wide range of dates.

Listing 3.7: Testing the DateTools Package

```
1  public class TestDateTools {
2    public static void main(String[] args) {
3
4      GregorianCalendar calendar = new GregorianCalendar();
5      calendar.setTime(new Date());
6      Date dt = calendar.getTime();
7      String dayDate = DateTools.dateToString(
8        dt, DateTools.Resolution.DAY);
9      System.out.println("Indexable day date: "
10       + dayDate);
11     String secondDate = DateTools.dateToString(
12     dt, DateTools.Resolution.SECOND);
13     System.out.println("Indexable second date: "
14       + secondDate);
15
16     long tm = calendar.getTimeInMillis();
17     String dayMDate = DateTools.timeToString(
18       tm, DateTools.Resolution.DAY);
19     System.out.println("Indexable day timestamp: "
20       + dayMDate);
21     String secondMDate = DateTools.timeToString(
22       tm, DateTools.Resolution.MILLISECOND);
23     System.out.println("Indexable second timestamp: "
24       + secondMDate);
25   }
26 }
```

The core Java `GregorianCalendar` (line 4) class has many methods to generate a `Date` using combinations of the year, month, day, hour, minute, and second. You can also specify a timezone or the time in milliseconds since the Unix epoch (Jan 1, 1970). The sample code uses the current time in a `Date` (line 5) object measured to the nearest millisecond to initialize the calendar time.

The `dateToString` (line 7) method of the `DateTools` package will convert a `Date` to a `String` with the specified date resolution. The core Java `toString` representation of a `Date` object cannot be used in the index since it includes alphabetic characters for the day of the week, the month, and the timezone. The methods to convert from a `String` to a `Date` and back in the `DateTools` package preserve a lexicographic sorting order. Notice, the output from the first two print statements.

```
Indexable day date:  20080502
Indexable second date:  20080502015901
```

The first date uses the `DAY` (line 8) resolution while the second date uses the `SECOND` (line 12) resolution to generate a string representation of the `Date`. The first eight digits in both timestamps are the familiar four digit year, two digit month, and a two digit day of month. In the second date, the last six digits are the two digit hour, minute, and second values. Internally, Lucene uses the GMT timezone and will convert the time from your current timezone using the `Calendar` methods.

The output from the `dateToString` methods represents the time (at GMT) in the `Date` object, which may differ from the output of the `toString` method in the `Date` class that does not adjust timezones. The methods to convert from `Date` to `String` and back keep the timezone conversion transparent, but you will need to choose the resolution of the timestamp, if you plan on creating a Date object with the exact same time.

The `Calendar` class has a method to extract the current time in milliseconds (since the start of the epoch). The current time is stored in a long number (line 16) and is an alternative to maintaining the current time in a `Date` object. The `DateTools` package contains a pair of methods to convert between `Strings` and long values of the current time that are similar to the methods to convert between `Strings` and `Dates`.

Lucene also has a `NumberTools` package to convert between `longs` and `Strings` such that lexicographic order is preserved. For example, the long number 9 is converted to a fixed size String 00000000000009 of length 14. The largest long number is 19 digits long and the `NumberTools` methods compress the numeric value to a 14 character String value by using the 26 alphabetic and 10 numeric characters in a base 36 representation. You will need a package like `DateTools` or `NumberTools` to handle any `Field` in a search that will be a sort key, or to find documents in a range. For example, if a *part number* will be searched by range, you will need methods to convert between the current representation and a `String` such that lexicographic order is preserved.

3.10 Metadata

The purpose of the index in a book is to quickly find locations in the text where a word, phrase, or a name is mentioned. Manually building an index for a book with several hundred pages is a tedious affair, and maintaining an index for a library of books is even more demanding. Indexing is also the most crucial task in building a search engine, since the index is the primary means used to locate documents. If your collection of documents is small, you may not need an index. It is possible to submit a regular expression query using a tool such as `grep` over the entire collection. `Grep` also does not handle boolean queries and returns a list of matching lines. In practice, few document collections remain small enough for these tools to be efficient.

3.10.1 Document Metadata

There are several text fields external to the contents of a document that serve as descriptors of the document. In a book, this would include the publisher, the author, title, table of contents, abstract, subject, number of pages, and place of publication. This information makes up the metadata of the book that is also found in other genres of text. For example, the metadata tags of a Web page can be used to describe the contents and help search engines build a more precise index. Consider a Web page on *horse riding* that may have the following metadata between the header tags.

- <META name="description" content="All about horse riding classes and competitions">

- <META name="keywords" content="dressage, eventing, reining, show jumping, vaulting">

The first META tag has the attribute *description*, whose value should contain a concise explanation of the contents of the page. Typically, explanations are less than 250 characters long. The second META tag uses the *keywords* attribute to describe a set of words and phrases that best characterize the content of the Web page. Accurate metadata is very valuable to a search engine since it is the author's, and possibly the best, description of the Web page. Unfortunately, on the Web this tag is open to exploitation, and as a result some search engines just ignore META tags entirely. It may be possible that if the text contents of the Web page and the metadata match, the search engine will use the author supplied metadata in the index. The contents of the *title* tag of a Web page is another source of metadata that can be used.

Lucene does not explicitly provide any guidelines to handle metadata and the developer of a search engine can choose to selectively include or exclude metadata based on the requirements of the user community. A developer may also be limited by the type of metadata available from a document filter. For example, the metadata from a plain text file will not include a *title* or an *author* that may be available in a PDF file.

On the desktop, there are many types of documents, including Web pages, emails, e-books, articles, letters, and so on. The metadata for each type of document is unique with different attributes. For example, an email has *subject* and *sender* attributes that are absent in a Web page. Similarly, e-books may have a *publisher* and an *ISBN* attribute. Almost any type of document will have some metadata that is of use in an index. Identifying these attributes before building an index can make your search engine more efficient and provide multiple ways of getting access to information. A comprehensive document filter will extract all possible metadata, which is then provided to Lucene to include in the index.

3.10.2 Multimedia Metadata

Multimedia files pose a significant challenge for automatic indexers. Image files downloaded from a digital camera do not contain any metadata that describes the contents of the image. The optional information captured in an image includes a timestamp, resolution, and other camera settings that are insufficient to find images with keywords. A brief sentence describing the image itself is usually sufficient to locate an image using a query.

Automatically building an index for such images is still very difficult, but through pattern recognition it is possible to recognize particular objects in an image. For example, it is possible to find files that contain images of a mountain, and maybe even a particular mountain, such as Mt. Everest. Nonetheless, these descriptions cannot match the manually generated description of an image which can be very precise. Unfortunately, manually generating a description for every image stored on a desktop is tedious and very few users will take the time to individually tag images. But, if you do take the trouble to organize your collection of images in folders and files with appropriate names, it will be easier to search your collection. Digital image organization software for the desktop gives you more control over your image collection with manual tags that can be searched and listed by date and creator. Some image formats such as the Exchangeable Image File Format (*Exif*) and Tagged Image File Format (*TIFF*) have fields to store a text description of the image that may be suitable for indexing within the image file itself. Many of the current digital cameras do allow you to attach metadata to captured images.

Web sites like Flickr (`http://www.flickr.com`) that catalog a huge collection of images distribute the task of assigning descriptions to images. Each image is initially manually tagged with a user based taxonomy (folksonomy) by the creator of the image and other users add comments to build a richer metadata description. Unfortunately, the relationship between tags is not known and most tags are shown in a flat list or a cloud (see Figure 1.4). The Web facilitates such massive collaborative projects to build a huge collection of organized multimedia files that would have been very difficult to accomplish otherwise. Critics argue that this unorganized method of assigning tags will be unreliable and inconsistent. This is because a single word can have more than one meaning. For example, the word *Lincoln* may mean the name of a place in Nebraska, the 16th President of the United States, or the name of a car made by the Ford Motor Company. The open source community has faced a similar problem of explaining the phrase *"free software"*, which could mean either that the software is without any cost, or that the software can be distributed freely. Despite these issues with an uncontrolled tag set, collaborative indexing does provide reasonably accurate results.

Web search engines have built automated collections of image, audio, and video files with a description taken from the Web page where the file was found. For example, if a Web page contained an IMG tag with an ALT attribute, then the image would be tagged with the description assigned to the ALT attribute. If no such text was provided, then a window of text in the neighborhood of the image would be substituted for the image description. This process is not guaranteed to produce the most accurate description of an image, but is probably the best that can be done from an HTML Web page.

3.10.3 Metadata Standards

Automatic methods to extract the contents of multimedia data have not been as successful as manual descriptions. An automated method relies on context and other sources of information that are typically not as reliable as a human generated explanation. Metadata standards provide a uniform way to generate descriptions of multimedia data. Implementations of these standards can process these descriptions and assign attributes to generate a precise description.

The Dublin Core (`http://dublincore.org/`) is a set of expandable metadata elements to describe multimedia and text files. An implementation of these elements may use XML and the Resource Definition Format (RDF) from the World Wide Web Consortium (W3C). The list of metadata elements was chosen by a community-based library organization. In 1995, the Online Computer Library Center (OCLC) defined a core set of 15 metadata elements which included elements such as *title*, *creator*, *subject*, and *description*.

The Resource Definition Framework (RDF) is another well known standard for creating metadata to describe multimedia and other types of data as well. It was designed to be used by applications to assign meanings to text fragments that would otherwise be difficult to grasp from the plain text context alone. For example, you can use RDF syntax to describe a car in detail. A car has many different attributes including the manufacturer, model, and type of engine. In RDF, the car is the *subject* which is being described by a set of attributes (properties), each of which has an associated value. The *subject*, *property*, and *value* form a triple and many such triples complete the description of the car.

The adoption of standards such as the Dublin Core and RDF would make the development of intelligent applications much easier than the current methods of guessing the most likely meaning of a text fragment from context. However, the success of these metadata models depends on the widespread adoption of standards, which has yet to happen. Sites like Flickr that use a simpler collaborative tagging model to assign a description have quickly become popular

3.11 Summary

This chapter has covered the creation of an index, which is the core of any search engine. Building the index of a search engine is analogous to loading the tables of a database. We need information in the index to begin searching. The boundary between databases and search engines has become somewhat fuzzy with databases handling some forms of full text search and a search engine like Lucene that can function as a database as well. If we consider each `Field` in Lucene to be a column, then a single `Document` represents a row. Although it may be tempting to use one or the other for managing all your information, each is best suited for its original purpose. A database is most efficient at handling data that can be fetched with keys, while a search engine is best at finding the documents that match a query. A hybrid approach combines the most efficient features of a search engine and a database. We can use a database to store metadata information that is useful at search time, but not used in a query, and use the search engine to find matching documents from indexed text.

4 Searching Text with Lucene

In the previous chapter, the importance of a high performance index for a search engine was described. This chapter covers the more visible search interface and is equally important for the successful implementation of a search engine. The chapter begins with an overview of search architecture and design followed by a description of Lucene query types and some query modification (spell checking and troubleshooting) using LingPipe and Lucene.

4.1 Lucene Search Architecture

The search user interface is built on top of the index that we constructed in Chapter 3 (see Figure 4.1). Lucene offers a rich collection of query types to fetch documents from the index. The purpose of the search user interface is to translate the text entered in a search box to a Lucene query that is submitted to an `IndexReader` that in turn finds a set of hits that match the query.

We considered the use of analyzers and text filters in Chapter 2 to tokenize text and feed the `IndexWriter`. An index is a set of files that may exist on a single directory, multiple directories, and even on multiple machines. In the simple case, we assume an index on a single directory of the local file system. The user interface is typically a search box on a Web page in which the user enters a query. Some filtering of the text of the query is advisable before submitting the query to Lucene, since practically any kind of text can be entered in the search box. The text entered in a search box is unrestricted in most cases and may include non-alphabetic characters that have a special meaning in a search engine. For example, the ":" character delimits a search field and the "?" character is a wildcard character for a partial query term. Unbalanced parentheses or quotes are also possible sources of error and may return unpredictable results.

Figure 4.1: Design of a Lucene-Based Search Engine

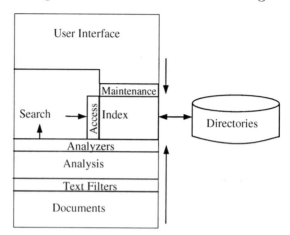

The user interface should provide read only access to the index and no harm can be done to the index by submitting queries alone. A tool like *Luke* is very handy to maintain and debug the index. There will be cases where documents that should match do not appear in a hit list for some reason. Luke can be used to debug and verify the index. The number of indexed documents, the number of terms, and other statistics are also useful to confirm that the index does actually represent the document collection (Figure 4.2).

Luke includes a browser to view the indexed documents by the unique Lucene document ID that was assigned when the document was indexed. The screenshot in Figure 4.2, shows the results of a query for the token lucene in the contents field. The results show the top six hits of the 29 documents that matched the query. The key field contains the name of the file whose contents contain the token lucene. Luke includes several other nifty features to -

- Browse the index by term or view the list of terms in alphabetic order

- Find the number of documents in which a term occurs

- Reconstruct and edit the contents of an indexed document

- Search for documents using one of several analyzers

Figure 4.2: A Screenshot of a Lucene Index using the Luke Browser

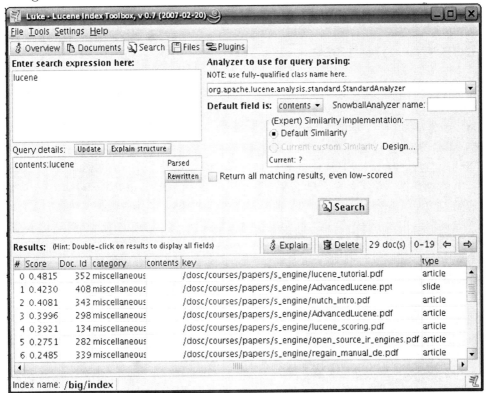

- Explain the score for a matching document (see section 4.6.2 Scoring Results in this chapter)

- Display the parsed query string generated from the user submitted query

- Several other tools to compare analyzers and view the growth of the index vocabulary

Lucene's Explain function, described later in this chapter, is very useful to understand how documents are ranked in a hit list and why one document is ranked higher than another document. This is a major benefit of using an open source search engine, since you can tweak the calculation of the score for a document to suit your requirements. The scoring and similarity calculations are transparent and you can build `Similarity` classes that are appropriate for your domain.

4.2 Search Interface Design

The user interface is an important part of the search engine that ultimately may determine the success or failure of the search engine. Lucene does not mandate any standard user interface and it is left to the creativity of the developer to build the interface that will satisfy the user community's requirements. The widespread use of search engines on the Web has led to a basic set of expectations that should be fulfilled in a search interface (see Figure 4.3). The search box is a simple text field in a form to enter an unformatted query text string. The novice user can submit a query without any knowledge of the syntax used to formulate specific queries. A knowledgeable user may combine boolean operators, use other search engine specific syntax such as domain restriction, or use nested queries to build a precise query.

The results page shown after the submission of a query contains many details that may be of interest to the user. Just below the search box is a summary of the number of hits found and the range of the hits shown in the current page. The "Expand Query" link will generate a broader query from the existing query. For example, the phrase "search engine" is a more general query than the specific query, *Lucene*. The next part of the results page is the hit list shown in descending order of score. The first part of a hit is the name of the file and a possible link to the file. A Web-based search engine would point to the Web page for the hit with the title text as the anchor. Next is a link to "Similar Pages".

There are several ways to find pages similar to an existing page. One way is to store a list of the top n pages that are most similar to a page in the index and return those pages when requested. This would require the computation and storage of similar pages for every document that is indexed. Matching a document against all other documents in a large collection can be time consuming and will slow down the index process. Instead, another method is to compute the pages similar to the selected document using another query. A query is constructed using the primary n words in the selected document and submitted to the search engine like any other query.

Figure 4.3: A Typical Search User Interface

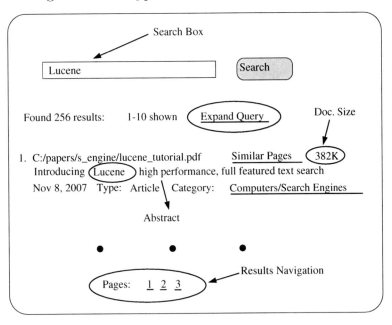

A hit should also provide the context for the matching document. In this case, the query contained the word *Lucene* and should have been found in the text of any matching document. A snippet of text from the document containing the term *Lucene* is shown with the query term highlighted using a different color or font to show the context. There are several types of indexed documents including – Web pages, articles, books, slides, email, spreadsheets, letters, and instant messages. The type of document based on an assigned category is stored in a database when the document is indexed. In this example, the hit belongs to the *search engines* sub-category under the *computers* category. Documents are classified into one or more categories at the time of indexing based on tokens that match the definition of a category (see Chapter 7). Finally links to additional pages of hits should be shown, if the number of hits exceeds the limit for the number of hits on a single Web page.

4.3 Search Behavior

The retrieval of data from a database table is very precise compared to document retrieval from a search engine. Queries submitted to database tables use Structured Query Language (SQL) with clear specifications to indicate which table to search, the number of fields to return, the order of the results, and any matching data requirements. Unfortunately, there is much less structure in a search engine that can be exploited and search engine queries are rarely as accurate as SQL queries. The index of a search engine is also viewed as a single entity with no clear boundaries to separate documents of different classes similar to the tables of a database. Lucene does have query features to dynamically partition the index based on a particular `Field`. Most users overlook the lack of precision compared to SQL queries and prefer the convenience of specifying a few keywords to form a search engine query. Users who are accustomed to the unrestricted search engine query format do not want to remember key fields and the associated values that are needed to generate an SQL query.

The boolean query that was originally created for information retrieval systems has become a standard on most search engines. The knowledgeable user can generate a precise query using the most suitable set of terms and operators. The three standard boolean operators – *AND, OR*, and *NOT* work with operands (terms) that may have further boolean sub-queries. Formulating a boolean query with operators requires some logical reasoning and over three fourths of the users of Web search engines do not use any operators (see Figure 4.4). It is also difficult for users not trained in logic or mathematics to understand the meaning of the operators. The inexperienced user may assume that the *AND* operator is actually an expansion of the query since more information is being requested. The *OR* operator is also sometimes interpreted as a mutually exclusive choice among two operands. Both these errors are contrary to a proper understanding of how boolean operators work and will lead to user dissatisfaction with a search engine.

Some search engines substitute the operators *AND* and *NOT* with the symbols + and – which are more intuitive. A search engine can assume a default *AND* or *OR* operation when multiple terms are specified in a query with no operator.

The data for the plot shown in Figure 4.4 was taken from a paper [Silverstein] published in 1999 at the SIGIR Forum. The query log contained entries from ap-

Figure 4.4: Frequency of Terms and Operators in Search Engine Queries

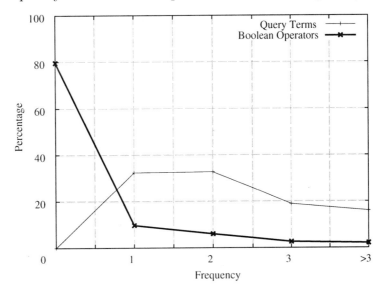

proximately one billion queries submitted over a period of six weeks. The main conclusions of the paper were that users tend to generate short queries and seldom scan results beyond the first page of hits. The average number of terms used in a query is roughly two and less than a quarter of all queries use an operator. Users tend to submit queries with 1-2 words to find results that are *"good enough"* and not necessarily the best results the search engine has to offer. The principle of least effort (Zipf's Law) that we saw in Chapter 3 for word usage in documents applies to queries as well. The typical searcher is economical in the effort required to describe an information need. The paper also studied the power law distribution of queries where a few queries tend to occur very often and the vast majority occur just once in the log.

Another study [Querylog] by the Patricia Seybold Group in 2006, found that the top four percent of all queries *"matter the most"*. That is, just four percent of all unique queries made up half of all submitted queries. In other words, optimizing a search engine for the several hundred terms from the top four percent of queries will improve the results for half the searches. The results of this study corroborate the findings from the analysis of the Web search engine query log. Optimizing a search engine for the few popular queries that make up the bulk of all queries will lead to better search results with less effort.

4.3.1 Intranets and the Web

Users accustomed to high performance Web search engines find it puzzling and frustrating when they cannot locate information on a much smaller scale. It seems to be easier to find answers to questions like the "number of steps to reach the top of the Sydney Harbor Bridge" (1439) on the Web than to find information at the workplace or even on the desktop. The answers to this puzzle lie in the differences between an Intranet and the Web. Typically, the size of the Web is much larger than an Intranet and the vocabulary on the Web is correspondingly large (see Figure 3.8). The result is that almost any query, even with spelling errors, will generate some results. On an Intranet, a much larger fraction of the queries will have zero hits, which may lead the user to give up or try an alternate query. Therefore, suggesting other terms and ways of finding information on an Intranet is more important than on the Web. Queries submitted to a small search engine must be expanded to link documents with words that are not explicitly mentioned in the document. This may include adding word stems and synonyms (see section 2.7.1) to the query.

Secondly, the results on a few Web search engines are often quite precise and relevant to the user's information need. This is not always the case with Intranet search engines. The best results from an Intranet search may be buried in a hit list and seen by only the most determined user. In Chapter 3, (Document Metadata) we saw that adding metadata to describe the content of a document was very useful to build an accurate index. Web search engines use the billions of links that are included in Web pages to create implicit metadata to describe and assign authority to a Web page.

We distinguish between inbound links (to a page) and outbound links (from a page). A Web page with many inbound links is potentially an authority on a specific topic. These inbound links are the basis for ranking algorithms such as the *PageRank* algorithm used by Google. A document x is recursively assigned higher importance based on the importance and number of the inbound links that point to x. This type of rich link structure is minimal in most Intranets. Other formats of documents such as email, PDF, or slides tend to contain fewer hyperlinks than a Web page. The typical desktop search engine will need to track these links in a database that is external to the index. So, it is not surprising that results from Intranet search engines do not have the same level of precision as a Web search engine, given the absence of the rich hyperlink structure that provides implicit metadata.

Users of an Intranet are a much smaller population compared to the users of the Web. They are usually more active consumers and producers within the smaller domain, and typically expect to be able to store and retrieve information on an Intranet with the precision of data in a database. And this is not an unreasonable expectation: Documents for an Intranet are transferred to a directory where the crawler for a search engine will find and index the information. The user expects the indexed document to appear in a hit list, when the keywords from the contents of the document are supplied in a query. The use of an internal search engine will be limited, if it does not perform this basic function of storage and retrieval.

A more complex but related issue is the location of the document in the hit list. More documents are published on the current hot topic than other subjects and in such cases there will be many documents that match a query. A list of hits for a hot topic may not appear in the order expected by a reader. The ranking algorithm has little or no metadata to differentiate between pages by author. Some authors may be known as experts in a community. A search engine cannot rank pages authored by such experts higher than other pages, without any metadata describing the expertise of the author.

Users may be curious to know why one page is ranked higher than some other page. This chapter will cover ranking, one of the most important parts of a search engine. In an open source search engine like Lucene, the ranking algorithm returns the computation of the score for any document in the hit list, and this algorithm can be tuned to return results with higher precision.

Note: Web search engines usually offer unrestricted search to all content to all users. In some cases, a search engine may be censored to show only results that are deemed appropriate—for example, a search engine designed for children. But for Intranet search engines, there are legitimate reasons for a company to block access depending on the user. There are several ways of controlling access to the

---

---

information available through an Intranet search engine and we will look at some of them in the Security Filter section 4.7.2 later in this chapter.

4.4 Searching the Index

The user interface to the search function is the primary means of accessing information from a search engine index. We continue with an existing index of 10K documents from the previous chapter. Now we would like to search it. The steps to execute a search and return a list of hits in Lucene are fairly simple (Figure 4.5).

Figure 4.5: Steps to Run a Search and Return Results

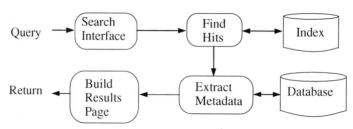

A query is first submitted from a search interface to find hits. We will initially use a simple query with just a single term and will cover more complex queries later in this chapter. The index is searched for matching documents and the associated metadata for each matching document is extracted from a database and returned to the user. The results page will show a subset of the hits for the query if the number of hits is very large. In Figure 4.5, we have shown a single index, but Lucene also supports the search of multiple indexes that are stored in separate directories (see Listing 4.2). Similarly, we can extract metadata from multiple databases. The index will typically contain information from fields that are made up of long text strings and could have been stored in a database. It is more efficient to search text strings with Lucene than with a relational database. The code in Listing 4.1 fetches a list of hits for a query. The SearchTools package is included in the software distribution that accompanies the book.

Listing 4.1: Search the Lucene Index for Matching Documents

```
1  public class SearchQuery {
2    private Searcher is = null; // index searcher
3    public SearchQuery() {
4      is = SearchTools.getSearcher(SE_INDEX_DIR);
5    }
6    public Hits getHits(String str) {
7      QueryParser qp = new QueryParser("contents",
8        new StandardBgramAnalyzer() );
9      Query query = qp.parse(str);
10     Hits hits = is.search(query);
11     return (hits);
12   }
13 }
```

The first step is to fetch a Searcher (line 4) using the index directory. The SearchTools class contains a getSearcher method (see Listing 4.2) to return an IndexSearcher or a MultiSearcher. The IndexSearcher is returned when a single index directory is provided, and the MultiSearcher is returned if a list of directories is passed to getSearcher. Both Searchers provide methods to search the index with a query.

The QueryParser (line 7) class is generated from a JavaCC (https://javacc.dev.java.net) specification to parse a query string. This class is useful to build a Query from a text string that can be passed to the search method of the Searcher. A query string extracted from a field on a Web page may contain any conceivable string of characters, and it is preferable to filter the input query before passing it to the QueryParser. The constructor for the QueryParser accepts the name of the default Field and an Analyzer. Every search in Lucene must be associated with at least one Field in the index. For example, the query — "contents:Kuwait" is a search for documents that contain the word Kuwait in the contents Field. Similarly, searches on other Fields such as title or author will have as the prefix of the query string, the name of the Field followed by a colon and the query value. The QueryParser will assume a default Field if none is provided in the passed query string.

In Listing 4.1, the default `Field` is the `contents` field and the analyzer is the `StandardBgramAnalyzer` we saw in Chapter 2. It is important to use the same analyzer that was used when constructing the index to build the query. This is because the decision to add a `Document` to the list of hits is based on matches between individual tokens in the query and the tokens generated from the text string of the `Field`. If different analyzers are used during indexing and searching, there is a possibility that the tokens from the query may not match the tokens from the document, even though there is a legitimate match. For example, if the `StandardAnalyzer` with the standard set of stopwords was used to build the index and the query was the phrase "*Kuwait a target*", no matches would be found since the stopword *a* would be removed from the index and the `StandardBgramAnalyzer` would include the word *a* in the phrase for the query.

The `parse` method of the `QueryParser` returns a `Query` that can be submitted to the `Searcher`. The `search` method of the `Searcher` returns a list of `Hits` which can be scanned to fetch text from matching documents. A `Searcher` is based on one or more index directories that can be searched concurrently (see Listing 4.2).

Listing 4.2: Return an IndexSearcher or a MultiSearcher Based on the Number of Index Directories

```
1   public static Searcher getSearcher(String indexDir)
2       throws IOException {
3     return new IndexSearcher(
4       FSDirectory.getDirectory(indexDir));
5   }
6
7   public static Searcher getSearcher(
8     String[] dirs) throws IOException {
9     IndexSearcher[] searchers =
10      new IndexSearcher[dirs.length];
11    for (int i = 0; i < dirs.length; i++)
12      searchers[i] = new IndexSearcher(
13        FSDirectory.getDirectory(dirs[i]);
14    //return (new ParallelMultiSearcher(searchers));
15    return (new MultiSearcher(searchers));
16  }
```

Consider the collection of 10K Reuters documents indexed in a single directory. Table 4.1 shows the times in milliseconds to fetch the hits for ten different queries from the same collection of 10K documents. An `IndexSearcher` was used when the index was stored on a single directory and in the other two cases with five and ten directories, a `MultiSearcher` was used. Notice, the time to search the index on more than one directory takes longer than on a single directory. This is intuitive since each searcher must sequentially run the query on multiple indexes and finally merge the results. A parallel version of the `MultiSearcher` (line 14) will start a separate thread for each `Searcher` and run the searches concurrently. The list of hits are collected in a common queue and returned to the caller.

Table 4.1: Times to Fetch Hits for Ten Queries from Different Numbers of Index Directories

No. of Index Directories	Time (msecs.)
1	102
5	129
10	146

The index should be stored in a single directory if possible, and the use of multiple searchers will be of benefit in a machine with more than one processor. The `Hits` object returned by the `search` method of the `Searcher` contains the IDs of matching documents. Each ID is an unique identifier that can be used to fetch the document and associated `Fields`.

4.4.1 Generating Queries with QueryParser

The `parse` method of the `QueryParser` class translates a query text string into a Lucene `Query`. For example, the query string, *"(disease OR ailment) AND heart"* is parsed to the `Query` — *"+(contents:disease contents:ailment) +contents:heart"*. Notice, every query term is prefixed with the `Field` name that should contain the term. In this example, all the query terms should appear in the `contents Field` alone. The symbol + means that the query term must occur in a matching document. Query terms should be in lower case unless the analyzer that you used to index text did not use a lower case filter. There are two ways of generating a query – the automatic method with a `QueryParser` and the manual method from individual query types (see Figure 4.6).

Figure 4.6: Automatic and Manual Methods of Generating Queries

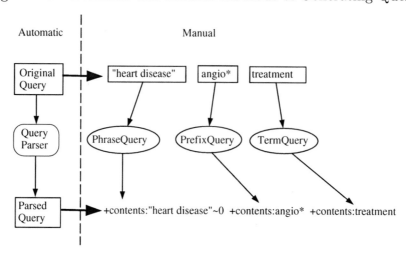

The QueryParser translates a given query string into a set of Lucene query types. In Figure 4.6 three different query types were generated from the query string. There are over ten different query types, each query type representing a particular class of queries. For example, the PhraseQuery type is used for all query terms enclosed in double quotes. The ~ character at the end of the phrase in the generated query represents a slop value or the maximum number of permissible word operations to form a match. We can manually create and combine queries in numerous ways that cannot be replicated with a QueryParser generated query. The task of the QueryParser is complex since it must handle all types of query strings and find which set of Querys is best suited to represent the user's original query. In QueryParser syntax, the symbol + represents a mandatory occurrence of a term and − the mandatory absence of a term. The terms of a query should occur, if no symbol is present before a Query and the value of the QueryParse.Operator is a boolean *OR*.

TermQuery and BooleanQuery

The QueryParser is a versatile class that works reasonably well for most types of queries, but there will be occasions where you will need to manually generate a query. We can manually generate the same parsed query "*+(contents:disease con-tents:ailment) +contents:heart*" with the code -

```
TermQuery tq1 = new TermQuery(
  new Term("contents", "disease"));
TermQuery tq2 = new TermQuery(
  new Term("contents", "ailment"));
TermQuery tq3 = new TermQuery(
  new Term("contents", "heart"));
BooleanQuery bq1 = new BooleanQuery();
bq1.add(tq1, BooleanClause.Occur.SHOULD);
bq1.add(tq2, BooleanClause.Occur.SHOULD);
BooleanQuery bq2 = new BooleanQuery();
bq2.add(bq1, BooleanClause.Occur.MUST);
bq2.add(tq3, BooleanClause.Occur.MUST);
```

Each query term is created in a separate `TermQuery` that accepts a `Term` in the constructor. A `Term` has two parameters, a `Field` name and a value. Here, we are searching the contents `Field` alone using three different terms. Each of the queries `tq1`, `tq2`, and `tq3` are independent Lucene queries that can be submitted to the index. The `BooleanQuery` class combines existing `Querys` or clauses into a composite `Query`. The `BooleanClause` class has fields to describe if a query term must occur, should occur, or must not occur in the text of a matching document.

We first construct the left boolean clause using the query terms *disease* and *ail-ment*. Next, the query generated from the term *heart* along with the left boolean clause are combined with the must occur flag to create the final query. The generated boolean query and the query returned from the `QueryParser` class are identical and will return the same set of hits. The `BooleanClause` parameter of the **add** method of the `BooleanQuery` class makes it easy to create fairly complex queries. The default maximum number of clauses in a `BooleanQuery` is 1024 and can be altered with the `setMaxClauseCount` method. The `String` representation of any `Query` can be printed with the `toString` method to view the submitted query.

PhraseQuery

A query stated in the form of a phrase is more specific than a combination of the individual terms that make up the phrase. For example, the query phrase "*heart disease*" is more specific than the boolean query - "*heart AND disease*". The text of a matching document for the query phrase should contain the words `heart` and `disease` in order, without any intervening terms. The latter boolean query is more loose and will match documents that have both the words *heart* and *disease* anywhere in the text.

```
PhraseQuery pq = new PhraseQuery();
pq.add(new Term("contents", "heart"));
pq.add(new Term("contents", "disease"));
pq.setSlop(0);
```

A `PhraseQuery` is first created and `Terms` are added in the expected order of the phrase. The word `heart` should occur before the word `disease` without any intervening terms. Note, that all `Terms` in the phrase should be from the same `Field` (`contents`). The `setSlop` method specifies the number of allowed words between the phrase words for a successful match. A zero (default) value for slop implies that the exact phrase should match. The slop or edit distance is the minimum number of edit operations that are needed to match two phrases. The edit operations are word-based operations to move or delete words in a phrase to find a match (see Figure 4.7).

Consider the first search phrase for "*native alaskan*". Text from a document x with the phrase "*alaskan native*" will not match with a slop of zero. A slop of two, which means a maximum of two edit operations is sufficient for document x to match the phrase. Two operations are needed since a single move operation will only change the position of one word. The second search phrase for "*heart disease*" is more complex. Consider the text chunk — "*heart and lung disease*", that was indexed using the `StandardBgramAnalyzer`. A set of six tokens is created from this text chunk with four of the tokens occupying two positions. The delete operation will remove the tokens in the middle position which then permits a match of the phrases "*heart disease*" or "*heart and disease*".

`PhraseQuerys` for simple phrases without stop words are not difficult to manually construct. The `QueryParser` handles longer and more complex phrases with stop

Figure 4.7: Phrase Matching with Move and Delete Operations

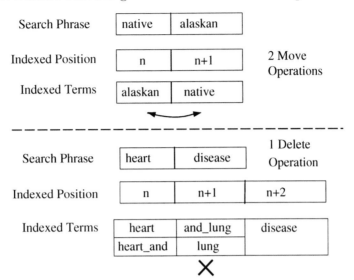

words. The analyzer passed in the constructor of the `QueryParser` builds the tokens that are used in generating the `Query` from the query string. The `QueryParser` contains a `setPhraseSlop` method that applies to all phrases in the query string.

```
QueryParser qp = new QueryParser(
  "contents", new StandardBgramAnalyzer());
qp.setPhraseSlop(1);
String qstr = "\"heart and disease\"";
Query q = qp.parse(qstr);
```

This example underscores the importance of using the same analyzers for indexing and submitting queries. The string representation of the query generated by the `QueryParser` is *"(heart heart_and) (and_disease disease)"~1*. The ~ character is the symbol for slop and the following numeric value is the degree of slop. The double quotes delimit the extent of the phrase and the parentheses contain one or more tokens that can occur at the same index position for a successful match. The score for a matching document is inversely proportional to the slop needed to find a matching phrase. A closer match will score higher than a match where the phrase's constituent words are further apart. The `MultiPhraseQuery` class has methods to build a search phrase which matches more than one combination of a phrase. For example, the phrases "alaskan native", "alaskan natives", "alaskan origin", and "alaskan born" can be combined into a single `MultiPhraseQuery`. A document that contains any one of the phrases will match the `Query`.

Any additional query terms in the query string will be combined with the default boolean operator of the `QueryParser`. The `setDefaultOperator` method of the `QueryParser` specifies the default boolean operator to combine individual `Querys`. The `QueryParser` class also contains methods to specify if the terms from expanded queries should be automatically lower-cased or not and if wildcards should be allowed in the first character of a query term.

4.4.2 Expanded Queries

There are at least four different types of `Querys` that will expand a given query term into a set of related terms. This is analogous to the word stemming that we saw in Chapter 2, where a single word stem represents one or more word forms. Here, the regular expression metacharacters — * and ? are inserted in a query term to form a `Query` that will match more than one term alone. For example, the query term *angio** will match the words *angiogram*, *angioplasty*, and *angiography*. The wildcard characters * and ? represent zero or more and zero or one characters respectively. Expanded queries may generate a number of `BooleanQuerys` depending on the number of leading characters before the first wildcard character.

WildcardQuery

The `WildcardQuery` allows the use of both metacharacters anywhere in a query term. A query term that begins with the metacharacter * will be extremely slow since the entire set of terms in the index needs to be scanned to check for a match. For example, if the query *angio?en** takes a millisecond to run, the query **angio?en** may take a hundred or more milliseconds. These types of time consuming queries can be disallowed in a `QueryParser`, which will then return a `ParseException` for any query starting with a wildcard character. The exception to this rule is the query *:* that will return a hit list with all documents and is useful to simply browse the documents in an index.

PrefixQuery

The `PrefixQuery` is a limited version of the `WildcardQuery`, and will only suffix the * character to the query term specified in the constructor. A search with a `PrefixQuery` will locate the offset of the greatest index entry that is less than or equal to the term without the last suffix character and check if the index term matches the root query term. A root term is also similarly created for queries constructed with a `WildcardQuery` by stripping off all the text that follows the first wildcard character. All matching terms will be combined in an *OR*ed `BooleanQuery`.

FuzzyQuery

The third type of expansion query is the more flexible `FuzzyQuery` that does not use wildcard characters. A `FuzzyQuery` finds term matches for a given query term based on the edit distance between the query term and an index term. The edit distance is the minimum number of character deletions, insertions or substitutions required to transform one term to the another term. For example, it takes a minimum of two character operations to transform the term *avalible* to the term *available* (see Figure 4.8).

The character labels of the rows and columns represent the characters of the target (transformed) and source (original) words respectively. The value of a cell (i, j) in the matrix is the minimal distance between the first i letters of the target word and the first j letters of the source word. For example, the value of the cell at position $(6, 5)$ is two, meaning that it takes two character operations to transform the source string *avali* to the target string *availa*. The first character operation is the insertion of the character i after *ava*, followed by a matching l, and a substitution of the trailing i in the source string with the character a. The row 0 and column 0 represent a sequence of j deletions and i insertions respectively. The value (2) in cell $(9, 8)$ is the number of operations to transform *avalible* to *available*. In general, there will be more than one way to transform a source word to a target word and we are mainly interested in the minimum number of character operations needed for the transformation. A fourth character operation transpose, to switch the positions of two adjacent characters may be considered one or two operations (a delete followed by an insert).

Figure 4.8: Edit Distance Matrix to Transform Avalible to Available

Source

Column		0	1	2	3	4	5	6	7	8
Row		null	a	v	a	l	i	b	l	e
0	null	0	1	2	3	4	5	6	7	8
1	a	1	0	1	2	3	4	5	6	7
2	v	2	1	0	1	2	3	4	5	6
3	a	3	2	1	0	1	2	3	4	5
4	i	4	3	2	1	1	1	2	3	4
5	l	5	4	3	2	1	2	2	2	3
6	a	6	5	4	3	2	2	3	3	3
7	b	7	6	5	4	3	3	2	3	4
8	l	8	7	6	5	4	4	3	2	3
9	e	9	8	7	6	5	5	4	3	2

(Target labeled vertically along the rows: T a r g e t)

By default the minimum fuzzy similarity for a match is 0.5, which means that the maximum edit distance for a source word is the truncated integer value of half of the length of the source word up to a maximum of five. A lower minimum fuzzy similarity value will loosen the matching criterion with a higher maximum edit distance. At first glance, the FuzzyQuery might appear to be an efficient way to handle spelling errors in query terms. However, the edit distance is a coarse grained property to control the degree of match between a pair of words (see Figure 4.9) and the performance of the FuzzyQuery is relatively slow compared to some of the other Querys.

The number of word matches from the WordNet dictionary increases rapidly as the minimum edit distance for a match increases. For example, the word *Lucene* has 2 word matches at a distance of one, 1 word at a distance of two, 15 words at a distance of three, 118 words at a distance of four, and 453 words at a distance of five. A spelling model (see section 4.8.1 Spell Check) is a better alternative to handling spelling errors than the FuzzyQuery. The primary use of a FuzzyQuery may be in matching alternate and legitimate spellings of the same term. For example, the word

Figure 4.9: Some of the Words within Edit Distance of 4 from the Word Lucene

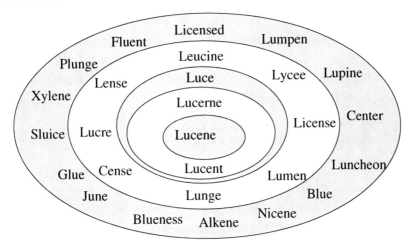

hi-fi can be written as *hifi*, *hi fi*, or even *hi+fi*. A `FuzzyQuery` with a minimum edit distance of two will find matches for all three forms of the word. The canonical form of a query term can be compared directly with terms in the index that have been similarly transformed to a single root word that represents multiple spellings for a fuzzy match. The `FuzzyQuery` will find weak or strong matches depending on the value of the maximum edit distance.

RangeQuery

The `RangeQuery` is used most often to find dates within a particular date range. Before searching a date range, the `Field` of the indexed document should be stored such that the lexicographic search will accurately find documents within the range.

```
GregorianCalendar cal = new GregorianCalendar();
cal.set( 2008, 12, 0);
doc.add( new Field("date",
  DateTools.dateToString(
    cal.getTime(), DateTools.Resolution.DAY),
  Field.Store.YES, Field.Index.UN_TOKENIZED) );
```

A `Date` is created using a `GregorianCalendar` and passed to the `Field` constructor which is then stored and indexed without tokenization. The `DateTools` class (see section 3.9) converts the `Date` into a suitable string that can be lexicographically sorted in the index. The resolution is set to day (eight character YYYYMMDD) to limit the number of characters stored in the index. A `RangeQuery` for the date `Field` is constructed by giving the constructor a start date, end date, and an indicator whether the range is inclusive or not.

```
RangeQuery rq = new RangeQuery(
  new Term("date", "19990101"),
  new Term("date", "20011201"), true);
```

This `RangeQuery` will search for documents that were indexed within the date range from January 1st, 1999 to December 1st, 2000 inclusive of the start and end dates. The first and last date will be excluded from the date range in a query that is *not* inclusive. A query with a higher precision start or end date that includes hours, minutes, or seconds will match the same documents as a query with an eight character *YYYYMMDD* date provided the date `Fields` of indexed documents are saved in day resolution. The `QueryParser` can generate expanded queries from a query string that are equivalent to a `Query` generated from individual query types.

```
// Query generated with query parser
QueryParser qp = new QueryParser("contents",
  new StandardBgramAnalyzer());
String qstr = "disease* angio?rap* availa~ " +
  "date:[19990101 TO 20011231]";
Query qq = qp.parse(qstr);

// Manually generated query
PrefixQuery pq = new PrefixQuery(
  new Term("contents", "disease"));
WildcardQuery wq = new WildcardQuery(
  new Term("contents", "angio?rap*"));
FuzzyQuery fq = new FuzzyQuery(
  new Term("contents", "availa"));
RangeQuery rq = new RangeQuery(
```

```
  new Term("date",  "19990101"),
  new Term("date",  "20011231"),  true);
BooleanQuery bq = new BooleanQuery();
bq.add(pq,  BooleanClause.Occur.SHOULD);
bq.add(wq,  BooleanClause.Occur.SHOULD);
bq.add(fq,  BooleanClause.Occur.SHOULD);
bq.add(rq,  BooleanClause.Occur.SHOULD);
```

The QueryParser uses the default *OR* operator to combine the four individual query terms in the string qstr. The default value for the minimum fuzzy similarity is 0.5 and can be altered to some other value using the FuzzyQuery constructor. The Query qq generated with the QueryParser is equivalent to the BooleanQuery bq that is generated manually, one query type at a time. The QueryParser offers less control over the query generation and is less flexible than the API generated query. It is also important to filter the query string before passing it to the QueryParser.

4.4.3 Span Queries

The queries that we have seen so far do not make use of the positions of matches found in the text. A boolean query with two phrases will not rank a document that has both phrases in closer proximity higher than a document where the phrases are spread apart. The assumption here is that documents where multiple phrases are close together in the text are more relevant than a document where the same phrases are scattered in the text.

A span query for a phrase is built using methods similar to the construction of a phrase query we saw earlier. Each constituent word of the phrase is added as a Term in order and a list of SpanTermQuerys are generated for the phrase.

```
SpanTermQuery[] heart_phrase = new SpanTermQuery[] {
  new SpanTermQuery( new Term("contents", "heart")),
  new SpanTermQuery( new Term("contents", "disease"))
};
SpanQuery[] sq = new SpanQuery[] {
  new SpanNearQuery(heart_phrase, 0, true),
  new SpanTermQuery( new Term("contents", "angiogram"))
};
SpanNearQuery snq = new SpanNearQuery( sq, 10, false);
```

The constructor of the first `SpanNearQuery` accepts a slop value, a flag indicating if the phrases should occur in the order they were built, and a list of `SpanTermQuerys`. The phrase "heart disease" should occur in the same word order without any intervening terms. The second `SpanNearQuery snq` includes a slop of ten positions and will allow matches of the word angiogram, ten words before or after the heart disease phrase. The slop in a `SpanNearQuery` is the difference in the positions of terms or phrases in the text. We do not need to store the character offsets to find close matches and instead the integer positions of tokens in text is sufficient to find phrase matches.

Note, you may find non-exact matches with a `PhraseQuery` generated from a `QueryParser` that are not found in a `SpanNearQuery`. For example, no matches would be found in documents that contained the phrase "*heart disease*" alone, if an additional `SpanTermQuery` for the term and was added between the `SpanTermQuerys` for the terms heart and disease, to create the phrase "*heart and disease*". A similar phrase in a query generated from the `QueryParser` may drop the term and in the query phrase. Essentially, `SpanQuerys` are built one `Term` at a time without an `Analyzer` and may produce different results from a generated query. Matches may also depend on whether an analyzer that dropped stop words accounted for their positions or ignored the stop word occurrences.

Every span of text in a document has a *start* and *end* position that was stored when the text was indexed. We have looked at two types of span queries and there are several other types of span queries that require span matches to occur within the first n positions of the text, disallow span matches that have overlapping positions, or combine the results of multiple span queries.

4.5 Query Performance

There are no explicit parameters to tune the performance of a query similar to the parameters to improve index performance. However, the performance of a query can be optimized by following a few guidelines when generating queries. We have looked at over eight different `Query` types, each of which will search a limited or large portion of the index. The simplest and fastest queries to process are plain `TermQuerys` that can be implemented with a single lookup of the term in the index. A `TermQuery` for a term from a `Field` with less text (such as the document title) will in general run faster than a term from a longer `Field` (contents). A `PhraseQuery` will take a little longer than a set of `TermQuerys` made up of the individual terms of the phrase.

Additionally, the expanded `Query` types usually take longer than the other `Querys`. A `RangeQuery` may take less time to search than a `FuzzyQuery` but more time than a `PhraseQuery` or a `TermQuery`. The list of `Terms` from a `Field` in a `RangeQuery` is usually small and can be searched faster than a search of a larger `Field` like the *contents* field. However, a `RangeQuery` can generate a large number of boolean clauses that may exceed the default limit of 1024. For example, a `RangeQuery` for documents over several decades in a big document collection will generate a huge number of date sub-queries. The slowest queries are those that start with a wildcard and need to search the list of all `Terms` for matches. The use of a `QueryParser` to generate queries adds minimal overhead compared to the manual generation of queries using the API.

A smaller index is always faster to search than a larger index and there are a few ways to reduce the size of the index. One way is to increase the number of stop words. The standard English stop word list is a generic list for all genres of the language and can be made larger with a custom set of stop words that are application specific. For example, a patent search engine would exclude words like *patent* or *feature* that occur in too many documents and therefore are of little value in the index. There is a trade off between adding an excessive number of stop words to the list and the search vocabulary. A rich set of search terms makes it easier to find documents in the collection, but at the same time will make the size of the index larger. The index will also be larger if the occurrences of stop words with non-stop words is being tracked to match search phrases that contain stop words.

Another way to reduce the size of the index is to limit the maximum text that will be indexed from a single document. The `maxFieldLength` parameter of the `IndexWriter` limits the size of the indexed text from a document. A small value will restrict the `IndexWriter` to index only a fraction of a large document which may limit its accessibility while a large value may index more text than necessary to retrieve the document. The default value of `maxFieldLength` is 10K bytes, which may be satisfactory for a collection consisting of Web pages and short articles but may not be appropriate for a collection of e-books. A large index can also be split over multiple disks in a multi-processor machine and searched concurrently. This has the added benefit of fitting more of the index in memory which should speed up the time to search.

Recall and Precision

The two metrics *recall* and *precision* were first used to evaluate IR systems and have been applied to measure the performance of text categorization, entity extraction, and Q&A systems. They have become standard measures for many NLP/IR tasks and other measures such as the F-measure (see section 6.4.2) are derived from recall and precision. To illustrate, we assume a collection of 100 documents. Based on prior knowledge, we know that 5 of the 100 documents are relevant for a particular query q. We can run the same query q against the document collection with an untested search engine that returns 12 hits (see Table 4.2).

Table 4.2: Contingency Table for a Query q

	Relevant	Not Relevant	Total
Retrieved	4	8	12
Not Retrieved	1	87	88
Total	5	95	100

Of the 12 hits, 4 are relevant and the remaining 8 are not relevant. Since we know that a total of 5 documents are relevant in the entire collection, the search engine failed to retrieve 1 additional relevant documents. A set of 87 documents that were not relevant was not returned. The *recall* is defined as the fraction of relevant documents retrieved out of all the relevant documents in the collection, 0.80 (4 / 5). The *precision* is defined as the fraction of relevant documents retrieved out of all retrieved documents, 0.33 (4 / 12). In general, the two measures recall and precision are inversely related. When we increase recall, the precision drops and if precision is raised, recall falls.

4.6 Organizing Results

In Listing 4.1, we ended the search with the retrieval of a **Hits** objects that contains a ranked list of matching documents for a query. The **Hits** object contains methods to find the total number of hits and to return a Document for any element of the hit list. Each stored document in our indexed collection has three stored fields – the *id*, the *filename*, and the *date*. The contents of these fields can be fetched from the Hits object returned from the search method of the IndexReader.

```
Hits hits = ir.search(query);
for (int i = 0; i < hits.length(); i++) {
   Document doc = hits.doc(i);
   String key = doc.get("id");
   String filename = doc.get("filename");
   String date = doc.get("date");
   float score = hits.score(i);
}
```

The get method of the doc object returns the stored strings by Field name. The list of hits returned is sorted in descending order by score. The score method returns a normalized score (between 0 and 1) for the ith document in the hit list. By default the matching documents are sorted in descending order of score.

4.6.1 Sorting Results

The search method of the IndexReader is overloaded to accept a Sort object in addition to the query parameter. The Sort object overrides the default sort-by-score ordering and can be customized to sort on any field. For example, we can sort the results in descending order of date.

```
Sort sort = new Sort("date", true);
Hits hits = ir.search(query, sort);
```

The first parameter passed to the Sort constructor is the name of the Field and the second optional parameter is a boolean flag to indicate if the sort is in ascending (false) or descending (true) order. We can similarly sort on any other Field such as the name or category of the file. Note, the output of the sort of String fields will be based on a lexicographic ordering of the field contents and may take longer than a sort by integer or float values. The Sort.RELEVANCE (default by score) and Sort.INDEXORDER (by Lucene's document id) are sorts by floating point and integer respectively. A multiple field sort order can be specified with the SortField class.

```
Sort sort = new Sort ( new SortField[] {
   new SortField("contents", SortField.SCORE),
   new SortField("date", SortField.INT, true)
});
Hits hits = ir.search(query, sort);
```

The `Sort` constructor accepts a single or a list of `SortFields`, each of which specifies a sort order based on a `Field`. The primary sort in this example is by the floating point score value of the document and the secondary sort is by the integer date value. Complex sorting orders will take longer to process than the fastest sort by relevancy. The type of `Field` that can be used in a sort order is restricted to non-tokenized Fields alone.

4.6.2 Scoring Results

The transparent ranking of results is one of the major benefits of using an open source engine. Lucene includes an `explain` function that clearly shows why one document was ranked higher than another. This allows the search engine administrator to understand the ranking algorithm and helps in tuning the search engine to provide the most relevant results. Every document that matches a query is assigned a score based on a formula that attempts to score documents that are more likely to be relevant higher than others. There are several components in the Lucene scoring algorithm, each one of which may alter the score substantially, and knowing the details of the formula makes it easier to debug the results of the search engine.

Every `Query` or `Document Field` is initially assigned a boost value of 1.0, that essentially means all `Fields` are equally important for the purposes of the scoring algorithm. A boost to assign a higher weight to a `Field` is possible during indexing and searching. A document that contains matching text from a `Field` such as the title may be more relevant than another document which contains matching text from the `contents Field` alone.

```
String title = "This is the title of the document";
Field fld = new Field("title", title,
   Field.Store.YES, Field.Index.TOKENIZED,
   Field.TermVector.NO);
fld.setBoost(1.5f);
```

```
doc.add(fld);
```

A separate `title` `Field` is created just like any other `Field` that was added to the document, with an additional call to the `setBoost` method that changes the boost value from the default 1.0 to 1.5 for the `title` `Field` alone. This boost value is taken into account when computing the `Field`'s normalization value (`fieldNorm`) that is used to compute the score of a document. The value of the boost to a query term is specified in the query string or through an API call.

```
PhraseQuery pq = new PhraseQuery();
pq.add(new Term("contents", "heart"));
pq.add(new Term("contents", "disease"));
pq.setSlop(1);
pq.setBoost(1.5f);
//equivalent to parsing the query string
// "heart disease"~1^1.5
```

The phrase *"heart disease"* is assigned a slop of 1 and a boost of 1.5. The boost value will alter the value of the query weight in the formula to compute the document score. The `setBoost` method of a `Document` will uniformly set the boost value of all `Fields` in the `Document`.

$$DocumentScore = coord \times \sum_i (q_i \times t_i) \tag{4.1}$$

The score of a document is the product of the coordination factor (*coord*) and the sum of the products of the query (*q*) and term (*t*) factors for all query terms that were found in the text of any `Field` of the document. The coordination factor is a fraction of the number of query terms found in the matching document. Consider the query string —

```
date:[19990101 TO 20011231] contents:disease* title:leaf
```

that contains three query terms from three separate `Fields`. A document that matched on the title `Field` alone would be assigned a coordination factor of 0.3333, since only one of the three query terms was matched. The coordination factor may be disabled in a `BooleanQuery`. The query weight qw_i is a measure of the importance of the query term i.

$$qw_i = boost_i^2 \times \sum_j (idf_j \times boost_j)^2 \tag{4.2}$$

Each query i may have j sub-queries that are either explicitly nested or implicitly defined in the form of an expanded query. For example, a date range query may match a hundred or more documents that contain dates within the specified range defined in the query. The idf and boost values are the inverse document frequency and boost values (from the `Query setBoost` method or default of 1.0) respectively. The inverse document frequency (see section 3.3.1) idf_j for any term j is defined as

$$idf_j = log(N) - log(n_j + 1) + 1 \tag{4.3}$$

where N is the total number of documents in the collection and n_j is the number of documents in which the term j occurs. One is added to the *log* of n_j to avoid errors when the number of documents containing term j is zero and one is added to the entire expression to preclude an idf value of 0 when N and $(n_j + 1)$ are equal. For example, the idf value for a term occurring in 11 out of 9858 documents in a collection is 7.71. The idf value of a phrase is the sum of the idf values of the individual terms. The query normalization qn is defined as the inverse of the square root of the sum of the squares of the individual query weights —

$$qn = \frac{1.0}{\sqrt{\Sigma_i \, qw_i^2}} \tag{4.4}$$

The query normalization is applied uniformly to all query terms and therefore does not play any role in the ranking of the hit list. It can be used to compare the results of two different queries. We can now define the query factor q_i as the product of the query normalization qn and the idf weight idf_i of the query term i as —

$$q_i = qn \times idf_i \tag{4.5}$$

The term factor t_i, the weight of the query term i in a matching document j, is the product of the term frequency tf_i, inverse document idf_i, and the field normalization of the `Field` j of the term in document i. The term frequency of a term i is by default the square root of the number of occurrences of term i in the document.

$$t_i = tf_i \times idf_i \times fieldNorm_{ij} \tag{4.6}$$

The field normalization is computed for every `Field` in every document in a *Doc-Field* byte table at the time of indexing and stored in an index file (see Figure 4.10). The number of terms that occur in every `Field` of all documents is computed and transformed into a field normalization value for the document. The field normalization values for the *Date*, *Contents*, and *Title* `Fields` for a document i are stored in a row of the *Doc-Field* byte table. The field normalization value for `Field` j in document i is computed as —

$$fieldNorm_{ij} = boost_j \times (\frac{1.0}{\sqrt{t_{ij}}}) \tag{4.7}$$

The $boost_j$ is the boost value for Field j and t_{ij} is the number of terms in `Field` j of document i. In Figure 4.10, the number of terms in the *date*, *contents*, and *title* fields of document i are 1, 90, and 10 respectively. The corresponding field normalization values for the three fields are 1.0, 0.1054, and 0.4743 where a boost of 1.5 has been applied to the *title* field. The three floating point values are compressed to a byte value to save space in the index. The byte table is stored in index files and recovered when a search is processed. An index file with a `nrm` suffix is created for all indexed Fields in Lucene 2.1. The three byte values of the fields of document i — 124, 110, and 119 are uncompressed back to floating point values that are close to the original values. The floating point value that was recovered from a decoding table is used to compute the term factor t_i that is utilized in the document score computation.

Notice, that two of the uncompressed floating point values 0.09375 and 0.4375 are not identical to the original floating point values of 0.1054 and 0.4743. They are reasonably close for the purposes of scoring documents. The field normalization is an important component of the score computation, since its value can have a significant effect on the score and therefore the rank of the document as well. For example, the field normalization value of the `Contents` field is less than one tenth the value of the `Date` field.

The idea behind the use of field normalization is to score matches from fields that have fewer terms higher than matches from a field with many terms. A match from the `Title` field should be given more weight than a match from the `Contents` field since the match occurred in a field with fewer terms. Field normalization also balances the term frequency which may be high in fields that have many terms. The

Figure 4.10: Computing the Field Normalization Values for a Matching Document

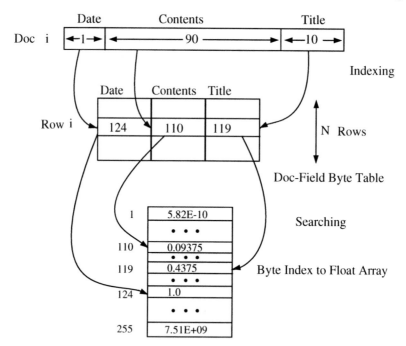

field normalization values cannot be changed during a search operation since these values are part of the index and not directly related to a search. An example of the output from the Explain function shows the use of the different scoring factors to compute the final score.

```
1   Query: contents:disease date:[19990101 TO 20011231] title:leaf
2
3   Explanation: 0.28264666 = (MATCH) product of:
4    0.42396998 = (MATCH) sum of:
5     0.0068300236 = (MATCH) sum of:
6      0.0068300236 = (MATCH) weight(contents:disease in 2960), product of:
7       0.03319009 = queryWeight(contents:disease), product of:
8        6.5851207 = idf(docFreq=36)
9        0.005040164 = queryNorm
10       0.20578502 = (MATCH)fieldWeight(contents:disease in 2960),product of:
11        1.0 = tf(termFreq(contents:disease)=1)
12        6.5851207 = idf(docFreq=36)
13        0.03125 = fieldNorm(field=contents, doc=2960)
14      0.41713995 = (MATCH) sum of:
```

```
15      0.41713995 = (MATCH) weight(date:20000422 in 2960), product of:
16       0.045852523 = queryWeight(date:20000422), product of:
17       9.097426 = idf(docFreq=2)
18       0.005040164 = queryNorm
19       9.097426 = (MATCH) fieldWeight(date:20000422 in 2960), product of:
20       1.0 = tf(termFreq(date:20000422)=1)
21       9.097426 = idf(docFreq=2)
22       1.0 = fieldNorm(field=date, doc=2960)
23     0.6666667 = coord(2/3)
```

The query string in this example contains three terms – a `TermQuery` for the term disease in the contents Field, a `RangeQuery` using the date `Field`, and a `TermQuery` for the word *leaf* in the title `Field`. The overall score of 0.2826466 (line 3) is obtained from the product of the sums of two term matches 0.0068 (line 5) and 0.4171 (line 14), and the coordination factor 0.666 (line 23). In the second match, the query weight of 0.458 (line 16) is the product of the idf weight and the query normalization factor. The docfreq value is 2 (line 17), meaning that two documents in the collection had a date `Field` value of 20000422. The field weight (line 19) is the product of three terms – the term frequency, the idf weight, and the field normalization for the date `Field` in this particular document. The term frequency (line 20) is one since only one term occurs in the date `Field`, the idf frequency is the same as the value used in computing the query weight, and the date field normalization for this document is 1.0.

Notice, the field normalization for the date `Field` (line 22) is over 10 times higher than the field normalization for the contents `Field` (line 13). This is because the number of terms in the contents `Field` is much higher than the number of terms in the date `Field`. The *"sum of"* value at the beginning of the term match will show the sum of multiple term matches for wildcard query terms like *disease** that may match more than one term. In our example, a single term matched both query term matches.

The explanations of the scores for two documents that match a particular query can be compared to identify why a document is ranked higher than another. The default `Similarity` class attempts to find a balance between the various factors that determine the relevance of a document such as the term frequency, inverse document frequency, and the number of terms in the `Field`. The functions from a custom `Similarity` class can be tuned to the requirements of a document collection such that a document which should rank higher than another document will appear in the same order in the hit list.

4.6.3 Customizing Query-Document Similarity Computations

The scoring algorithm has many components from the document and the query that contribute to the final score for a matching document. The Similarity class contains abstract methods that define the functions to compute the term frequency, inverse document frequency, query normalization, and field normalization. A custom SearchSimilarity class to extend the Similarity class will provide specific implementations for each function. The same custom SearchSimilarity class is used when indexing and searching.

```
// code to set the Similarity class during indexing
Directory dir = FSDirectory.getDirectory(SE_INDEX_DIR);
IndexWriter writer = new IndexWriter(dir,
  new StandardBgramAnalyzer(), true);
writer.setSimilarity(new SearchSimilarity());

// code to set the Similarity class during search
Searcher is = SearchTools.getSearcher(SE_INDEX_DIR);
is.setSimilarity(new SearchSimilarity());
```

The methods from the custom implementation of the Similarity class (see Listing 4.3) will be called when searching for and indexing documents.

Listing 4.3: A Customized Similarity Class for Searching and Indexing

```
1  public class SearchSimilarity extends Similarity {
2    public float lengthNorm(String fieldName, int numTerms) {
3    //return (float) (1.0 / Math.sqrt(numTerms)); // default
4      return (1.0f);
5    }
6    public float queryNorm(float sumOfSquaredWeights) {
7      return (float) (1.0 / Math.sqrt(sumOfSquaredWeights));
8    }
9    public float tf(float freq) {
10   //return (float)Math.sqrt(freq); // default
11     return (freq > 0 ? 1 : 0);
12   }
13   public float sloppyFreq(int distance) {
14     return 1.0f / (distance + 1);
15   }
16   public float idf(int docFreq, int numDocs) {
17     return (float) (Math.log(numDocs
```

```
18        / (double) (docFreq + 1)) + 1.0);
19    }
20    public float coord(int overlap, int maxOverlap) {
21      return overlap / (float) maxOverlap;
22    }
23  }
```

Two of the six functions are overridden with a custom implementation. The `lengthNorm` (line 2) function returns 1.0 in all cases and effectively nullifies the effect of field normalization during a search. The `tf` (line 9) function implements a binary count that indicates the presence or absence of a term. The `sloppyFreq` (line 13) function assigns a higher weight to phrases that have closer matches based on the edit distance between the query phrase and matching text. Note, that the `lengthNorm` is the only function called during indexing and all the other similarity functions are used to compute the score for a matching document during a search.

4.7 Filtering Queries

The early IR systems based on mainframes viewed a typical search as the submission of a series of increasingly specialized queries till the user was satisfied with quality and number of hits. The results of queries were numbered sequentially and the results of say the third and fourth query could be combined to form a new query – *Combine 3 AND 4* (results common in queries 3 and 4) or *Combine 3 NOT 4* (results from query 3 that are not present in query 4). This is unlike the modern day Web search engine where each query is treated independently and the results from prior queries in a session are typically not used in the current query. Lucene use `Filters` to save the results of a query that can be used in a subsequent query.

4.7.1 Range Filter

A fairly common query requirement is to filter results by a date range. For example, a boolean query for the phrase "heart disease" in the date range from January 1st 1999 to December 31st, 2001 inclusive would be generated using a `PhraseQuery` and a `RangeQuery`.

```
PhraseQuery pq = new PhraseQuery();
```

```
pq.add(new Term("contents", "heart"));
pq.add(new Term("contents", "disease"));
RangeQuery rq = new RangeQuery(
   new Term("date", "19990101"),
   new Term("date", "20011231"),
   true);
BooleanQuery bq = new BooleanQuery();
bq.add(rq, BooleanClause.Occur.MUST);
bq.add(pq, BooleanClause.Occur.MUST);
```

An equivalent query can be submitted using a `RangeFilter`. The constructor of the `RangeFilter` accepts five parameters – the name of the `Field` (date), the start value, the end value, a boolean to include the start value, and a boolean to include the end value.

```
RangeFilter rf = new RangeFilter(
   "date", "19990101", "20011231", true, true);
Hits hits = is.search(pq, rf);
```

The `RangeFilter` is supplied as a parameter to the `search` method of the `Searcher` class along with the `PhraseQuery`. The results from both the `BooleanQuery` and the `Query` with a `RangeFilter` are identical but may be ranked in different orders. The use of a `RangeFilter` may have advantages over a `BooleanQuery` in terms of query performance. A filter reduces the size of the search space for the `PhraseQuery` by setting a bit mask of the documents that are in the specified range of dates. The number of computations to check for matching documents is higher with a `BooleanQuery` than a `RangeFilter`. Another advantage of using a `Filter` is that a large date range can be used in the query without considering the maximum limit on the number of boolean clauses in a query. The `RangeFilter` is not limited to date ranges alone and can be used with any other `Field` that can be searched with a `RangeQuery`.

The difference in the scores of documents matching a `BooleanQuery` and a query with a filter can alter the ranking of documents. In a `BooleanQuery`, the score of the matches with *date* query term is added to the score of the match with the phrase to build the overall matching score for a document. The score of the date query term is absent in a query with the `RangeFilter`, since the *date* term is not part of the submitted query. This makes a difference in ranking, since the contribution from the *date* query term to the overall score, dominates the score of the document. A single date that occurs in more than one document will have a lower IDF value than a date which is found in only one document and the difference in these partial scores between documents is added to the score computed from the matching query terms. Therefore, the final ranked list of documents can be different in queries that use a `Filter` and those that do not.

4.7.2 Security Filter

In a database, security mechanisms are built-in and handled by the database administrator who creates accounts and sets privileges to access database tables. Most databases provide fine grained control to grant browse, insert, update, and delete privileges on sets of tables to individual users. In a search engine, no such security mechanism exists and the search engine administrator has to integrate external access control methods to restrict access to indexed documents. The issue of access control is more important in Intranet search engines, where documents may contain information that not everyone is authorized to view, than in Web search engines, which typically do not restrict access to indexed documents based on the user.

Consider a simplistic access control mechanism for the indexed documents in a search engine. Every document is assigned one of three security groups – *admin*, *restrictive*, or *general*. All users of the search engine must be authenticated with an *userid* and *password*. The search engine administrator assigns every userid to one or more groups. The custom `Filter` class in Listing 4.4 will accept a *userid* and restrict access to the indexed documents based on the groups to which the *userid* belongs. The `secgroup` `Field` of the `Document` contains the name of the group to which the document belongs.

Listing 4.4: A Custom Security Filter to Restrict Access to Documents

```
1  public class SecurityFilter extends Filter {
2    private String userid = "";
3    private int[] docs;
4    private int[] freqs;
5    public SecurityFilter(String userid) {
6      this.userid = userid;
7    }
```

```
8    public BitSet bits (IndexReader ir)
9       throws IOException {
10      int numDocs = ir.maxDoc() - 1;
11      BitSet bits = new BitSet(numDocs);
12      docs = new int[numDocs];
13      freqs = new int[numDocs];
14      bits.set(0, ir.maxDoc(), false);
15
16      // find the set of groups to
17      // which the userid belongs
18      String[] groups = {"general"};
19      for (String group: groups) {
20        TermDocs tdocs = ir.termDocs(
21          new Term("secgroup", group));
22        int size = tdocs.read(docs, freqs);
23        for (int i = 0; i < size; i++)
24          bits.set(docs[i], true);
25      }
26      return bits;
27    }
28 }
```

The SecurityFilter class implements the bits (line 8) method from the abstract Filter class to set the bits of the documents in the collection that can be viewed by the given *userid*. A BitSet (line 11) of size n is allocated where n is the number of documents in the collection. The BitSet is initialized to disallow access to all documents. Next, the groups (line 18) for the *userid* are extracted from an external source like a security database or an access control list. In this example, a single group *general* is assigned to all *userids*. The termDocs (line 20) method of the IndexReader returns an interface to fetch the list of documents that contain the Term from the secgroup Field with the value *general*. The Lucene document *ids* that have a *general* security group are returned in the docs parameter of the read (line 22) method of the TermDocs class. Finally, the bits of the BitSet of the matching document *ids* are set and returned to the caller. The filter is used exactly like the RangeFilter we saw earlier.

```
SecurityFilter sf = new SecurityFilter("joe");
Hits hits = is.search(query, sf);
```

Another way of providing search engine security is to limit access at the page level. An user can only view a page after providing authentication information. This may not be entirely satisfactory, since a searcher can extract useful information from the knowledge of the file name and the text that it matches. Random searches for matching documents are sufficient to know if a particular fact is documented or not. An integer security value instead of a group name, makes it possible to use a RangeFilter to restrict access instead of the custom filter. A default integer security level of zero is assigned to all documents and restricted documents are assigned higher numbers. Every userid is assigned a security level that limits the set of viewable documents.

There are other security issues related to the creation and modification of documents. A confidential document may be posted on a Web site and automatically indexed by a spider that does not use any filters to verify if the document should be indexed and does not assign the appropriate security group to the document. Most search engines accept links from anyone with few restrictions that are fed to the crawler. It is easy to post a confidential document on a server and add a link to the crawler's list of initial links. A crawler blindly scans all documents that can be indexed from the initial list of links. This type of security breach is harder to detect until it is publicized, and is easier to handle at the source when links are provided to the crawler.

4.7.3 Query Filter

Lucene provides a FilteredQuery class that reverses the order of applying a Filter and then a Query. Instead the Query is first submitted, followed by the Filter (see Figure 4.11).

The FilteredQuery is exactly like any other Query except that the constructor of the Query requires a Filter parameter. At the time of execution, the Filter will be applied after the results of Query have been identified.

```
SecurityFilter sf = new SecurityFilter("tom");
FilteredQuery fQuery = new FilteredQuery(
    query, sf);
```

Figure 4.11: Three Ways to Submit Filtered Queries

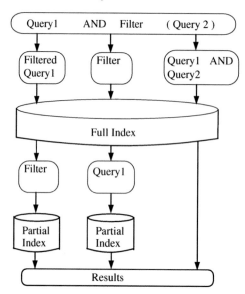

```
Hits hits = is.search(fquery);
```

The results are identical from all three methods, however, the order of the results and the query performance will vary. The use of filters is usually faster than the equivalent query with a boolean AND operator. The order of applying the filter may not matter as much as the use of a filter to speed up a query. The order of results from a query that uses filters will not be different, since the IDF values for matching query terms will be the same, even though one query uses a partial index and the other uses a full index.

4.7.4 Caching Filters

A cached `Filter` can be re-used to handle multiple queries that must be filtered identically. Consider the custom security filter we saw earlier — an user may submit many queries in a single session and for every submitted query, the same security filter is applied to remove documents that the user is not authorized to view from a hit list. The results of the security filter for a user can be cached and re-used for better performance instead of repeatedly running the same filter.

```
SecurityFilter sf = new SecurityFilter("joe");
CachingWrapperFilter cf =
   new CachingWrapperFilter(sf);
Hits hits = is.search(sq.query, cf);
```

The security filter is built just as before and passed to a caching filter wrapper that is then used in the `search` method of the `IndexSearcher`. The bitset returned from the security filter will be re-used in successive `search` method calls from the same instance of the IndexSearcher, saving the time needed to run the filter in all subsequent search requests submitted by the same user.

4.7.5 Chained Filters

Consider a Web site selling digital cameras. Every camera has attributes (`Fields`) such as the name of the manufacturer, price, weight, resolution, and the optical zoom. One way of searching the collection of digital cameras is to ask the user to fill up a form with a value for every attribute that is converted to a query. This approach is likely to overwhelm the novice photographer who may not know which values are appropriate for all attributes. It is the fastest way for an expert user who has precise requirements and will quickly lead the user to relevant results in a single link. The slower method will direct the user iteratively to more specific results, till detailed information is available. This process of browsing a collection has been called *faceted browsing* and is distinct from a taxonomy-based search.

Users iteratively combine attributes in combinations that are best suited for their requirements with a default value for unspecified attributes. A taxonomy is predefined and the user has to select categories from a hierarchy with little flexibility to remove attributes to broaden a search or to add attributes to narrow a search (see Figure 4.12). A search for cameras in a taxonomy is restricted to searching the pre-defined tree of attributes. Faceted browsing is more flexible and lets the user select just the attributes that are necessary to issue a query.

For example, assume a digital camera with three attributes — the manufacturer, resolution, and price range. All cameras in the collection are listed, if none of the attributes are specified. The user can select values from known attributes that best characterize the description of the buyer's need and leave other attributes with default values. Typically, the default for an attribute will match all values. Matches from all price ranges will be returned, if no single price range is selected.

Figure 4.12: Faceted Browsing for Digital Cameras

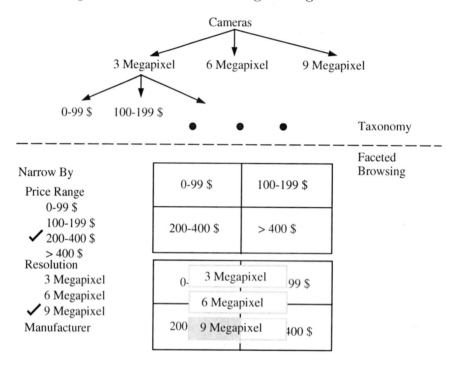

The use of faceted browsing makes it easier for the naïve and expert user to search for items in a collection with multiple attributes. Conceptually, faceted browsing can be viewed as the boolean AND of multiple sets where each set represents an attribute. This is fairly simple to implement in a database with an SQL Select statement that specifies values for selected attributes. We can create a similar query for a search engine with a boolean *AND* of multiple TermQuerys. Instead, we will use a ChainedFilter to run the equivalent query. The ChainedFilter (from Kelvin Tan) in the misc directory of the *sandbox* (the contrib directory of the Lucene distribution), allows multiple filters to be linked sequentially in order with a boolean operator.

```
QueryFilter qf1 = new QueryFilter(
  new TermQuery(new Term(
    "price_range", "200-400")));
QueryFilter qf2 = new QueryFilter(
  new TermQuery(new Term(
    "resolution", "9 Megapixel")));
ChainedFilter cf = new ChainedFilter(
  new Filter[] { qf1, qf2}, ChainedFilter.AND);
Hits hits = is.search(
  new TermQuery(new Term("*", "*")), cf);
```

The `QueryFilter` wraps a `Filter` around a `Query` (a `TermQuery` in this example) and is similar to the `RangeFilter` and `SecurityFilter` filters we saw earlier. The constructor of the `ChainedFilter` accepts a list of `Filters` that will be executed in the order of the list using a boolean operator (*AND*). The `search` method of the `IndexSearcher` uses a query that will match every document in the collection, along with the `ChainedFilter` to get a list of matching documents in the specified price range and resolution. The performance of queries using specific attributes can be improved with a set of equivalent cached filters for attribute values.

4.8 Modifying Queries

The generation of queries is open-ended and there are infinite ways of combining operators and query terms. A subset of these queries will return satisfactory results and the remaining queries may return very few or even zero hits. This is more likely to occur in a small or medium sized Intranet search engine than in a Web search engine. Almost any query term returns at least a few hits on a Web search engine and even query terms with spelling errors, return hits from documents that contain text with the same spelling error. One of the goals of a responsible search engine administrator is to improve user satisfaction by tracking the number of zero hit queries and queries that do not return relevant results. Some zero hit queries may be legitimate, but others may be due to a spelling error or the use of the wrong term. We first look at the correction of spelling errors.

4.8.1 Spell Check

Most Web search engines correct the spelling of query words with a *"Did you mean"* prompt. For example, the mis-spelled query word *speling* will be corrected to *spelling*. For simplicity, we will only consider spell check in English. Spelling is a challenge in English with its large vocabulary and inconsistencies in how letters and sounds are used in words. We first tried to solve this problem with the `FuzzyQuery` earlier in this chapter to find new query terms within a short edit distance range of the original word. This method is slow and does not use any model to predict the most likely correct word. A probabilistic spelling correction model uses the combination of the likelihood of the corrected word and the probability of the sequence of correction operations. Consider a spelling error *Leucine* for the intended word *Lucene* (see Figure 4.13)

Figure 4.13: A Spelling Error and Correction

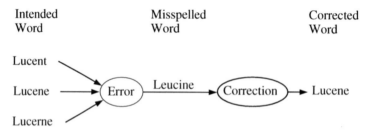

The search engine receives a misspelled word *Leucine* and must guess the intended word. In Figure 4.9, we saw that the number of words in the edit distance boundary of Lucene increases rapidly at higher edit distances (> 2). A reasonable initial assumption would be to choose the intended word with the minimum edit distance from the misspelled word. There are five different character operations – *match*, *insert*, *delete*, *substitute*, and *transpose* to calculate the edit distance between two words.

In Table 4.3, three of the five character operations were used to compute the edit distance between *leucine* and *lucene*. The insert operation adds a new character and the transpose operation reverses the order of a two character sequence ($ab \rightarrow ba$). Notice, the cost of a substitution is double that of an insert or delete operation and the total cost for the transformation is three. The costs of the other two possible intended words, *lucerne* and *lucent* is four and five respectively. In this case, the intended word was the one with the minimum edit distance, but the intended word is not always found at the minimum edit distance from the misspelled word. The default implementation in Lucene uses a cost of one for all non-match operations.

Table 4.3: Edit Distance Between Leucine and Lucene

Error	Correction	Operation	Cost
l	l	match	0
e	-	delete	1
u	u	match	0
c	c	match	0
i	e	substitution	2
n	n	match	0
e	e	match	0

Both LingPipe and Lucene include spell check classes and use somewhat similar methods to correct misspelled words. We have two possible sources to identify corrections, a dictionary or the collection of indexed documents (see Figure 4.14). Here, a dictionary is simply a flat file consisting of a list of words that will be used to find corrections. Another source is the text from the collection of indexed documents that may contain the correct spelling of a word.

We first consider the text from the collection of indexed documents that is tokenized and used to create a spelling model (LingPipe) or a spelling index (Lucene) from character-based ngrams. Alternatives for a misspelled query term are extracted from the model or index. In Lucene, a query is submitted to the SpellChecker index and the returned ranked hits are possible corrections. LingPipe uses a probabilistic model to find the most likely correction.

Lucene SpellChecker Index

In Lucene, the spell checker index is generated after the search engine index is created. A list of all the words in the search engine index is extracted and added to a new ngram-based SpellChecker index. Words that are less than three characters

Figure 4.14: Spell Check Process in LingPipe and Lucene

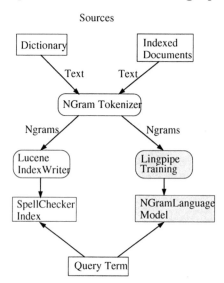

long are excluded from the spell index. The length of ngrams range from 1-2 for short words to 3-4 for the long words. A Lucene `Document` is generated for every word in the index with separate `Fields` for the text of the word and ngrams. The size of the SpellChecker index will be larger than the original index due to the large number of `Documents` and ngrams. The code to create the SpellChecker index is fairly straightforward.

```
// SE_INDEX_DIR is the name of the original index
// SPELL_INDEX_DIR is the name of SpellChecker index
IndexReader ir = IndexReader.open(SE_INDEX_DIR);
Dictionary dictionary = new LuceneDictionary(
  ir, "contents");
Directory spellDir = FSDirectory.getDirectory(
  SPELL_INDEX_DIR);
//Dictionary dictionary = new PlainTextDictionary(new
// File(SPELL_TRAIN_MODEL));
SpellChecker spellChecker = new SpellChecker(spellDir);
spellChecker.indexDictionary(dictionary);
```

The dictionary is an interface to browse the words stored in the index. The `indexDictionary` method loops through the list of all index words for a `Field` (contents) and creates a separate index. We usually pick the `Field` with the largest number of words to train the spell checker. An alternative is to use a dictionary of words in a flat file (`SPELL_TRAIN_MODEL`) that are indexed exactly like the words from the original index. The index created from the list of words fetched from the dictionary file may be smaller than a similar spell index for a large document collection.

Lucene SpellChecker Search

Consider the indexed word *Lucene*. The `SpellChecker` class will create a `Document` with seven `Fields`. The first `Field` is the word itself and the remaining six `Fields` are ngrams (see Table 4.4). The size of the ngrams for the word *Lucene*, range from three to four. Three `Fields` named *startx*, *endx*, and *gramx* are created for each ngram of length x. The purpose of breaking up a word into multiple ngrams is based on the idea that some parts (ngrams) of a misspelled word will match the ngrams of the correct word. Words from the spell index with large fractions of matching ngrams are candidate correction words.

Table 4.4: Field Names and Values for a Document created from the Word *Lucene*

Field Name	Field Value
word	lucene
start3	luc
end3	ene
gram3	luc uce cen ene
start4	luce
end4	cene
gram4	luce ucen cene

The ngrams of a fixed length x are divided into three categories to make it possible to assign higher weights to the ngrams at the beginning or ending of the word. We make the assumption that the characters of the misspelled words are more likely to be found in the inner ngrams (*gramx*) than the outer *startx* or *endx* ngrams. The

171

code to find a correction first creates a `SpellChecker` from the SpellChecker index and then uses the `suggestSimilar` method to find alternate queries.

```
Directory spellDir = FSDirectory.getDirectory(
    SPELL_INDEX_DIR);
SpellChecker spellChecker = new SpellChecker(spellDir);
String[] altWords = spellChecker.suggestSimilar(
    "lucine", 2);
```

The `suggestSimilar` method accepts the misspelled query term and the number of alternate words that should be returned. The list of returned alternate words is ranked in descending order of similarity to the misspelled word from a generated boolean query. The generated boolean *OR* query for the misspelled word Lucine is made up of 11 `TermQuerys` from six ngram `Fields` (see Table 4.5).

Table 4.5: Query Terms Generated for the word *Lucine*

Field Name	Query Terms	Boost
start3	luc	Yes
end3	ine	No
gram3	luc uci cin ine	No
start4	luci	Yes
end4	cine	No
gram4	luci ucin cine	No

The highest ranking document from this query returns the word *lucene* that has a matching ngram (*luc*) in the *start3* and *gram3* `Fields`. This method of spell correction is dependent on the number of common ngrams between the misspelled word and the correct word. We need to find an optimized size of ngrams since long ngrams may limit the number of matching ngrams and short ngrams may generate a number of misleading hits.

Ngrams and Spelling Errors

This experiment uses a sample of about 2500 spelling errors collected from Wikipedia [SpellError], where each entry had an unique correct word and a misspelled word to describe the relationship between ngrams and spelling errors. We also assume that the spelling error represents the most frequent way of misspelling the correct word. Over 92% of the misspelled words were within an edit distance of two or less from the correct word, assuming a cost of two for substitutions and transpositions and a cost of one for insertions and deletions. The average length of the correct word was about 9 characters long and the maximum edit distance for a spelling error was limited to four.

In all cases, a shorter ngram had more overlap between the misspelled word and the correct word than a longer ngram, which is intuitive since a longer ngram will include multiple shorter ngrams. The number of overlapping ngrams of length two was almost twice the number of overlapping ngrams of length four for misspelled words of all edit distances. Similarly, the number of overlapping trigrams was more than double the number of overlapping ngrams of length five. In Table 4.6 we look at the distribution of the ngram mismatches of the 2500 misspelled words.

Table 4.6: Percentage of Mismatched Words for Ngrams of Different Lengths

Ngram Size	First Ngram	Middle Ngrams	Last Ngram
2	6	84	10
3	10	77	13
4	13	73	14
5	18	63	19

The percentage of mismatches in the first and last ngrams is the least in the shorter ngrams compared to the longer ngrams. This also appears to be intuitive since we would expect more errors to appear in longer ngrams and within the interior of a word. The middle ngrams make up most of the errors in all cases and are usually more numerous than the first or last ngrams. The collection of all mismatched ngrams represent an *error model* indicating the frequencies of spelling errors and the collection of all overlapping ngrams represents a *term model*. LingPipe combines these two models to create a probabilistic method to find corrections for spelling errors.

LingPipe SpellChecker

We draw an analogy from the communication of messages over a channel that is prone to randomly garble characters. In the late 1940s, Claude Shannon [Pierce] developed a theory to compute the maximum capacity of a channel given a model of the channel's noise. The surprising results of this theory meant that any message could be transmitted over a channel with a negligible fraction of errors. The representation of errors using this method is called the *noisy channel model*. The first part of this model represents the most common spelling errors due to typos or assumed spelling from the sound of a word or prior experience. The second part of the model represents the expected spelling from the collection of indexed documents. If e is the misspelled word, then the probability that the word w was intended can be stated using Bayes' Theorem (see Appendix B).

$$argmax_w p(w|e) = argmax_w p(e|w) \times p(w) \qquad (4.8)$$

The probability on the left hand side of the equation is the probability that the user intended the word w, but mistakenly used the word e. We are interested in the most likely word w out of all possible intended words. This probability is a combination of the two probabilities on the right hand side that represent the error model and term model (see Figure 4.15).

It is easier to find the most likely intended word with a probability model than a simple edit distance calculation. Often, there are multiple words that are within the same edit distance from the misspelled word and there is no way to discriminate between the choices to identify the best correction. Further, the word with the minimum edit distance from the misspelled word is not always the best choice for a correction. For example, the edit distance of the correct word *receipt* for the misspelled word *reciet* is three, while the word *recite* has a closer edit distance of two. A probability model will rank corrections for the misspelled word based on the error and term models. Fortunately, the LingPipe spell checker uses a probabilistic model to find the most likely correction.

LingPipe SpellChecker Model

The code to create the model in LingPipe is broken into three steps. In the first step, the spell checker is created with specific weights for edit distances. The trained

Figure 4.15: Error Model and Term Model for Spelling Correction

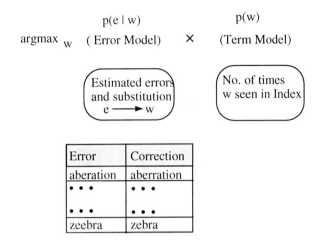

model is generated in the second step from the text of the indexed documents. A file containing the compiled model is written to disk in the last step.

```
1   // Step 1. Create spell checker
2   FixedWeightEditDistance fixedEdit =
3     new FixedWeightEditDistance(
4     MATCH_WEIGHT, DELETE_WEIGHT, INSERT_WEIGHT,
5     SUBSTITUTE_WEIGHT, TRANSPOSE_WEIGHT);
6   NGramProcessLM lm = new NGramProcessLM(NGRAM_LENGTH);
7   TokenizerFactory tokenizerFactory =
8     new StandardBgramTokenizerFactory();
9   TrainSpellChecker sc = new TrainSpellChecker(
10     lm, fixedEdit, tokenizerFactory);
11
12   // Step 2. Train the spell checker
13   sc.train(txtDoc.getContents());
14
15   // Step 3. Write the spell checker model to a file
16   ObjectOutputStream objOut = new ObjectOutputStream(
17     new BufferedOutputStream(
18     new FileOutputStream(SPELL_CHECK_MODEL)));
19   sc.compileTo(objOut);
20   objOut.close();
```

The set of weights (lines 4-5) are constant values for the five character operations to compute edit distances between words. The match weight is usually set to 0 and the other weights can be set to -5.0. A negative number is used for these weights since they are used in calculations based on the logs of probability values. The length of ngrams (line 6) is the number of characters per ngram in the term (language) model, and it can range from 5 for small collections to 7 or higher for large collections.

The trained spell checker (line 9) is created using the language model, the weights for the edit distances of the error model, and a tokenizer factory. We use the same tokenizer factory that was used to build the index of the search engine such that the indexed tokens match the tokens used in the language model. The model is trained (line 13) in step 2 from the plain text contents of a document. The passed string is normalized by substituting consecutive white spaces with a single white space, adding a start and end whitespace, and verifying that all generated tokens are separated by white spaces. The `train` method keeps track of the number of `NGRAM_LENGTH` ngrams seen in the character sequence and is usually found within an indexing loop that scans the collection of indexed documents. The third and final step dumps a compiled version of the spell checker model to a file.

LingPipe SpellChecker Search

The first step to find an alternative word for a misspelled word is to read the spell checker model from a file and create a compiled spell checker. Next, we use the `didYouMean` method of the spell checker to find the best alternative word. If no better alternative is found in the language model, then a null is returned.

```
// 1. Read the compiled spell checker model from a file
ObjectInputStream objIn = new ObjectInputStream(
  new BufferedInputStream(
   new FileInputStream(new File(SPELL_CHECK_MODEL))));
CompiledSpellChecker sc = (CompiledSpellChecker)
  objIn.readObject();
objIn.close();

// 2. Check for an alternative
String alt = sc.didYouMean("lucine");
```

The `didYouMean` method performs a series of operations looking for best possible alternative in the language model. A higher penalty is assigned to character operations performed on the leading two characters of the misspelled word. This assignment is similar to the higher query boost assigned to the *startx* `Field` in Lucene. Next, the four character operations are performed on the misspelled word in sequence starting from the leftmost character to the end of the string and the best possible match is sought in the language model.

The main advantage of a character-based language model is that the error correction is based on patterns in parts of tokens as well as across all tokens. The misspelled phrase "supreme cout" will be corrected to "supreme court". A second advantage is that the corrections are based on the words created from indexed documents and will return a set of hits for a query. The third advantage is that corrections are based on the domain of the document collection. For example, the misspelled word *sulfer* may be corrected to either the word *sulfur* (American) or *sulphur* (British) based on the frequencies of the correct word in the language model.

Spelling correction has been a research topic since the 1960s and there are more subtleties to suggest and improve the accuracy of a spell checker. The highest ranking correction may not be appropriate in all cases and we should consider the frequency of occurrence, edit distance, neighboring words, and usage patterns to more accurately identify the best alternative. The implementations in Lucene and LingPipe both find reasonable alternatives for misspelled words from the index or a language model.

4.8.2 Finding Similar Documents

A link to *"Similar Documents"* is often seen in every hit returned by a search engine. In a large search engine, this computation is rarely performed when documents are indexed. Instead, the set of similar documents are fetched from a separate query at search time. It would take too much time and space to pre-compute all document similarities and save the results in the index. An easier solution is to build a query for similar documents only when requested.

We can build a vector of the terms from the document text and use the set of terms that occur more frequently than others, in a generated query to find similar documents. Lucene includes an option to store a term vector that contains a list of words and associated frequencies for any `Field` of a document at index time. The size of the index can be significantly larger ($> 50\%$) when term vectors are stored. An alternative is to dynamically build a term vector at run time.

```
Token[] tokens = LuceneTools.tokensFromAnalysis(
  analyzer, docText);
Map <String, Integer> tVector =
  new HashMap<String, Integer>();
for (Token token: tokens) {
  String word = new String(tokens[i].termBuffer(),
    0, tokens[i].termLength());
  int value = (tVector.containsKey(word))
    ? tVector.get(word) + 1:
    1;
  tVector.put(word, new Integer(value));
}
```

The term vector tVector is created in a Map from the list of tokens returned from analysis where the key is the term and the value is the number of occurrences of the term in the document. We make the assumption that stop words and other words are removed in the analysis and build a boolean query from the most frequent terms in the term vector. The term vector is first sorted by descending order of value.

```
List <Map.Entry<String, Integer>> tlist =
  new Vector <Map.Entry<String, Integer>> (
    tVector.entrySet());
java.util.Collections.sort(tlist,
  new Comparator<Map.Entry<String, Integer>>() {
    public int compare(
      Map.Entry<String, Integer> e1,
      Map.Entry<String, Integer> e2) {
      return (e1.getValue().equals(e2.getValue()) ?
          0 : (e1.getValue() > e2.getValue() ?
          -1 : +1));
    }
  }
);
```

A `List` of map entry objects is created from the term vector and sorted using the `sort` function of the `Collections` class. The `compare` function orders the map entry objects in descending order of the number of term occurrences. We can now create a new `BooleanQuery` made up of the top n frequently occurring terms in the document.

```
BooleanQuery query = new BooleanQuery();
for (Map.Entry <String, Integer> entry : tlist ) {
  TermQuery tq = new TermQuery(
    new Term("contents", entry.getKey()));
  query.add(tq, BooleanClause.Occur.SHOULD);
}
```

The number of `TermQuerys` added to the boolean query can be truncated to a reasonable number. The number of tokens from a large document may exceed a 1000 and the generated query from the text of such a document may be very broad. Instead of a fixed limit, the number of tokens used to generate the query can be limited to the square root of the total number of tokens. The method described here to find similar documents is simple and a more accurate method would use the links that point to the document and from the document. The anchor text for links is another valuable source for query terms.

4.9 Troubleshooting a Query

The absence of a known relevant document from a hit list is probably the biggest source of frustration for a searcher using an Intranet search engine. Compare this situation to a database, where the user provides a key and fetches one or more rows. There is little room for error given a precise key for a database table. Searchers using a search engine may need to expand a query term using a set of synonyms, hypernyms, or even hyponyms to check for the existence of other words in the neighborhood of the query term that may exist in the index. Search engines can automatically expand queries using the query itself or the terms from a set of documents that have been judged relevant.

Sometimes, a long hit list may contain a few documents that are relevant and a new expanded query can be generated using the terms from the few relevant documents to return a hit list with higher precision. In a large search engine, the ranking algorithm may set scores based on the default formula that is not appropriate for the application. The score of a matching document in Lucene is made up of several parameters.

- Boost for the matching query term

- Boost for the matching Field

- Overall fraction of number of matching query terms in the document

- Normalization of the matching Field

- Normalization of the Query

- Frequency of query term in the document

- IDF frequency of query term

The `Explanation` for a matching document shows the values for each parameter and how they contribute to the final score. It is much easier to debug an open source search engine like Lucene, given the values for each of the score parameters, than a proprietary search engine that hides the workings of the ranking algorithm. A more precise ranking algorithm will use other parameters such as the *currency* and *authority* of the document. The score of a recent document can be boosted by generating a set of boolean queries for a range of timestamps with higher boost values for the more recent timestamps. The authority of the document is computed using a more complex algorithm (see Chapter 8). Finding an optimal set of scoring parameters for a test set of queries is an NP-complete problem. An optimized set of scoring parameters should return the most relevant documents that users expect for a test set of queries.

4.10 Summary

Search is a crucial part of information management within an organization and for external clients. The information indexed by a search engine is of little use unless it is easily made available when requested through queries. The expectations of clients using a search box has risen with the increased sophistication of Web search engines; the typical user expects to type in a few words and find relevant hits early in the results page. The success of the search engine depends on the user having confidence that the search engine will take the least time to find information compared to any other method. The typical user should find the search engine simple to use and the addition of new features should increase the average user satisfaction.

Lucene has many features that can be tweaked to return a list of hits that are more relevant. This is an iterative process since altering the values of a feature can improve the results of a few queries but may lower the precision of other queries. The user's search experience can be improved by providing suggestions such as alternate or related queries, when the user enters a query that does not appear to generate enough hits. Error analysis from the study of failed searches can give valuable information on user expectations and the types of zero-hit queries.

5 Tagging Text

Search engines work well for questions like "*What did Vasco Da Gama discover?*", with a singular answer. These types of factoid questions can be answered with a single word or a short phrase. The answer to a more complex question like - "*What are the locations of Ethanol Producers in the United States?*" cannot be answered in a similar manner. Let's reconsider a query discussed earlier in Chapter 1: "*List the Textile companies in South Carolina*". Ideally, an intelligent search engine should return a list of company names and not a list of documents that may contain the names of candidate companies.

A generated search engine query for the list of textile companies question, would simply list the nouns and adjectives of the question and rank documents with a larger fraction of these query terms higher than other documents. The problem with this query is that documents containing the names of textile companies in South Carolina, may not use the term "*South Carolina*". Instead a city (*Greenville*) in South Carolina may be mentioned in the text and the search engine has no way to link the place with the name of the state. A search engine would first need to identify the type of questions (factoid, list, or other) before processing a request. Questions that are specialized will be treated differently than a simple factoid question. Other question categories include why questions that are typically requests for a moderately detailed explanation.

Similarly, the query for the locations of Ethanol producers will find documents that contain the words *located, Ethanol, major,* and *producers*. A rare document may exactly match this list of query terms, but more often the answers to this question are found in documents that mention the name of an Ethanol producer and the name of a place. Clearly, matching documents and queries based on the query terms alone is not sufficient. The search engine needs to know that certain fragments of text refer to the name of a place, an organization, or a person. If the names of all places have been tagged in the text, then we can transform the query term *located* to a generic query term *place*. The word *place* will not be matched, instead the documents that contain text tagged with the *place* entity and which also match the remainder of the query will be listed.

The task of finding such entities in text is called *Information Extraction* and is a sub-field of NLP. The goal of information extraction is to build structured information from unstructured text by assigning text fragments a meaning or interpretation. For example, meaning of the phrase "*Addis Ababa*" would be interpreted as the name of a place. Similarly, the phrase "*Abraham Lincoln*" would mean the name of a person. Such entities extracted from text would be added to the metadata of a document and used to find responses for a query.

The tools in this chapter will explain the building blocks to create applications that exploit the meaning of phrases in text, using the open source tools LingPipe and Gate. We will look at the extraction of sentences, entities, parts of speech, and phrases. The results of the extraction are typically stored in a database from which Web applications can extract and synthesize information from other sources to generate a more informative and usable tool.

5.1 Sentences

We need to extract sentences from text to implement a question and answer (Q&A) engine or a document summarizer. The results from a Q&A engine are a list of sentences that most likely answer a given question. A document summarizer will identify the most important sentences in a document and return a handful of such sentences that are sufficient to grasp the contents of a document. We use the same model that we developed to find tokens in text to extract sentences. A sentence extractor reads a text stream and constructs a sentence when a sentence boundary is encountered. In English the period (.), exclamation point (!), and question mark (?) are the typical sentence boundary characters analogous to the whitespace character that separates tokens.

5.1.1 Sentence Extraction with LingPipe

LingPipe uses a heuristic sentence model to detect sentence boundaries. The problem of finding these boundaries is a difficult one: A sentence boundary character like the period may be used for other token types such as abbreviations, Internet host names, an initial, and a decimal point. To further complicate things, the period of an abbreviation located at the end of a sentence represents an abbreviation and is also an end-of-sentence indicator. Any period that is preceded by a non-abbreviation token is most likely an end-of-sentence indicator, however a period preceded by an abbreviation token may also be an end-of-sentence indicator. LingPipe's heuristic algorithm will attempt to resolve the ambiguity of sentence boundary characters by examining the context of neighborhood tokens and pre-defined tokens. The lists of pre-defined tokens include a list of all *possible stop tokens, impossible start tokens, and impossible penultimate tokens.* (Start and stop tokens are the first and last tokens in a sentence respectively. Penultimate tokens are the second-to-last tokens in a sentence.)

The list of possible stop tokens includes - . (single period), .. (two consecutive periods), ! (exclamation point), ? (question mark), " (double quotes), ' ' (two consecutive single quotes), ' (single quote) and). (close parentheses followed by a period). A list of all known abbreviations would be difficult to maintain since the list is open ended and instead it is easier to track known abbreviations that are unlikely to be seen just before the end of a sentence. These abbreviations (such as e.g. or Mr.) form the impossible penultimate token set. The list of all possible opening tokens for a sentence is similarly open ended. The last token set is a list of tokens such as) (close parentheses), . (period), and ! (exclamation point) that are unlikely to found at the beginning of a sentence.

There are several other clues to detect sentences such as unbalanced quotes or parentheses and the case of the first character of a potential sentence. We also depend on a tokenizer to retain embedded periods in real numbers, IP addresses, and URLs. Consider a sample of three sentences (see Figure 5.1).

Every token in the text segment is assigned one of four types – *stop, start, penultimate,* or *miscellaneous.* The *stop* token type is assigned by comparing a token with a standard set of seven stop tokens for English, while the *start* and *penultimate* token types are identified from stop lists. A sentence break is defined only when the token before and after the sentence boundary token are penultimate and start tokens respectively. An extra whitespace character is padded after the last character of the text segment. The code to extract a list of sentences is shown in Listing 5.1. The

Figure 5.1: Sentence Extraction using Token Types from a Text Segment

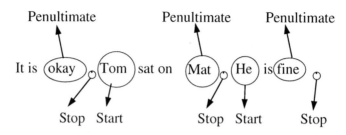

LingpipeTools package is included in the software distribution that accompanies the book.

Listing 5.1: Extract Sentences from a Text Segment using LingPipe

```
1  public class ExtractLingpipeSentences {
2    private static LingpipeTools lt =
3      new LingpipeTools();
4    public static void main(String[] args) {
5      String text =
6        "It is okay. Tom sat on Mat. He is fine.";
7      lt.buildSentences(text);
8      String sentence = "";
9      for (int i = 1;
10       ((sentence = lt.nextSentence()) != null); i++) {
11       System.out.println(i + ": " + sentence);
12     }
13   }
14 }
15
16 Generated Output
17 1: It is okay.
18 2: Tom sat on Mat.
19 3: He is fine.
```

The three sentences (lines 18-20) in the text segment will be returned with the sentence boundary defined correctly at the period character. The first and second

186

sentence will be combined into a single sentence, if we replace the word *okay* in the first sentence with the abbreviation *OK*. The token *OK* is an abbreviation for the state Oklahoma and is included in the list of disallowed penultimate tokens that includes all alphabetic letters, honorifics, state abbreviations, military ranks, month abbreviations, and location suffixes. Optionally, sentences can be formed from a list of tokens that contains unbalanced parentheses and the last token in the segment can be forced to be a stop token. The `LingpipeTools` package includes parameters to restrict the length of sentences within a particular range.

5.1.2 Sentence Extraction with Gate

Gate uses a rule-based method to extract sentences in contrast to the heuristic method in LingPipe. A rule-based sentence extractor looks for patterns in the text to identify potential sentence boundaries. Gate uses a list of abbreviations like LingPipe, but splits text into sentences based on termination patterns and a list of exceptions. The code to extract sentences using Gate is quite similar to the code in Listing 5.1. Nonetheless, the methods used in Gate are based on the annotations of tokens, a regular expression like language for annotations called Jape, and a gazetteer (see section 5.4.2 Entity Extraction with Gate). Let's try extracting the same three sentences using `GateTools` in Listing 5.2.

Listing 5.2: Extract Sentences from a Text Segment using Gate

```
1  public class ExtractGATESentences {
2    private static GateTools gt;
3
4    public static void main(String[] args) {
5      gt = new GateTools();
6      text = "It is okay. Tom sat on Mat. He is fine.";
7      gt.setforSent();
8      gt.buildSentences(text);
9      String sentence = "";
10     for (int i = 1;
11       ((sentence = gt.nextSentence()) != null); i++) {
12       System.out.println(i + ": " + sentence);
13     }
14   }
15 }
```

Rules similar to the ones in LingPipe to detect sentence boundaries are encoded in Gate using the Jape language that defines regular expressions over annotations to create new annotations. The list of abbreviations are saved in a flat file and can be easily extended. The rules for sentence extraction allow a period that ends an abbreviation, in numbers and for a middle initial without creating a sentence boundary. We can identify the sentence boundaries in a text fragment in three steps (see Figure 5.2).

Figure 5.2: Identifying Sentence Boundaries with Gate

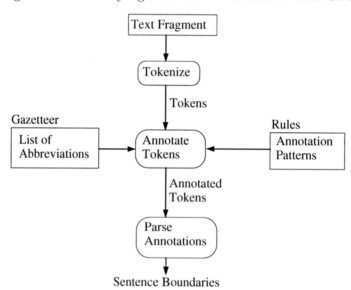

In the first step, the text fragment is tokenized and passed to the next annotation step. The annotation process uses the pattern matching rules specified for sentence boundaries together with a gazetteer that includes a list of abbreviations. The annotated tokens are passed to a XML parser that returns the locations of sentence boundaries in the list of tokens. A gazetteer can include many other lists such as the names of companies and people that will be used to extract entities (see section 5.4.2). The rules in Jape are flexible and can be customized to annotate groups of tokens with any arbitrary annotation type. The following rule is a simple rule to prevent the creation of a sentence boundary at a period that belongs to a numeric value or an Internet host name. This rule (**Fake**) will fire when a sequence begins with any token and is immediately followed by a period and either a word or a number.

```
Rule:Fake
// Left hand side
(
  ( {Token} {Token.string == "."} )+
  ( {Token.kind == word} | {Token.kind == number} )
):fake
-->
{}
```

A rule is made up of a left hand side that describes the matching pattern and the right hand side that inserts the annotation. In this case, the right hand side is made up of the empty brackets {} and the left hand side will match an Internet host name like *www.yahoo.com* or a decimal number like 3.1415926. The *kind* field of the Token is a numeric value that defines the type of token and the *string* field returns the contents of the token. The next rule (**Fake1**) skips periods that occur in a sentence and that are followed by a word that starts with a lower case letter.

```
Rule:Fake1
(
  {Token.string == "."}
  ({SpaceToken.string == " "}) +
  {Token.orth == lowercase}
):fake1
-->
{}
```

The **Fake1** rule fires when at least one or more space characters separates the period from the word in lower case. The *orth* field of the Token defines whether the token starts with an upper case letter, consists of only upper case letters, or consists of lower case letters alone. The sentence extractor in Gate can be modified to recognize a period that is part of an abbreviation and also ends a sentence. For example, if the word *okay* in the text string is replaced with the abbreviation *OK*, the sentence extractor should detect the abbreviation and the end of the sentence. The rule to detect abbreviations that can also be found at the end of a sentence is

```
Rule: Split_Abbrev
// Start of left hand side
(
 {Lookup.majorType == "abbreviation"}
 {Token.string == "."}
 ({SpaceToken.string == " "})*
 {Token.orth == "upperInitial"}
):splitAbbrev
-->
// Start of right hand side
:splitAbbrev {
 FeatureMap features = Factory.newFeatureMap();
 features.put("kind", "Split");
 Node first = splitAbbrevAnnots.firstNode();
 Node start = splitAbbrevAnnots.nextNode(first);
 Node end = splitAbbrevAnnots.nextNode(start);
 annotations.add( start, end, "Split", features);
}
```

The left hand side should match an abbreviation from a pre-defined list in the gazetteer followed by a period character, zero or more spaces, and a token that begins with an upper case letter. We make the assumption that every valid sentence starts with an upper case letter. The right hand side contains the Java code to insert a Split annotation between the period character of the sentence. A feature map is a mapping between attributes and values passed to the add method of the set of annotations. The add method accepts the start location, end location, and name of the annotation. The start and end locations of the annotation are just before and after the period which is the character range 8-9 in the first sentence -

Sentence:

It is OK. Tom sat on Mat.

Annotated Sentence:

It is OK <Split>.</Split> Tom sat on Mat <Split>.</Split>

A period token that was not consumed by any one of the earlier rules will be considered a sentence boundary. A sentence boundary will also be added when punctuation tokens such as the question mark and exclamation point are preceded by a token. The Split annotations alone have been shown in the annotated sentence that may include annotations for other token types such as the SpaceToken. The indices of sentence boundaries are identified from the `Split` annotations with an XML parser and passed back to the caller.

Note, applying the rule indiscriminately will lead to bad sentence breaks. For example, an honorific such as *Mr.* or a middle initial followed by a token that begins with an upper case letter is not a sentence break. The list of abbreviations followed by a token with an upper case letter that should not be split must be selected based on prior knowledge. For example, the list of abbreviations will include most honorifics such as *St, Prof,* or *Gen.* This list of abbreviations is embedded in the Indo-European sentence model in LingPipe, while in Gate an equivalent list is built in the gazetteer. A more detailed description of the use of rules in Gate to annotate text is included later in this chapter (see section 5.4.2 Entity Extraction with Gate).

5.1.3 Text Extraction from Web Pages

In the preceding examples, we have considered text that is well-formed. The text extracted from Web pages is often chunks of text from a list or box structure without punctuation. Text that was laid out in a table may not be extracted in the same visual order that it appears in a browser. Often, there is no separation between text chunks and the tags that define space in the Web page are not retained in the extracted text. The result is that the extracted text is a collection of words with little indication of boundaries.

The simple method to segment such text is to use the same algorithms used earlier for well-formed text with a limitation on the maximum length of a sentence. A sentence break will be added when the length of the extracted sentence exceeds a limit. The arbitrary location of the sentence boundary means that the returned list may contain multiple sentences in a single entry and a legitimate sentence may be split.

An alternate method to segment text without any explicit sentence boundaries is to locate the parts of text where there is a topical shift. These shifts are identified by the introduction of new vocabulary as the text begins a new topic. The locations of such shifts are possible text boundaries. The term *sentence* is not appropriate in this context since it implies a well-formed structure with nouns and verbs. Instead, we refer to a *block* that mainly describes a single topic.

The entire block of text is tokenized and divided into chunks of n tokens where n is large enough to hold the smallest block. All blocks are compared with their immediate neighbor blocks before and after using a similarity measure (see section 6.2.2). The value of the similarity between the two blocks represents the degree of cohesion. A low degree of cohesion means that a boundary is more likely to be found between two blocks. Large changes in the relative cohesion of the token sequences are also potential boundaries.

The previous method works well provided there is sufficient text, but often a Web page may contain several images and animations with minimal text. Web pages also contain text that is of little use in segmentation. Copyright messages, navigational links, and headers are of little use to identify topical boundaries. The text shown in a Web page may be ordered for visual presentation, for example, text chunks from adjacent columns of a Web page may appear far apart in the extracted text. Vision based segmentation is more appropriate to find boundaries in the text of a Web page.

5.2 Part of Speech Taggers

Part of speech (POS) tagging is an intermediate task performed before the interpretation of text chunks. A POS tagger assigns a tag to every token in the text. These tags are used to find referential proper nouns, phrases, and detect events in the text (see Figure 5.3).

Nouns and adjectives make up most of the entities in text. For example, a *Person* pattern to tag the text string - *"Jones, F. W. Jr."* would consist of a proper noun followed by a comma, one or more initials, and an optional suffix to differentiate the name. There are many different patterns to identify a *Person* entity, since there are numerous ways of stating a person's name in text. Patterns to tag a text chunk as an *Entity* or *Organization* will similarly use the POS assigned to a token when appropriate.

A POS tagger assigns the most likely tag to every token in the text using a tagger model. The eight standard set of POS tags are adjectives, adverbs, conjunctions, determiners, nouns, prepositions, pronouns, and verbs. Interjections and punctuation marks are two other tag types to classify any word or character that does not fit in the standard set of POS tags. Unfortunately, some words have more than one POS and therefore a simple lookup in a dictionary is not sufficient. For example, the

Figure 5.3: A Part of Speech Tagger used to Extract Structured Information

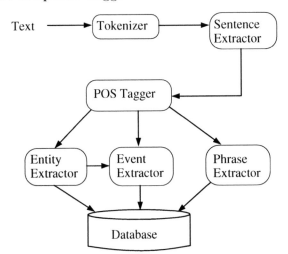

word *round* has four different parts of speech in the WordNet dictionary. We need to select the most likely part of speech based on the local context and topic of the source document.

5.2.1 Tag Sets

The eight standard POS are coarse grain descriptors of the parts of speech and are sufficient for tasks that need to identify nouns or adjectives without any further qualification. The tag sets used to identify parts of speech at a more detailed level may have 100 or more parts of speech that describe a part of speech in more detail. For example, an adjective may be a comparative adjective, superlative adjective, or a numeric adjective. These examples are limited to English and other languages will have different parts of speech and qualifications based on the grammar of the language.

The Brown tag set was an influential tag set used for tagging the American Brown Corpus [Brown]. The corpus was made up of about a million words from a wide variety of carefully selected sources including fiction, newswire, and humor with over 170 different tags (see the Appendix A for a sample list of Brown Tags). The more recent British National Corpus is a much larger corpus with about 100 million words tagged with the Claws tag set. The Penn Treebank set is another tag set that has been popular in computational linguistics. There are high level similarities between the tag sets, but the codes used for tags are usually different and cannot be mixed. (see Table 5.1). LingPipe includes a tagger model that has been trained on the Brown tag set and Gate uses the Hepple tagger trained on the Penn Treebank tag set.

Table 5.1: POS Tagging with different Tag Sets

Word	Brown Tag	Claws	Part of Speech
The	AT	AT0	Determiner,article
company	NN	NN0	Noun
said	VBD	VVD	Verb(past)
information	NN	NN0	Noun
management	NN	NN0	Noun
products	NNS	NN2	Noun Plural
will	MD	VM0	Modal Verb
be	BE	VBI	Auxiliary verb form of be
the	AT	AT0	Determiner, article
focus	NN	NN0	Noun
.	.	PUN	Full stop

Each tag is a short coded description of the part of speech. The code *AT* or *AT0* represents an article, *NN* or *NN0* a noun, *NN2* or *NNS* a plural noun, and so on. A larger tag set will make more fine grained distinctions between parts of speech and may have more tags in one particular part of speech than another. The purpose of a tag is to provide the grammatical class of the word and some predictive features indicating the behavior of other words in context. For example, given the tag *AT*, we can reasonably expect the next word to be an adjective or noun in a sentence from the Brown corpus.

The best tag set depends on the application and often you may not have a choice since the tag set is prescribed by the training data. The type of tag set may not make a difference, if an application uses the coarse grain parts of speech such as nouns, adjectives, and verbs alone. We will look at two different ways of extracting parts of speech from text. One is based on the Markov model and the other is based on transformation rules.

5.2.2 Markov Models

Andrei Markov originally created the Markov Model to study letter sequences in Russian literature. For example, the letter sequence *th* is far more common than the letter sequence *te*. The Markov model captures this uneven distribution of letter sequences and is the basis for predicting the next letter given the current letter. The chain of letter sequences represents a Markov chain, where each letter is conditionally dependent on the previous letter. The letter dependencies are expressed in the form of probabilities.

The application of the Markov Model to find the parts of speech in text was partly based on the success of its use in speech recognition problems. The speech recognition Markov model associated a phoneme with an audio signal pattern that was dependent on the speaker's utterance and the prior phoneme. The phoneme and audio pattern of the speech recognition model was replaced by a part of speech (state) and a word (observation) respectively, in a POS tagger model.

We distinguish between *states* and *observations* in a Hidden Markov Model (HMM). The states are the unknowns that we estimate from the observations and represent the parts of speech, while the words are the observations in the POS tagging problem. The training data contains both the observations and the states and the test data contains just observations alone from which we estimate the most like sequence of states that would have generated the set of observations (see Figure 5.4). Some words may have more the one possible POS (state) from which we select the most likely part of speech using the model probabilities.

The use of the HMM for POS tagging depends on two assumptions. First, we assume a *"limited horizon"* when considering dependencies between states. A state is dependent only on its immediate predecessor in a first order HMM. The model generates a following state or the previous state given the current state using a distribution that has been trained with a large number of state sequences. Second, the computed probabilities of the model do not change with time. These assumptions are satisfactory in most cases and Hidden Markov Model-based POS taggers have high precision comparable to other taggers. There are a few long distance relationship

between states that will not be saved in the model. For example, in the two sentences
-

> The *football* player ran and scored a *goal.*
> The *baseball* played ran and scored a *run.*

There is a dependency between the sport (football / baseball) and the scoring unit (goal / run). The word run in this context is a noun and not a verb. In a dynamic language, vocabulary and syntax changes over time and a model trained on out-dated language usage will not perform as well. The model stores the probability estimates of state sequences and the state given a word.

Figure 5.4: Training and Testing a Markov Model

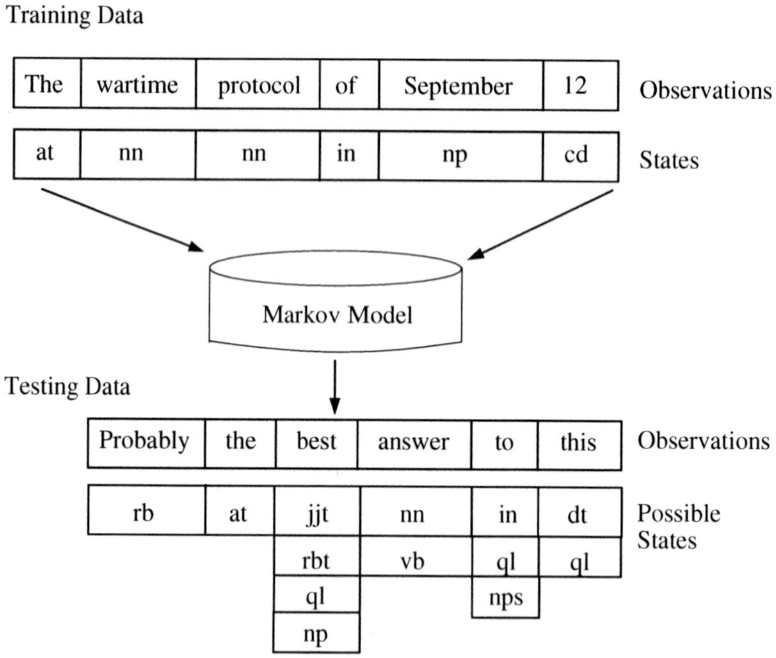

Training Data

The	wartime	protocol	of	September	12	Observations

at	nn	nn	in	np	cd	States

Markov Model

Testing Data

Probably	the	best	answer	to	this	Observations

	rb	at	jjt	nn	in	dt	Possible States
			rbt	vb	ql	ql	
			ql		nps		
			np				

The training data for the Markov model-based POS Tagger consists of a large set of tagged sentences like the first sentence shown in Figure 5.4. These sentences make up the model that is used to predict the tags of words from sentences in the testing data. Notice, some words may belong to just one POS (state) and others belong to more than one POS. The word *best* has at least four possible POS, of which the model must select one. Similarly, the words *answer* and *to* also have more than one POS. The number of occurrences of the word *best* as an adjective (jjt) is typically far more frequent than as a noun, verb, or adverb. We can use this uneven distribution of tags to words to find the most likely tag.

The POS tagging problem can be stated as the identification of the most likely set of tags $t_{1,n}$ given the words $w_{1,n}$ from a sentence of length n. Notice, that the model finds the most likely tag sequence for the entire sentence and we can apply Bayes' Rule (see Appendix B) to define the problem as

$$argmax_{t_{1,n}} p(t_{1,n}|w_{1,n}) = argmax_{t_{1,n}} p(w_{1,n}|t_{1,n}) \times p(t_{1,n}) \qquad (5.1)$$

$$= argmax_{t_{1,n}} \prod_{i=1}^{n} (p(w_i|t_i) \times p(t_i|t_{i-1}))$$

The first expression in the right hand side of the equation represents lexical information that gives the probability of a word sequence being seen given a tag sequence and the second expression is the probability of the tag sequence. The right hand side has been expanded using the chain rule to compute probabilities that are dependent on a single tag and not a sequence of tags. The maximum of the product of these two probabilities gives the most likely tag sequence that would have generated the observed word sequence. The number of possible combinations of tag sequences of length n is large and it would be time consuming to find the best of all such possibilities. Instead, we make a few assumptions to simplify the computation. We assume that words are conditionally independent of each other given a tag and a tag depends only on its previous tag. The probability $p(t_1|t_0)$ is computed from the estimated likelihood of a state being an initial state in the training data.

Based on these assumptions, we can estimate the probability of a word w given a tag t as the ratio of the number of times the word w was seen with tag t and the number of occurrences of the tag t.

$$p(w|t) = \frac{Count(w,t)}{Count(t)} \qquad (5.2)$$

The probability of tag sequences is computed from the ratio of the number of times a tag t_j followed a tag t_i to the number of times the tag t_i was seen.

$$p(t_j|t_i) = \frac{Count(t_i, t_j)}{Count(t_i)} \qquad (5.3)$$

One is usually added to all counts to handle cases of unseen words in both probability estimates. This operation (adding one to all counts) is called *Laplace smoothing* and distributes some probability uniformly across all unseen words. Consider a sentence with three words w_1, w_2, and w_3. We can compute the probability that the tag sequence t_1, t_2, and t_3 generated the sentence, from the product of the individual probabilities for the words given the tags and the tags given the previous tag.

$$\overbrace{p(w_1|t_1) \times p(w_2|t_2) \times p(w_3|t_3)} \times \overbrace{p(t_0) \times p(t_1|t_0) \times p(t_2|t_1) \times p(t_3|t_2)} \qquad (5.4)$$

These probabilities are estimated from the training data. A dummy tag t_0 is inserted at the beginning of a sentence. Two additional probabilities $p(t_0|first)$ and $p(last|t_3)$ are added to compute the probability across all sequences, where *first* and *last* are the start and end states of a sequence. These two probabilities model the begin and end of sentence effects such as capitalization of letters and the use of periods in English. Both the word-tag and tag sequence probabilities are computed from the set of individual training sentences. Table 5.2 contains a small subset of the counts for the word-tag probabilities from the Brown Corpus.

Table 5.2: Some Word Counts for Tags from the Brown Corpus

Word	at	nn	vbd	vbn
the	69,013	0	0	0
company	0	218	0	0
said	0	0	1,747	213
information	0	243	0	0

The counts for four words and tags are shown in Table 5.2. Notice, the word *the* occurs with tag *at* alone. The tag *at* occurs 99,077 times in the corpus and therefore the estimated probability of seeing the word *the* given the tag *at* is $\frac{69,013}{99,077}$ or about

0.70. We can construct a similar table for the counts of tag sequences (see Table 5.3) where the tags in the rows represent the first tag and the columns the following tag.

Table 5.3: Some Tag Sequence Counts from the Brown Corpus

Tag	at	nn	vbd	vbn
at	0	48,638	0	0
nn	0	11,625	3,306	0
vbd	3,910	0	0	0
vbn	0	0	0	0

The tag *at* was followed by another tag in 80K training examples, of which 48,638 subsequent tags were nouns. The estimated probability of seeing a noun given the current tag is *at* is about 0.60. A dummy start tag inserted at the beginning of a sentence precedes the first tag. The set of tags is finite and we can compute a probability for every pair of tags. The number of words in unbounded and therefore it is quite likely that a tagger trained on a finite set of words will need to compute the probability of a tag given an unknown word. The accuracy of a tagger is often determined by how well it handles probabilities of unknown words. The orthography of the word can give hints of its POS, for example, a capitalized word is more likely to be a noun.

The two Tables 5.2 and 5.3 represent the probability values for a state transition probability matrix A and an observation probability matrix B. A third vector not shown here is the probability of seeing a tag in the first state of the sentence. These three parameters are supplied to the Viterbi [Viterbi] algorithm to find the most likely state sequence that generated the observation sequence. The algorithm works by recursively finding the most probable path through a trellis of all possible state sequences. The total number of paths that need to be examined is bounded by the square of the number of states that is typically a smaller number than all possible paths (bounded by the product of the number of states and number of observations).

5.2.3 Evaluation of a Tagger

A small part of the training data is set aside for testing the precision of the tagger. The tagger may be trained on 90% of the training data and then tested on the remaining 10%. We pick a large enough fraction of the training data to build an accurate model and larger fractions of training data typically lead to better models. Following testing, the final model can be trained on 100% of the training data to utilize all possible examples. Testing on a very small data set may give misleading results. The small sample of testing data may not be representative of the training data and the precision of the tagger may be either underestimated or overestimated.

A general way to overcome any bias caused by a non-representative testing sample is to test the tagger on more than one sample. All of the training data is divided into some number, say ten folds (equal sized partitions). The tagger is trained on nine tenths of the training set and tested on the remaining one tenth. There are ten ways of picking nine tenths of data and the final accuracy of the tagger is the average precision of ten runs, each with a unique training set. This type of evaluation is called ten fold cross validation and uses the entire data set for training and testing. In the limit, we leave out exactly one test sample and train on the remaining $n - 1$ test samples. This is called n fold cross validation where n is the number of test samples.

The choice of a fraction (10%) of testing data may also affect the precision of the tagger. The precision values for larger or smaller fractions of testing data can be averaged in two ways. The *macroaverage* is the average of the precision results from runs with different fractions. The *microaverage* is a weighted average that takes into account the size of the testing data set. The precision from a run with a large testing set will have more weight than a run with a smaller testing set. The macroaverage assigns equal weight to all runs regardless of the size of the testing set.

5.2.4 POS Tagging with LingPipe

We skip the training process and assume an existing model that has been trained on the Brown corpus. The code to extract the parts of speech from a text chunk with LingPipe is shown in Listing 5.3. The sample text contains two sentences and is passed to the `extractPOS` method in the `LingpipeTools` package.

Listing 5.3: Extract the POS Tags from a Text Chunk

```
1  public class ExtractLingpipePOS {
2    private static LingpipeTools lt = new LingpipeTools();
3
```

```
4    public static void main(String[] args) {
5      String text = "Time flies like an arrow. "
6                     + "This is a second sentence.";
7      lt.extractPOS(text);
8      String[] tags = lt.getTags();
9      String[] tokens = lt.getTokens();
10     for (int i = 0; i < tags.length; i++)
11       System.out.println(tokens[i] + "/" + tags[i]);
12   }
13 }
```

The output from this program is a list of tokens and their associated POS tags. Two sentences are passed in a single text chunk and the POS tagger must first segment the text into sentences and then tag each individual sentence separately. The tagger model was trained on tagged sentences and makes probability assumptions based on the locations of tokens at the beginning or end of a sentence.

```
Time/nn
flies/vbz
like/cs
an/at
arrow/nn
./.
This/dt
is/bez
a/at
second/od
sentence/nn
./.
```

The tag codes shown are part of the Brown Corpus tagset and you can translate the codes to nouns, adjectives, or verbs. Notice, the first sentence is ambiguous. The sentence has the popular meaning that time passes more rapidly than we think, but it could also be an instruction to measure the movement of flies. The second interpretation is of course almost meaningless, but is syntactically valid. The model indicates that the tag sequence from the first interpretation is more probable.

The code in LingpipeTools (Listing 5.4) initializes and makes calls to LingPipe functions on behalf of the caller. The constructor for LingpipeTools reads the

Markov Model from a file and creates a `HmmDecoder` object (lines 8-12). The HMM decoder contains methods to find the best tag sequence or the n best tag sequences for a sentence.

Listing 5.4: POS Tagger using a HMM Model in LingPipe

```
1   public class LingpipeTools {
2      private HmmDecoder decoder = null;
3      protected String[] tokens = null;
4      protected String[] tags = null;
5
6      public LingpipeTools() {
7        SENTENCE_MODEL = new IndoEuropeanSentenceModel();
8        ObjectInputStream oi = new ObjectInputStream(
9          new FileInputStream(POS_TAGGER_MODEL));
10       HiddenMarkovModel hmm =
11         (HiddenMarkovModel) oi.readObject();
12       decoder = new HmmDecoder(hmm);
13     }
14
15     public void extractPOS(String text) {
16       buildSentences(text);
17       String sentence = "";
18       List<String> ltags = new ArrayList<String>();
19       while ((sentence = nextSentence()) != null) {
20         // first get the tokens
21         char[] cs = sentence.toCharArray();
22         Tokenizer tokenizer =
23           tokenizer_Factory.tokenizer(cs, 0, cs.length);
24         String[] tokens = tokenizer.tokenize();
25         // then get the tags
26         List<String> tempTags = Arrays.asList(
27           decoder.firstBest(tokens)) ;
28         ltags.addAll(tempTags);
29       }
30       tags = new String[ltags.size()];
31       ltags.toArray(tags);
32     }
33   }
```

The `extractPOS` (line 15) method first creates sentences from the text chunk and passes each sentence to the tagger. The sentence is tokenized (line 24) and the list of tokens are passed in order to the decoder. The decoder returns a list of tags, one for every token passed, that is appended to a list of all tags from every sentence and finally returned to the caller. The `firstBest` (line 27) method finds the best tag sequence out of all possible tag sequences.

The decoder begins by creating lattice and backpointer matrices of size m by n, where m is the number of tokens (5) in the sentence and n is the number of tags (93 in this model). The lattice matrix keeps track of the products of probabilities for each state as the algorithm proceeds from one token to the next (see Figure 5.5). The backpointer matrix tracks the best previous tag from which the current tag was reached.

Figure 5.5: The Lattice Matrix to Find the Best Tag Sequence Path for the Sentence

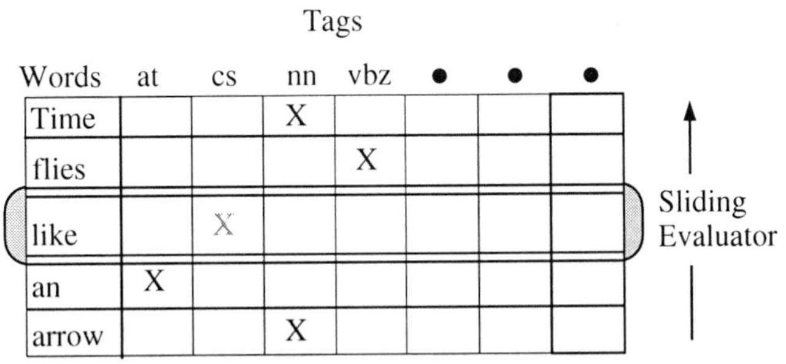

A sliding evaluator finds the best state from the products of the tag sequence probabilities starting from the rightmost token. The first token in the sentence is a special case and the top row of the lattice matrix is computed using the probabilities of words and the first tag in a sentence. In this example, it is the product of the probability of seeing the word *Time* given a tag x with the probability that the first tag in a sentence is of type x. The lattice probabilities in rows 2-5 are computed using the product of the tag probability computed in the row above the current row, the probability of the transition from the previous tag to the current tag, and the probability of the current word given the current tag.

The tag of the last token in the sentence is extracted from the tag column with the highest probability in the last row of the lattice matrix. The backpointer matrix keeps track of the tag sequences in reverse order and we move up the matrix one row at a time, till the top row, marking a tag at each row. The backpointer matrix identifies the previous tag at each row, with the highest probability of leading to the current tag. The list of tags from first to last are returned to the caller. The implementation of the Viterbi algorithm in hmm.HmmDecoder.Viterbi does more than the description here to keep track of the different solutions starting from the most likely in descending order of probability.

Evaluation

LingPipe includes functions to evaluate and compare the results of the tagger. The getPOSDump method of LingpipeTools accepts a sentence and dumps an evaluation of the top three tag sequences (see Table 5-4). Consider the same sentence we used in the earlier example.

Table 5.4: Evaluation of Tag Sequences for a Sentence

Token	First	Second	Third
Time	nn	nn	np
flies	vbz	nns	vbz
like	cs	cs	cs
an	at	at	at
arrow	nn	nn	nn
p	0.56	0.21	0.08
$log(p)$	-0.83	-2.22	-3.58

The first, second, and third columns represent the top three tag sequences returned by the tagger. There are just 1-2 differences between the tag sequences. The word *flies* that is correctly tagged as a verb in the first sequence is tagged as a noun in the second sequence. The third tag sequence incorrectly tags the word *Time* as a proper noun. The bottom two rows represents the scores for each tag sequence. The scores are the conditional log (base 2) probabilities of the tag sequence given the observation (token) sequence from the sentence. The probability of the first tag sequence (0.56) is more than twice the probability of the second tag sequence (0.21). There are a large number of tag sequences with very low probability that cover the remaining probability space. In general, the tagger has correctly tagged a sentence when the difference between the first and second tag sequences is relatively large and the absolute probability of the first tag sequence is high. The scores for sentences which cannot be unambiguously tagged will have a larger number of tag sequences with close probabilities.

LingPipe XML Tagged Sentences

Applications that need to identify just nouns, adjectives, or verbs can use the `extractXMLPOS` method in `LingpipeTools` to generate XML tagged sentences. For example, the two sentences in Listing 5.3 would be tagged as follows.

```
String xmlPOS = lt.extractXMLPOS(text);
System.out.println(xmlPOS);

Generated Output:
<Noun>Time</Noun><White> </White><Verb>flies</Verb>
<White> </White>like<White> </White>an<White> </White>
<Noun>arrow</Noun><White></White>.<White> </White>This
<White> </White>is<White> </White>a<White> </White>
<Adjective>second</Adjective><White> </White>
<Noun>sentence</Noun><White></White>.<White></White>
```

One problem with HMM models is the large number of training examples needed to estimate the values of the cells of the tag-sequence and word-tag matrices. When the sizes of the matrices are huge, it will not be possible to build accurate estimates, unless the training set is proportionately large. Another criticism of HMM-based POS taggers is the limited dependency on just the previous tag alone. A higher order tagger that takes into consideration a wider neighborhood of tags would need estimates to populate an even larger number of cells in a 3D matrix. Rule-based tagging is a simpler solution to these problems.

A Lucene POS Analyzer

An application that uses the Lucene API can embed a POS tagger in a part of speech analyzer. Every `Token` has a `type` field that was earlier (see section 2.2.1) used to indicate a company name, an acronym, or a word . A POS analyzer uses this field to save the POS type for every token.

```
public class TestPOSAnalyzer {
  public static void main(String[] args) {
```

```
String sentence = "Time flies like a rocket.";
POSAnalyzer posAnalyzer = new POSAnalyzer();
Token[] tokens = IndexTools.tokensFromAnalysis(
  posAnalyzer, sentence);
for (Token token : tokens) {
  String tokenText = new String(
    token.termBuffer(), 0, token.termLength());
  System.out.println("Type: " + token.type() +
    " Token: " + tokenText);
}
}
}

Generated Output:
Type: noun Token: time
Type: verb Token: flies
Type: conjunction Token: like
Type: determiner Token: a
Type: noun Token: rocket
```

The output from this code is a list of tokens and associated part of speech types. The constructor of the POSAnalyzer reads the Brown part of speech tagger model and creates a HMM decoder. The Brown corpus parts of speech are translated into one of the standard eight parts of speech using a properties file. A default *noun* part of speech is assigned to any token that was not given a Brown corpus POS.

5.2.5 Rule-Based Tagging

The use of a tagger with rules is based on the observation that close to 90% of words can be correctly tagged with the most frequent tag for the word and a small set of rules are sufficient to correct the remaining 10%. A rule-based tagger is conceptually simpler than a HMM-based tagger. Rules can be added, modified, or deleted to improve the accuracy of the tagger. A relatively small set of rules is sufficient to obtain precision up to 90%. It takes many more rules to cover the large number of exceptions in the remaining 10% of words that are incorrectly tagged. The rules can model dependencies between tags and words that are extracted from a larger word neighborhood.

Training

We first need to train the tagger to generate the set of correction rules. The input to the training algorithm is a tagged corpus as before and a dictionary. The dictionary consists of words and the most frequent tag in the corpus. Every word is initially assigned the most frequent tag from the dictionary and evaluated against the tag in the training corpus. The output of the comparison is a set of words, wrongly assigned tags, and the correct tags.

A rule is constructed from the context of the wrongly tagged word and the triplet consisting of the word, wrong tag, and the correct tag. The context of a word is the text window ±n words centered on the current untagged word. An example of a rule is "change the tag from verb to noun, if the preceding word is a determiner". Consider the two sentences below with the word *run*.

- The *run* was too long.

- They *run* two miles a day.

The most popular tag for the word *run* is a verb. The verb tag is correct in the second sentence, but a noun tag should be assigned to the word *run* in the first sentence. The rule to transform a verb to a noun given a preceding determiner (*the*) will correct this error. The use of a rule can correct some errors, but may introduce new errors and therefore the inclusion of a rule in the set of correction rules is conditional on a reduction in the overall number of errors. The training and use of the tagger is shown in Figure 5.6.

Eric Brill [Brill] first proposed a POS tagger based on a set of correction rules and a dictionary. The dictionary is first constructed from the tagged corpus and an initial set of correction rules is generated. The number of mis-tagged words is computed and in the next iteration, the rule that corrects the highest number of mis-tagged words is added to the rule set. This process continues in a loop till there is no further reduction in the number of mis-tagged words. The dictionary and the final set of rules, together form the tagger. The set of transformations are applied in batch after all possible transformations have been identified.

Figure 5.6: Training and Tagging using a Rule-based Tagger

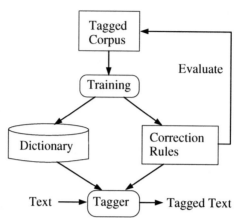

The rule-based tagger has problems similar to the HMM-based tagger with unknown words. Words that do not exist in the dictionary are hard to tag accurately. An initial guess is to simply assign the most popular tag (*nn* in the Brown corpus) to the unknown word. Other methods use word features such as the suffixes, prefixes, and capitalization to guess the most likely tag.

5.2.6 POS Tagging with Gate

Gate uses a POS tagger (based on the Brill rule-based Tagger) that was trained on a large corpus taken from the Wall Street Journal. The Penn Treebank tagset was used to tag words. The ruleset to tag words and the lexicon (dictionary) is included in the `data/gate/plugins/ANNIE/resources/heptag` directory. The lexicon contains a list of words and the most popular part of speech for each word. Three sample entries from the lexicon are shown in Table 5.5.

The most popular tag for the word *rebate* is a noun, but the same word can be used a verb as well. The lexicon differentiates between words that begin with an upper case or lower case letter. For example, the lower case word *works* is tagged *VBZ* while the word *Works* is tagged *NNP*. The size of the lexicon for all words is over 60K. By contrast, the ruleset is much smaller with about 750 rules. A sample set of three rules is shown in Table 5.6.

Table 5.5: Sample Entries from the Lexicon for a Rule-based Tagger

Word	Tag	Description
rebate	NN	noun, singular
stipulate	VB	verb, infinitive
ten	CD	adjective, cardinal number

Table 5.6: Sample Set of Rules for a Rule-based Tagger

Error Tag	Correct Tag	Type	Context
JJ	NN	nextwd	is
NN	VBG	prevwd	by
JJ	VBD	nexttag	DT

The first rule states that if the next word is the word *is* and the current word is tagged *JJ* (adjective), then correct the tag to *NN* (noun). The last rule states that if the next word is tagged *DT* (determiner) and the current tag is *JJ*, then correct the tag to *VBD*. The code to dump the list of tags for a given sentence using Gate is shown in Listing 5.5.

Listing 5.5: Extracting POS Tags from Text using Gate

```
1  public class ExtractGATEPos {
2    private static GateTools gt;
3    private String out = "";
4
5    public static void main(String[] args) {
6      gt = new GateTools();
7      text = "Time flies like an arrow.";
8      gt.setforPOSDump();
9      gt.getPOSDump(text);
10   }
11 }
```

The `GateTools` package contains methods to extract the parts of speech from text. The method `setforPOSDump` allocates the resources and methods needed to run the

POS tagger. The `getPOSDump` method returns a list of tokens, the associated tags, length of each token, and the token offsets. The output from the listing is shown in Table 5.7. The POS tags alone are shown for every token in the passed text chunk.

Table 5.7: List of POS Tags for a Sentence from LingPipe and Gate

Word	LingPipe	Gate
Time	NN	NNP
flies	VBZ	VBZ
like	CS	IN
an	AT	DT
arrow	NN	NN

The POS tags extracted with LingPipe, for the same sentence is shown in the Table 5.5 for comparison. Notice, that some of the tag codes are different but both POS taggers have identified the same nouns, verb, determiner, and conjunction. `GateTools` includes methods to dump the tagged text in an XML format.

Gate XML Tagged Sentences

The `setforPOS` and `getPOS` methods (line 8, listing 5.5) together are used to return a tagged sentence. A set of tokens from the passed sentence are tagged with noun, adjective, adverb, or verb annotations. These annotations make it easy for a subsequent function to identify the nouns or verbs in a sentence. The tagged sentence from the earlier example would look like -

```
<Noun>Time</Noun> <Verb>flies</Verb> like an
<Noun>arrow</Noun>.
```

The use of a gazetteer in Gate does allow for extending the set of words in the dictionary to include multi-word or collocations for some parts of speech. For example, some collocations such as "out of the question", "part of speech", or "hit the books" are simpler to handle as an unit instead of assigning tags to each of the component words. Take the following sentence - "Timing flies is out of the question", for which the tagged sentence is -

```
<Noun>Timing</Noun> <Verb>flies</Verb>
```

```
<Verb>is</Verb> <Adjective>out of the
question</Adjective>.
```

The number of such collocations in text is typically minimal and tagging these collocations as an unit, is of benefit to applications that require the meaning as well as the POS tag of tokens.

5.2.7 Markov Model vs Rule-based Taggers

The design of the Markov model-based tagger differs significantly from the rule-based tagger. A model-based tagger uses stochastic methods and probabilities to tag a sequence of words in a sentence. The success of this method depends on the availability of sufficient training data to accurately construct probability estimates for the model. The model-based tagger can achieve accuracies of over 96% given enough training data. A rule-based tagger also requires adequate training data to build the dictionary of words and POS tags and the set of correction rules. Conceptually, the rule-based tagger is easier to understand and examine. The set of rules can be extended as needed to correct as many as errors as possible.

We have looked at the use of the HMMs in POS tagging alone. A HMM can also be used at a higher level (sentences or lines of text). A line of email can be tagged as new text, part of the signature, Ascii art, or quoted replies. The lines of text in an article can be tagged as part of the bibliography to extract a list of citations in the article. The next section discusses an application to find phrases in text using a POS tagger.

5.3 Phrase Extraction

Phrase extraction can be defined as the automatic selection of important words that best describe the contents of a document. The selected phrases are extracted from the text of the document itself and are not generated. A short list of 5-15 noun phrases are typically used to capture the main topics in a news article. We use the term *phrase*, since most of the entries will consist of two or more words. Typically, the individual words of these phrases cannot be substituted with their synonyms to obtain the same meaning. For example, the word *judgment* in the phrase *"pass judgment*" cannot be replaced by the synonym *opinion* to form the phrase "*pass opinion*" which does not have the same meaning.

5.3.1 Applications

There are several reasons to automatically find key phrases. One of the most popular uses of phrases is to summarize a document with a list of phrases, that are most likely to represent the content of a document. Other uses of phrases include improving the precision of a search engine and identifying new terminology.

Web Page Summarization

The list of phrases for a Web page or an article is an extreme form of summarization. A summary based on the top n phrases is the most succinct abstract that can be generated. Such a summary will enable a reader to quickly decide if an article is of interest or not. The extracted phrases can also be shown highlighted in context within the text of the document. This would be comparable to a reader manually highlighting sections of text. The set of automatically extracted phrases can also be included in an index for an article or an e-book. The number of extracted phrases is usually much higher when the intent is to build an index from phrases. By contrast, the number of phrases needed to describe a typical Web page is much smaller.

Search Engine Optimization

The precision of a search engine can be increased if the key phrases for a document are saved in a Lucene `Field` with a higher boost (see Chapter 4). The phrases from a boosted document's `Field` that match query terms will be ranked higher than matches from other terms located elsewhere in the document. The *log* of a search engine is a valuable source to find the current popular query phrases. These query phrases can be used to suggest alternative queries. For example, the queries "*web mining*", "*text mining*", "*mining equipment*", or "*mining engineering*" are all alternate queries for a simple *mining* query. These queries refine the user's original query and are suggestions to narrow the query for higher precision. Query refinement is fairly important for a search engine, given the tendency of most users to supply a limited number of query terms.

The current search engine log contains a list of query terms that are currently popular and represents a snapshot of the users' interests. Recent topics that are gaining popularity can be found by comparing the frequency of phrases in the current log with the frequency of phrases in an older log. The phrases for new topics that are of growing interest will be seen more often in recent Web logs and are potential queries that can be optimized by a search engine administrator.

Lexicography

Lexicographers have the harder task of identifying words and phrases that should be included in a dictionary, in a much larger context. Computational lexicography can simplify the task by automatically analyzing large volumes of text for potential phrases that are absent in a dictionary. It is also simpler to automatically identify words that exist in the dictionary and are seen infrequently in text. Such words can be potentially removed from the dictionary.

Phrases in Books

Amazon.com includes a set of Statistically Improbable Phrases (SIPs) with the description of some books. SIPs are extracted from the text contents of a book and represent the phrases that occur more often in a particular book than other books. These phrases are typically indicative of the type of content and may be the smallest possible summary of a book. The reader can quickly scan the list of SIPs and decide if a detailed summary is worth reading. Matching hits from a search of all the SIPs may be more precise than a search of the titles alone. Along with SIPs, Amazon.com includes Capitalized Phrases (CAPs) that are often the names of people, places, or events. A search with a CAP such as *"Charles Darnay"* will return a list of hits for the book, *"A Tale of Two Cities"* with links to references in the book where the name is mentioned.

5.3.2 Finding Phrases

The simplest method to find phrases is to rank a list of all bigrams (two word phrases) found in the text in descending order of frequency. Consider a collection of 10K Reuters news articles that consists of about 1.9 million tokens. We build a bigram for every unique pair of tokens and count the number of bigram occurrences in Table 5.8.

Table 5.8: List of Sample Bigrams in Descending Order of Frequency

Rank	Bigram	Frequency
1	of the	9145
2	in the	8176
4	mln dlrs	5025
8	will be	2600
26	last year	1576
39	the dollar	1045
95	New York	588

A sample from the list of top ranking bigrams is shown in Table 5.8. Notice, the bigrams at the top of the list are mainly made up of function words such as *of* and *the*. These bigrams are not very useful since they do not indicate the contents of the text. We can filter this list to find more descriptive bigrams that can represent the content. A simple filter is to only keep the bigrams that consist of nouns, adjectives, adverbs, or prepositions. Some of the patterns for common phrases include two consecutive nouns, an adjective followed by a noun, or a preposition between two nouns. Another pattern would exclude all phrases that do not end with a noun. The use of upper case letters in a token is a strong hint that the token is more likely to be a noun. Alternatively, we could drop all bigrams that have one or both words that appear in a stop list. In a collection of 1.9 million tokens, we have sufficient data to get a reasonable list of bigrams using these simple methods.

5.3.3 Likelihood Ratio

The number of tokens in a typical Web page is several thousand or less and we can use a statistical method that works well with sparse data, to extract phrases. The main purpose of the statistical method is to verify that two words did not occur in sequence just by chance and are actually seen more often together than as separate words. The steps to extract such phrases are shown in Figure 5.7.

Figure 5.7: Phrase Extraction using Likelihood Ratios

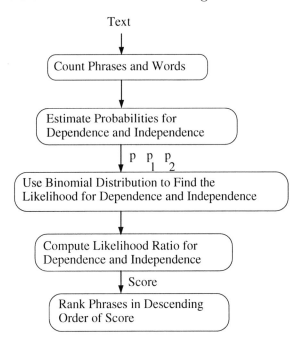

We begin by tokenizing the text and counting the number of bigrams and words. In this example, we use a collection of 10K Reuters news articles with a total of 1.9M tokens. Bigrams that contain tokens that are either too short or begin with a non-alphanumeric character are excluded from the list. Consider the two words *New* and *York*, that we would expect to be seen in a phrase. We can count the number of occurrences of the individual tokens *New* and *York* and the token sequence "*New York*" (see Table 5.9).

The counts for the term "¬*New York*" is the number of times the word *York* is preceded by any word except *New*. These counts are used in the following step to compute probability estimates that are used to compute the likelihood that the words *New* and *York* are dependent or independent. Assume the words of the phrase are independent, which means that the probability p of the word *York* being preceded by the word *New* is the same as the probability of being preceded by any word except *New* (see Table 5.10).

Table 5.9: Frequencies of the Words *New* and *York* and the Phrase "*New York*"

Term	Count	Value
New	c_1	1,044
York	c_2	597
New York	c_{12}	588
¬New	$N - c_1$	$1,900,000 - 1,044$
¬New York	$c_2 - c_{12}$	$597 - 588$
All	N	1,900,000

Table 5.10: Estimated Probabilities for Dependence and Independence Assumptions

Hypothesis	New York	¬New York
Independence	$p = \frac{c_2}{N}$	$p = \frac{c_2}{N}$
Dependence	$p_1 = \frac{c_{12}}{c_1}$	$p_2 = \frac{c_2 - c_{12}}{N - c_1}$

The dependence hypothesis assigns different probabilities p_1 and p_2 for the two phrases in Table 5.10. Notice the probability p_1 is much higher than the probability p which means that the two words are more likely to appear together in a phrase than as separate words under the dependence assumption. The difference in the probabilities alone is not sufficient to draw a conclusion. The likelihood of dependence between the two words is computed from a binomial distribution and the ratio of the dependence and independence likelihoods.

The binomial distribution is a popular statistical test to verify that a result did not occur by chance. For example, if we toss a fair coin 10 times, the binomial predicted probability of getting five heads is 0.246, seven heads is 0.117, and nine heads is 0.010. Notice, the probabilities for more extreme results is less given a fair coin. The binomial expression to compute the probability of getting five heads from ten tosses of a fair coin is *b(5; 10, 0.5)*. We use the binomial distribution since it adjusts for the variance of the frequencies of words. The binomial probability estimates from the probabilities computed in Table 5.10 are shown in Table 5.11.

The observation of a token is the equivalent of a coin toss in our example. The upper left cell estimates the probability of observing 588 occurrences of the preceding word *New* from 1044 occurrences of the word *York* with a probability p of 0.0003.

This is a very low value, since the value of p is low and the number of occurrences of *New* is more than half the number of occurrences of the word *York*. The probability value for the left cell in the second row under the dependence assumption is much higher, since the probability p is 0.5632, which more closely matches the proportion of observed word frequencies. (The probability values and frequencies in Table 5.11 are computed using the results and observations in Tables 5.9 and 5.10).

Table 5.11: Estimated Likelihoods for Dependence and Independence Assumptions

Hypothesis	New York	¬New York
Independence	b(588; 1044, 0.0003)	b (8; 1.9M − 1044, 0.0003)
Dependence	b(588; 1044, 0.5632)	b(8; 1.9M − 1044, 0.0000045)

The products of the binomial probabilities in each row gives the estimated likelihood for the dependence and independence assumptions. The binomial probability values are typically very small and the logs of the probabilities are used to compute the ratio of the independence likelihood to the dependence likelihood. The final result is multiplied by -2 to give a number that can be interpreted from statistical tables. For example, the final ratio value for the phrase "*New York*" is 578, which implies that *York* is far more likely to follow *New* than any other word. The code to run this algorithm is shown in Listing 5.6.

Listing 5.6: Extract Phrases from a Text File using Likelihood Ratios

```
1  public class ExtractPhrases {
2  ...
3    public static void main(String[] args) {
4      ExtractPhrases pt = new ExtractPhrases();
5      String textFile = DATA_DIR + FS + "textfiles" + FS
6        + "kodak_article.txt";
7      String text = Files.readFromFile(new File(textFile));
8      String[] phrases = pt.getPhrases(text, 10);
9      for (int i = 0; i < phrases.length; i++) {
10       System.out.println("Phrase " + i + ":" + phrases[i]);
11     }
12   }
13 }
```

The text passed to the phrase extractor contains a news article announcing a set of new products. The top three phrases out of the ten extracted phrases from the text are shown below.

```
Phrase 0:  information management systems
Phrase 1:  kodak divisions
Phrase 2:  optical disks
```

The algorithm uses only adjective and noun tokens to form phrases. The token and bigram frequencies are computed from the list of tokens and the ratio of the likelihood values for each bigram is assembled in a ranked list. A final step is added to combine any bigrams into trigrams. For example, the two bigrams *information management* and *management systems* have been combined into a single trigram. Several other phrase extraction methods are covered in detail in the textbook, *"Foundations of Statistical Natural Language Processing"* [Manning]. In the next section, we will look at a different method to find phrases using LingPipe.

5.3.4 Phrase Extraction using LingPipe

The extraction of phrases in LingPipe is based on a chi-squared statistic to verify that two words are more likely to be seen in a phrase. The chi-squared statistic is computed from a set of observation and expected values. We can construct a two by two observation table that contains the frequencies of four phrases. The observation table for the phrase *"New York"* is shown in Table 5.12 from the same collection of 10K Reuters news articles.

Table 5.12: Observation Values for the Words **New** and **York**

	$w_2 = $ **York**	$w_2 = \neg$**York**	Total
$w_1 = $ **New**	588	456	1,044
$w_1 = \neg$**New**	9	1,592,697	1,592,706
Total	597	1,593,153	1,593,750

Each cell of the table contains the frequency of occurrences for the row and column types. For example, the number of occurrences of a phrase where the first word was not *New* and the second word was *York* is 9. Similarly, the number of phrases where the first word was *New* and the second word was not *York* is 456. The observation table shows the distribution of the words *New* and *York* in the document collection. We can generate a set of expected values in a new Table 5.13 from the Total columns in Table 5.12.

Table 5.13: Expected Values for the Words **New** and **York**

	$w_2 = $ **York**	$w_2 = \neg$**York**	**Total**
$w_1 = $ **New**	0.4	1,043.6	1,044
$w_1 = \neg$**New**	596.6	1,592,109.4	1,592,706
Total	597	1,593,153	1,593,750

The expected value of a cell i, j in Table 5.13 is computed by multiplying the total of the row i with the total of the column j and dividing by the grand total $(1,593,750)$. The number of expected occurrences of the phrase "*New York*" is $597 \times \frac{1044}{1,593,750}$ or 0.4. Notice, this is a much smaller number than the value 588 for the same cell in Table 5.12. The expected value is calculated from the proportion of the frequency of a word w_1(using the marginal totals) and the marginal total for the word w_2. For example, we compute the distribution of the 1044 occurrences of the word *New* in proportion to the total number of observations. We would expect the preceding word *New* to occur just 0.4 times in 597 occurrences of the word *York*. We can now calculate the chi-square statistic as the sum of the squares of the differences between the observed and expected cells scaled by the value of the expected cell.

$$\chi^2 = \sum_{i,j} \frac{(O_{i,j} - E_{i,j})^2}{E_{i,j}} \tag{5.5}$$

The chi-squared value for our example from Tables 5.12 and 5.13 is 864,094 indicating that the words *New* and *York* are almost certainly seen in a phrase (based on confidence levels from a chi-squared Statistics table) . The code to run the phrase extractor is shown in Listing 5.7.

Listing 5.7: Extract and List Phrases from Text Files in a Directory

```
1  public class ExtractLingpipePhrases {
2     private static int NGRAM = 3;
3       // length of token ngrams
4     private static int NGRAM_REPORTING_LENGTH = 2;
```

```
5       // length of reported ngrams
6     private static int MIN_COUNT = 50;
7       // min. number of occurrences
8     private static int MAX_COUNT = 5000;
9       // max. number of occurrences
10
11    public static void main(String[] args)
12        throws IOException {
13      IndoEuropeanTokenizerFactory tokenizerFactory
14        = new IndoEuropeanTokenizerFactory();
15      // Train the model with directory files
16      TokenizedLM model = buildModel(tokenizerFactory,
17        NGRAM, new File(TESTING_DIR + FS + "txt"));
18      model.sequenceCounter().prune(3);
19      ScoredObject[] coll = model.collocations(
20        NGRAM_REPORTING_LENGTH, MIN_COUNT,MAX_COUNT);
21      for (int i = 0; i < coll.length; i++) {
22        String[] toks = (String[]) coll[i].getObject();
23        System.out.println("S: " + coll[i].score()
24          + " " + toks[0] + " " + toks[1]);
25        if ( (i == 99) || ((i+1) == coll.length) ) break;
26      }
27    }
28
29    private static TokenizedLM buildModel(
30      TokenizerFactory tokenizerFactory,
31      int ngram, File directory) throws IOException {
32      TokenizedLM model = new TokenizedLM(
33        tokenizerFactory, ngram);
34      for (String file: directory.list())
35        model.train(Files.readFromFile(
36          new File(directory, file)));
37      return model;
38    }
39  }
```

A tokenizer factory, ngram size, and source directory are passed to the `buildModel` (line 16) method that returns a tokenized language model. The tokenized model tracks the number of sequences of tokens of length three from the text in all files of the passed directory. The `collocations` (line 19) method returns a list of two word phrases sorted in descending order of score. The score for each phrase is computed from observed values as shown in Table 5.12. In Table 5.14, the scores using LingPipe and the likelihood ratio method for a sample set of phrases are shown.

Table 5.14: Scores for Five Sample Phrases using LingPipe and the Likelihood Ratio

Phrase	LingPipe Score	Likelihood Ratio
Wall Street	1,784,040	581.7
Hong Kong	1,703,633	579.2
New York	1,059,338	578.3
Kiichi Miyazawa	854,255	407.7
Middle East	549,652	330.8

The scores of the phrases for both methods are in the same order and should find similar phrases given the same text. However, LingPipe needs a substantial amount of text to build accurate observed and estimated frequencies of phrases, while the Likelihood Ratio method can work with smaller data sets. The performance of phrase extraction is faster in LingPipe and can be scaled to handle large corpora.

5.3.5 Current Phrases

Dynamic information sources on the Web like news sites and blogs change content periodically and it is difficult to manually track or evaluate new information. A small part of a Web page may change or the topic of popular queries on a search engine may have changed. The Yahoo! search engine includes a *buzz index* to show which queries are gaining or losing popularity.

A tokenized language model in LingPipe includes a method `newTerms`, that returns a list of terms and scores based on the currency and frequency of the terms in a new model. We build two models, one model from the past data and a new model from the current data. The phrases from both models are compared to identify the most frequent and new phrases. A *z-score* is assigned to each phrase in the new model.

The *z-score* quantifies the amount by which the number of occurrences of the phrases differs with the mean of the past model.

$$z = \frac{x - \mu}{\sigma} \qquad (5.6)$$

The difference between x the number of current occurrences and μ the mean number of past occurrences is scaled by the standard deviation σ. For example, consider the phrase that was seen 588 times in a collection of 1.9 million tokens in the old model. We can say the probability p of seeing the phrase in the old model is $\frac{588}{1,900,000}$ or 0.0003. Consider a smaller new model with 983,000 (n) tokens and 325 occurrences of the phrase "*New York*". The phrase should occur 295 times in the new model, if the probability of seeing the phrase is the same as the old model. The values 295 and 325 represent the mean and current numbers of occurrences of the phrase respectively.

The standard deviation is calculated using a formula for a binomial distribution. In a binomial distribution of tokens, every successive token from the list of tokens is either a success or a failure. A success represents the occurrence of the phrase "*New York*". The square root of the product of n, p, and $(1 - p)$ is the standard deviation. Now, we have all the values to compute the *z-score*.

$$z = \frac{329 - 295}{\sqrt{983,000 \times 0.0003 \times 0.9997}} = 1.75 \qquad (5.7)$$

When the *z-score* is positive, the number of occurrences in the new model is larger than the expected number of occurrences. A list of phrases in the new model sorted by the z-score is an ordered list of phrases based on *freshness* in the new model. The following code when added to the end of the main function in Listing 5.6 will return a list of `ScoredObjects` from which the tokens and scores can be extracted.

```
TokenizedLM newModel = buildModel(tokenizerFactory,
  NGRAM, new File(TESTING_DIR + FS + "txt2"));
newModel.sequenceCounter().prune(3);
ScoredObject[] newTerms = newModel.newTerms(
  NGRAM_REPORTING_LENGTH, MIN_COUNT, MAX_COUNT, model);
```

The new model is trained exactly like the old model from a directory containing a set of files with the current content. The `newTerms` method accepts the same list of parameters as the `collocations` method with the addition of a parameter to specify the old model. The *z-score* for a new phrase is computed using the total number of tokens in the new model, the number of occurrences in the new model, and the probability of a success in the old model. The ranked list of phrases is returned in descending order of score.

5.4 Entity Extraction

Entities in text are words or phrases that have been interpreted for applications that use semantics to make inferences about the text. An entity is typically a name of a person, place or organization. The extraction of entities is the categorization of small chunks of text into one of these name categories. The term named *entity recognition* is also used for the same task.

5.4.1 Applications

The use of entities extracted from text makes it a little simpler to build an application that use some semantics, without a complete parse of the text or significant knowledge. Some of the applications that use entities include Question & Answer systems, the organization of health records, academic literature search, and e-commerce applications.

Question & Answer Systems

We began this chapter with a discussion about questions that are difficult to answer with a search engine query alone. These questions cannot be answered purely by matching keywords from the question and text from documents alone. The answer to a question may require searching for entities and not keywords. For example, an intelligence analyst may be interested in finding the locations of all violent incidents over a period of six months in and around *Najaf, Iraq*. It would be difficult to generate a precise search engine query to find the answer to this question.

Database queries are far more precise than search engine queries, since the keywords used in the search must match the text for a particular attribute. We can generate a precise database query for the previous question with a date range, longitude and latitude range, and a list of keywords for violent incidents such as bombings or riots. Entity extraction is the task of populating such a database table with specific text chunks from the unstructured text of news articles (see Figure 5.8). In this example, we extract the list of places and timestamps from articles along with a list of keywords and synonyms. The list of places is further differentiated into longitude and latitude values. The list of keywords and synonyms are indexed using a search engine like Lucene.

Figure 5.8: Searching Text using Database Tables and a Search Engine

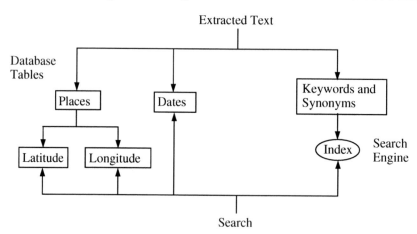

A question is translated into one or more database queries and a search engine query. The results from a search of the database tables will return a set of articles A, that mention places in and around *Najaf* within the specified date range. A search engine query will return a set of articles B, that include keywords such as bombings in the text. The intersection of the sets A and B should return the articles that are most likely to be relevant to the question.

Health Records

Examples of other applications include tracking health care records, academic papers, e-commerce Web pages, and e-recruitment Web pages. Massive amounts of information from patient records in hospitals are collected and stored. These records contain valuable notes written by doctors in unstructured text. It is hard to summarize and evaluate hospitals, without creating a database from extracted information that contains attributes, such as the severity of a case, a numeric code for the type of ailment, and dates.

Academic Papers

Academic research papers are typically published in a standard format with metadata in the header of the paper to describe the title, authors, email addresses, organizations, dates, and abstract. A database table of papers populated with this metadata would make it much easier to search a document collection. Unfortunately, the extracted text from papers does not contain demarcations to separate the different types of metadata and we need models to extract the title, authors, and other header fields.

Web Pages

The text from e-commerce Web pages contains a list of products, features, and the cost. Again, there is little indication of when the description of one product ends and another product begins. An initial solution would be to build a regular expression based on either a text or HTML pattern in the Web page. This solution is not reliable, since the format and content pattern of a Web page can change rendering the regular expression unusable. Manually generating a regular expression to handle all possible cases is also difficult and not easily verified. E-recruitment pages may similarly contain a group of job listings with descriptions for each job. The description may include a region, skill requirement, salary, job title, contact email, and a phone number or URL. In the following sections, we will look at two ways to extract this information using a model and a regular expression-like language.

5.4.2 Entity Extraction with Gate

Gate consists of an architecture and framework to build language processing applications. In this section, we will look at the use of just the entity extractor called A Nearly-New Information Extraction (ANNIE) system. The components that make up ANNIE are called *resources* (see Figure 5.9).

Figure 5.9: Extraction of Entities from Text using ANNIE

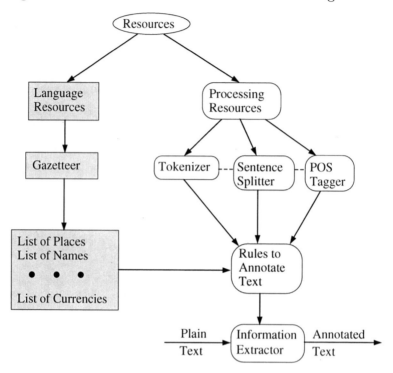

Gate uses resources for maintaining lexicon data (language resources) and common algorithms (processing resources). Both types of resources can be found in the data/ gate/plugins/ANNIE directory. The language resources contain a gazetteer that is made up of many lists and can be found in the resources/gazetteer sub-directory. Processing resources are the algorithms that we discussed earlier in this chapter to extract sentences and parts of speech. The core of ANNIE is found in the rules to extract entities. The list of rules is specified in files in the resources/NE sub-directory are used to annotate plain text.

Gazetteer

We begin with the set of lists in the `gazetteer` sub-directory. The file `lists.def` is the list of all lists in the directory. This file has one entry for each list file in the directory. An excerpt from the `lists.def` file is shown below.

```
city.lst:location:city
company.lst:organization:company
country.lst:location:country
day.lst:date:day
hour.lst:time:hour
jobtitles.lst:jobtitle
```

Each line of the file may contain two or three fields separated by colons. The first field is the name of the file containing the list of entities. The second field is the *major* entity type of the entries in the file and the third optional field is the *minor* entity type. For example, the file, `city.lst` is a flat file containing a list of cities from *Accra* to *Zurich*, one line per city. The major entity type for any city in this list is *location* and the minor type is *city*. The other entries in the `lists.def` file are files containing lists of other entity types such as the names of people, organizations, and countries. The lists are used in the set of rules to annotate entities. For example, the condition for a set of tokens to match one of the entries in the `city.lst` or `country.lst` files is

```
{Lookup.majorType == location}
```

Similarly, the condition to match one of the numeric descriptions for the hour is

```
{Lookup.minorType == hour}
```

All entries in the `hour.lst` file, such as one, three, or five have a minortype of *hour*. Notice, the location condition may match one or more tokens, with a preference for a longer match over a shorter match. For example, the longer text fragment "*St. Petersburg*" will be matched instead of just the single token *Petersburg*. The conditions are part of a pattern that must be matched for an annotation.

Rules for Extracting Entities

We use regular expressions to build patterns to match individual characters from text. Gate includes a Java Annotation Pattern Engine (JAPE) to build similar patterns with the use of more complex data structures. A pattern in JAPE may include

- The comparison of the part of speech of a token with a POS tag

- An annotation from a prior rule

- Comparison of a token's contents with a literal

- Comparison with one or more lists from a gazetteer

- A check for a numeric or word token

- A check for a token that begins with an upper case or lower case letter

- Regular expression quantifier metacharacters (?, *, +)

Some patterns are quite simple and unambiguous. For example, a pattern to match the text string "*University of South Carolina*" would be stated as

```
{Token.string == "University"}
{Token.string == "of"}
( {Token.category == NNP} )+
```

The `string` property and the `category` properties of the `Token` return the text contents and the part of speech respectively. One or more proper nouns may follow the string "*University of*" for a successful match. Note, the same pattern also matches "*University of* Texas" or "*University of* Illinois", but not "*University of California, Los Angeles*". A separate pattern to handle handle noun phrases with embedded commas will identify these special cases. An implicit space is assumed between the matches of individual tokens unless `SpaceTokens` are used in the input for the pattern. The + character is the regular expression quantifier for one or more occurrences of the condition.

A rule in JAPE is made up of a pattern and Java code that typically inserts an annotation enclosing the matching tokens. Each rule is saved in a list of rules called a phase. The entire entity extraction process consists of many such phases that are executed sequentially. An ordered list of phases can be found in the `main.jape` file

Figure 5.10: Entity Annotation using Phases and Rules

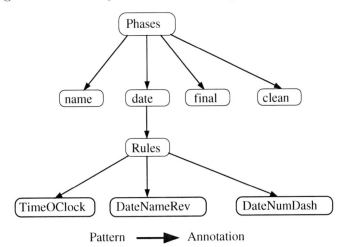

in the `resources/NE` sub-directory. A sample list of four phases from the entire list is shown in Figure 5.10.

A separate jape file must exist for every phase listed in the `main.jape` file. The `date.jape` file has a set of rules to construct annotations to identify text segments that may represent a date. The last phase is the `clean` phase that removes any temporary annotations created from the application of rules in earlier phases. Intermediate temporary annotations, that are removed in the cleanup phase are inserted when there is some ambiguity that cannot be resolved with a pattern.

A rule is made up of a pattern on the left hand side and an annotation on the right hand side. The `TimeOClock` rule is one of the rules in the date.jape file that identifies text segments which describe time using the o'clock short form (see Figure 5.11).

The pattern for the rule begins with a lookup of the `minorType` that will match tokens that contain a numeric description of any one of the numbers in the range 1-12 followed by the string "o'clock". All the text between the left and right parentheses are saved and associated with the annotation label `time`. The annotation type `Time`, is the annotation that will enclose the matching text segment. The annotation

Figure 5.11: The Components of a Rule to Match a Time Entity

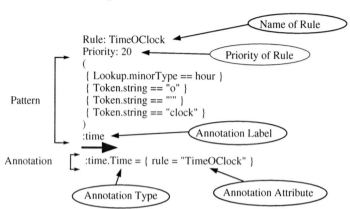

attribute will include values for properties such as the name of the matching rule and the kind of annotation.

In some cases, the conditions for more than one rule may be satisfied and it is not obvious which rule should be fired. There are several alternatives to handle multiple matching rules. One, all matching rules can be fired, which may result in multiple annotations for a single text segment. Two, only the first matching will be fired or finally, we can use a priority to decide which rule should be fired. The use of a priority value for a rule makes it easier for JAPE to select a rule from all possible matching rules. JAPE will select a rule at random when multiple matching rules exist with the same priority. We have used the priority of a rule to select the best matching rule.

In each phase, text is scanned from left to right for a match with each pattern of a rule in the phase. Any rule that is fired, consumes that text segment and is not considered in the remaining rules. All the matching text between the first opening parentheses and the corresponding closing parentheses will be annotated. The other rules in the `date.jape` file such as the `DateNameRev` and `DateNumDash`, tag dates that are specified in the form, *Wed, July 2nd, 2008* and *07-02-2008* respectively. We may need many rules to handle all possible cases of describing a date. For example, the date *August 15th, 2010* can be stated as *Sun, Aug 15th, 2010* or *Sunday, 15 / 08 / 2010*, or *Sun 15th August, 2010*.

The description of patterns in the list of rules can be simplified through the use of macros. For example, a four digit pattern for the year will be common in many date rules. Similarly, the pattern for the day of the week and the two digit patterns for the month and day can also be stated in macros.

```
Macro: ONE_DIGIT
 ({Token.kind == number, Token.length == "1"})
Macro: TWO_DIGIT
 ({Token.kind == number, Token.length == "2"})
Macro: FOUR_DIGIT
 ({Token.kind == number, Token.length == "4"})
Macro: DAY_MONTH_NUM
 (ONE_DIGIT | TWO_DIGIT)
Macro: DASH
 {Token.string == "-"}
Macro: YEAR
(
 {Lookup.majorType == year} |
   TWO_DIGIT | FOUR_DIGIT |
 {Token.string == "'"}
  (TWO_DIGIT)
)


Rule: DateNumDash
// 15-08-2010
(
 ( DAY_MONTH_NUM DASH DAY_MONTH_NUM DASH YEAR )
)
:date
-->
:date.TempDate = {rule = "DateNumDash"}
```

The first five macros are self-descriptive. The *YEAR* macro pattern matches text segments that consist of a year in the list of acceptable years from the gazetteer, a two digit or four digit number, or a two digit number preceded by a single quote ('98). The *DateNumDash* rule matches both the *mm-dd-yyyy* and *dd-mm-yyyy*

231

date formats. Note, this pattern will also match the rather odd *mm-dd-'YY* date as well. The code to extract person, date, and location entities is shown in Listing 5.8.

Listing 5.8: Entity Extraction using Gate

```
1  public class ExtractGATEEntities {
2    private static GateTools gt;
3
4    public static void main(String[] args) {
5      gt = new GateTools();
6      gt.setforIE();
7      text = "Mr. Smith went to Washington D.C. in 2010.";
8      String out = gt.getEntities(text);
9      System.out.println("Tagged Text: " + out);
10   }
11 }
```

The constructor of the `GateTools` (line 5) package loads resources that will be needed to startup Gate and sets the directory paths for the entity extractor. The `setforIE` (line 6) method creates a controller from a pipeline of allocated processing and language resources to run the entity extractor. Finally, the `getEntities` (line 8) method accepts the passed text string and uses the controller to tag entities and return the tagged string to the caller. The output from the execution of this class is

```
Tagged Text: <Person>Mr. Smith</Person> went to
<Location>Washington D.C.</Location> in <Date>2010</Date>.
```

The rule-based method in Gate is a flexible approach to find text segments that represent entities. New rules and entity types can be added as needed, provided the patterns to identify the entities are unambiguous and consistent in the text. The lists in the gazetteer can be customized for known entities and types, that will be used in the set of rules. In the next section, we will look at a model-based method to extract entities in LingPipe.

5.4.3 Entity Extraction with LingPipe

There are several ways to extract entities in LingPipe using `chunker`s. We will look at three different ways, including the simplest regular expression-based `chunker`, a dictionary-based `chunker`, and finally the model-based `chunker`. The process of extracting entities in all three methods is the same.

1. Create a `chunker`.

2. Use the `chunk` method of the `chunker` to get a `chunking`.

3. Fetch an `iterator` from the `chunkSet` of the `chunking`.

4. Loop through the set of `chunks` using the `iterator`.

   a) For each `chunk`, return the type and text fragment.

A `chunker` is first created and the `chunk` method of the `chunker` is used to get a `chunking`. The bulk of the processing time will be spent in step 2 to create the `chunking`. The loop scans an ordered list of `chunks` stored in a linked list. The type of `chunker` used is the only difference in the three methods described in this section.

Regular Expression-based Chunker

Consider the regular expression-based chunker. We can scan the passed text using a regular expression to tag matching text fragments. This method of extracting entities is quite similar to the regular expression tokenizer we saw in Chapter 2. A list of emails are extracted using a `chunker` in Listing 5.9.

Listing 5.9: Extract Entities using a Chunker

```
1  public class ExtractLingpipeChunk1 {
2    private final static String EMAIL_REGEX =
3      "\\b[\\w.%-]+@[\\w.-]+\\.[a-zA-Z]{2,4}\\b";
4    private final static String CHUNK_TYPE = "email";
5    private final static double CHUNK_SCORE = 0.0;
6
7    public static void main(String[] args) {
8      Chunker chunker = new RegExChunker(
9        EMAIL_REGEX, CHUNK_TYPE, CHUNK_SCORE);
10     String text = "Mr.Smith's email is smith@yahoo.com.";
11     Chunking chunking = chunker.chunk(text);
12     Iterator it = chunking.chunkSet().iterator();
13     while (it.hasNext()) {
14       Chunk chunk = (Chunk) it.next();
15       String tchunk = text.substring(
16         chunk.start(), chunk.end());
```

```
17           System.out.println(chunk.type() + ": " + tchunk);
18       }
19    }
20  }
```

A RegExChunker (line 8) is first created using an email regular expression, a chunk type, and a chunk score. The passed regular expression is converted to a Java pattern and all matching chunks will be assigned the chunk type and score assigned in the RegExChunker constructor. The chunk (line 11) method populates a linked list of Chunks that match the given Pattern in the text string.

The collection of chunks is scanned using an Iterator from the chunk linked list. Each Chunk has a start index, end index, a score, and a type. The output from this class will be the single email address in the text string.

Dictionary-based Chunker

The dictionary-based chunker uses a dictionary to identify entities in a text string. A dictionary is made up of a list of DictionaryEntrys, each of which consists of a phrase, a category, and a score. The chunker is created from the dictionary that is populated one entry at a time.

```
1  MapDictionary<String> dictionary =
2    new MapDictionary<String>();
3  dictionary.addEntry(
4    new DictionaryEntry<String>(
5      "Smith", "PERSON", 1.0) );
6  dictionary.addEntry(
7    new DictionaryEntry<String>(
8      "Washington", "LOCATION", 1.0));
9  dictionary.addEntry(
10   new DictionaryEntry<String>(
11     "Ford", "PERSON", 1.0) );
12 dictionary.addEntry(
13   new DictionaryEntry<String>(
14     "Ford Motor Co.", "AUTO", 3.0));
15 boolean overlap = false;
16 boolean caseSensitive = false;
17 ExactDictionaryChunker chunker =
18   new ExactDictionaryChunker(dictionary,
19     IndoEuropeanTokenizerFactory.FACTORY,
```

20   `overlap , caseSensitive ) ;`

The dictionary in our example is made up of just four entries, but a real world dictionary would include hundreds or thousands of entries. The constructor of the chunker uses the dictionary, a tokenizer factory and two flags. The dictionary can be loaded from a serialized version stored in a file and need not be repeatedly created entry by entry. The `IndoEuropeanTokenizer` creates tokens from the text that are used to lookup the dictionary for matching entries. The dictionary can handle multi-token entries such as the "*Ford Motor Co.*". The last two flags in the constructor (lines 18-20) are options for case sensitive and overlapping matches. A token may be used in more than one category in overlapping matches. For example, the single token *Ford* will match the `PERSON` category, in addition to an existing match in the `AUTO` category.

When a phrase is assigned to two or more categories, the `chunker` will first prefer a longer chunk over a shorter chunk and selects the category with the higher score, when the phrase span is identical. The `chunker` does not use context to identify the more likely category. A dictionary is useful when the set of entities that are to be identified are known, much like the gazetteer that we used earlier to find entities. In LingPipe, all entries are saved in a single dictionary, unlike the gazetteer that was made up of many different lists. The `ApproxDictionaryChunker` identifies chunks based on a fuzzy match that is evaluated using an edit distance computation (see section 4.8.1). The approximate dictionary is built with individual entries similar to the exact dictionary and a `WeightedEditDistance` instance returns the degree of similarity between a chunk and a dictionary entry.

Model-based Chunker

A model-based chunker is a more complex chunker than the previous two chunkers. The code to use this chunker is identical to the earlier chunkers. The first line of the `main` function in Listing 5.8 is replaced with the following statement to create the chunker.

```
Chunker chunker = (Chunker)
AbstractExternalizable . readObject (
  new File(ENTITY_MODEL ) ) ;
```

The best `chunking` is returned from a pre-compiled `chunker` that was read from the `ENTITY_MODEL` file. This file was created from a HMM model trained on a tagged data set. The training data set contains a large number of tagged sentences, each one of which contains tagged tokens. For example, consider the sentence "Mr. Smith goes to Washington." shown in Table 5.15.

Table 5.15: List of Tokens and Associated Entity Tags for a Sentence

Token	Tag
Mr	B_PERSON
.	M_PERSON
Smith	E_PERSON
goes	BB_O_PERSON
to	EE_O_LOCATION
Washington	W_LOCATION
.	WW_O_OOS

Every tag is made up of a prefix and suffix that indicates the tag of the current, preceding, or following token. The prefixes $B\_$, $M\_$, and $E\_$ represent the beginning, middle, and end tags respectively of a multi-token entity. The BB_O prefix means that the previous token was part of an entity, but the current token is not part of an entity and the EE_O prefix means that previous and current tokens are not part of an entity, but the following token does belong to an entity. The $W\_$ prefix indicates that the current token is a single token of the given entity type. Finally, the WW_O prefix means the current token is not part of an entity, the previous token did belong to an entity, and the tag of the following token is included in the suffix. The OOS tag is a tag added to represent the out-of-sentence position. The W_OOS tag is a dummy tag inserted at the beginning and ending of a sentence. The names of tags are arbitrary and different training data sets can use different tag sets.

The three suffixes in the collection of tags are *PERSON*, *ORGANIZATION*, and *LOCATION*. A total of 25 different tags are used in the entire training data set. This data set was made available for the Message Understanding Conferences held during the 90s, sponsored by the Defense Advanced Research Projects Agency (DARPA). This training data set has properties similar to the Brown corpus we saw earlier, that assigned a POS tag to every token. We can build a HMM model from the training data set to tag tokens with entity tags. The training model keeps track of the number of transitions from one tag to another and the number of occurrences of a word given a tag. Consider the sentence "Mr. Smith goes to Washington." that is made up of seven tokens (see Figure 5.12). We can set entity tags for the given sentence from a table of seven rows and twenty five columns. The Figure 5.12 shows just four of the twenty five columns for brevity, where each column represents an entity tag.

Figure 5.12: Table of Tokens and Entity Tags Generated from a HMM Model

Token	B_O_PERSON	M_O_PERSON	E_O_PERSON	• • •	W_O_LOCATION
Mr	✗				
.		✗			
Smith			✗		
goes					
to					
Washington					✗
.					

The values for the first row are computed from the product of the probability of starting in a column x and the probability of the word *Mr* from the language model for the entity tag x. The remaining cells of the table in Figure 5.12, with the exception of the last row, are calculated from the product of transition probabilities from entity tag x to entity tag y and the probability of the token from the language model for the given entity tag. The last row in the table is product of the probability of ending with an entity tag x and the probability of a period character from the language model for x.

The set of tags for the seven tokens in the sentence are extracted from the table starting with the last token and working backwards to the first token. At each token, we compute the most likely entity tag using the table of probabilities in Figure 5.12. The tags output from this algorithm cannot be used directly and the `HmmChunker` class handles the decoding of these tags to the general PERSON, LOCATION, and ORGANIZATION tags that are returned in the chunks.

5.4.4 Evaluation

We can evaluate a model-based entity extractor since training data is necessary to build the model. Typically, a small part ($> 10\%$) of the training data (see section 5.2.3) is set aside to evaluate the entity extractor. The results of the evaluation are compared with the tags in testing data to generate precision estimates of the extractor. The accuracy of the extractor is based on the number of entities and non-entities correctly identified out of all possible tokens. An error is one or more tokens wrongly identified as an entity or the absence of an entity tag for a token that should have been tagged as an entity. In the absence of training data, it is difficult to evaluate an entity extractor.

The methods used in Gate and LingPipe for entity extraction are analogous to the methods to used for part of speech tagging. Earlier, we used the Brown corpus to create a POS tagging model. There are several other larger POS tagged corpora for English that are sufficient for most tasks. Entity extraction can be more specific than what we have seen so far. For example, we may need to extract timestamps, currency amounts, dimensions, or addresses. In a model-based algorithm, we would need to train a model with a sufficient volume of training data to estimate probabilities for all types of tags. This can be cumbersome process, but is necessary for the accuracy of the model-based method.

The rule-based method transfers the burden of creating training data to the generation of a set of rules that are sufficient to handle all types of cases. A rule-based system does appear to offer flexibility in the addition of new rules and new entity types to customize and improve the precision of the extractor. For example, we can add a new rule to ensure that an entity that should be extracted from the text is correctly tagged based on an observed pattern. The success of the rule-based system depends on correctly identifying all such patterns that are sufficient to extract all possible entities in a given text.

5.4.5 Entity Extraction Errors

Entity extraction continues to be a harder problem than POS tagging. One reason is that entities can span multiple tokens. For example, the use of the conjunction and in "`Cable and Wireless`" should not be treated as a separator for two entities, `Cable` and `Wireless`, while the text fragment "*IBM and Google*" should generate two separate entities. Other complex entity structures include prepositions such as *of* and *for*. The phrase "*City University of New York*" is a single entity, while "*Macy's of New York*" should return two separate entities.

A person entity such as "*Professor Calculus*" may be initially expressed with the honorific *Professor* at the beginning of an article. Later mentions of the same entity may not use the honorific, making it harder for an entity extractor to disambiguate the use of the word *Calculus*. The first occurrence of such entities is usually a formal introduction and includes the honorific and the following mentions should be collapsed into a single class. The root of the possessive form can also be sometimes collapsed into a single form. For example, the use of *Ford* and *Ford's* in a single article probably refers to the same entity and while the trailing *s* of *Macy's* should not be stripped.

Capitalized words are more likely to represent entities, but often may not represent a person, place, or organization. They may be found in the title of an article or represent a financial, medical, or legal term that is not included in the entity extractor's lexicon. An extractor can also be misled into interpreting entities such as "*General Electric*" or "*St. Luke's Hospital*" as *PERSON* entities based on the use of the honorific. Other similar errors include creating *PLACE* entities for "*New York Times*" and the "*Chicago Board of Trade*". Many of these errors can be resolved by using a dictionary or gazetteer to handle all known entities. Note, we do not resolve multiple mentions of the same person (co-reference) such as "John Smith", "J. Smith", or "John S." to a single entity.

5.5 Summary

This chapter has covered the extraction of sentences, parts of speech, phrases, and entities. In each case, we have looked at two ways of doing the same task. A paper by Mikheev in the Computational Linguistics journal [Mikheev] describes the disambiguation of sentence boundaries and capitalized words in more detail. Jeff Reynar's PhD thesis from the University of Pennsylvania published in 1998, explains detection of topic boundaries in text. By itself, entity extractors or POS taggers have little value. Typically, these tools are embedded in a larger application such as a specialized search engine or a Q&A system. The use of these tools is the first step to add semantic information to text that is not included in the metadata. The precision of an entity extractor is highly dependent on training data or lists of specified entities. A POS tagger may have high precision, provided the text is not very specialized. The extraction methods used in Gate and LingPipe are quite dissimilar and performance is also varied. In general, LingPipe methods are faster than Gate methods. No attempt has been made to formally compare the two software tools, but hopefully we have illustrated the use of extraction methods in both tools.

Gate includes many other features to build text applications not described in this chapter; to explore its full capabilities, the official documentation is available at `http://gate.ac.uk/documentation.html`. In the following chapters, we will look at two methods of organizing information, text categorization and clustering.

6 Organizing Text: Clustering

Building groups is one of the fundamental ways of organizing a collection of items. We learn to group everyday items by their attributes, such as color, size, or shape, at an early age. And generally speaking, it is easier to study smaller groups of items than a much longer list of items. Clustering, or the organization of items into smaller groups, has been successfully applied in many subjects including astronomy (identifying stars and galaxies), medicine (categorizing and treating similar symptoms and diseases), and market research (predicting the behavior of consumers with similar attributes). For example, retailers build customer groups based on the similarity of purchases. Customers from the same age or income groups tend to have similar buying patterns and customized marketing tailored to a group's interests is more likely to succeed than a broad advertising campaign.

The results from a search engine can also be clustered into groups based on shared terms (see `http://www.clusty.com`). The list of hits for the query *"Iraq War"* may be grouped into clusters representing pages that oppose the Iraq War, discuss the cost of the Iraq War, and cover the involvement of Iran in the Iraq War. A small set of 10-20 such clusters is easier to assimilate than a larger collection of several hundred Web pages. In this chapter, we consider clustering a collection of documents. Multiple similarity measures, link types, and clustering algorithms are covered. An agglomerative clustering using LingPipe is implemented and evaluated.

6.1 Applications

At the lowest level, we can cluster the individual words or tokens in a document. We can identify all words that share the same neighboring left and right tokens. The words that share the same neighbor possibly belong to the same group (part of speech or entity). For example, all words that are preceded by the words *in* or *on*, are usually followed by an article or a noun phrase. A cluster analysis of words may also identify semantic families of words such as time or place .

In the previous chapter, we saw that the same entity, *Mr. Smith* may be referred to in more than one way within the same document and a collection of documents. Clusters of the documents may reveal which documents refer to the same person entity. Sometimes, the same name *John Smith* in multiple documents refers to different people and the only way to differentiate between identical mentions of the name is to relate the words in context. Clusters of the context words may separate the documents into groups that refer to the same individual who shares a common name.

Clustering can also speed up the time to browse a list of documents. Typically, after reading a few sentences from a document, it can be judged as relevant or not. The reader's time is saved by extracting the most appropriate sentences that describe the content of the document. These extracted sentences represent a summary of the document for the purposes of just identifying the type of content. Sentences can be extracted (see Chapter 5) from a document and clustered into groups of sentences. The primary summary sentence from each of the top n clusters is a potential summary of the document. All sentences that belong to a group share a common topic and therefore one sentence from the group should suffice to briefly describe the topic.

Some Web search engines [Cluster] return the list of hits for a query in the form of clusters. A query token such as *Jaguar* has more than one meaning. It could mean an automobile, an animal, the name of an operating system, or a football team. Clusters of the hits for the token should reveal the different meanings making it easier for the searcher to identify the intended meaning. Similarly, the query "*text mining*" has clusters for conferences, solutions from vendors, and related data mining Web pages.

News organizations publish a stream of articles that are broadly categorized under terms such as *Business*, *Sports*, or *Health*. These individual terms are insufficient to identify the popular sub-topics of recent articles published. A review of the clusters of the *Business* articles for a day quickly show which particular events captured the interest of the financial news media. Multiple news organizations tend to cover the same events; there is often considerable overlap between articles in a topically-oriented cluster. A reader can choose to read just one article from a cluster and save the time needed to browse articles with similar content. A quick glance of the list of cluster titles is also sufficient to learn the main events mentioned in the news.

6.2 Creating Clusters

Clustering data is a technique to analyze a large data set in a simpler and more convenient format. It has been commonly used with a visual to examine and understand data. Researchers have conceived of many creative ways to display clusters within a data set that include the use of faces, scatter plots, and star charts. Clustering is distinguished from text categorization (see Chapter 7) that uses prior classifications to populate pre-defined categories. The terms *unsupervised learning* and *supervised learning* are used to describe clustering and text categorization respectively. The primary difference is the absence of any training examples and a set of categories in unsupervised learning. We will look at methods to categorize documents in the next chapter and the remainder of this chapter will cover clustering alone.

We can use simple methods to manually identify clusters when the number of dimensions in a data set is limited. Consider the plot in Figure 6.1 of 24 stars of different luminosities shown in their x, y position. Each star has three dimensions - a luminosity, a x position, and a y position.

A symbol based on the luminosity of a star is shown at its x, y position. From the plot, we can check if stars with the same luminosity are located close together, far apart, or are uniformly distributed. We have manually created three clusters using the x, y location of stars. Notice, that clusters are not obvious and it is easy to think of a new set of clusters that may appear to be more appropriate. There are also a handful of stars that do not belong to any clusters.

This example illustrates some of the problems with clustering. In many cases, it is difficult to compute the perfect cluster arrangement since the number of possibilities is very large. For example, consider a collection of 50 objects from which we create five groups of objects. There are 8.9×10^{34} ways of selecting five groups from 50 objects. In general, the number of groups examined is a much smaller percentage of the total number of possibilities and it is not difficult to find a reasonably good cluster arrangement without exhaustively searching all possibilities. Clustering algorithms differ in their methods and the time to find a near optimal solution from the multitude of solutions.

Figure 6.1: Plot of the Positions of 24 Stars of Different Luminosities

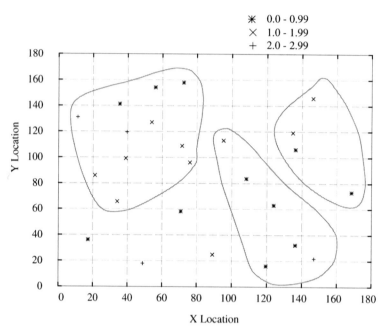

Many visual clustering algorithms (scatter plots, Chernoff faces, Andrews plots, star plots, and bubble plots) were designed for multivariate data sets with fewer than ten dimensions (a dimension is an attribute that has a value in every object.) For example in Figure 6.1, a star has three attributes or dimensions. In a vector representation of a document, each unique word is considered to be a dimension. A news article may have one hundred or more unique words and it is very difficult to conceive of visual methods that will show clusters in this high dimensional space. Instead, we simplify the problem and use a *distance* measure that compares all dimensions at once. We lose some information by not comparing all possible combinations of dimensions to identify the ideal set of dimensions that separate documents into clusters, but gain the ability to make sense of grouped documents. The latent semantic indexing method (see Section 3.3.1) uses the singular value decomposition method to find a set of orthogonal dimensions to represent documents. We can cluster documents using modified representations of documents that have been projected on the set of orthogonal dimensions alone. Here, we use a simple document representation based on the frequency of word occurrences in a document to build clusters.

6.2.1 Clustering Documents

The input to our clustering process is a list of n documents and the output is a list of k clusters (see Figure 6.2). In general, n should be much larger than k. The minimum and maximum limits for the number of clusters is 1 and n respectively. Both a single cluster of all n documents and n clusters (with one document each) are not useful. The ideal number of clusters is some number k between 1 and n, that is sufficient to identify all possible groups and at the same time, does not sub-divide any logical group. For example, we can group the 24 stars in Figure 6.1 into three or more clusters. The optimal number of clusters is not known before we cluster the items and most algorithms search for a number k, such that each group is cohesive and does not include items that should belong in a different cluster. We may need to try several values of k to find a near optimal set of clusters for a particular application.

Figure 6.2: Building Clusters from a List of Documents

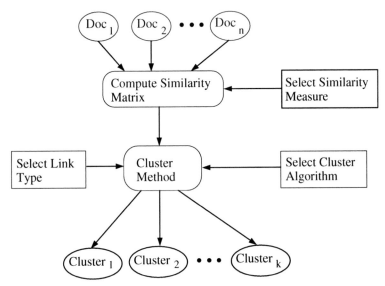

There are a few choices that need to be made, before we can construct clusters from documents. We have several similarity measures to choose from, when comparing one document with another. The similarity values returned by these measures are not identical and the results of the clustering algorithm are dependent on the type of similarity measure selected. A similarity matrix contains the similarity computations of all possible unique pairs of documents from the list of n documents. Some cluster methods such as *K-Means* do not compute every possible pair of inter-document similarity. A cluster method can also assign a document to more than one cluster.

The cluster link type dictates the quality of the cluster, a high quality cluster will require all documents in a cluster to be highly similar to each other. A lower quality cluster may include documents that are similar to just one other document in the cluster. There are multiple clustering algorithms that we can use to build a set of clusters from the similarity matrix. Later in this chapter, we will compare some of the similarity measures, cluster link types, and clustering algorithms. We have also made the assumption that a document will belong to exactly one cluster, it is also possible to assign a document to more than one cluster, when there is sufficient similarity between a document and the individual clusters. For simplicity, we consider document memberships in one cluster alone.

6.2.2 Similarity Measures

The first step in building clusters is to compare all unique pairs of documents. There are many ways of comparing documents and we will look at a few of them. In most cases, the comparison between documents is not performed using the raw text itself, instead we compare a representative of a document with the representative of another document.

Document Representation

At first, the representation of a document as an unordered list of words may not seem appropriate. This representation is also called a "*bag-of-words*", since the list of word positions are not maintained. There is no indication of punctuation to separate chunks of text and the meaning of the text cannot be extracted from just a list of words. The use of a dimension for each unique word in the text is based on the assumption that words occur independently and that there are no relationships between words. In reality, this is not true. The benefits of using more complex models such as letter and token ngrams to include the relationships that are missing in the bag-of-words representation to find or compare documents has been significant.

We will use a simple list of words (a vector) with optional weights for each word as the representation of a document in the rest of this chapter. The direction and magnitude of the vector are the dimension and weight of the word respectively. A binary vector will only indicate if words are present or not in the document. The optional weight for each word denotes the importance of the word in the document. In general, a term that occurs often in a document is given a higher weight than a term that occurs infrequently.

In Chapter 3, we saw that most frequent words in a document tend to be function words such as *and, the,* and *of* that do not reveal the contents of the document. These stop words should not be included in a document representative since most documents will contain these words. A direct comparison of representatives without filtering stop words will give a misleading higher degree of similarity in all inter-document comparisons. Removing these *noisy* words does improve the accuracy of the similarity computations.

Bayesian methods to tag tokens and classify documents are based on the assumption of the independence of features. These methods have become quite popular because of their relative simplicity and the precision of the results. We can consider each unique word in a document to represent a feature of the document and the set of features for a document is a reasonable representation for the purposes of comparing documents to build clusters.

Distances between Documents

Consider two documents with just two words that can be shown in a 2D plot (see Figure 6.3). The document points i and j are shown based on the number of occurrences of the terms represented by the x and y dimensions. The distance c between any two points i and j in a two dimensional Cartesian coordinate system is the square root of the sum of the squares of the differences between their x and y locations.

$$\sqrt{(x_i - x_j)^2 + (y_i - y_j)^2} \tag{6.1}$$

This formula is also called the Euclidean distance between the two points i and j and is derived from the Pythagorean theorem. Other distance formulas include the Manhattan or City-Block distance that represents the distance in terms of the absolute distance to travel from point i to point j along the lines of the grid.

$$|x_i - x_j| + |y_i - y_j| \tag{6.2}$$

For example, the Manhattan and Euclidean distances between the points i and j in Figure 6.2 are the 3 and $\sqrt{5}$ respectively. The values of the distance measures do not matter in a clustering method, but will affect the number and size of clusters for a given distance threshold. These same formulas can be conveniently extended to handle n dimensions, making it amenable to compare high dimensional document vectors. We will look at three different similarity measures starting with the most popular *Cosine* similarity measure followed by the *Jaccard* and *Dice* similarity measures. All three measures use similar pair-wise methods to measure the degree of overlap and differ in how the overlap is scaled.

The similarity measures that we will look at are symmetrical. The similarity $sim(i, j)$ between documents i and j is the same as $sim(j, i)$. An asymmetric similarity measure may have value in finding documents that are part of another document to build a cluster hierarchy. In most cases, the similarity computations are also normalized to a value in the range 0 to 1 or -1 to $+1$. In the former case, we can easily compute the dissimilarity or distance between documents as $1 - sim(i, j)$. The latter case is equivalent to the correlation between two documents. A value of $+1$ means that the documents i and j are positively correlated, when any word x occurs in document i, it also occurs in document j. A negative correlation means that many words occurring in document i are not found in document j. The absence of some words in both documents can also be a source of similarity. In general, we only consider the presence of words when computing the similarity between documents. The absence of words is typically a weaker signal of document similarity.

Note, a similarity measure assigns a *higher* value and a distance measure assigns a *lower* value, when documents are more similar. We can convert between normalized similarity and distance values by simply computing the absolute difference with 1.0. Unnormalized or raw values are harder to convert and it is preferable to create a similarity matrix with normalized similarities. In our clustering implementation using LingPipe, the two similarity measures, *Jaccard* and *Cosine* are normalized, while the *Edit Distance* measure is not.

Cosine Similarity

Consider a plot of two documents shown in Figure 6.3. The lines a and b from the origin to the points i and j that represent the pair of documents are vectors separated by the angle θ. The documents i and j have two and four word occurrences in the x dimension; three and two word occurrences in the y dimension respectively.

Figure 6.3: Distance between Two Points and the Angle between Two Vectors

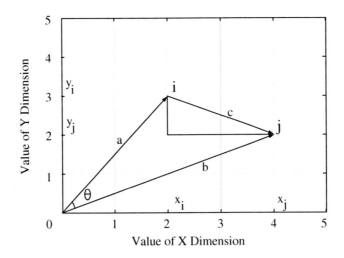

The three points i, j, and the origin form a triangle with the three sides a, b, and c. The law of cosines allows us to measure the angle θ between the two sides a and b of the triangle.

$$cos(\theta) = \frac{a^2 + b^2 - c^2}{2ab} \tag{6.3}$$

The values in the numerator and denominator can be replaced with expansions using the Pythagoras theorem and simplified to

$$cos(\theta) = \frac{x_i x_j + y_i y_j}{\sqrt{x_i^2 + y_i^2} \times \sqrt{x_j^2 + y_j^2}} \tag{6.4}$$

The denominator is the product of the lengths a and b of the two vectors. The numerator is the product of the values of the vectors in the same dimensions. This expression is commonly called the *cosine similarity* between two vectors. Notice, if we compute the similarity of a document with itself, we get a value of 1, which is the same as the cosine of a zero degree angle. The value of the cosine similarity increases as the angle between the two vectors becomes smaller to a maximum of one. Vectors that are similar to each other will have smaller angles than dissimilar vectors.

The cosine similarity is a very popular measure to compare two documents because it can be easily extended from the two dimensions in Figure 6.3 to n dimensions and the similarity values are always normalized in a range from zero to one. The computation of the similarity between documents with a hundred or more dimensions is quite feasible and represents the cosine of the angle between two large multi-dimensional vectors.

Jaccard and Dice Similarity

Consider the list of words (*time, flies, like, an, arrow*) from document i as a set A and the list of words (*how, time, flies*) from document j as the set B. The Jaccard similarity is defined as the ratio of the size of the intersection to the union of the sets A and B. The equation to compute the Jaccard Similarity is

$$Jaccard(A, B) = \frac{|A \cap B|}{|A \cup B|} \tag{6.5}$$

The numerator is similar to the numerator to compute the cosine similarity except that the frequencies are discarded and merely the presence or absence of terms is counted. Two words, *time* and *flies* are common in both sets. The union of the sets is the sum of the number of terms (5 and 3) from each set and the difference of the number of terms (2) in the intersection.

$$Jaccard(i, j) = \frac{2}{5 + 3 - 2} \tag{6.6}$$

The Dice coefficient is related to the Jaccard coefficient and uses the same numerator with twice the weight for instances where the sets share common terms. The denominator is the sum of the number of terms in each set.

$$Dice(A, B) = \frac{2|A \cap B|}{|A| + |B|}$$

$$Dice(i, j) = \frac{2(2)}{5 + 3} \tag{6.7}$$

The three similarity coefficients all evaluate the degree of overlap, but differ in how the value of overlap is scaled. In the next section, we will compare the similarity coefficient values for the same sets of documents.

Edit Distance

The last similarity measure is the edit distance. This measure computes the number of character insertions, deletions, and substitutions to convert one string to another (see Section 4.4.2). The text from both documents are converted to character sequences and passed to the `editDistance` method of the `EditDistance` class in LingPipe. The returned integer value is number of character operations needed to convert the first string to the second string. The computation is symmetric and therefore the order of the string parameters is not important.

The values returned from the edit distance calculation are the number of integer operations needed for the conversion and will typically be much larger than the values computed using the Jaccard, Cosine, or Dice similarity measures. For example, the edit distance between a 4K and a 1K character string may be 3000 or greater. The values from these distance calculations are important when deciding a threshold value for cluster membership. The edit distance measure is more suitable for clustering small text strings such as tokens or phrases. For example, you could cluster addresses, named entities or titles to find near duplicates.

6.2.3 Comparison of Similarity Measures

The choice of a similarity measure can affect the set of clusters generated from the similarity matrix and therefore it is important to carefully select the similarity coefficient based on the application. Similarity computations using the Jaccard measure are generally less than identical computations with the Cosine measure. The time required for the Cosine similarity computation is typically more than any of the other similarity measures. In a large document collection, the time to compute the similarity matrix may dominate the overall time to build clusters.

In this example, we use a simple binary count to compare two similarity coefficients. A word is either present or absent in a document and we do not assign any weight to the word based on the number of occurrences in the document. Consider a set of ten words that occur in two documents i and j shown in Table 6.1.

Table 6.1: Distribution of Ten Words in Documents i and j

	w_1	w_2	w_3	w_4	w_5	w_6	w_7	w_8	w_9	w_{10}
Document i	0	0	0	0	1	1	0	0	1	0
Document j	1	0	0	0	1	0	0	1	1	0

A 1 indicates the presence and 0 the absence of a word in a document. We can construct a two by two table to compute the number of overlapping words in documents i and j. The upper left cell in Table 6.2 is the number of words a, that are present in both documents (w_5 and w_9). The upper right cell is the number of words b, that are present in document i, but absent in document j (w_6).

Table 6.2: Two by Two Table Showing Presence and Absence of Words in Documents

		Document j		
		1	0	Total
Document i	1	$a(2)$	$b(1)$	3
	0	$c(2)$	$d(5)$	7
	Total	4	6	10

The Jaccard similarity between documents i and j is $\frac{a}{a+b+c}$ or 0.40, the Dice similarity is $\frac{2a}{((a+b)+(a+c))}$ or 0.57, and the cosine similarity is $\frac{a}{\sqrt{a+b}\times\sqrt{a+c}}$ or 0.58. The cosine similarity is scaled by a smaller value, the square root of the products of the lengths of the documents, and is therefore larger than the Jaccard similarity. Consider another example with documents that are made up of either 100 or 20 words. A comparison between documents of the same size and differing sizes is a *comparable* and *uneven* evaluation respectively. The degree of overlap varies from a minimum (20%) to a maximum (80%) with an average (50%) between the two limits (see Figure 6.4). Both similarity measures generate values that are identically ordered in all cases. A similarity computation between a long and a short document is always lower than a computation between documents of comparable lengths, which is intuitive since the length of the longer document reduces the similarity value. The cosine similarity is larger than the Jaccard similarity in all cases for the reasons mentioned earlier. The similarity values increase in roughly the same proportion as the degree of overlap in all cases.

Figure 6.4: A Comparison of Similarity Values for the Jaccard and Cosine Measures

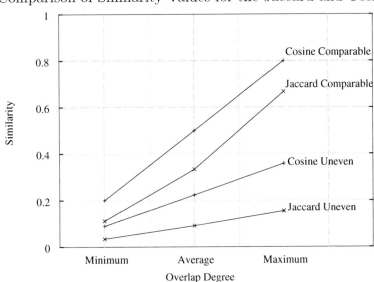

The values for the Dice coefficient not shown in Figure 6.4 are higher than the Jaccard measure, but less than the Cosine measure. Since, all three coefficients are jointly monotonic, the choice of any one of these coefficients will return similar sets of clusters, provided the thresholds for cluster membership are adjusted appropriately. The threshold for cluster membership is the minimum similarity required to include a document in a cluster. For example, a lower threshold would be more suitable, if the Jaccard measure is used to compare documents.

Document Normalization

The binary representation of a document treats all dimensions uniformly. In most cases, there will be a few dimensions (words) of a document that are more important than others. For example, consider a collection of ten documents, each with a hundred words. The word *Ford* occurs in just two of the documents while the word *automobile* occurs in nine out of ten documents. The occurrence of the word *Ford* in a document should be given more weight than the occurrence of the word *automobile*, since it is sparsely distributed in the collection. In Chapter 3, we used the inverse document frequency (IDF) to assign such words a higher weight.

The frequency (TF) of a term can be computed as the raw count of the word, a function (square root) of the raw count, or a normalized count. The raw counts of words can distort the similarity value when a large number of occurrences of a single word is compared with much fewer occurrences in another document. The square root of the number of word (term) occurrences is a damping function to limit the influence of a large term frequency count in the similarity computation. The third method divides every term's frequency by the total number of word occurrences in the document limiting the TF to a value between 0 and 1. The document vector created from this new representation has real values that are used identically in the similarity computations described earlier. The binary values for x_i, y_i, x_j, and y_j are replaced with real TF/IDF values.

6.2.4 Using the Similarity Matrix

The input to a clustering method is a similarity matrix and a cluster link type. Consider a set of 12 documents, for which we compute a similarity matrix. The 12 documents are shown in Figure 6.5.

The collection of 12 documents are arranged in a circle in an arbitrary order. Each document is assigned a number and a link is established between any two documents whose similarity exceeds a threshold. For example, document 1 is similar to documents 2, 5, 7, and 8. We can re-arrange the circle such that documents which are similar to each other are closer than other documents. The lower arrangement of documents in the circle has three distinct clusters that can be visually identified. A clustering algorithm automatically identifies such clusters. The distances of lines

Figure 6.5: List of Documents Before and After Clustering

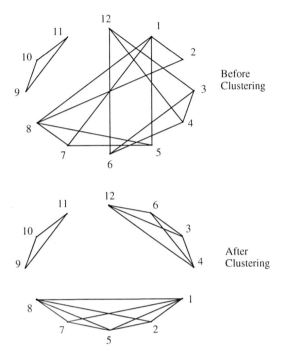

shown in the Figure 6.5 do not represent the degree of similarity and merely indicate that the similarity between a pair of documents falls within a threshold.

Every document in our example belongs to a cluster. In a real-world example, this may not happen. A few isolated documents may not have a similarity that exceeds the threshold, with any other document in the collection. These types of documents form a separate *singletons* cluster that consists of all the documents that are unrelated to the rest of the collection. Each document in the singletons cluster represents a cluster with a single document. In Figure 6.5, every document in a cluster was related to every other document in the same cluster. This is one method of building clusters and in the next section we look at three different ways of creating clusters based on the links between documents.

6.3 Cluster Algorithms

Many clustering algorithms have been proposed to build clusters from a group of items. Broadly, clustering algorithms can be divided into *top-down* and *bottom-up* (agglomerative) techniques. In a top-down clustering algorithm, we begin with one or more clusters and improve the set of clusters by splitting a cluster, combining two clusters, or re-arranging document memberships in a cluster. An improvement to a solution is computed from the overall quality of all clusters. A measure of the quality of a cluster is based on the sum of all pairs of inter-document similarities or the similarity between every member document and an average cluster document (centroid). The centroid of a cluster is a representative of a composite document made up of all member documents. A centroid is easy to assemble when documents are represented in the form of vectors.

Heuristic algorithms that iteratively assemble clusters of higher quality have been successful in finding near optimal clusters. Some of the reasons that clustering is difficult using top-down methods include -

- The number of clusters, k is unknown and the ideal number of clusters can only be estimated at run-time. Typically, an initial estimate of k is used and modified at run time when better solutions are found.

- The size of each of the k clusters is also unknown. We can initially either assume that all clusters are of the same size or use some other distribution of sizes to account for large and small clusters.

One solution to these problems is to begin with an initial guess of the number of clusters and sizes and subsequently search for alternate values that give better results. This may take a long time for a large document collection, since the number of combinations is huge. Further, some multi-topic documents may belong to more than one cluster and the degree of allowed cluster overlap is unspecified.

The bottom-up methods begin with one cluster per document and merge clusters that are *close* (based on a similarity computation). This process is repeated till a single cluster or some number k clusters are left. The next section covers some of the top-down heuristic methods followed by an implementation of an agglomerative technique using LingPipe.

6.3.1 Global Optimization Methods

Global optimization methods such as K-Means and the expectation maximization algorithm attempt to minimize the overall intra-cluster variance. The final set of clusters is returned when the algorithm converges and there is no further improvement in the quality of the clusters. Convergence is not guaranteed and an algorithm may oscillate between two solutions.

K-Means

The K-Means method is one of the simplest clustering algorithms. It begins with the selection of k centroids, where k is chosen based on n, the number of documents. The $\sqrt{n}$ is a reasonable initial number for k, when there is no prior information to select k. Each centroid is initially a document selected from the collection, such that all selected centroids are as far away from each other as possible.

Next, each of the n documents is compared with all k centroids to find the closest centroid. Every document is assigned to one of the k clusters and a new set of k centroids are computed based on the current member documents. This step is repeated till there appear to be few or no changes in the composition of the clusters.

This algorithm works because at each iteration, we find a better set of centroids that fits the collection of documents. The centroids move from their initial position to a more central location where a neighborhood of documents that are similar can be assembled. The K-Means algorithm will always terminate, but does not guarantee an optimal solution. The algorithm is sensitive to the initial centroids and the best results may be found from multiple runs with different initial centroid sets.

6.3.2 Heuristic Methods

The use of heuristic methods is common when the number of possible solutions is excessive and an exhaustive search is infeasible. Heuristic methods such as genetic algorithms, simulated annealing, and neural networks find near optimal solutions. Typically, these methods construct an initial solution from a random selection or an informed guess, apply improvements by altering the solution, and continue till a sufficiently good solution has been found. A near optimal solution is often good enough for most applications.

Simulated Annealing

We begin by creating an initial solution of k clusters. The number k is selected carefully based on the number of documents and the size of each cluster. Every document is initially randomly assigned to one of the k clusters. Two documents from clusters i and j are randomly selected and swapped. The new clusters i' and j' created after the swap are compared with the original clusters i and j to check for an improvement. The new cluster arrangement is kept, if there is an improvement. A degradation in the quality of the clusters is more likely to be accepted during the initial iterations of the cluster than near the end of the algorithm.

The run terminates after a sufficient number of iterations and returns a set of near optimal clusters. These clusters can be further improved in a post-processing step. Every cluster generated from the simulated annealing algorithm can be checked for quality and documents that have low similarity with the centroid can be moved to a singleton cluster. Small clusters could be potentially combined into larger clusters to reduce the number of overall clusters.

Genetic Algorithms

This algorithm [Genetic] is a form of evolutionary computation that attempts to build a better solution in every generation (iteration). An initial population of solutions is created, where each solution is a random arrangement of the collection of documents. Our aim is to find an ideal arrangement of the documents such that documents that are close (similar) to each other are also near each other in the arrangement (see Figure 6.5). Once we have this arrangement, we can then find key documents and build clusters around these central documents.

A new generation is created by randomly selecting two parents (arrangements) from the current population and splicing parts of the parent to make a new child. The new child arrangement is added to the next generation and a number of such children are created to build the population for the next generation. The algorithm terminates after a sufficient number of generations and the best solution from the population of the last generation is returned.

6.3.3 Agglomerative Methods

The clustering methods we have seen so far return a set of clusters with no indication of the relationships between the clusters. A flat arrangement of clusters is reasonable, when the number of clusters is few. A hierarchical arrangement is more appropriate and easier to browse, when the number of clusters is large. An agglomerative method builds clusters bottom-up, starting from a set of single document clusters. A new larger cluster z is built by combining the two nearest clusters x and y. At each step, the number of clusters is one less than the number in the previous step. There are several ways to link two clusters.

Cluster Link Types

We look at three different methods of evaluating the similarity between clusters based on the number of links between member documents. The first method *single link*, is a simple method that combines clusters by identifying the closest pair of documents in two separate clusters. Notice, the other documents in the cluster may be weakly related and the only consideration when combining the cluster is the inter-document similarity. This method does have an weakness, in that a cluster can become diluted, since the documents found at either end of a chain of links may be unrelated (see Figure 6.6).

Figure 6.6: Three Cluster Link Types

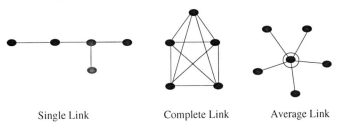

Single Link   Complete Link   Average Link

We can join two single link clusters x and y when any one of the member documents from cluster x is similar to a member document from cluster y. The requirements to merge two complete link clusters are more stringent. All documents of one complete link cluster must be similar to all documents of another complete link cluster. This ensures that at any given threshold, the quality of the complete link clusters will be higher than that of the single link clusters. Finally, all member documents should be similar to a centroid in an average link cluster. A document is added to a cluster when it is similar to the centroid. A new centroid is built from the updated list of member documents. The distance between two single link clusters is the minimum distance separating all pairs of member documents and between two complete link clusters, it is the maximum distance separating all pairs of member documents.

At first, it may appear as if complete link clusters should always be chosen over single link clusters. The choice of the type of cluster link depends on the similarity distribution of documents. The results of a clustering method with complete links, when applied to a document collection that is weakly related, may not be as useful as the use of the same method with single links. The complete link method will generate a larger number of clusters than the single link method at the same similarity threshold. One of our aims in building clusters is to reduce the time required to browse a document collection and a very large number of small clusters defeats the purpose of clustering. The complete link type is suitable for spherical distributions of documents and the single link type is more appropriate for linear document distributions.

Single Link vs. Complete Link Clusters

Consider a small collection of four documents a, b, c, and d with the similarity matrix (based on distance) shown in Table 6.3. Each document consists of a single sentence.

Name	Contents
a	A cow jumped over the moon made of green cheese.
b	At once a cow with green cheese jumped over the moon.
c	At once a cow jumped on the moon, but fell down.
d	At once an orange cow leaped, but fell down.

In an agglomerative method, we combine clusters with the highest similarity first and continue till a single cluster made up of all the documents is generated. The two closest clusters in the first step are the documents a and b that are separated by the least distance (2). For simplicity, we define distance between two documents a and b as $(10 - x)$, where x is the number of common words between a and b.

Table 6.3: The Distance Similarity Matrix for a Set of Four Documents

Document	a	b	c	d
a	0	2	5	9
b	2	0	3	7
c	5	3	0	4
d	9	7	4	0

In Figure 6.7, the complete and single link cluster types are compared, when applied to the similarity matrix in Table 6.3. The first step (*a-b* cluster) is identical in both link types. In the single link method, the *a-b* cluster is combined with *c* cluster, since the distance between *b* and *c* is the second lowest value (3) in the matrix.

We cannot combine the same two clusters in the complete link method, since the distance between documents *a* and *c* is 5, which is greater than the similarity (4) between documents *c* and *d*. The final step in the single link method combines document *d* and the document *c* from the cluster created in the second step. Note, the maximum threshold (4) using the single link method is less than the maximum threshold (9) in the complete link method, to create the final cluster in step 3 (see Figure 6.8).

A *dendrogram* is the representation of cluster analysis in a tree-like structure. The root of the tree is a single cluster made up of all the documents in the collection and the lower branches divide the collection into progressively smaller clusters. In general, the similarity required to form clusters is higher in the complete link than the single link method. The height of nodes in the tree corresponds to the similarity required to merge a pair of clusters. Every cluster contains a single document at the leaf level. The clusters at higher levels in the tree are more broad compared to the clusters at lower levels.

Notice, the arrangement of clusters in the form of a dendrogram makes it easy to find a variable number of clusters. Imagine a horizontal line drawn at a fixed distance of 2.5 in either the single or complete link dendrograms. This line cuts three vertical lines, each line leading to a separate cluster. We can move this line higher or lower in the dendrogram to get fewer or more clusters.

Figure 6.7: Comparison of the Single Link and Complete Link Cluster Types

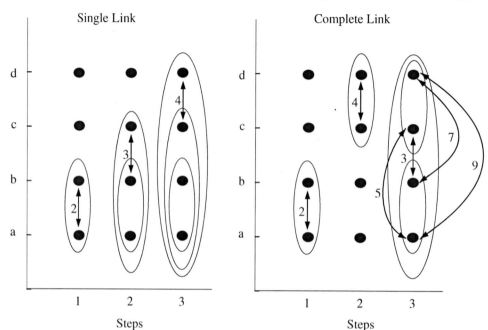

6.4 Building Clusters with LingPipe

LingPipe includes classes to build complete link and single link clusters from a collection of objects. In the first example, we build clusters of documents from a collection that has been organized in separate sub-directories. The clustering algorithm views the documents from all sub-directories in a single Set without any distinction. The results from the clustering algorithm can be compared with the pre-defined organization to evaluate the quality of the clusters.

Consider a collection of 36 documents in three sub-directories, coffee, sugar, and cocoa of the cluster directory. We first (see line 4, Listing 6.1) create a referencePartition that contains the organized collection of documents in three separate Sets. Each Set of the referencePartition contains a list of documents from a single topic (sub-directory). A Document is an inner static class that contains information about a single document including the name of the file, the text contents

Figure 6.8: Single Link and Complete Link Dendrograms

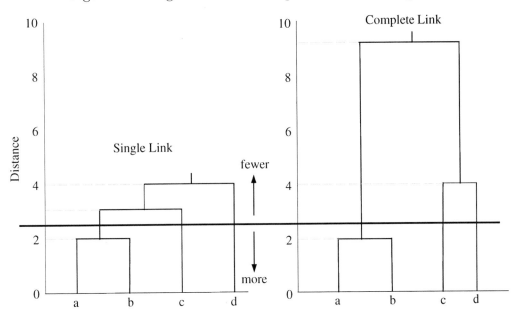

of the file, the length of the file, and a counter for document tokens. The list of tokens from the document text is generated with a default Indo-European tokenizer and a filter for stop words.

Listing 6.1: Cluster a Collection of Documents using Complete Links

```
1  public class TestCluster {
2    public static void main(String[] args) {
3      File dir = new File(TESTING_DIR + FS + "cluster");
4      Set<Set<Document>> referencePartition =
5        new HashSet<Set<Document>>();
6      for (File catDir : dir.listFiles()) {
7        Set<Document> docsForCat = new HashSet<Document>();
8        referencePartition.add(docsForCat);
9        for (File file : catDir.listFiles()) {
10         Document doc = new Document(file);
11         docsForCat.add(doc);
```

```
12          }
13        }
14        Set<Document> docSet = new HashSet<Document>();
15        for (Set<Document> cluster : referencePartition)
16          docSet.addAll(cluster);
17        HierarchicalClusterer<Document> clClusterer =
18          new CompleteLinkClusterer<Document>(COSINE_DISTANCE);
19        Dendrogram<Document> completeLinkDendrogram =
20          clClusterer.hierarchicalCluster(docSet);
21        for (int k = 1; k <= docSet.size(); ++k) {
22          Set<Set<Document>> clResponsePartition =
23            completeLinkDendrogram.partitionK(k);
24          System.out.println("Clusters: "
25            + clResponsePartition);
26        }
27      }
28    }
```

Next, the collection of all documents are added to a `docSet` (line 16). A complete link clusterer (line 18) is created and used to generate a dendrogram from the documents in `docSet`. The final loop in Listing 6.1 is equivalent to moving a horizontal line from the top of the dendrogram to the leaf level. The number of required partitions (clusters) is passed to the `partitionK` (line 23) method of the dendrogram, that returns a `Set` of `Sets`, where each of the `Sets` contains a list of member documents in the cluster. For example, when k is five, we get the following output

```
Clusters: [
1. [coffee/f4, coffee/f1, cocoa/c7, sugar/s14],
2. [sugar/s9, coffee/f8, sugar/s2, sugar/s6, sugar/s8,
   sugar/s5, sugar/s4, sugar/s7, sugar/s15, sugar/s13,
   sugar/s3, sugar/s11, sugar/s1],
3. [coffee/f5, cocoa/c5, sugar/s10, coffee/f9, coffee/f2,
   cocoa/c6, coffee/f3, coffee/f6, cocoa/c2, cocoa/c3,
   coffee/f10, cocoa/c4, coffee/f12, cocoa/c8, cocoa/c1,
   coffee/f11, cocoa/c9],
4. [coffee/f7],
5. [sugar/s12]
]
```

The `partitionDistance` method (not shown in the listing) can also generate partitions at specific distances. This would be the equivalent of setting the bar in Figure 6.8 at the given distance on the y-axis and returning the clusters that intersect the bar. Every cluster has a list of file names and associated sub-directories or categories. Notice, the non-singleton clusters are made up of documents from more than one topic. This does not necessarily mean that the algorithm itself is faulty. The clustering algorithm uses a matrix of the similarities between all unique pairs of documents to build a dendrogram. The results of the clustering algorithm are dependent on accurate similarity computations to identify clusters. In Listing 6.1, we used the *Cosine* similarity to compare two documents, alternatively the *Jaccard* similarity can be used as well. The `cosine` method is implemented (not shown in the listing) in the **Document** class.

```
static Distance<Document> COSINE_DISTANCE =
  new Distance<Document>() {
    public double distance(Document doc1, Document doc2) {
      return 1.0 - doc1.cosine(doc2);
    }
};

static Distance<Document> JACCARD_DISTANCE =
  new Distance<Document>() {
    public double distance(Document doc1, Document doc2) {
      return 1.0 - doc1.jaccard(doc2);
    }
};
```

The constructor for the clusterer accepts an implementation of a **Distance** interface that contains a single `distance` method to compare any two objects. The example here compares two **Documents**, but we could also compare two **City** objects in another implementation of the **Distance** interface. The `distance` method would return the great circle distance between two **Citys**, assuming that each **City** contains fields for longitude and latitude.

6.4.1 Debugging Clusters

The accuracy of the clustering algorithm is dependent on the inter-document similarity computations and potential errors should first be identified in the similarity matrix. The `prettyPrint` method of a `Dendrogram` returns the similarities between documents and the order in which the clusters were merged. A partial listing from the output of the `prettyPrint` method is shown below.

```
0.620   -- cluster z
  0.524   -- cluster y
    0.451   -- cluster x
        coffee /f9
        coffee /f10
    coffee /f6
  0.480   -- cluster w
    coffee /f5
    coffee /f12
```

Two documents `f9` and `f10` that are separated by a distance of 0.451, are first combined into a cluster `x` which is then combined with the document `f6` to form a cluster `y`. A cluster `w` from the combination of documents `f5` and `f12` is combined with cluster `y` at a distance of 0.620 to form a cluster `z`. The nodes on the right most side of the output represent the leaves of the dendrogram and we move up the tree from right to left in the dendrogram listing. Notice, the distance values increase from right to left representing weaker cluster combinations at higher levels.

A further examination of the output reveals that mixed clusters are found at higher levels in the dendrogram, leading to lower precision. Clusters with low similarity can be prevented from merging with a threshold parameter in the constructor of the clusterer to set the maximum allowable distance between two clusters that can be merged. The distances between a pair of clusters is based on the link type (single or complete). LingPipe version 3.4 includes a K-Means clusterer and a multi-topic classifier based on the Latent Dirichlet Allocation model [LDA].

6.4.2 Evaluating Clusters

The code in Listing 6.1 began with a set of documents that were pre-assigned to categories. The clustering algorithm created a set of clusters that in the ideal case would mimic a pre-defined cluster arrangement. The algorithm will rarely find the perfect set of clusters, for several reasons including the accuracy of the similarity computation, noisy data, and the large number of reasonably good solutions.

Clusters are evaluated by identifying the location of pairs of documents in clusters. For example, we would record a *true positive*, if the pre-defined or reference partition contained two documents x and y in the same category and both x and y were also assigned to the same category by the clustering algorithm. The list of all possibilities for the occurrence of a pair of documents x and y in the reference and assigned partitions are -

- **True Positive**: x and y were found in a single cluster in the reference and assigned partitions.

- **False Positive**: x and y were found in different reference clusters, but in a single assigned cluster.

- **False Negative**: x and y were found in same reference cluster, but different assigned clusters.

- **True Negative:** x and y were found in different clusters in the reference and assigned partitions.

Consider the cluster measures for a set of five clusters generated using the code in Listing 6.1. A set of 36 documents with a total of 36×36 (1296) pairs, were clustered. A document paired with itself is counted as a true positive. A two by two table (see Table 6.4) with counts for the four possibilities of the occurrence of a document pair is sufficient to compute cluster evaluation measures for the given arrangement.

Table 6.4: Number of Document Pairs in Assigned and Reference Partitions

		Reference Partition	
		Same	Different
Assigned Partition	Same	254 (true positive)	162 (false positive)
	Different	196 (false negative)	684 (true negative)

We look at just three of the large number of possible evaluation measures – *recall*, *precision*, and *accuracy*. The recall is the ratio of the number of true positives (254) to the sum of the numbers of true positives and false negatives (450) or 0.56. The precision is the ratio of the number of true positives (254) to the sum of the numbers of true and false positives (416) or 0.61. Finally, accuracy is the ratio of the number of correct classifications (true positives + true negatives, 938) to total number of classifications (1236) or 0.72. The accuracy measure does not assign a higher weight to the number of true positives that is more valuable than the number of true negatives. The *F-measure* (*F*)combines the recall and precision measures into a single value.

$$F = \frac{2}{\frac{1}{Recall} + \frac{1}{Precision}} \tag{6.8}$$

This formula is the harmonic mean of the recall and precision with equal weights for both measures. A modified F-measure may assign more or less importance to either recall or precision. The evaluation results depend on the number of clusters that in turn depends on the distance threshold in the dendrogram. A clustering algorithm can only guess the number of clusters that would return the highest evaluation. The code in Listing 6.1 builds clusters for the entire range of clusters from a minimum of one to the maximum of 36, the number of documents. Consider the plot in Figure 6.9 that shows the recall, precision, and F-measure values for the range of clusters.

The precision is low and recall is high when the number of clusters is low. This corresponds to the clusters that are found near the root of the dendrogram, which will include most of the documents (high recall) in the collection, but in diffuse clusters (low precision). The recall is lower and precision is higher when the number of clusters is near the maximum. A fine balance between recall and precision is found with about five clusters that represents a near optimal solution. The number of clusters that corresponds to the peak value for the F-measure is also a reasonable number to assume for the final set of clusters.

Cluster Evaluation without a Reference Partition

All the calculations we have made so far to evaluate clusters, are based on the assumption that a reference partition with the correct document assignments for clusters exists. Often, the input to a clustering algorithm will be a set of documents with unknown properties, making it impossible to compute precision or the F-measure. We cannot estimate the number of clusters that would best fit the document collection, without an evaluation measure.

Figure 6.9: Recall, Precision, and F-Measure Values for a Range of Clusters using an Agglomerative Clusterer

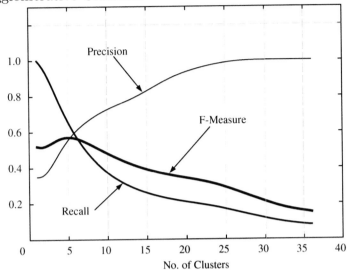

We use a new evaluation measure that is based on a property of the clustering itself. The quality of a cluster is the sum of all the similarities between every pair of member documents. A cluster that contains a set of related documents, should have a lower score than a diffuse cluster. Our aim is to find an optimal number of clusters such that all clusters have closely related documents. The `withinClusterScatter` method of a `Dendrogram` returns a scatter score given a number of clusters and a `Distance` instance. The scatter score is the sum of the distances of all pairs of documents in every cluster. A plot of the scatter score vs. the number of clusters is shown in Figure 6.10.

The scatter score reduces as the number of clusters increases, since the number of document pairs in every cluster decreases with smaller clusters. The number of clusters (3-4) that intersects the *knee* of this curve is a reasonable estimate of the number of clusters (k) for a near optimal solution. The knee of this curve is found at the range of consecutive x values where there is a large difference in the scatter score.

Minimizing the scatter score alone does not give an optimized solution, since the lowest score (zero) occurs when every document belongs to a separate cluster. This solution is obviously not very useful and we need to balance the number of clusters with the scatter score. We can add a penalty proportional to the number of clusters to compensate for the lower scatter score. As the number of clusters increases, the scatter score decreases, but the penalty increases to return a balanced score that can be minimized. This is a statistical criterion [Kmeans] to find an optimal number of clusters.

Figure 6.10: Scatter Score for all Clusters vs. Number of Clusters

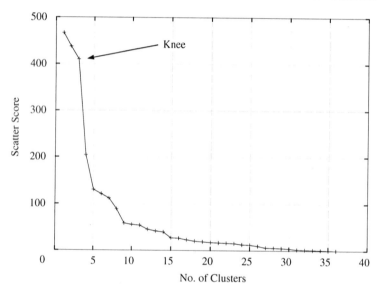

6.5 Summary

Many of the current clustering algorithms for documents were originally designed to mine numeric data and have been adapted to handle text data from documents. There is no ideal clustering algorithm that can be uniformly applied to all document collections. Some of the parameters that we can tweak to improve performance include the distance computation, limits on the number of clusters, limits on the size of a cluster, and the type of cluster link

Two implementations (Jaccard and Cosine) of similarity computations are included in the sample code. A third computation based on the edit distance is more suited to compare short text strings to find clusters of words. Limits on the number of clusters and size of clusters are constraining parameters to find a set of clusters that are easier to manage. A large number of small clusters is not very beneficial since clustering has not substantially reduced the time to browse the collection. On other hand, a very large cluster may be diffuse and is similarly not very useful to the reader. The complete link method does return clusters of higher quality than the single link method, but is not necessarily the first choice in all cases. A complete link method would return a larger number of small clusters than the single link method for a collection that contains documents from many topics that may be loosely related. The scatter score that includes a penalty proportional to k, the number of clusters is one way of comparing different cluster parameters.

7 Organizing Text: Categorization

In the previous chapter, we covered clustering, a way of organizing a set of documents into a more manageable and smaller collection of groups of documents. This chapter will explain the use of text categorization to assign documents into pre-defined categories. The primary difference between clustering and text categorization is the use of prior information to build categories (groups) of documents. This information is provided in the form of sample documents that have been assigned to a set of known categories before categorization. We begin the chapter with a description of the problem and a sample set of text categorization applications. Several types of classifiers (categorizers) using LingPipe are implemented and evaluated. Finally, we cover the extraction of features (unique characteristics) for categorization.

7.1 Categorization Problem

A model for all categories is created from training data that defines the main characteristics or features of items belonging to the category. There are two types of categorization models that we can use to assign items to categories. The first type is a composite model that assigns one of n categories to an item. The other type is based on the use of multiple models, each of which simply indicates if an item belongs to a single category or not. We have considered non-overlapping categories, i.e. every document is assigned to a single category.

A composite model is a multi-classifier that will assign scores to each of the n categories based on the likelihood that the item belongs to the category. A binary model uses a single model to either accept or reject an item from a category.

7.1.1 Applications for Document Categorization

We have used the term *item* to describe the unit of categorization. In this chapter, an item is a document, but an item could also be a token or even a book. For example, a library is possibly the most well-known and oldest example of categorization. Every book is assigned a unique call number or an ISBN number based on the assigned category. The prefix of the call number in the U.S. Library of Congress code refers to the name of the category. A book on information retrieval would have a call number that starts with the prefix *Z699*. The call number for all books that belong to the same category will be categorized with the same prefix. The rest of the characters of the call number following the prefix, define the sub-category of the book.

Often, the physical organization of books in a library is based on the logical organization created with assigned call numbers. For example, all books on information retrieval are physically located in the same or neighboring shelves, making it easy for a reader to find related books while browsing. This type of organization is mirrored in a computer-based hierarchical user interface to locate documents. The arrangement of items in this manner is called a *taxonomy*. It complements an initial query on a search engine and is also beneficial for the beginner who is unfamiliar with terminology or the types of books available. A hierarchical organization makes it simple to follow a path to identify relevant books.

Organizing the Web

The initial attempts at organizing the Web (such as Yahoo! and the Open Directory Project) followed a hierarchical model. The task of categorizing every Web page appeared manageable in the early 90s, when the size of the Web was in the thousands of pages. Later, it became impractical for a single organization to manually categorize all Web pages; instead a combination of collaborative and automated methods to find and organize Web pages was successful. The organization of the Web in a taxonomy was of use to both the beginner and the expert user of the Web. A novice user of the Web found a list of categories more appealing than the empty search box of a search engine to find information. An expert user could search for a specific topic within a category with higher precision than a broad search across the entire Web.

The classification of Web pages into a large taxonomy was feasible, provided the number of pages per category was limited to a manageable size. The use of a taxonomy was also a scalable solution to handle the large number of Web pages. Subcategories were created when the number of pages in a single category exceeded a threshold. This solution accommodates the rapid growth in the number of pages for popular or hot topics. Building a taxonomy for a large document collection is a complex task that is accomplished through a combination of user feedback, manually defined categories, and automated methods. In this chapter, we will only consider automated methods to find the category of an unknown document.

Detecting Spam

An estimated half to three fourths of all email transmitted on the Internet is *spam* or junk email. Most of these emails are solicitations for products that are usually not of interest to the recipient. The transmitter (spammer) of these emails sends messages to as many recipients as possible. The spammer receives a commission for every email recipient who responds to the spam message by visiting a Web site advertised in the message. This cheap and annoying form of advertising through email has become very difficult to prevent due to evolving nature of spam.

Spammers and spam detectors have been battling each other since the early 90s, when spam first became noticeable [?]. The task of spam detection is essentially a binary categorization of a message into either a *reject* (spam) or *accept* (legitimate) category. An accurate spam detector must constantly evolve to keep up with spam messages whose content is also constantly changing. The first goal of a spammer is to prevent a message from being categorized as spam, using a variety of cunning methods to deceive the detector. There is a higher possibility of getting a response, if a spam message ends up in the *Inbox* and not a *Bulk* or spam folder of the recipient.

It has become very affordable for a spammer to send thousands or even millions of email messages because of the low cost of hardware and Internet bandwidth. A spammer usually profits even when 99.99% of the recipients do *not* respond to the spam. The higher accuracy of a spam detector only forces the spammer to send a larger volume of email. The number of new users on the Web continues to increase worldwide. Most beginners on the Web create an email account and automatically become potential email targets for a spammer. Currently, there appears to be no solution to remove spam completely. Instead, spam filters have become increasingly sophisticated and savvy email users are learning to train a personal filter that reduces spam to nearly nil.

Filtering News

It is hard to keep up with the large number of news sources on the Web without any tools. With limited time, most readers use information that is easily accessible and ignore the rest. This approach restricts the users' view of the news to a partial list of sources. Consider a profile created by the user, that may consist of a list of terms or even a list of documents (or hyperlinks) that have been categorized as relevant to the user's interest. A detector scans the profile and uses the profile terms to decide if a news article is relevant or not. A large number of news articles are compared with the profile and assigned ranks. The list of high ranking news articles are returned to the user. An user can continually train a profile by removing or adding terms and documents. Here, categorization saves the readers' time by finding just the news articles of interest. The Google news Web site (`http://news.google.com`) collects articles from many sources and categorizes articles by region, subject, and sub-topic.

Tagging

We can tag one or more tokens with a part of speech, entity, or even a phrase type. Consider the simple list of eight parts of speech. POS tagging can be defined in terms of categorization as the selection of one of the eight parts of speech for every token. The assignment of a POS to a token is made on the basis of the token's features and context. Similarly, one or more tokens are assigned an entity type. An entity token may be categorized into one of several entity types such as person, place, or organization. Extracting entities can be considered as a two step categorization process, with the first step being the identification of an entity and the second step the assignment of a type to the entity.

Tokens that are part of phrases have some common syntactic features, such as an initial upper case letter or all upper case letters. These features are hints that can be combined to build a binary categorizer that specifies if a token should be part of a phrase or not. Finally, words such as *round* and *bank* have many senses and a categorizer can rank the list of senses based on contextual and syntactic features.

Language Identification

The identification of the language of a document is necessary in a multi-lingual document collection to restrict searches to a specific language. A language is assigned to every indexed document of a search engine. It is not feasible to manually assign the language of individual documents, when the number of documents in a collection is in the thousands or millions. We can accurately identify the language of a document with a multi-classifier that has been trained with text from a number of languages. Many languages have distinct character sets and even languages that share the same character set have many unique character sequences (ngrams) that are seen more often in one language than another. The accuracy of a language classifier is typically much higher than other types of classifiers due to the large number of distinguishing features in each language.

Author Identification

This classifier returns a list of possible authors for a given text, from a model that has been trained with a collection of documents from a set of authors. This problem is harder than language identification, since the features to distinguish between authors is more subtle than between languages. Authors tend to have unique habits in the use of vocabulary and style that are usually sufficient to build a model to identify the source of a given text. The Federalist Papers [Federalist] are a set of 85 essays were published in 1787-1788 to persuade voters to ratify a new constitution. Each of the essays was signed with a common pseudonym and there has been some debate on the true identity of the authors. Automated methods use models built from the writings of each author to estimate the likelihood that a particular author did write an essay. This likelihood together with the common belief can reveal the true identity of the author. Claims of the appearance of a new document written by an author such as Shakespeare, can also be similarly verified using a trained model. This chapter will deal with the categorization of documents alone. The model used here can be adapted to handle other categorization problems.

Other Applications

There are many other categorization applications in domains such as medicine, law and finance. A complaint written in an emergency room is usually a short chunk of text that is categorized into a one of several medical syndrome categories. Similarly, the text from a patient record is automatically categorized into a ICD-10 (International Classification of Diseases) code to compile statistics at the state or national level. An abstract of an article is classified as relevant to a particular topic such as genetics or cancers. At a lower level, individual sentences of an article can also be classified as relevant to the study of genes and relations between genes. A paragraph of text from an article can be assigned to the introduction, body, results, or conclusion categories.

Classification is also used in Information Retrieval to find documents similar to a document. The category of a selected document and the associated terms are used to find other related documents. The search for documents in a collection can also be cast as a classification of all documents into a relevant or irrelevant category.

7.2 Categorizing Documents

We categorize documents using a model trained on the set of n possible categories. A set of training documents are manually selected for each possible category (see Figure 7.1). In general, a large number of training documents for each category should lead to a more accurate model. This assumes that the training documents per category are fairly distinct with minimal overlap. The separation between categories is based on the occurrences of unique features (words or any other characteristics) in a particular category. Documents belonging to categories that have overlapping features will be difficult to categorize. We have considered categories organized in a list and not a hierarchy.

The first step of selecting the most appropriate training documents for a category is also the most important, since the remainder of the categorization task largely depends on the model generated from these documents. Ideally, a balanced model that represents all categories is preferred. The number of training documents per category should not be skewed in favor of one or more categories. Unfortunately, a collection of training documents is rarely uniform and documents from one or categories are more popular than other categories. This results in a bias in favor of terms from the more numerous training documents for a category that may not be reflected in a general language model. In many cases, the length of training documents is also not uniform. The text from a long document has a greater influence

Figure 7.1: Training a Model and Document Categorization

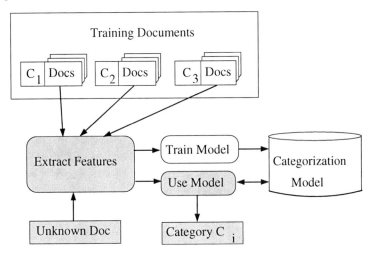

on the probability of the document belonging to a category than the text from a short document.

The second step to extract features uses the text of the training documents to build a model. Finding the best features that distinguish between categories has been the subject of research and is critical to the success of the model. Later in this chapter, we will look at methods to identify features that distinguish categories. Once a set of good features have been identified, most of the standard machine learning techniques such as K-nearest neighbor, decision trees, neural networks, or naïve Bayes classifiers categorize documents with reasonably good accuracy. A feature is some unit of the document contents that separates one category from another. Examples of features include individual tokens, character ngrams, token ngrams, tokens and part of speech, or even a pattern of musical notes from an audio file.

7.2.1 Training the Model

The extraction of good features is language specific and depends on methods such as stop word lists, stemming, and word orthography. Languages such as Chinese, with no clear word boundaries are dependent on a pre-segmentation step to build tokens from text and consequently errors in segmenting text are inherited by the feature extraction process. The importance of all features is not uniform for all end uses. For example, in the authorship identification task, linguistic features such as the length of sentences or vocabulary size are more important than in other categorization tasks. The document categorization task uses a bag of words with optional weights in a vector to assign importance based on the number of occurrence of words in categories. The representation of a document in a word vector is one form of representation and others may include phrases, bigrams, parts of speech, and other features.

Each word is a feature and a weight is typically assigned using the TF/IDF measure. We can concatenate the text from all training documents for a category into a single document and use the TF/IDF measure to compute the weight of words across all categories. A word seen often in a single category will have both a high TF and IDF values. These types of words are good indicators of a category and are responsible for the successful categorization of a document. The number of features in a moderate sized document collection is fairly large and there will be few features that have a high TF/IDF value. Cumulatively, the numerous features with medium or low scores also contribute to the overall category score for a document.

7.2.2 Using the Model

The categorization model is a collection of profiles for each category. Each profile is made up of a list of features and weights for the category. The features of an unknown document are extracted using the same procedure that was used when building the categorization model from training documents. The extracted features of the unknown document are compared with the profiles of all categories. We use the same types of similarity measures from chapter 6 to compare a document vector and a profile. The category with the highest score above a threshold is returned.

This method of categorization has some limitations that were mentioned earlier. One, is the identification of features that requires customization for every language. Two, most text categorization models use tokens alone and ignore linguistic features such as punctuation. These non-alphabetic features may have importance in a classification task like author identification. Finally, the number of features per category is usually limited to keep computational costs low.

We can also use a search engine to build a categorizer. Consider the Lucene API (see Chapters 3 and 4) that we used to index and search a document collection. The collection of training documents are assembled into a smaller collection of composite pseudo-documents, one for each category, with the appropriate boost for text from the individual document titles. The text of all training documents for a category is indexed as before, except that in this case, a document actually represents a category. Next, the text from an unknown document is converted into a boolean query made up of the main terms in the document and submitted to the search engine. The list of hits (categories) returned represents the potential document categories in descending order of score. In the next section, we will look at an implementation with LingPipe that uses an alternate character-based ngram model for classification.

7.3 Categorization Methods

We will use LingPipe to classify a small collection of documents using several classifiers. The first two classifiers are ngram-based and the remainder use tokens or generic features to categorize documents. The training directory, `/data/training/tcat` is a collection of 36 documents that are distributed across three categories – *sugar*, *coffee*, and *cocoa*. A collection of 23 documents in the testing directory, `/data/testing/tcat` are distributed over four categories that include an additional *miscellaneous* category. This is a very small collection of documents and the results shown here will most likely be not identical to the results from tests with larger collections of many thousands of documents.

The contents of files in a testing dataset are typically more broad than the files in a training dataset, which are carefully selected to represent a set of categories. Files in a training dataset can be excluded or included depending on the set of categories and classifier. A real-world example will have files that cannot be accurately categorized into any one of the set of *trained* categories. Such files are placed in a miscellaneous category, that is not present in the training set of categories. Documents that belong to the miscellaneous category are harder to classify, since we have no training examples to evaluate. Therefore, assignments to the miscellaneous category are made when no other category appears appropriate for a document. The reason it is difficult to train a miscellaneous category is because the set of documents that can represent such a category is potentially infinite. All the classifiers in the following sections use the same training and testing datasets.

7.3.1 Character-based Ngram Models

The descriptions of the binary classifier and the multi-classifier that follow, both use character-based ngram language models. The successful use of these models in speech recognition to predict the probability of word sequences has led to their implementations in text classification . A language model will assign a high probability to word sequences that occur in training text and a low probability to other word sequences. We use a language model in text classification to find the most likely category for a document from a given set of categories C.

$$cat = argmax_{cat_i \in C} p(cat_i|cs) \tag{7.1}$$

The most likely category cat_i, is the category with the highest conditional probability given a character sequence cs. The text of any document can be represented as a character sequence cs. We use Bayes' theorem (see Appendix B) to find this probability and restate the conditional probability as

$$p(cat_i|cs) \approx p(cs|cat_i) \times p(cat_i) \tag{7.2}$$

The probability of a character sequence given a category cat_i is based on the probability of ngram character sequences in the language model for cat_i. A separate language model is created for each trained category from the training dataset. The *cross entropy* is a measure of how likely the character sequence was generated from the language model for the category and is represented as the negative of the log likelihood of the character sequence. The cross entropy rate is the cross entropy of the character sequence divided by the length of the character sequence.

$$\frac{-(log(p(cs|cat_j)) + log(p(cat_j)))}{length(cs)}$$

A small probability is allocated to ngrams that were not encountered in the training data to avoid zero probabilities for such ngrams. The estimated probability is based on lower order ngrams with a base uniform probability for individual characters.

The probability of a category cat_i is based on the fraction of training instances that belonged to the cat_i. The *logs* of these probabilities are used in the final calculation to avoid underflow errors due to low probabilities.

7.3.2 Binary and Multi Classifiers

A binary classifier is trained on a single category and is equivalent to a *yes/no* classification decision. The best category for a document is identified from a series of classification decisions, one for each possible category. The two models in a binary classifier are the *accept* and *reject* models. The training data for a category is used to generate the *accept* model and the *reject* model assumes uniform estimates per character. The code in Listing 7.1 creates and dumps a language model for a single category to a file.

Listing 7.1: Build a Binary Classifier for a Single Category

```
1  public class TrainBClassifier {
2    private static File TDIR = new File(
3      TRAINING_DIR + FS + "tcat");
4    private static String CATEGORY = "sugar";
5    private static int NGRAM_SIZE = 6;
6
7    public static void main(String[] args) {
8      BinaryLMClassifier classifier =
9        new BinaryLMClassifier( new NGramProcessLM(
10         NGRAM_SIZE), 100.0);
11     File classDir = new File(TDIR, CATEGORY);
12     for (File file : classDir.listFiles()) {
13       String text = Files.readFromFile(file);
14       classifier.train("accept", text);
15     }
16     String modelFile = TRAINING_DIR + FS + "tcat"
17       + FS + "tcat_bclassifier";
18     ObjectOutputStream os = new ObjectOutputStream(
19       new FileOutputStream(modelFile));
20     classifier.compileTo(os);
21     os.close();
22   }
23 }
```

An ngram process language model with a given ngram size (6) and a cross entropy threshold (100.0) is passed to the constructor (line 9) of a binary classifier. The text from every file in the training category is extracted and passed to the **train** (line 14) method of the classifier. Finally, the classifier model is compiled and dumped to a file (line 20). We can now test this model with a different set of files from the same category and a *miscellaneous* category (see Listing 7.2).

Listing 7.2: Test the Binary Classifier using a Mixed Collection of Documents

```
1   public class TestBClassifier {
2     private static File TDIR = new File(
3       TESTING_DIR + FS + "tcat");
4     private static String[] CATEGORIES = { "sugar", "misc" };
5
6     public static void main(String[] args){
7       String modelFile = TRAINING_DIR + FS +
8         "tcat" + FS + "tcat_bclassifier";
9       ObjectInputStream oi = new ObjectInputStream(
10        new FileInputStream(modelFile));
11      LMClassifier compiledClassifier =
12        (LMClassifier) oi.readObject();
13      oi.close();
14
15      for (int i = 0; i < CATEGORIES.length; ++i) {
16        File classDir = new File(TDIR, CATEGORIES[i]);
17        String text;
18        for (File file : classDir.listFiles()) {
19          text = Files.readFromFile(file);
20          JointClassification jc =
21            compiledClassifier.classifyJoint(
22              text.toCharArray(), 0, text.length());
23          String bestCat = (jc.score(0) < -2.5) ?
24            CATEGORIES[1]: CATEGORIES[0];
25        }
26      }
27    }
28  }
```

The binary classifier created in Listing 7.1 is read from a file (lines 11-12) and used to classify the text from each of the files. The files from two categories – *sugar* and *miscellaneous* are passed to the classifier. The files in the miscellaneous category may contain text from any topic except *sugar*. The classifier returns a `JointClassification` that includes information such as the scores for categories and the best category. An empirical threshold score of -2.5 was selected to separate the two categories (line 23). The score per category is a log value of a probability and therefore a better score is closer to zero.

The multi classifier is similar in many ways to the binary classifier. We use the `createNgramBoundary` method of the `DynamicLMClassifier` class to create the classifier. The ngram size and the list of categories is passed as parameters.

```
DynamicLMClassifier classifier =
  DynamicLMClassifier.createNGramBoundary
    (CATEGORIES, NGRAM_SIZE);
```

Each file is trained as before using the **train** method of the classifier and the model is compiled and dumped to a file. The multi-classifier builds a single composite model for all categories that is used to categorize the text of an unknown document. The text from all files of each of the training categories is passed to the the train method with the name of the appropriate category.

```
classifier.train(CATEGORIES[i], text);
```

The code (Listing 7.3) to run test the classifier is similar to the code in Listing 7.2 with the exception of a confusion matrix to evaluate the classifier. We use the same three training categories and add a miscellaneous folder with four test files.

Listing 7.3: Test the Multi-Classifier using a Mixed Collection of Documents

```
1  public class TestMClassifier {
2    private static File TDIR = new File(
3      TESTING_DIR + FS + "tcat");
4    private static String[] CATEGORIES = {
5      "sugar", "coffee", "cocoa", "misc" };
6
7    public static void main(String[] args) {
8      String modelFile = TRAINING_DIR + FS + "tcat"
9        + FS + "tcat_mclassifier";
10     ObjectInputStream oi = new ObjectInputStream(
11      new FileInputStream(modelFile));
12     LMClassifier compiledClassifier =
13       (LMClassifier) oi.readObject();
```

```
14        oi.close();
15        ConfusionMatrix confMatrix =
16          new ConfusionMatrix(CATEGORIES);
17        for (int i = 0; i < CATEGORIES.length; ++i) {
18          File classDir = new File(TDIR, CATEGORIES[i]);
19          String text;
20          for (File file : classDir.listFiles()) {
21            text = Files.readFromFile(file);
22            JointClassification jc =
23              compiledClassifier.classifyJoint(
24                text.toCharArray(), 0, text.length() );
25            confMatrix.increment(
26              CATEGORIES[i], jc.bestCategory());
27          }
28        }
29      }
30    }
```

The `classifyJoint` (line 23) method of the classifier is used as before, to return a `JointClassification`. The results of the classifier are evaluated using a confusion matrix. This matrix shows the number of documents that were correctly categorized and the number of errors. In addition, the types of errors can also be identified. The confusion matrix for a testing set of 23 documents is shown below in Table 7.1.

Table 7.1: A Confusion Matrix for a Multi-Classifier with Four Categories

Category	Sugar	Coffee	Cocoa	Miscellaneous
Sugar	7	0	0	0
Coffee	1	5	0	0
Cocoa	0	0	6	0
Miscellaneous	4	0	0	0

In a perfect classifier, the confusion matrix should be a diagonal matrix. In Table 7.1, 18 out of 23 documents have been correctly classified and all the miscellaneous documents have been mis-categorized. A single document out of six *coffee* documents was also wrongly categorized. Clearly, categorizing *miscellaneous* documents is difficult without a well-defined model for the *miscellaneous* category.

Binary Classifier vs. Multi-Classifier

The problem with the use of a multi-classifier is that categorization is exhaustive. Every document must belong to a category that has been trained. A model for the *miscellaneous* category must match any document that does not fit in any trained category. In some cases the miscellaneous category may be well-defined and it is not very difficult to find training documents. However the set of training documents for an undefined miscellaneous category is very large. We can use a binary classifier to overcome this problem. Consider a binary classifier trained with the single category, *sugar*. The results from this classifier are shown in a two by two confusion matrix. The testing dataset is a collection of *sugar* and *miscellaneous* documents.

Table 7.2: Confusion Matrix for Sugar and Miscellaneous Documents with a Binary Classifier

Category	Sugar	Miscellaneous
Sugar	6	1
Miscellaneous	0	4

All the documents with the exception of one *sugar* document were correctly categorized. We can repeat this same process with the two other categories – *cocoa* and *coffee*. A separate training model is created for each category. The results from the separate evaluations with each category are shown in Table 7.3.

Table 7.3: Confusion Matrices for Categorization of *Coffee*, *Cocoa*, and *Miscellaneous* Documents

Category	Coffee	Miscellaneous
Coffee	4	2
Miscellaneous	0	4

Category	Cocoa	Miscellaneous
Cocoa	6	0
Miscellaneous	0	4

The use of the binary classifier is a better method to handle documents that cannot be categorized into any one of the trained categories. It also handles documents that may belong to more than one category. For example, a *sugar* document may also include features from the *coffee* category and therefore can be categorized under both categories. The binary classifier can correctly categorize a mixed document that has content from more than one category.

An *anti-model* for a category is a classifier created from all the documents that do *not* belong to a category. For example, the training documents for the *sugar* anti-model is the set of all documents that are not *sugar* documents. This set of documents may be large and the size of the ngram can be lowered to build an anti-model from the larger training data set. An unknown document is evaluated against a set of anti-models to eliminate categories. A document belongs to the categories that have not been eliminated in the evaluation. The remaining classifiers in this chapter use tokens instead of ngrams for document features.

7.3.3 TF/IDF Classifier

The TF/IDF classifier uses *feature vectors* to represent categories and documents. A feature vector is a list of features such as tokens and associated frequencies. Consider a list of training documents for multiple categories (see Figure 7.2). The list of tokens extracted from the text of training documents and frequencies for a category, is accumulated in a vector. The vector created for each category is then normalized using the token and inverse document frequencies.

The square root of the token frequencies is used instead of the raw counts to dampen the effect of large frequencies. The inverse document frequency (IDF) of a token x is

$$idf(x) = log(\frac{N}{df(x)}) \qquad (7.3)$$

where $df(x)$ is the number of vectors (categories) in which the token x appears and N is the number of vectors. Notice, the minimum IDF is zero for a token x that occurs in all categories and the maximum is $log(N)$ when a token occurs in exactly one category. In Listing 7.4, the TF/IDF classifier uses a `handle` (line 9) method instead of a `train` method to create the classifier model.

Figure 7.2: Categorization with the TF/IDF Classifier using Feature Vectors

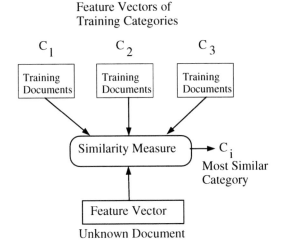

Listing 7.4: Training a TF/IDF Classifier

```
1  TfIdfClassifierTrainer<CharSequence> classifier = new
2    TfIdfClassifierTrainer<CharSequence>(
3      new TokenFeatureExtractor(
4        new IndoEuropeanTokenizerFactory()) );
5  for (int i = 0; i < CATEGORIES.length; i++) {
6    File classDir = new File(TDIR, CATEGORIES[i]);
7    for (File file : classDir.listFiles()) {
8      String text = Files.readFromFile(file);
9      classifier.handle(text,
10       new Classification(CATEGORIES[i]));
11   }
12 }
```

The first parameter of the **handle** method is a character sequence made up of the text from the training document and the second parameter is a **Classification** with the name of the category. The code (not shown) to dump the model to a file is identical to the binary and multi-classifiers. In Listing 7.5, we use a **ScoredClassification** (line 7) instead of a **JointClassification** to test the **classifier**.

Listing 7.5: Testing a TF/IDF Classifier

```
1  ConfusionMatrix confMatrix =
2    new ConfusionMatrix(CATEGORIES);
3  for (int i = 0; i < CATEGORIES.length; ++i) {
4    File classDir = new File(TDIR, CATEGORIES[i]);
5    for (File file : classDir.listFiles()) {
6      String text = Files.readFromFile(file);
7      ScoredClassification classification =
8        compiledClassifier.classify(text);
9      confMatrix.increment(CATEGORIES[i],
10       classification.bestCategory());
11   }
12 }
```

The `classify` method of the `classifier` returns a ranking of categories by score. The name of the top category is returned from the `bestCategory` method. The score of a category is a measure of the similarity between the feature vectors for the document and the category. In the binary and multi-classifiers, a score was the conditional probability of the category given the document. The distance between two vectors is calculated using the Manhattan distance (see Section 6.2.2) or the sum of the absolute differences between every dimension.

7.3.4 K-Nearest Neighbors Classifier

The K-Nearest Neighbors (Knn) classifier also uses feature vectors to compare documents. However, classification is based on the comparison of inter-document vectors and not document-category vectors. The vector of an unknown document is compared with all training document vectors. The most popular category of the k most similar documents is selected (see Figure 7.3).

Training in this classifier is simply the memorization of the category for each document. Classification with a *Knn* classifier has also been called memory-based classification. The time to test an unknown document is longer in this method than any of the previous methods, since the vectors from each one of the training documents must be compared with vector of the unknown document. The number of training documents is usually much larger than the number of categories. The code to train the *Knn* classifier is very similar to the training code for the *TF/IDF* classifier and the only difference is in the constructor.

Figure 7.3: Categorization with the Knn Classifier using Feature Vectors

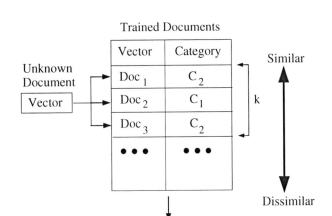

```
KnnClassifier<CharSequence> classifier =
  new KnnClassifier<CharSequence>(
    new TokenFeatureExtractor(
      new IndoEuropeanTokenizerFactory()),
    k, new EuclideanDistance() );
```

The second parameter in the constructor is the integer k representing the number of documents that participate in the classification. The simplest method to assign a category is to build a histogram of the frequencies of categories in the top k documents and find the most popular category. An alternate method uses a weighted average of the inter-document similarities to locate the best category. The category from a training document that is closer to the unknown document is given a higher weight than the category from another document that is weakly similar to the unknown document. We have used the standard IndoEuropean tokenizer to extract features from the text.

The third parameter is the `Distance` function to compare two vectors. The number of vector comparisons per document is $O(n)$ and therefore a simple Manhattan distance measure is used over the more computationally intensive cosine measure to compute distances. The code to categorize a document is identical to the code for the TF/IDF classifier.

7.3.5 Naïve Bayes Classifier

The Naïve Bayes classifier is a probabilistic classifier similar to the binary and multi-classifiers. Here, we use tokens instead of ngrams to compute the probability of a category given a document. Training consists of creating separate tokenized language models for each category (see Figure 7.4).

Figure 7.4: Categorization with Naïve Bayes Classifier using Tokens

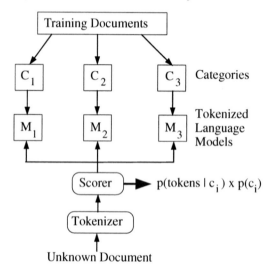

A tokenized language model contains probability estimates for tokens that have been seen in the text of the training documents for a category. The probability of a category c is based on the proportion of the number of training documents allocated to c. The constructor for a Naïve Bayes classifier accepts a list of categories and a tokenizer factory.

```
NaiveBayesClassifier classifier =
  new NaiveBayesClassifier(CATEGORIES,
    new IndoEuropeanTokenizerFactory());
```

A custom tokenizer factory can also be used that may implement stemming and removal of stop words to constrain the number of tokens. The score for a category is the product of the individual probabilities of tokens given the category and the probability of the category itself. The `classifyJoint` method of the classifier returns a `JointClassification` from the which the best category is identified. The tokens from an unknown document may not have been seen in the training dataset and we assume an uniform character model for such tokens. The probability of unseen tokens is proportional to the number of characters in the token and inversely proportional to the size of the character set.

7.3.6 Evaluation

We have described five classifiers that can be implemented with LingPipe. The following evaluation is a simple evaluation with 23 testing and 36 training documents from three categories; the evaluation is not a recommendation of any particular classifier. The list of results with the five classifiers is shown in Table 7.4. A single test was conducted and a more thorough evaluation would use a larger set of categories and training documents with cross-validation.

There are several options to obtain a higher accuracy by using a higher order ngram or a customized tokenizer factory that filters tokens. A higher order ngram may need more training data to build the language model. A custom tokenizer factory may limit the set of tokens used in creating feature vectors to just the ones that are useful to assign categories. The `Similarity` class used in the classifiers can also be modified to refine the comparison between feature vectors. The accuracy is the percentage of testing documents that were correctly categorized. The accuracy of the binary classifier is the microaverage of three categorizations.

The majority of errors in all classifiers were caused by *miscellaneous* documents that were wrongly categorized. The binary classifier is possibly the best of the five classifiers to handle the documents from the miscellaneous category. The other classifiers will perform well, when the categories are exhaustive and every category includes a sufficient number of examples to build an accurate model. Note, the accuracy rates shown in Table 7.4 should *not* be generalized to other larger document collection. Typically, a set of 10-50 training documents or 100 kilobytes to 1 megabyte of training data per category is good enough to create a model.

Table 7.4: List of Results from Five Classifiers for a Sample Collection of 36
Documents

Classifier	Unit	Type	Accuracy %
Binary	Ngram	Probabilistic	87
Multi	Ngram	Probabilistic	78
Knn	Tokens	Similarity	65
Naïve Bayes	Tokens	Probabilistic	78
TF/IDF	Tokens	Similarity	83

In a probabilistic classifier like the Binary classifier, a threshold is specified to decide if a document belongs to a category or not. This threshold is estimated empirically and may need to be adjusted to fine tune the classification. The best threshold is one which works for multiple sets of testing data in a cross-validation. It may be tedious to find thresholds for a dataset with many hundreds of categories. One alternative is to build a hierarchy of categories and find thresholds at each level of the hierarchy.

The Knn classifier is the only classifier without a model for each category. Instead, an unknown document is compared with individual documents to find the most likely category. This of course, limits the scalability of the algorithm due to the large number of computations needed per categorization. The other classifiers do not have this limitation and will scale with larger numbers of categories. It is possible to limit the number of training instances that need to be considered using pruning strategies that have not been covered in this discussion. In our limited experiment, there is little indication of the level of expected accuracy from these classifiers in larger datasets. High levels of accuracy can only be achieved when the features of documents and categories are representative and do provide sufficient evidence to distinguish between categories.

7.3.7 Feature Extraction

A small set of 10-20 unique words are typically sufficient to represent a category. Phrases have a lower frequency than individual words and are therefore not as popular as content indicators compared to words. A feature is not necessarily a word alone. For example, we can classify a document as a *letter* by examining the header and signature information alone. We would expect a header to contain a *from* and *to* address, *date*, and a *greeting* with punctuation. This set of features is unique to the *letter* category.

Similarly, a spam detector uses a set of features that are mostly unique to spam messages. There are several ways to identify these *"category features"* and we will look at one method using the chi-square score. The inverse document frequency score does not give an indication of the likelihood of the dependence between the category and the feature. The value of the chi-square score specifies the level of confidence for a category-feature dependence.

Consider the training set of documents we used to evaluate the five classifiers. A standard tokenizer will generate a large number of tokens that we can prune based on frequency. The ideal set of tokens for a category will have a high chi-square score and co-occur in the same category. For example, the word *bank* was found more often in the *coffee* category than any of the other categories. Table 7.5 shows a two by two table with the observed frequencies of the word *bank* in the *coffee* category.

Table 7.5: Observed Word Frequencies and Occurrences in Categories

Category	Word Feature		
	Bank	Not Bank	Total
Coffee	14	4254	4268
Not Coffee	5	9588	9593
Total	19	13842	13861

We can calculate a chi-square score (24.66) for the word *bank* occurring in the *coffee* category using the observed frequencies in this table and the expected frequencies (see Chapter 5). This score is sufficient to state with a 99.9 % confidence level that there is a dependency between the word *bank* and the category *coffee*. On the other hand, a word like *price* is seen more widely across all categories and has a chi-square score of 0.15, which is not sufficient to identify any dependency. A set of n features in descending order of chi-square score is a good representative for a category.

7.4 Summary

In this chapter, we covered a number of categorization methods based on probability and the use of similarity measures. LingPipe has several classifiers that can be customized with special tokenizers and distance computations. A small set of documents was used to evaluate five methods of classifying documents in LingPipe. The binary classifier had the best performance in this experiment, but tests with larger collections may differ. The online tutorial documents included in the LingPipe distribution has more information on the use of various classifiers.

Feature extraction is an important part of categorization and is the basis for comparing documents, building representatives of categories, and estimating probabilities. We can use a measure like the chi-square score or the inverse document frequency to find the best set of features for a category. A few good features are sufficient to make accurate categorization decisions. The Naïve Bayes classifier has reasonably good performance despite the assumption of feature independence. There are several other categorization methods such as decision trees, logistic regression, support vector machines, perceptrons and multi-layer neural networks that we have not covered in this chapter.

8 Searching an Intranet and the Web

The Web continues to be the most widely used source of information on almost any topic. In this chapter, we will cover the use of some of the tools used to organize, rank, and search the Web. The tools to make the Web a more reliable source of information have evolved with the rapid growth of the Web. We will use the Nutch search engine that is based on the Lucene API to crawl and extract information from sources on an Intranet. This chapter should be useful to anyone interested in building a search engine for an Intranet or a desktop. The methods to organize and rank Intranet sources is loosely based on similar methods for Web sources. We begin with a description of the early Web and the problems faced by the first Web search engines.

8.1 Early Web Search Engines

The initial Web search engines of the mid-90s were similar to contemporary IR systems. But, the Web was unlike any of the other document collections seen earlier. There was no central authority to accept, categorize, and manage documents. Anyone could publish documents on the Web and the accompanying metadata was not always trustworthy. Add to it, the Web was growing exponentially and simultaneously the number of users who wanted to use the Web was also growing rapidly.

It is not surprising that many of the first Web search engines have faded away, since they had to confront a series of difficult problems. Returning results with high precision was hard even with high performance hardware to handle the large volume of information and queries. The size of the Web was becoming overwhelming and it was challenging to fix these problems without completely re-designing a search engine to handle the unique features of finding precise information on the Web. Most early Web search engines ignored the rich metadata embedded in the huge number of links in Web pages. These links play a valuable role in extracting useful documents from a large set of matching documents. Further, users on the Web were accustomed to free search services unlike the subscriber-based IR systems of the past. The developers of early search engines had to design new revenue models in addition to scaling the size of the search engine index and the number of visitors.

The first Web spammers tricked search engines by simply repeating a search term n times in a background color. The initial simple ranking algorithms assigned weights to documents based on the frequency of occurrence of terms. This assumption was perfectly valid in a closed document collection, where the contents of all indexed documents were reviewed. On the Web, spammers manipulated the ranks of hits matching a particular query term, by fudging the contents of the document. This of course made users frustrated with the initial results of a search engine.

The *term vector* model used in IR systems assigned weights to hits based on the number of occurrences of query terms in a document. A simple query like *"White House"* would match thousands of documents that may have simply mentioned the phrase, but are not relevant to the user's request. These hits were of little use to the searcher who was probably interested in accessing the home page of the White House. The developers of Google incorporated a ranking algorithm that used the metadata in the links of the Web in addition to the text of Web pages to return more accurate results than an algorithm based on text alone.

The use of the *recall* measure to evaluate the results of a Web search engine is not very useful, since most searchers do not have the time to scan all relevant hits. However, *precision* is far more important to users who may not look at hits beyond the first page of results. In fact, the location of hits in a results page is also important. So, even though two search engines return the same set of results in the first page, the search engine that returns more relevant documents *early* in the list of hits is ranked higher than the another search engine, where the most relevant documents are not shown early in the list.

8.2 Web Structure

During the mid to late-90s, the Web became extremely popular. Commercial, non-profit, and government organizations of all sizes found it affordable to publish information on the Web. Large numbers of individuals began using the Web as the primary source of information. The principal gateway to this information was the

Web search engine. Organizations quickly realized that the rank in a list of hits for a relevant query term was important to attract Web traffic. A searcher is more likely to visit pages listed earlier than later in a list of hits. This behavior is apparent from search engine logs and reflects a tendency to spend more time reading than locating a good source.

The term *"Search Engine Optimization"* (SEO) was coined to name the process of attracting Web traffic to a site using search engines. The common methods include making it easy for a search engine spider (see section 8.3 Crawlers later in this chapter) to collect and find information on a site. Other methods that are not approved include hiding a large number of keywords in a page that will not be visible in a browser and the use of thousands of pages that reference each other specifically to generate a higher search engine rank. This is a relatively new industry and a few commercial organizations provide SEO services that are customized for particular products. In this chapter, we have not considered SEO methods to optimize the rank of a site and instead focus on the Web link structure, ranking algorithms, and crawlers.

It is not practical to build and show a graph of every link in the Web. Instead, we can estimate the nature of links in the Web from a large number of samples. We cover two visuals of the Web, one was a snapshot of the Web taken in 1999 and the other in 2006. The purpose of trying to understand the nature of the links of the Web is more than just a curiosity. Some parts of the Web are more popular (and therefore more important) than others and knowing where your site is located on the Web is a good indicator of its accessibility and fame.

8.2.1 A Bow-Tie Web Graph

At first, the Web appears to be a chaotic environment with billions of links between pages and little discernable structure. The initial impressions of the Web graph led to the idea that all pairs of pages were linked by a path with a maximum length that would grow logarithmically with the size of the Web. A later study revealed that this was not true and the Web was not as tightly linked as expected. Rather, the Web had a well-defined structure and ease of access to a page depends on the location of the page in the graph. The paths to some Web pages that were highly

linked and centrally located were shorter than other Web pages on the periphery of
the graph.

There is a well-defined core in the Web that most users of the Web visit frequently.
This popular part of the Web that forms the heart of the Web was described in
a study [Broder] by Altavista, IBM and Compaq (now part of Hewlett Packard)
published in 2000. The study from a dataset with over 200 million pages and 1.5
billion links found that the Web resembles a bow tie with peripheral tendrils (see
Figure 8.1). Some of the interesting conclusions in this study, apart from the visual
of the Web graph, were the use of *power laws* to predict the number of incoming
links in a page. The power law expresses the large number of pages with very few
or no incoming links and the rare page that has many incoming links, in a simple
equation $i^{-2.1}$, where i is number of incoming links (ranging from 0 to 10,000+).

Components of the Web

We distinguish between incoming links that refer to a page and outgoing links from
one page to another. This distinction is important since over 90% of the Web is linked
in an undirected graph and less than half of the Web is connected in a directed graph.
About 28% of Web pages, form a central component of the Web, where every page is
connected to every other page along a directed link. This 28% of the Web forms the
Strongly Connected Component (SCC) or the core of the Web. None of the other
four components of the Web are as large as the SCC.

The second and third components called IN (22%) and OUT (22%) are the pages
that can reach the SCC and pages that are reachable from the SCC respectively.
The set of IN pages may be new sites that are not part of the SCC yet. The pages in
OUT may be corporations or organizations that do not link externally. Finally, the
last two components, tendrils (22%) and disconnected components (6%) are more
isolated and less visible than the SCC. Note, a new page cannot become part of the
SCC by simply linking to well known pages such as the Yahoo! or CNN home pages.
A link back from these popular pages to the new page is required to join the SCC.

This study was the first large scale experiment to analyze the graph structure of
the Web and the numbers of links between pages. Earlier studies concluded that
the Web was very well connected. This is true only if the Web is considered an
undirected graph. The percentage of pages connected dropped significantly in a
directed graph. Only one out of four pairs of randomly selected pages were linked.

Figure 8.1: A Map of the Links in the Web

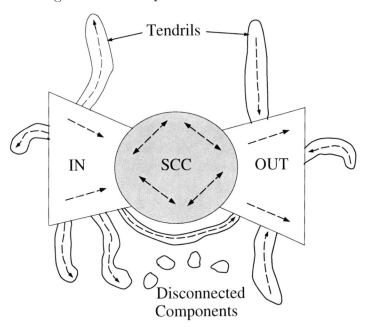

This means that many parts of the Web are not connected. We define the *diameter* of the Web graph as the expected length of the shortest path between between two linked pages. Based on a sample of 200 million Web pages, the diameters of the Web and the SCC are roughly 500 and 28 respectively.

Other interesting results of the study include the use of power laws to compute the number of links and the resilience of the Web graph. Power laws characterize the use of links to create the Web graph. In general, Web page authors create more links to popular pages than other pages. This leads to a skewed distribution of incoming links for any given page that can be described by a power law. So, roughly 0.233, 0.034, and 0.016 of all Web pages have two, five, and seven incoming links respectively. Similarly, the number of outgoing links per Web page also follows a power law distribution. A few pages have a large number of outgoing links, most pages link to a few pages. Power laws were observed for inter-site as well as the set of all links.

Graph Structure

The Web's resilience (paths between any pair of nodes) in an undirected graph does not appear to be due to a few pages with a large number of incoming or outgoing links. We use the term *hub* and *authority* for pages with many outgoing and incoming links respectively. The Web consists of a well-connected graph with embedded hubs and authorities. The use of hubs and authorities plays a very important role in estimating the rank of a given page and in crawling the Web. The removal of these hubs and authorities does not break up the Web graph into disconnected components. These sites are the most easily accessible pages from a search engine.

A complete crawl begins with an initial set of URLs from which all possible links are followed recursively till every possible page that can be reached in a directed graph from the initial set is fetched (see Figure 8.2).

Figure 8.2: A Crawl from an Initial Set of URLs

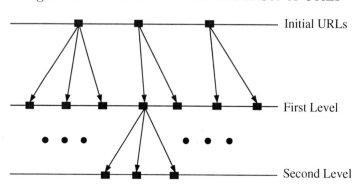

Notice, the initial set of URLs are key to the final set of URLs returned from the crawl. A crawl can either end prematurely or explode and cover a large portion of the graph. A successful crawl should include all major hubs in the initial set of URLs. A single crawler can quickly get bogged down fetching one page at a time and typically large scale crawlers run in parallel to speed up the time to complete the crawl.

A follow on study [Donato] examined the details of each of the Web components in the bow tie pattern of Figure 8.1. Separate studies of crawls on a smaller scale revealed a similar bow tie structure in each crawl, with a power law distribution for the number of incoming and outgoing links. An examination of the individual components did not reveal a fractal like structure. In other words, the bow tie pattern was not seen in the IN, OUT, SCC, and TENDRIL components.

The links from the IN and OUT components to the SCC were examined. Most of the IN and OUT pages were found in close proximity to a SCC page. About 80-90% of the OUT pages were found within five links from a SCC page. More than half the pages in the OUT component were just one link away from a SCC page. The links from the IN component to pages in the SCC were similarly distributed.

These results are useful in building a crawler strategy. There are two possibilities to crawl the Web – a depth first or a breadth first method. The depth first method will follow a link to as many levels as necessary, till a leaf page that contains zero unvisited links is found. The breadth first method will fetch all pages at a given level (see Figure 8.2) before moving deeper into another set of pages. We can say that the breadth first method is a better approach to crawl the Web than the depth first method from our knowledge of the structure of the SCC, IN, and OUT components. A wider variety of pages will be found sooner in a breadth first than a depth first search. Both crawl methods will eventually return the same set of pages.

A Jellyfish Internet Graph

The physical graph of links in the Internet does not have a bow tie structure similar to the logical graph we saw earlier. A study [Carmi] of the physical links in the Internet revealed a jelly fish like structure (see Figure 8.3). The collection of physical route information for this experiment was distributed across several thousand clients. Each of the clients periodically validated a route to a randomly selected host, using either the *traceroute* or *ping* utilities. Millions of such measurements were collected, categorized, and analyzed. Each measurement was categorized into an autonomous system based on the IP address. An *autonomous system* is a collection of IP networks and routers under the control of one or more entities. The analysis of the Internet at a coarse grain autonomous system level was simpler than an analysis at the detailed IP level.

Each autonomous system was made up of about 20K nodes. We use the term *node* to represent a single IP address. The K-Shell decomposition method to organize a network, works by repeatedly removing nodes from degree 1 to k, till no more nodes exist in the graph. First, all nodes with only one link are removed to create the 1-

Figure 8.3: Jellyfish Structure of the Internet at the Autonomous System Level

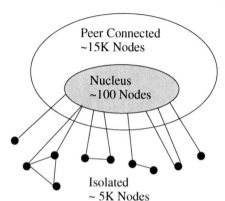

shell. Next, nodes with two links are removed, and so on. The value of k is increased till some threshold and any remaining nodes in the graph form the *k-core*. The size of the nucleus or *k-core* varied from 50 to 2500 nodes depending on the autonomous system.

All nodes in the nucleus are separated by one or two links. The nodes outside the nucleus are divided into two categories, a large set of peer connected nodes and a smaller set of isolated nodes. The set of isolated nodes connect through the nucleus with paths made up of two or three links. The links between nodes in the peer connected component are longer (three to four links). Understanding where a crawler is physically located in Figure 8.3 is useful to speed up the collection and assembly of information. Equally important is the inclusion of hubs in the initial set of URLs to begin a crawl.

8.2.2 Hubs & Authorities

We saw earlier that important pages that are relevant to the user's need are not distinguishable from other pages based on textual features alone. For example, the phrases "*White House*" or "*Harvard University*" are found in thousands of documents. The number of occurrences of these phrases alone in the extracted text from their respective home pages, is typically not sufficient to assign a higher rank than other pages. This is a much bigger problem on the Web than on an Intranet, due to the abundance of matching documents on the Web.

The creation of a link from a page p to a page q can be viewed as a measure of authority assigned by the author of page p to q. However, not every link is an assignment of authority and many links exist purely to assist in the navigation of a site. One solution to this problem is to only consider intra-site links to compute the rank of a page. But just counting the number of incoming links to a matching page is not enough to find the most relevant page. Pages from universally popular sites like Yahoo! or Google are not necessarily the most relevant pages.

The Hubs & Authorities model is based on the relationship that exists between a set A of authoritative pages for a topic and those pages (hubs) that link to the pages in A. This relationship is exploited in an algorithm to find both types of pages from a Web graph. Consider the sample graph in Figure 8.4 of twenty linked pages.

Figure 8.4: A Web Graph of Twenty Pages

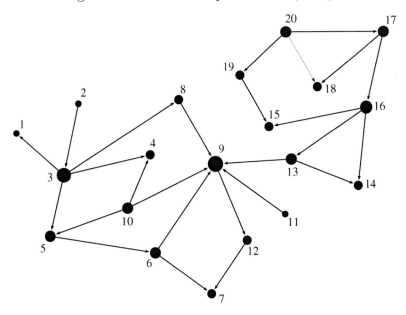

Such a graph could conceivably be generated from a set of 20 hits for a query. The directed graph consists of 26 links between pages that are distributed unevenly.

Pages with many incoming and outgoing links are potential authorities and hubs respectively. All pages in this graph are relevant, but a few pages do stand out in the graph. We can iteratively compute a hub and authority score for every page in the graph. The authority score measures the number of incoming links weighted by the hub score of the referring page. The hub score is based on the sum of the authority scores of linked pages from the hub. Notice, the mutual relationship between a good hub and authority. The algorithm is defined as follows.

1. Assign identical hub and authority scores to every page in the graph.

2. Run a loop till convergence

   a) Compute the authority score for a page x from the sum of the hub scores of the set of pages found in incoming links of x.

   b) Compute the hub score of a page x from the sum of the authority scores of the set of pages found in outgoing links of x.

   c) Normalize the hub and authority scores of all pages.

   d) Terminate when there appears to be no change in the hub and authority scores of pages.

The first step assigns an uniform value of one, to the hub and authority scores of all pages. Next, we compute new hub and authority scores using link information in the graph. The authority score of a page x depends on the hub scores of pages that link to x. Conversely, the hub score of a page x is the sum of the authority scores of linked pages from x. Finally, the hub and authority scores of all pages are normalized to a value between 0 and 1. The computation of the algorithm can be represented using a matrix A of all incoming links and vectors $\vec{a}$ and $\vec{h}$ for the authority and hub scores respectively.

$$\vec{a} = A^T \times \vec{h}$$

$$\vec{h} = A \times \vec{a}$$

The algorithm runs this pair of matrix computations in a loop, till an *equilibrium* is found. An equilibrium is found when the hub and authority scores converge to

Table 8.1: Top Ranking Authorities and Hubs for the Web Graph in Figure 8.1

Authorities		Hubs	
Number	Score	Number	Score
9	0.50	10	0.43
4	0.33	13	0.37
5	0.33	6	0.36
14	0.30	3	0.35

a set of scores that remain constant over multiple iterations. The results of the algorithm are shown for the top ranking hubs and authorities in Table 8.1.

The top ranked authority 9 with the highest number (5) of incoming links seems like an obvious choice. There are several choices for the remaining authorities since six of the pages have two incoming links. The three pages 4, 5, and 14 are ranked higher than the remaining three pages since they are linked to the highest ranking authority 9. The top ranking hub pages have two and three outgoing links. Notice, the hub page 3 with three outgoing links is ranked lower than the remaining three pages that have just two outgoing links. The reason for the higher weights of pages with fewer outgoing links is the distribution of the weight of the dominant authority 9 to the hubs 10, 13, and 6. The use of links to rank pages is an improvement over purely text based methods alone and in the next section we will look at an algorithm that combines these two measures into a single score.

8.2.3 PageRank Algorithm

The PageRank algorithm assigns a score similar to the hubs and authorities scores based on the link structure of the Web graph. A single score based on incoming links is computed for every page in the graph. Earlier, we saw that simply counting the number of incoming links is not an accurate measure. For example, there is a substantial difference between an incoming link from the Yahoo! home page and a similar link from a personal home page. The link from the Yahoo! home page should be given greater importance than the link from a personal home page. The PageRank score of a page depends not just on the number of incoming links, but also on their quality. For example, the PageRank score R_5 of page 5 in Figure 8.4 is

$$R_5 = c(\frac{R_3}{4} + \frac{R_{10}}{3}) \tag{8.1}$$

The ranks of the incoming links from pages 3 and 10 that link to page 5 are added and normalized. The contribution of an incoming link of a page x is inversely proportional to the number of outgoing links from x. The ranks of pages 3 and 10 are divided by the number of outgoing links, four and three respectively. A page with exactly one outgoing link will transfer its entire rank to the linked page. Pages like the Yahoo! home page with many outgoing links that have a high rank will distribute its large score among many hundreds of pages.

Note, the equation to compute a PageRank is recursive. We need an initial PageRank for each page to begin computing successive PageRanks. This model does not take into account pages that may have zero incoming links which results in a zero PageRank for such pages. This is undesirable since these pages do have some value. A modified equation for the PageRank is a weighted sum of the ranks of incoming links and a constant value of $(1 - c)$.

$$R_5 = c(\frac{R_3}{4} + \frac{R_{10}}{3}) + (1 - c) \tag{8.2}$$

The weight c is chosen to balance the amount of constant rank with the rank contributed by incoming links. The values of 0.85 or 0.9 for c have been found to work reasonably well. We can consider the value of $(1-c)$ as the initial rank assigned to every page. Contrast this assignment with the uniform assignment of 1.0 in the hubs and authorities algorithm. A simple description of the PageRank algorithm follows.

1. Assign a constant PageRank, $(1 - c)$ to every page.

2. Repeat till convergence.

   a) Compute a new page rank for every page using the set of incoming links.

   b) Check if the difference between the old and new page ranks is minimal or not.

The initial PageRank of every page is 0.15 or 0.1. The PageRank of all pages are computed in a loop till the difference between PageRank scores of all pages has converged. The table of all incoming links for every page is saved in a matrix. The computation of a new set of PageRanks is the equivalent of a matrix computation using the matrix A of all incoming links. The list of ordered PageRanks forms a vector $\vec{r}$.

$$\vec{r'} = c \times A \times \vec{r} + (1 - c) \times \vec{1} \qquad (8.3)$$

A new PageRank vector $\vec{r'}$ is computed using the existing PageRank vector $\vec{r}$ and the matrix A. The repeated calculation of this equation converges when the difference between the values of the new and existing PageRank vectors is minimal. A parallel implementation of this equation 8.3 uses multiple threads to compute the new PageRank vector where each thread calculate the PageRank for a fraction of all pages.

This method of finding principal eigenvector is called the *Power Method*. We are essentially trying to find the best set of values for twenty unknowns (PageRanks). The values returned by the principal eigenvector is the closest approximation to the twenty PageRanks. The Power Method transfers the initial value of the PageRanks through the directed links to other pages till a "steady state" is reached. The PageRanks for the top scoring pages in Figure 8.4 is shown in Table 8.2.

Table 8.2: Top Ranking Pages and PageRanks

Page Number	PageRank
7	0.734
12	0.576
9	0.529
15	0.264

The top ranked page is not intuitive from the figure of the graph. The page 9 has a high rank due to the large number of incoming links, that is then transferred to page 12 and finally to page 7. Page 7 is ranked higher than page 12 since it has an additional source of rank from page 6. Notice, the PageRank score for a page is sensitive to small changes in the graph. A PageRank in a sense is an indicator of how easy it is find a page on the graph. The PageRank is just one component of the overall rank of a page that includes the textual features, the font of specific sections of text, and the anchor text of incoming links.

8.2.4 PageRank vs. Hubs & Authorities

The use of links to improve the precision of search engine results is based on a link model in the citation of research papers. A paper that was cited often in a particular context is analogous to an authority in a Web graph. Similarly, a survey paper that includes many of the popular references for a topic is equivalent to a hub. We would expect a few papers to have many incoming links and the remaining papers to have a few or no incoming links. This is based on statistics from citation analysis that revealed that a quarter of all published papers were never cited and of the remaining 75%, half were not cited within a year. Three quarters of the remaining papers were cited just once a year and less than 5% of all publications were cited at least three times a year.

We can use this natural citation model in academia to find the Web pages that are relevant based on textual features and that also appear in the most referred section of the Web. Both the Hubs & Authorities and PageRank algorithms use the citation model in the Web graph to return results with higher precision. However, there are several differences between the two algorithms (see Table 8.3).

Table 8.3: Main Differences between Hubs & Authorities and PageRank Algorithms

Hubs & Authorities	PageRank
Algorithm is run at search time.	PageRank scores are pre-computed before a search.
Each page is assigned a separate hub and authority score.	A page is assigned a single PageRank score.
The query-based Web graph is typically not very large.	The Web graph to compute PageRank is usually much larger than a query-based graph.

One of the criticisms of the PageRank algorithm is that it is not associated with any query. Clearly, the static PageRank score of a document is not appropriate for all possible matching queries. It is therefore only one component of the final rank of a matching document. Pre-computed PageRank scores of all matching documents are combined with other features to generate the final set of ranks. The other components include the use of title text, anchor text of incoming links, and various textual features.

The Hub & Authorities algorithm starts with an initial set of URLs that match the query and then builds an expanded set of URLs from the initial set. The algorithm is run against the graph of the expanded set to find hubs and authorities. Every page has a hub and authority score. A page can be both a strong hub and a strong authority. Some hubs may also be mixed; a page may contain links to multiple topics. This means that both relevant and non-relevant pages are linked through the same hub. Therefore, the authority score of a mixed hub leaks from the relevant to non-relevant pages leading to lower precision in the list of hits for a query. One method of solving this problem is to verify that a page with a large hub score is focused on a single topic; otherwise the page is segmented based on common terms. A single mixed hub is split into multiple pages before the computation of hub and authority scores.

Both algorithms treat all outgoing links uniformly. There is no distinction between links based on proximity to matching query terms. Links that are found closer to a query term may have greater relevance than a link located elsewhere in a page. Further, the location of the link on a Web page is also ignored. A reader is more likely to notice links at the top or side of a page. The Hubs & Authority algorithm is also susceptible to changes in the link structure. It is dependent on bipartite cores to reinforce the hub and authority scores (see Figure 8.5).

Figure 8.5: Bipartite Cores and Nepotistic Links

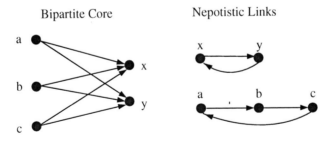

A bipartite core represents links between pages that may not be linked directly, but share a common interest. These types of links are found in many Web-based communities. We can say that pages a, b, and c are implicitly linked through pages x and y and vice versa. The co-citation of the same paper x in academic literature is an indicator of similarity between papers, that is modeled here with links to the same pages. New and emerging communities can be identified from a Web graph containing a list of bipartite cores.

Consider a search for the term *physics*. The results of a search for bipartite cores (Hubs & Authorities) in the Web graph for this query, would reveal smaller communities such as academic departments, associations, and other groups engaged in research on sub-topics like string theory or sub-atomic particles. Hubs and authorities correspond to the nodes a,b,c and x,y for a bipartite core in Figure 8.5. Similarly, the hubs and authorities extracted from a Web graph for the query *"gun control"*, would return two communities, one *for* and the other *against* gun control.

Link Spamming

The central assumption that all links are added to pages by authors to refer the reader to another page that is related, is not always valid on the Web. Link spamming is the addition of incoming links to a page, purely to obtain a higher search engine rank. Many hundreds or even thousands of Web pages are artificially generated for the sole purpose of boosting the rank of a set of pages. Each of these generated pages contain numerous links to a set of target pages. The rank of a page can be manipulated by adjusting the number of incoming links. Several commercial organizations specialize in this activity, building artificial pages to direct Web traffic to customer pages. Developers of Web search engines are aware of link spamming and penalize sites that build a large number of highly linked artificial pages by dropping such sites from the list of indexed pages.

The initial attempts to filter links, excluded all links between pages on the same host. This is based on the assumption that pages on the same host are more likely to be authored by the same person or are included for navigational purposes. Links that are added explicitly to raise the rank of a page are called nepotistic links (see Figure 8.5) and are contrary to our assumption that a link is equivalent to a citation in academic literature to confer authority to a related paper. Nepotistic links are found between two and multiple sites that collaborate to boost the rank of a set of pages and even within a single page that refers to itself. A *"clique attack"* is a group of sites that together build a dense network of inter-site links that serve no purpose in a browser. The effect of multiple links to a target page from a single host can be minimized by assigning duplicate links a fraction instead of an unit weight.

Another method of manipulating Web links is through the use of misleading anchor text. Search engines like Google assign a higher weight to the anchor text of a link, than the text contents of the linked page. This is a fair assumption to make since most genuine authors will include a concise description of the page in the anchor text accompanying the link. However, this also allows a group of collaborators to use this assumption to boost the rank of an unrelated page.

For example, some of the phrases in anchor text used to direct Web traffic to unsuspecting sites include "miserable failure" and "weapons of mass destruction". The text contents of these targeted pages may have none of the phrases, but will rank high in the list of hits for these queries. Search engine developers use empirical data to filter the results from queries with such phrases. Most crawlers simply collect and store information, the analysis for nepotistic links and other forms of spamming are performed post-retrieval. Oddly enough, the query "miserable failure" now returns links to pages that explain why pages about George Bush are linked to the query. The phrase "Google Bomb" was coined to explain this type of activity, although the results from other search engines that use the number of links to compute the rank of a hit are similarly affected.

8.3 Crawlers

We need a crawler in a Web-based environment to store and collect distributed information. Prior to the Web, information was manually submitted to an IR system and made available through a search interface. In a large corporate Intranet, it is difficult to visit hundreds of sites and manually collect all pages from these sites to build a search engine. Instead we use a crawler that *visits* all pages that can be accessed from an initial set of URLs (pages). The steps to run a crawler that fetches all possible pages from an initial set of pages is quite simple (the terms *bot*, *spider* or *robot* are often used to describe a crawler).

1. Load the initial set of URLs into a list of pages to be indexed.

2. Run till completion

a) Find an unindexed page, fetch and store the page, extract the out going links and add to the list of pages to be indexed

b) Exit the loop, if a time limit for the crawler is exceeded or there are no more unindexed pages left.

Most crawlers maintain a list of pages that have either been indexed or are yet to be indexed in a database. The list is initially loaded with the set of pages from which the crawl will begin. This set of pages determines the rest of crawl and is selected in such a way that the crawler will be able to access all visible pages in the environment using the out going links of the initial pages. An unrestricted crawler on the Web may run for days or even weeks, unless some termination conditions are included. A crawl will end, if all the pages in the list have been indexed or if the crawl time has exceeded a limit.

8.3.1 Building a Crawler

A single crawler takes a long time to run for several reasons. One, the time to fetch a page is based on the network bandwidth and the load on the host. Some hosts that are overloaded may take a long time to respond to a request. Secondly, every page that has not been visited before may have to be resolved to an IP address using a Domain Name Service (DNS) request. The time to perform a DNS lookup for a page can be substantial compared to the time to actually download the page. Finally, the number of unindexed pages in the list grows rapidly in a large Web-based environment, overwhelming the crawler.

Most large scale crawlers run in parallel. The collection and DNS lookups of pages is performed on multiple crawlers that share a common list of unindexed pages. The basic design of a parallel crawler is shown in Figure 8.6. Multiple crawlers interact with a shared list through a load manager that assigns URLs to crawlers and adds new unindexed URLs to the list.

The load manager has the important task of balancing the load across multiple crawlers and adding new pages to the list of URLs. Two crawlers should not attempt to fetch the same page and all crawlers should be kept busy with a stream of URLs to fetch and store. The load manager marks URLs that have been fetched in the list and assigns unique URLs to individual crawlers. Each crawler extracts the links

Figure 8.6: The Basic Design of a Parallel Crawler

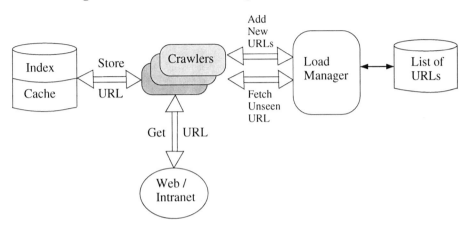

from the text of a Web page and creates a new set of pages that can be added to the list. Before adding a link to the list, the load manager must ensure that a duplicate link does not exist. Relative links (without the host name) must be converted to absolute links.

All links should be converted to a standard form made up of three parts. The first part is the name of the protocol (http for Web pages) in lower case followed by the canonical host name and an optional port number. A default port number (80) is used unless some other port number is specified. A single host may have multiple aliases. For example, the host sourceforge.net may use the alias sf.net. The use of a canonical host name prevents a crawler from storing duplicate links from the same host, even though the URLs are not identical. The last part of the URL is the path name on the server. A path name should be normalized to handle paths that link to the same page, for example the path s2/../s1/a.html should be converted to s1/a.html.

Crawler Traps

A crawler can find itself stuck in an endless loop building a long path from two or more directories that contain pages linked to each other. A simple solution to this problem is to limit the number of directories in the path of any URL. Web servers like Apache disallow symbolic links by default, in source directories. Two Web source directories with symbolic links to each other form an infinite loop of links. A crawler may also encounter URLs with a large number of extraneous characters. A different type of crawler trap is the endless cycle of requests for information from the Web server that the crawler is unable to provide. The server may eventually terminate the connection after many unsuccessful attempts by the same crawler.

Crawler Etiquette

A polite Web crawler follows some standards when fetching information from a Web server. A robot that submits a high number of requests in a short period is easily noticed in a Web log. A person using a browser will typically submit requests with some gap between successive requests. A polite parallel crawler will attempt to spread requests over multiple servers to avoid overtaxing a single server with many simultaneous requests. Some areas of the Web server that are available to the public may be off limits to a crawler. A Web server can issue a set of optional guidelines to crawlers in a `robots.txt` file found at the root directory of the server. For example, part of the `robots.txt` file for the `groups.google.com` site is shown below.

```
User-agent: *
Allow: /searchhistory/
Disallow: /news?output=xhtml&
Allow: /news?output=xhtml
Disallow: /search
Disallow: /groups
Disallow: /images
. . .
Disallow: /blogsearch?
Disallow: /blogsearch/
Disallow: /blogsearch_feeds
Disallow: /codesearch?
Disallow: /codesearch/feeds/search?
```

The first line describes the user agent or crawler to which the following guidelines apply. In this case, the * character implies that the following directives apply to all crawlers. A crawler is identified by the value of the *User Agent* attribute. For example, the names of some of the popular crawlers includes *GoogleBot*, *Nutch*, and *Scooter*. The directives for a specific crawler are listed separately with the associated crawler name as the *User Agent*. Most of the directories in this example are restricted to all crawlers with the exception of the `searchhistory` and `news` directories. These guidelines are optional and it is up to the discretion of the designer of the crawler to follow or ignore this protocol. All directories are presumed to be accessible to a crawler, if a `robots.txt` file is not found on the server. Finally, individual pages can be excluded from a crawl with a `robot` metatag in the header of a Web page.

Crawler Management

Most organizations work in a dynamic environment, where new Web pages are added or existing Web pages are modified. These changes can occur at any time and rarely will a crawler be notified of new or modified content. The only way for a crawler to find out what has changed since the last crawl is to run the crawler all over again.

We have seen that power laws explain the distribution of outgoing links, incoming links, and the sizes of pages on the Web. We can expect a similar distribution of dynamic Web pages. A few pages change frequently, while most pages are modified occasionally or not at all. A crawler may track the period between successive modifications to a page, to identify the set of pages that are being frequently modified. Most Web servers return a header containing metadata describing the contents of the page requested. The first two lines in the listing below are issued by the client and the remaining lines are returned by the server (`www.yahoo.com`).

```
GET /index.html HTTP/1.1

Host: www.yahoo.com
HTTP/1.1 200 OK
Date: Mon, 20 Aug 2008 06:53:45 GMT
Cache-Control: private
Vary: User-Agent
Last-Modified: Mon, 20 Aug 2008 06:33:52 GMT
Accept-Ranges: bytes
Content-Length: 9461
```

```
Connection: close
Content-Type: text/html; charset=utf-8
<html>
. . . . . .
</html>
```

The html contents of the page have been excluded for brevity. The metadata includes a timestamp of the last modification to the page. A crawler can move a page into a *"less frequently visited"* page category, if there appear to be no changes since the last crawl. The set of pages to visit in a crawl may be determined by the period between modifications and the time since the last visit. Pages that are rarely changed will be visited less often than others. Some search engines create two crawlers, a fast crawler for the sites that change often and a slower and larger crawler for other sites. The types of sites visited in a fast crawler would include weather, news, or blog sites.

A crawler may even use external search engine statistics to decide which page to visit. The URL of a page that was never seen in the hit list of any query within the last six months, may be a candidate for removal from the list of URLs. These types of URLs are not very popular and their removal from the index may make room for other URLs that are more likely to be fetched. The crawler will exclude these types of pages from the crawl.

Highly popular sites are often mirrored to speed up the distribution of information. A crawler visiting these mirror sites has no way of knowing that a page contains content that was seen earlier, from the URL string alone. We can store 128 bit MD5 signatures of the contents of every captured page along with other metadata. The signature of the contents of a newly fetched page is compared against the set of all signatures in a database to identify a duplicate. This is an added overhead for the crawler, since a check must be performed for every retrieved page. However, it may be worthwhile to perform this check at index time to prevent the generation of a hit list with multiple URLs, but the same content.

A Guided Crawler

The crawlers that we have described so far, collect every page that can be accessed without examining the text contents of the pages. A guided crawler is more selective in fetching pages. A guided or focused crawler attempts to download pages that are relevant to a set of topics and excludes all other pages. The guided crawler works exactly like the general Web crawler we saw earlier, but differs in how new pages are added to the list of URLs. The general crawler adds any link that was not seen to the list. A guided crawler must make a decision to add or ignore an unseen link based on a topic profile.

We can view the topic specific information used to guide the crawl as apriori relevance feedback or training data. Every extracted link that has not been seen, is either relevant or not. This is a form of binary classification and we can use the categorization methods we saw earlier in Chapter 7 to classify a link. We have several information sources to classify a link.

- The relevancy of the source page that contains unclassified outgoing links

- The anchor text of the outgoing link

- The location of the link in the pruned Web graph

We make the assumption that a highly relevant page based on the topic profile is more likely to contain outgoing links that are relevant than other pages. Secondly, the tokens used in the anchor text of an outgoing link are strong hints that describe the contents of the page. Finally, we can rank pages in the pruned Web graph using the PageRank or Hubs & Authorities algorithms to find key sources of relevant pages.

8.3.2 Search Engine Coverage

Every crawler begins with an initial set of URLs. On the Web, it is very likely that search engines will use different sets of initial URLs and therefore visit different parts of the Web. We can conclude that some parts of the Web are not accessible using links from the core of the Web alone, based on the bow tie picture of the Web graph (Figure 8.1). All the URLs and the associated outgoing links in the Strongly Connected Core (SCC) make up just about half of the pages on the Web. The remainder can only be accessed from URLs that are explicitly added to the initial list of URLs. Many search engines do allow for the manual addition of pages, to the list of indexable URLs.

One of the first systematic studies [Lawrence] of search engine coverage found that most search engines covered less than 40% of the Web. This is not surprising since most search engines index the popular pages on the Web that are found in the SCC. Consider an Intranet that is a much smaller version of the Web with a similar bow tie graph. We will have a similar pattern in search engine coverage starting from a given initial set. However, Intranets can be searched more thoroughly than the Web. It is relatively easy to build a file scanner that simply scans the list of viewable directories on a Web server to generate the initial set of URLs. Therefore, every page that can be accessed on an Intranet can be indexed.

Hidden Web

The term *"Hidden Web"* has been used to describe the large number of pages that can only be accessed through queries. A searcher must generate a specific query that is submitted to a search engine. The page returned by the search engine contains a list of hits or information relevant to the query. A crawler cannot fetch these types of pages, since an outgoing link to the result of a search engine query may not exist in a page. Further, it is almost impossible for a crawler to guess every possible query that can be submitted to a search engine, to retrieve all accessible pages.

The estimated size of the Hidden Web is many times the size of the static Web. A few sites like NASA's Earth Observing and Data Information System and the National Climate Data Center contain many hundreds of terabytes of data. A search engine is the most efficient way to distribute this large volume of information. It would be cumbersome to generate and store every possible Web page that could be created. Many of these types of search engines are specialized to handle one particular topic.

For example, the Medline Web site deals almost exclusively with medical information. This site is an authoritative source for information on clinical trials, case studies, and drugs. A query for the term *prozac* on a general purpose Web search engine like Google returns eight commercial hits out of ten. The first Web page from Medline was only found in the top 20 hits. A general purpose Web search engine serves a wide audience and is mainly supported by sponsors with commercial interests.

Some organizations have begun to scan the entire contents of libraries to build a single interface to search a huge collection of books, papers, or magazines. The conversion of print to digital media is a Herculean task with accompanying privacy and copyright issues. Specialized search engines that index specific collections of information may have more value than a general purpose engine, for some queries. Many medium to small organizations have smaller collections of information to organize and make available, compared to a large government agency. The open source Nutch project is an implementation of a scalable search engine built using the Lucene API.

8.4 Nutch

The initial motivation for the Nutch project (`http://www.nutch.org`) was to create a transparent alternative to the few commercial Web search engines. These large scale Web search engines are the gateways to information on the Web, for a majority of users. The average user does not have the time to browse beyond the initial page or two of results for any query. Therefore, Web search engines can largely control an user's view of information on the Web by ordering (ranking) the initial n results for a query.

The ranking algorithms of commercial Web search engines are generally proprietary and it is not possible to analyze why a matching document x was ranked higher than another matching document y. The code that ranks documents is hidden from outsiders to avoid spammers from manipulating text and links to specifically boost the ranks of a set of pages.

Therefore, a primary goal of the Nutch project was to provide a detailed explanation of how the score for any given matching document was computed. Nutch uses the Lucene search engine API (see Figure 8.7) to create and search an index. The explanation of the rank of a document is based on a calculation using the term weights, term frequencies, and field normalization values (see section 4.6.2, Scoring Results for details). Building and operating a large scale Web search engine is a substantial challenge. The crawler must fetch and index several billion pages per month. Many hundreds of queries must be simultaneously processed with minimal response times. It is difficult for a non-commercial organization to raise funds to run such a search engine. Consequently, the Nutch organization has de-emphasized the large Web search engine in favor of smaller Intranet and even personal desktop installations.

The Nutch architecture has been designed to implement parallelization techniques to scale the size and speed of the search engine. However, Nutch can also be used on a single server to manage the information of an individual or a small organization. In this chapter, we will focus on running Nutch on a single server. Nutch is distributed in a *tar* file and can be installed on Linux or Windows. In Windows, you will need *Cygwin* or an equivalent *nix* environment to run Nutch.

Figure 8.7: High Level Design of the Nutch Search Engine

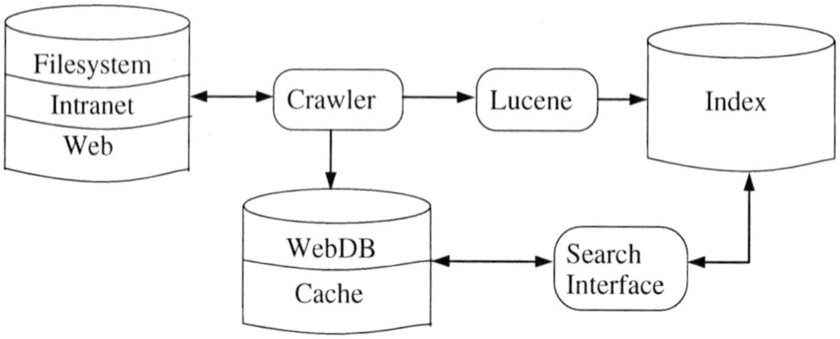

The operation of Nutch can be divided into two parts, a crawler and a search interface. Both components share an index created with the Lucene API. In addition to the index, Nutch also maintains database tables of URLs and links and a cache of indexed pages. The crawler first creates the index and database.

8.4.1 Nutch Crawler

The Nutch crawler uses a file containing seed URLs to start the crawl and returns three data structures (directories) – a Web database, a set of segments, and a Lucene index. The Web database is maintained by the crawler and consists of URL and link information. The information pertaining to an URL or page includes the address, an MD5 signature of the contents, the timestamp of the next retrieval, the number of outgoing links, and a score. Pages with the same content, but with different URL addresses are fetched and will have the same MD5 signature. All pages are initially assigned a default score of 1.0, that is later adjusted to reflect the importance of the page based on its location in the Web graph.

The term *segment* in Nutch is distinct from the Lucene *segment* we saw in Chapter 4. Here, a *segment* is a set of pages that are fetched in a single iteration of the *generate-fetch-update* cycle (see Figure 8.8). A segment includes the URLs to fetch, contents of URLs, and the Lucene index of fetched pages.

Figure 8.8: The Generate-Fetch-Update cycle of the Nutch Crawler

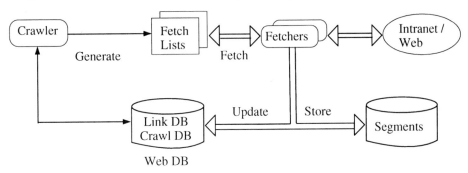

A crawl runs over as many *generate-fetch-update* cycles as required. The *generate* function to create a set of fetch lists, is the first step in the cycle. Each fetch list is organized such that the crawler load is distributed evenly. All pages from a single server will typically be found in a single fetch list to avoid overloading a host with an excessive number of requests in a short period. Collecting pages from an unique host in a single fetch list is considered good crawler etiquette. The Nutch crawler also observes the robot exclusion protocol, that we covered earlier to permit administrators to control which parts of a host are collected.

Directory Structure

The fetch list is generated from the list of URLs in the Web DB. Any URL that has not been fetched within the scheduled timestamp of the next retrieval is a candidate for the fetch list. The initial fetch list in the first cycle will contain the seed URLs provided to the crawler. A set of ten (default) fetcher threads will be assigned to process the fetch lists. Each fetcher thread works with a single fetch list. A fetcher retrieves the page associated with the URL from the Web or Intranet, extracts and saves the list of outgoing links in a Crawl DB and Link DB, and saves the contents with associated metadata of the page in the **segments** directory for the current iteration of the cycle. The CrawlDB keeps track of the URLs for the current cycle and the linkDB maintains a list of incoming links to pages. The initial list of URLs are saved in a file called **urls** in the **seeds** directory. The command to run a crawl from the top level nutch directory up to the third level is

```
bin/nutch crawl seeds -dir results -depth 3
```

The nutch shell script in the **bin** directory runs specific tools based on the command parameter. The crawl command accepts arguments that specify the name of the directory (**seeds**) of the initial urls file, the name of the directory (**results**) for the results of the crawl, and the depth (3) of the crawl. The directory structure after the crawl has completed is shown in Figure 8.9. Note, the directory structure below is valid for Nutch version 0.8. and is subject to change.

Figure 8.9: Directory Structure after Completion of Crawl

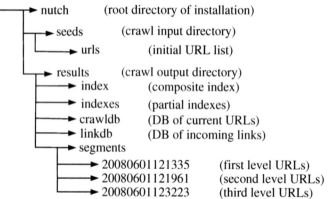

The name of a segment is the timestamp of the start of the crawl iteration. The results of each iteration are stored below the **segments** directory. The **indexes** directory contains the partial indexes created by fetchers that is merged into a composite index in the **index** directory. There are many different options to configure a crawl.

8.4.2 Crawl Configuration

An unrestrained crawler can quickly get bogged down with a long list of URLs that need to be fetched. Nutch includes a set of default directives in a `nutch-default.xml` file of the `conf` directory to control the crawl. These directives (properties) are typically overridden in the `nutch-site.xml` file of the same directory. For example, the `fetch.server.delay` property to specify the delay between requests to the same server is

```
<property>
<name>fetcher.server.delay</name>
<value>1.0</value>
<description>The number of seconds the fetcher will delay
between successive requests to the same server.
</description>
</property>
```

The default value of 1.0 seconds can be set lower on a minimally loaded Intranet host. The `fetch.max.crawl` delay is the maximum number of seconds the crawler must wait before skipping a page. The default of 30 seconds can be increased, if bandwidth is limited and to accommodate pages on slower connections to the Internet. A skipped page will be fetched a maximum of n times, where n is the number specified in the `db.fetch.retry.max` property. The number of fetchers (default 10) is described in a `fetcher.threads.fetch` property. This value is also the maximum number of concurrent connections that will be made by the crawler. The number of threads (default 1) that can concurrently access a host is represented in the `fetcher.threads.per.host` property. A higher value may overload a single host.

The `db.ignore.internal.link` is a boolean property used to force the crawler to only follow outgoing links to an external site. Earlier, we saw that link analysis tools like the Hubs & Authorities algorithm use intra-site links alone in the Web graph. The value of this property would be set to *true* to run such link analysis algorithms. A *true* value for this property can also substantially limit the total number of URLs fetched. The counterpart to this property is `db.ignore.external.link` that restricts a crawler to pages located in the same site as the current page.

The `db.default.fetch.interval` property is the number of days between successive fetches of the same page. This interval is uniformly applied to all fetched pages. Ideally, the crawler should dynamically set the interval for each page based on the time between changes to the content of the page. A short interval is more appropriate for a dynamic page from a news or weather site.

The `http.agent.name` property is the name of the crawler that will be provided to crawled sites, when a page is initially requested from the site. For example, `Googlebot` and `Scooter` are the names of two crawlers we saw earlier. This field cannot be null and is usually named after an organization. A description, version, email address, and URL of the crawler can be optionally specified using other http properties.

```
<property>
<name>http.agent.name</name>
<value>nutch</value>
<description>
   HTTP 'User-Agent' request header. MUST NOT
   be empty - please set this to a single word
   uniquely related to your organization.
</description>
</property>
```

Two proxy properties, `http.proxy.host` and `http.proxy.port` must be set to run a crawler behind a firewall. The `http.content.limit` numeric property limits the size of the content downloaded from a single page. The default value for this property is 64 kilobytes and should be appropriately adjusted for a collection of books or long documents. The `http.timeout` property is the time in milliseconds to wait before a http request times out. The default of ten seconds may not be sufficient to fetch pages from slower sites on the Web. The crawler will try to fetch a page from a busy site with a maximum of `http.max.delays` retries.

A crawler can sometimes get bogged down in a single large site. The pages of a single large well connected site will dominate the crawl database, confining the crawler to pages from a single source. This may be undesirable crawl behavior on the Web and the `generate.max.per.host` property limits the number of pages from any single host.

The properties to restrict the crawler to internal and external links alone, may not be sufficient on an Intranet with multiple hosts. You can specify the URL pattern (filter file) that must be matched, before a link is added to the list of crawl URLs, in a file specified by the `urlfilter.regex.file` property. The contents of the URL filter file (`crawl-urlfilter.txt`) in the `conf` directory for an Intranet crawl of the `nutch.org` site would look like the following.

```
1   # skip file:, ftp:, & mailto: urls
2   -^(file|ftp|mailto):
3   # skip image and other suffixes that
4   # can't be parsed
5   -\.(gif|GIF|jpg|JPG|....)$
6   # skip URLs containing certain characters as
7   # probable queries, etc.
8   -[?*!@=]
9   # skip URLs with slash-delimited segment that
10  # repeats 3+ times, to break loops
11  -.*(/.+?)/.*?\1/.*?\1/
12  # accept hosts in nutch.org and localhost alone
13  +^http://([a-z0-9]*\.)*nutch.org/
14  +^http://localhost.*/
15  # skip everything else
16  -.
```

Every line of code in the file represents a regular expression pattern (*regex*) for an URL. The first character is either a plus or minus sign (a line that begins with the # character is a comment). A plus sign means that the URL must match the regex, to be included in the list of URLs. Any URL matching the regex following a minus sign, will be excluded from the list. The process of matching an URL against the list of patterns is executed in order from the first to last pattern and terminates at the first successful inclusion or exclusion match. The regex patterns are built using the standard regex metacharacters. Note, matching is purely character based and some URLs that use IP addresses (like `192.168.1.*` or `127.0.0.1`) that point to hosts included in the crawl, will be excluded. URLs that point to themselves will be excluded after two successive crawls to the same page. Pages with duplicate content are removed at the end of the crawl.

Every page saved in the database is assigned a score. Several properties set the scores of seed URLs, pages linked across sites, and pages linked within a site. Nutch uses a version of an Adaptive Online Page Importance Calculation (OPIC) algorithm [Abiteboul] to calculate the scores of pages from the Web graph of a crawl. The idea behind the OPIC algorithm is similar to other link analysis tools like PageRank and Hubs & Authorities. Pages with a higher number of incoming links are more likely to be assigned a higher score than other pages. The score of a page can be used in two ways. One, the pages with higher scores may be re-crawled before other pages. This is based on the assumption that the important pages should be current. A score of a page can also be used to boost the rank of the page. We would expect pages with higher scores that represent authorities to have a proportionately higher relevance.

Minimal Configuration

Nutch includes a number of properties to restrict the number of outgoing links per page, the number of incoming links per page, and the maximum number of characters used in the anchor text. The default values for most of these properties is sufficient in most cases. The minimum configuration to run a crawl requires a name for the crawl agent and a change to the URL filter file (`crawl-urlfilter.txt`) in the `conf` directory. The `http.agent.name` property must be set before you can run a crawl with Nutch. The default URL filter value in the `crawl-urlfilter.txt` file is set to `MY.DOMAIN.NAME` and should be changed to the appropriate domain.

Plugins

Nutch uses plugins to add external tools such as indexers and text filters to handle different document formats. Plugins are based on the specifications given in the Eclipse development platform (`http://www.eclipse.org`). The `parse-plugins.xml` file in the `conf` directory is a cross reference of mime types [Mime] to plugins. For example, the mime type `application/msword` is associated with the plugin `parse-msword`. Similarly, plugins for other document types such as PDF, Excel, and OpenOffice.org files are specified in the same file. A default `parse-text` plugin is assumed when no mime type is given.

A text filter plugin is the name of a directory in the `plugins` directory. The `parse-pdf` directory contains specifications in an xml file that include the dependencies and libraries needed for the text filter. The PDFBox [Pdfbox] open source Java library is one of the dependencies to run the pdf parser. Many of the other document file types are similarly parsed with external libraries integrated with Nutch using plugins. New file types can be parsed by adding a plugin and modifying the `parse-plugins.xml` file. The default list of plugins includes many of the popular document formats and Javascript source code. All plugins are not used by default and can be enabled via the `plugin.includes` property in the `nutch-site.xml file` (see Desktop Configuration).

Desktop Configuration

Nutch can also be used to crawl and search a local file system. The list of files to scan is provided just as before in the `seeds/urls` file, except that each entry is the name of a local file specified with the `file` protocol. For example, the entry for the `readme` file in the `nutch` directory would be given as `file:///nutch/README.txt`. Two other files, the `nutch-site.xml` and `crawl-urlfilter.txt` files need to be changed to handle local files. The `plugin.includes` property is overridden in the `nutch-site.xml` file with `protocol-file` plugin added to handle `file` URLs.

```
<property>
<name>plugin.includes</name>
<value>protocol-file|protocol-http|urlfilter-regex|parse-(text|html|
    js|pdf)|index-basic|query-(basic|site|url)|summary-basic|scoring
    -opic</value>
</property>
```

The default `crawl-url-filter.txt` file skips URLs that begin with file. The regular expression is modified to skip `mailto` and `ftp` URLs alone. The following regular expression is added to accept all `file` URLs.

```
-^(ftp|mailto):
+file://.*
```

A desktop crawl is unlike a Web or Intranet crawl. In most cases, there are few outgoing links to extract from files and a crawl based on extracted links alone will end abruptly without fetching all possible files. An alternative is to recursively scan the list of index directories using a Perl script (see `filelist.pl` in `src/org/btext/ch8`) to build the list of seed URLs. The crawler then simply reads and fetches the list of all files in the `nutch/seeds/urls` file, without using any links to find additional files.

8.4.3 Running a Re-crawl

Unfortunately, we cannot run a re-crawl with the same `crawl` command that we used to initially build the database and segments. Each execution of `crawl` creates a brand new directory to save the results of the crawl. It may be more efficient to re-crawl a site instead of repeatedly starting a fresh crawl. The same functions that the `crawl` command executes are run in a shell script, `recrawl.sh` (in the `src/org/btext/ch8` directory) without creating a new directory to store the results. The existing database is used to find the list of URLs that are due to be crawled based on the next fetch date. The url filter file, `crawl-urlfilter.txt` is used by the crawl tool alone. A similar file `regex-urlfilter.txt` used by all other tools to filter URLs, must be modified to use the same patterns as the `crawl-urlfilter.txt` file, before running a re-crawl.

The `recrawl.sh` script first runs n fetch-generate-update cycles where n is the depth specified in an argument to the script. The *generate* function accepts an `adddays` parameter that can be used to re-crawl pages sooner than specified in the next fetch date. The number of `adddays` will be added to the current time and compared with the next fetch date to decide if a page should be re-fetched or not. All pages will be re-fetched, if the value of adddays is greater than 30 and the fetch interval is 30 days.

A new temporary segment is created to save the results at each iteration of the fetch-generate-update cycle. The temporary segments are merged into a single segment and deleted after all iterations of the fetch-generate-update cycles are complete. Each of the segments are indexed and duplicates are removed. Finally, all indexes are combined into a single index.

8.4.4 Search Interface

The Nutch distribution includes a `war` file to run searches from a browser. We use the Tomcat servlet container in this example. The `nutch-0.8.1.war` file is copied to the `webapps` sub-directory of the root Tomcat directory. The war file is unzipped at the next server restart to create a `nutch-0.8.1` sub-directory under the `webapps` directory. This sub-directory contains the files needed to run the search interface. The files include JavaServer pages and configuration files. The `nutch-site.xml` file in the `WEB-INF/classes` directory must be modified to specify the search (crawl results) directory with the following property.

```
<property>
<name>searcher.dir</name>
```

```
<value>/big/nutch-0.8.1/results</value>
</property>
```

This property reflects the name of the directory that contains all the results from a Nutch crawl. The search interface can be launched with the following URL – `http://localhost:8080/nutch-0.8.1`, assuming that Tomcat has been restarted to use the changes made in the `webapps` directory. A query is re-directed to the `search.jsp` page that runs the query and returns the results. The results of a sample query are shown in Figure 8.10.

Figure 8.10: Results of a Sample Query using the Default Interface

The interface includes a list of standard items for each hit including the title, URL, and a snippet of text that contain the query terms. The cached link fetches the page from the stored text content of the page using the `cached.jsp` page. The two other links for the *anchors* and *explain* functions use some of the special features of Nutch. The *explain* function returns the score for the matching hit with a detailed explanation of how the score was computed (see section 4.6.2, Scoring Results). The *anchors* function will list the anchor text of links that point to the page. The default interface is typically sufficient to verify that the search engine is working.

Custom Search Interface

In most cases, a custom implementation of the search interface would be preferable. The `custom.jsp` file in the `src/org/btext/ch8` directory contains a simple custom interface. The header of the file is shown in Listing 8.1.

Listing 8.1: Source to Generate Header of Custom Search Interface

```
1  <html>
2  <meta http-equiv="Content-Type"
3    content="text/html; charset=utf-8">
4  <head>
5  <title>Nutch</title>
6  </head>
7  <%
8  Configuration nutchConf =
9    NutchConfiguration.get(application);
10 NutchBean bean = NutchBean.get(
11   application, nutchConf);
12 String queryString = request.getParameter("queryString");
13 if (queryString == null) queryString = "";
14 %>
```

The static `get` (line 8) method of the `NutchConfiguration` class returns a configuration using the `ServletContext` passed in the `application` parameter. The `NutchConfiguration` class is an utility to create Hadoop Configurations that include Nutch-specific resources. We need the configuration to create a `NutchBean` (line 10) that contains several types of search methods. The `queryString` (line 12) is a form parameter in the search interface. The remainder of the `custom.jsp` file is shown in Listing 8.2.

Listing 8.2: Source to Generate Body of Custom Search Interface

```
1  <body>
2    <form name="search" action="./custom.jsp">
3    <input name="queryString" size=44
4      value="<%=queryString%>">
5    <input type="submit" name="type" value="SEARCH"
6       class="button">
7    </form>
8  <%
9    Hits hits;
```

```
10    Query query = Query.parse(queryString, nutchConf);
11    hits = bean.search(query, 10);
12    Hit[] show = hits.getHits(0, hits.getLength());
13    HitDetails[] details = bean.getDetails(show);
14    Summary[] summaries = bean.getSummary(details, query);
15    for (int i = 0; i < hits.getLength(); i++) {
16      HitDetails detail = details[i];
17      String title = detail.getValue("title");
18      String url = detail.getValue("url");
19      String summary = summaries[i].toHtml(true);
20      // print HTML to display a hit
21    } %>
22  </body>
23  </html>
```

Listing 8.2 is a skeleton JSP to build the search engine interface. The first part of the listing contains standard HTML to display a query field and a search button (lines 2-7). The remainder of the listing dumps the series of hits in a loop. The `Hits` and `Query` classes in Nutch are not the same as the Lucene classes with the same name. The `NutchBean` (line 11) is used to run the query and fetch a list of hits. The `getHits` (line 12) method of the `Hits` classes returns a subset of the hit objects in the specified range.

The `HitDetails` (line 13) class is used to fetch the values of `Fields` stored in the Lucene index. The stored `Fields` in the index include the *URL*, *title*, and *name* of the segment for an indexed page. Nutch includes two summarizers – a basic and the Lucene summarizer. One of the two summarizers is selected in the `plugin.includes` property of the `conf/nutch-default.xml` file. Both, the `BasicSummarizer` and `LuceneSummarizer` classes implement the `Summarizer` interface. The `getSummary` (line 14) method of these classes is called from the Nutch bean to build a list of `Summary`s.

Each summary is a list of excerpts that are sorted based on the number of unique tokens. Two properties, the `searcher.summary.context` (default 5) and `searcher.summary.length` (default 20), specify the number of tokens before and after a query token in an excerpt and the maximum number of tokens in the summary. The *title*, *URL*, and *summary* are extracted for every hit in a loop and should be dumped in the generated page that is sent to the browser. A complete search interface would include JavaServer pages to generate a header and a footer.

8.4.5 Troubleshooting

The absence of any hits for a query term that is known to be present in an indexed document is a typical problem after running a Nutch crawl. There are several reasons why a document does not appear in a hit list. The first place to check for an error is the `hadoop.log` file in the `logs` directory of the Nutch installation. This log file contains a list of log entries for the entire crawl including all generate-fetch-update cycles, the removal of duplicates, and index merge.

An error in the parse of a document will be mentioned in this log file. For example, the text of some PDF files cannot be extracted, since the text is encrypted and requires a key or the PDF document is made up of scanned pages and optical character recognition software is needed to extract the text. Similarly, the text from some Microsoft Office documents such as Word or PowerPoint files may not be extracted due to format problems that cannot be handled by the extractor.

One solution to this problem is to manually extract the text from these problem files and then run the crawl against the plain text copies of the original file. Another solution is to check the parser plugin. New versions of text filters that can be used in Nutch are published by the Apache Jakarta POI project (see Chapter 2). A custom plugin using external software for a Word or PowerPoint document can also be created.

There are primarily two data structures in Nutch – the Web database and the Lucene index. We used the handy index browser Luke (see Section 4.1) to examine Lucene indexes. This tool is very useful to check if a document has been successfully indexed by running interactive searches using terms that appear in the document. We can also verify the number of indexed documents and check the contents of some `Fields` stored in the index. Luke has several other features that are easy to explore from the GUI.

Unfortunately, there is no tool like Luke to examine the Web database. Instead, we use a series of command line utilities to check the status of the database. Most of these utilities can be run from the `nutch` shell script in the `bin` directory. The list of some of the major debug tools are shown in Table 8.4.

The `nutch` shell script runs specific Nutch classes based on the name of the first parameter. For example, the `readdb` and `readlinkdb` parameters call the Nutch `CrawlDbReader` and `LinkDbReader` classes respectively. The following `readdb` com-

Table 8.4: List of Debug Utilities, Options, and Description

Name	Data Structure	Options	FunctionDescription
readdb	crawldb	stats	List the number of fetched URLs and score information.
readdb	crawldb	dump	Dump the status and metadata of each URL to a file
readdb	crawldb	url	Print the status and metadata of a specific URL
readlinkdb	linkdb	dump	Dump the list of incoming links for all URLs
readlinkdb	linkdb	url	Print the list of incoming links for a specific URL
readseg	segment dir.	dump	Dump the entire contents of a segment to a file
readseg	segment dir.	get	Print the URL specific contents of a segment
readseg	segments	list	List the status of segments

mand returns statistics that describe the total number of URLs, the number of fetched URLs, and score details.

```
bin/nutch readdb results/crawldb -stats
```

The `readdb` command also accepts a `dump` option that prints the status and metadata of all URLs in the crawl database (`crawldb`) to files in a directory that is specified in an additional parameter. The metadata for an individual URL will be printed to standard out when the `url` option followed by the name of a specific URL is used in the `readdb` command.

The `readlinkdb` command performs functions similar to the `readdb` command on the link database (`linkdb`). We can print the list of incoming links for any particular URL or dump the entire list of incoming links for every URL to a set of files in a directory. The following command dumps the list of incoming links of all URLs to a set of files to the `linkout` directory.

```
bin/nutch readlinkdb results/linkdb -dump linkout
```

The **readseg** command calls the Nutch **SegmentReader** class to summarize the status of segments, print the entire contents of a segment, and print specific URL contents from a segment. The commands to run these function are

```
bin/nutch readseg -list -dir results/segments
bin/nutch readseg -dump results/segments/20080904112819
   segout
bin/nutch readseg -get results/segments/20080904112819 \
   http://textmine.sourceforge.net/cluster.html
```

The output of the first command returns the start and end fetch times, the number of generated URLs, and the number of parsed URLs by segment. The second command dumps outgoing and incoming links, the entire contents, the metadata, and the parsed text for every URL in the segment. Naturally, this file can be very large for a segment with many URLs. The third command returns similar results for a single URL. This command is useful to debug the status of a single URL in the segment.

We have primarily used Nutch to scan the desktop or an Intranet. There is a lot to more to Nutch that has not been covered in this section including running Nutch on a cluster of machines. Nutch also supports language detection and custom analyzers to handle different languages. The OPIC scoring algorithm for link analysis uses less space and runs faster than the PageRank algorithm.

8.5 Summary

In this chapter, we saw that the Web is not a giant collection of pages arbitrarily linked together, but instead follows a pattern found in social networks. Some pages have more importance than others and out going links from such pages confer more authority to a linked page than others. The importance of a page is also roughly proportional to the number of incoming links. The numbers of out going and incoming links and the sizes of Web pages follow Power laws.

The logical Web graph has a bow tie structure and the physical Internet connections between servers resembles a jellyfish. We described two algorithms, the Hubs & Authorities and PageRank algorithms to rank pages based on the location in the Web graph. Both algorithms recursively compute a score for a page based on the link structure of the graph.

Web crawlers are programs that automatically visit sites and collect information. These crawlers are also known by terms such as robots, bots, or spiders. Servers that provide information on the Web are monitored to detect excessive load due to a crawler. A well-behaved crawler follows a Robots Exclusion protocol to only visit authorized pages and limits the number of requests within a given period.

We have discussed the use of Nutch to crawl an Intranet and scan a desktop. Both Google and IBM offer similar products to find, index, and search information. Google's desktop search [Google] runs on Linux and Windows. The configuration and search tools run on a server that is managed from a browser. Version 1.0.2 of Google Desktop on Linux, handles information sources that are accessible through the `http` and `file` protocols.

IBM distributes the Omnifind Yahoo! Edition (OYE) [Omnifind] to search an Intranet or a file system. The basic edition of OYE includes features to crawl the Web or an Intranet, text filters for 200+ file formats, a search API, and multi-lingual support. The basic edition of OYE limits the number of indexable documents to 500K and does not include functions to integrate search across structured and unstructured information, security functions, and eCommerce search. OYE is based on Lucene and may be easier to install and operate than Nutch.

9 Tracking Information

There are many different forms of online information that we can track. Examples include the monitoring of the status of a customer's order, the location of a package, and information relevant to a topic or a product. In this chapter, we will look at ways to monitor information published on the Web, detect plagiarism and offensive content, and analyze the sentiment of text. The vast quantities of published information relevant to almost any topic on the Web is difficult to monitor using manual methods. Tools to sift through this information can make it easier to understand the general sentiment of a large audience and understand the public perception of a product or topic. We begin with the collection and tracking of news articles published on the Web.

9.1 News Monitoring

Much of the information that was earlier distributed exclusively in print media is now available on the Web. Most media organizations have Web sites and publish information that can be downloaded using a crawler. The typical method to distribute information on the Web, that is frequently updated like news, is through a Web feed. Interested readers subscribe to news feeds on the Web through a client (news reader or aggregator) that may run on a browser. A reader can select a subset of news feeds from which to periodically download articles, without providing personal information such as an email address to each of the news feeds.

9.1.1 Web Feeds

A Web feed is usually a XML-based document that provides a brief description, the title , a timestamp, and a link to the contents of the listed article. The two popular Web feed formats are *Atom* [Atom] and *Really Simple Syndication* (RSS) [RSS]. The extraction of attributes and values from a Web feed is precise since the contents of a Web feed are machine readable. The `news.xml` file in Listing 9.1 is a sample file that illustrates some of the RSS attributes and values.

Listing 9.1: A Sample news.xml RSS file

```
<?xml version="1.0" encoding="utf-8"?>
<rss version="2.0">
<channel>
 <title>Mustru RSS 2.0 Feed</title>
 <link>http://mustru.sf.net/</link>
 <description>Mustru rss 2 feed description</description>
 <lastBuildDate>Mon,6 Oct 2008 18:37:00 GMT</lastBuildDate>
 <language>en-us</language>

 <item>
  <title>Title of first item</title>
  <link>http://test.com/articles/08_10/123.html</link>
  <guid>http://test.com/articles/2008-10-123</guid>
  <pubDate>Mon, 6 Oct 2008 18:37:00 GMT</pubDate>
  <description> Description of first item </description>
 </item>
 . . .
</channel>
</rss>
```

The two main elements in this file are `channel` and `item`. Typically, we would have one channel element and many item elements. Each of these item elements can have many sub-elements. For example, the `channel` element has required `title`, `description`, and `link` sub-elements, that describe the feed. The `link` refers to a Web page that contains a detailed description of the source of the feed. In addition to these sub-elements, there are others such as an image link, copyright statement, and a ttl (time to live).

An `item` contains a reference to an article and includes sub-elements such as the `title` of the article, a `link` to the article, a `guid` or globally unique ID of the article, a short description of the article, and the `pubDate` or published date of the article. This information is repeated for every article in the channel. An item has other elements including a `category`, `comments`, and `author` to further describe the article.

One of the criticisms of RSS is the lack of compatibility between the many versions that were created following its introduction in 1999. The Atom publishing protocol was developed to counter the compatibility problems of RSS. Currently, the community has not adopted either protocol and both RSS and Atom feeds can be found on the Web. We have not compared protocols and instead focus on the collection and organization of dynamic information from the Web.

There are a number of commercial news readers to manage news feeds. These readers organize articles by news feed, date, and even category. Some readers also keep track of popular topics, popular news feeds, and other statistics. A good news reader makes it easy to read, cache, and search articles. The next section explains a server based tool to analyze news feeds in a collaborative environment with shared and personalized categories.

9.1.2 NewsRack

We will look at an implementation (`http://newsrack.in`) of a news filter that makes it easy to monitor sources on the Web. A typical searcher is interested in tracking information from a subset of news sources that frequently publish relevant articles. A monitoring tool in its essence, is simply a filter and categorizer of articles (see Figure 9.1). At first, the text categorization methods that we learned in Chapter 7 may seem appropriate. To recap, any document could be categorized into one or more categories using a model or profile. A model was trained using a set of pre-categorized documents.

Figure 9.1: A Categorizer for News Articles from News Feeds

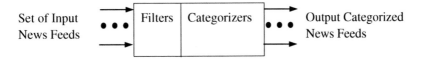

One of the problems with a general purpose categorizer for news, is that although many searchers share a common interest, the same topic may be defined with different sets of keywords. For example, every searcher interested in *"nuclear energy"* may not be interested in articles that include the terms *Iran* or *North Korea*. A personalized categorizer is more appropriate, when a single category can be defined in multiple ways. First, a searcher selects a set of news feeds to monitor. Next, a set of *concepts* are defined where each concept is a group of keywords that define the concept (see Figure 9.2).

Figure 9.2: A Personalized Categorizer using Concepts and Keywords

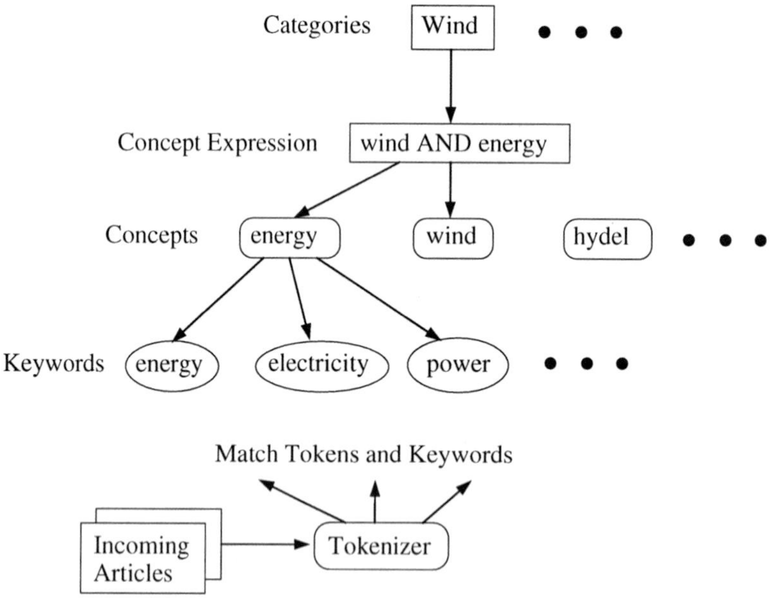

For example, the *energy* and *wind* concepts consist of keywords like *electricity* or *power* and *wind-power* or *windmill* respectively. The tokens generated from incoming articles are compared with concept keywords to assign concepts to an article. A category is defined by combining concepts using boolean operators AND/OR. The NOT operator can also be used in the boolean concept expression to exclude particular types of keywords. An article can be assigned to more than one category. Listing 9.2 contains a sample user profile that defines three categories – *Wind, Nuclear,* and *Carbon Trading* using five concepts.

Listing 9.2: A Sample User Profile to Define Concepts and Categories

```
1  DEFINE SOURCES {my_sources}
```

```
2    bbc = http://newsrss.bbc.co.uk/rss/.../rss.xml
3    google = http://news.google.com/?output=rss
4  END SOURCES
5
6  DEFINE CONCEPTS {energy}
7    <energy> = energy, electricity, power
8    <nuclear> = nuclear, nuke power
9    <wind> = wind-power, wind, wind-mill
10   <carbon-trading> = carbon credit, carbon trading,
11                     carbon market
12   <ignore> = iran, korea, iranian, korean
13 END CONCEPTS
14
15 DEFINE ISSUE Energy
16   MONITOR SOURCES {my_sources}
17   ORGANIZE NEWS INTO CATEGORIES {
18     [Wind] = wind AND energy
19     [Nuclear] = nuclear AND energy AND -ignore
20     [Carbon Trading] = carbon-trading
21   }
22 END ISSUE
```

The first definition describes the list of monitored news feeds. In this example, two news feeds from the BBC and Google are defined (lines 2-3). The next definition describes a set of five concepts and associated keywords. The final definition uses the concepts to create three categories – *Wind*, *Nuclear*, and *Carbon Trading*. Notice, the *Nuclear* category uses the minus sign to filter out articles that contain keywords from the ignore concept (line 12). The flat list of categories in Listing 9.2 can be organized into a hierarchy For example, articles on *nuclear energy* can be tracked by country using the profile below.

```
[Nuclear] = {
  [By Country] = {
    [Australia] = {
      [Debate] = nuclear AND debate AND australia
      [Research] = nuclear AND ansto AND research
                   AND australia
    }
    [Japan] = {
      [Safety] = nuclear AND (aec or nsc) AND japan
      [Plants] = nuclear AND power_plants AND japan
```

```
    }
 . . .
   }
}
```

A large number of collected articles organized in this fashion can be more easily browsed with a taxonomy than a single list of categories. A concept can be made up of single terms, phrases, and even multi-lingual terms. This design allows individual searchers to dynamically build personalized categories from pre-defined or new concepts. Existing concepts and categories can be shared among many searchers.

The text of collected articles is typically indexed to find relevant articles with a query. A group of users may also collaboratively rank and annotate articles. Markup and discussions related to an article add value in understanding a group's perception of a topic. A summary of the article is usually stored in addition to the description and title. In many news articles, the first sentence is typically a good summary sentence.

A number of statistics can be derived from the collection of articles over a period of time. For example, we can observe the rise and fall in the popularity of a topic. Most topics have a limited period of interest during which many related articles are published. Articles related to weather related disasters or anniversaries of events last from a few week to several months. Other articles on events like a long running court case or a war may remain popular for several years. We can also collect statistics that describe the focus of a particular media organization, based on the number of published articles per topic. Most news readers do not analyze the content of articles. In the next section, we will look at ways to automatically decide if a document that describes a product or event is written with a positive or negative sentiment.

9.2 Sentiment Analysis

The Web allows anyone to instantly share their anger with a company's product on a blog or a message board. It is unclear how much damage is caused from such negative information to a company's reputation. In any case, it is in the best interest of a company to monitor such information. The number of blogs and other outlets on the Web available for a person to post negative or positive information are too numerous to be monitored manually. There are several reasons that may motivate authors to publish such information. A small community of individuals who share a common interest in a particular product may collaboratively evaluate and generate feedback that a larger group finds useful. Misleading information can also be deliberately published. For example, a person seeking to temporarily boost the price of a stock may distribute false information promoting a company.

E-commerce sites like `Amazon.com` maintain customer reviews that can influence the sales of a product. A review is feedback generated by a customer that can determine the success or failure of a product to some degree. A site may include a ranking of reviewers, but it is difficult to compute the importance of a reviewer using an algorithm like Hubs & Authorities or PageRank, due to the absence of links between reviewers. Other sites like recommender systems suggest suitable movies or music based on a subscriber's interest. These sites use the evaluations of many individuals to find products that a particular customer may find attractive. Editorial sites collect the opinions of domain experts who assign ratings to articles, books, music, movies, and other products. Information from these types of sites may be particularly influential in directing the general perception of a product.

Many organizations conduct periodic employee surveys to evaluate the collective perceptions of employees. The format of these surveys is typically a series of questions and answers. The answers for some questions may be given in free form text that cannot be easily automatically tabulated. The text from these answers can be automatically classified by sentiment to quickly evaluate if the general opinion is positive or negative.

9.2.1 Automatic Classification

Sentiment analysis is the automatic identification of the viewpoint in a single text span or an entire document. The document should represent a consistent viewpoint in favor or against. We initially look at the simple problem of defining if a review is positive or negative and leave the problem of assigning a numeric rating (1-5) later in this chapter. We can use the text categorization algorithms that we described in Chapter 7, if we define sentiment analysis as a classification problem.

A review is classified into a *positive* or *negative* category. A single classification model or two separate models can be used. In a single model, a document is assigned to either a positive or negative category using a single evaluation. Two separate models, one for positive and the other for negative documents, is appropriate when a review may not be sufficiently positive or negative to be categorized into one of the two categories. Such documents are assigned to a third *neutral* category.

The success of any text categorization algorithm depends on the quality of the extracted features. Most algorithms will do reasonably well, when the types of extracted features are sufficient to make clear distinctions between documents in separate categories. Our first step is to find good features before we apply any categorization algorithm.

Subjective vs. Objective Sentences

We are mainly interested in the subjective sentences in a document. These types of sentences usually express the opinions of the author and are the most useful sentences to determine a document's sentiment. We first classify every sentence in a document into a subjective or objective category. The first two sentences in Table 9.1 are examples of subjective sentences. These sentences state the opinions of a group or individual. An opinion may be positive, negative, or neutral. By contrast, an objective statement simply presents factual information. The following sentences are examples of objective and subjective sentences.

Table 9.1: Two Subjective and Two Objective Sentences

No.	Type	Sentence
1	Subjective	I am *positive* that we will succeed.
2	Subjective	The mainstream argues that people are not *thrifty*.
3	Objective	Behavioral economic is a discipline that combines psychology and standard economics.
4	Objective	Economists have struggled to explain the characteristics of overspending and undersaving.

Objective sentences report known facts and cannot be classified into positive or negative categories. Such sentences are not useful in characterizing the sentiment expressed in a document and are usually removed before classifying a document. Subjective sentences can also be used in other applications such as a Q&A system, or a summarizer. A Q&A system may exclude subjective sentences from the list of potential answers in response to a factual question. Similarly, a summarizer will also exclude subjective sentences from a document summary, since a reader may be more interested in the facts mentioned the article.

Adjectives and Ngrams

All assertions by a group or person cannot automatically be classified as subjective sentences. The presence of a subjective element (adjective) with a source and target is a good indicator to identify a subjective sentence (see Table 9.2).

Table 9.2: Examples of Source, Target, and Adjectives from Two Sentences

Sentence No.	Source	Adjectives	Target
1 (Table 9.1)	I	positive	we
2 (Table 9.1)	mainstream	thrifty	people

The presence of adjectives alone is a good indicator of subjectivity. A study [Wiebe] estimated the probability of a subjective sentence was 0.58, given the presence of at least one adjective in the sentence. The probability of a subjective sentence increased from 0.58 to 0.62 with a test for the presence of WordNet synonym sets (see section 2.7) in addition to the adjectives in the sentence. However, adjectives like *thrifty* or *positive* can also occur in objective statements. For example, the sentences

- Integers consist of *positive* and *negative* numbers.

- Visit our Web site for *thrifty* office furniture.

are objective statements. A word sense disambiguator may help in improving the accuracy of a subjective / objective sentence classifier. The types of adjectives used in reviews is also dependent on the genre. Reviewers of a particular genre tend to use a popular subset of adjectives and may follow a pattern specific to the genre. Some adjectives are used more often in movie reviews, than say a book review. For example, the word *unpredictable* may be a positive adjective in a movie review, but not in a product review. A sample list of positive and negative adjectives for several genres is shown in Table 9.3.

Table 9.3: Sample of List of Positive and Negative Adjectives by Genre

Genre	Positive	Negative
General	inspirational, truly, achieve	depraved, disastrously, depress
Movie Review	compelling, passionate, mind-blowing	redundant, obvious, boring
Product Review	easy to, a great, for the price	the worst, not worth, what a joke
Messages	awesome, fun, :-)	crappy, dumb, :-(,

Newswire articles tend to be more formal than other genres like movie or product reviews and the least formal genre is email or instant messages. Therefore, it is important to create a training set of documents that is domain specific. For example, a classifier trained on product reviews may not perform well on a testing set of movie reviews. Some genres like instant messages and emails use emoticons that are good indicators of sentiment. Adjective features alone are not sufficient for all types of reviews. In particular, word ngrams are good features in product reviews. Trigrams such as *"is a great"* (positive) and *"taking it back"* (negative) are strong indicators of sentiment. We can extract such distinctive features directly from the text of reviews.

Training Documents

We use training documents for each sentiment category to build a model that will be used by a classifier. A custom classifier is built for each product type. For example, we can have separate classifiers for digital cameras and Personal Digital Assistants (PDAs).

Ideally, all categories should have a sufficient number of training documents. But, popular products like digital cameras, may have many reviews that can be used to train a precise classifier, while less popular products like PDAs are not reviewed as frequently and may have a corresponding less accurate classifier. The number of positive and negative reviews is also not uniform. In general, roughly three fourths of all product reviews on the Web are positive. Finally, the length of reviews is also not uniform. Some reviews may be just a single sentence, while other reviews are elaborate multi-paragraph descriptions. These differences in the training document set per product type, mean that all classifiers will not have the same precision. Two readers may disagree over the sentiment expressed in a review that is not strongly positive or negative. These differences in human interpretation mean that the automatic categorizer is also likely to make classifications that are not universally acceptable.

Extracted lexical features like adjectives and word ngrams exclude the relationships between documents. The features of each document are considered in isolation. The relationships between documents is an extrinsic feature that can increase the precision of a classifier. Product reviews that have been submitted over a period of time may refer to earlier reviews. The links between reviews may represent agreement or disagreement. Closely associated reviews that belong to a category x should be used to bias the categorization of a review that is also similar to the group in favor of category x. The inter-review similarity is an added feature to improve the precision of the classifier.

Finally, the importance of a sentence in a review depends on its location in the document. A sentence near the beginning or the end of the document may represent a possible summary statement. For example, if the last sentence of a movie review is -"*avoid this film at all costs*", then this statement should be assigned greater importance than other sentences in the review.

Classifiers

In Chapter 7, we tested several classifiers including the Naïve Bayes, K-Nearest Neighbor, and TF/IDF classifiers. Here, we use the Naïve Bayes classifier to separate subjective and objective sentences and to assign the polarity of a subjective sentence. Consider a simple sentiment analyzer shown in Figure 9.3.

The text of a document is first split into sentences (see section 5.1.1 Sentence Extraction). Next, we use the presence of adjectives to find subjective sentences. Earlier, we saw that the probability of a subjective sentence was over 0.5, given the presence of one or more adjectives in the sentence. Other features to identify subjective sentences may include unigrams, bigrams, trigrams, and parts of speech. These features are extracted from the training documents for a category and are dependent on the genre (see Table 9-2). We can state the probability p of a subjective (*subj*) sentence as

Figure 9.3: A Sentence-based Sentiment Analyzer

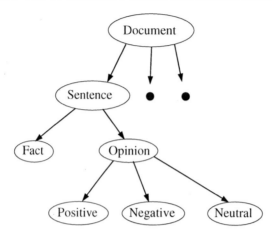

$$p(subj|d) = \frac{p(subj) \times p(d|subj)}{p(d)} \approx p(subj) \times \overbrace{p(f_1|subj) \times \ldots p(f_n|subj)} \qquad (9.1)$$

The simplified calculation shown on the right hand side of the equation assumes independence of features f_i and an uniform probability $p(d)$ of a document d. The probability p is computed for every sentence and evaluated against a threshold to separate the objective and subjective sentences. We can similarly construct a polarity classifier to identify the positive and negative sentences among the subjective sentences alone. The features of a polarity classifier are the set of positive and negative adjectives.

The use of adjectives alone may not be sufficient to make accurate sentiment predictions. The use of the word neighborhood [1]of the set of adjectives or adverbs is a larger set and will increase the number of matching features in a sentence and the model. This expansion is made based on the assumption that positive or negative words tend to co-occur more often than simply by chance and therefore are good indicators of sentiment. Recall in Chapter 5, we used a log likelihood ratio to find bigrams like "New York" and "Information Management". The co-occurrence of

---

[1]A word neighborhood for an adjective is the set of n words before and after the adjective.

words in these phrases is analogous to the co-occurrence of positive or negative words. The average log likelihood ratio comparing the collocation frequency with positive to negative adjectives per word of a sentence is a sentiment indicator. Finally, the sentiment indicator values for every sentence is totaled to compute the overall sentiment of the document.

Consider the use of separate classifiers for the positive and negative categories. Documents can be either positive, negative, mixed, or neutral. A binary classifier will only return the probability of a document belonging to a single category. The use of separate custom classifiers for the positive and negative categories makes it feasible to assign a document to one of four categories (see Table 9.4).

Table 9.4: Assignment of a Document to Mixed, Positive, Negative, or Neutral Categories

		Negative	
		Yes	No
Positive	Yes	Mixed	Positive
	Negative	Negative	Neutral

A document whose sentiment score exceeds the threshold for both the positive and negative categories is classified as a *mixed* document. Documents whose sentiment scores exceed the threshold of either the positive or negative categories are assigned to their respective categories. Finally, a document that does not match any category is a *neutral* document. In the next section, we will look at an implementation using LingPipe to evaluate the sentiment of a document.

9.2.2 An Implementation with LingPipe

We use two classifiers, one to separate subjective and objective sentences and the other to identify the polarity of a document from its subjective sentences alone. This hierarchical approach, using two separate classifiers is based on a prior study [PangLee] that was successful in categorizing movie reviews by category. Figure 9.4 illustrates the use of two classifiers to find the sentiment of a document.

The subjective classifier is first used to remove the objective sentences and is followed by the polarity classifier. Although, the implementation in LingPipe uses

Figure 9.4: Assigning the Sentiment of a Document

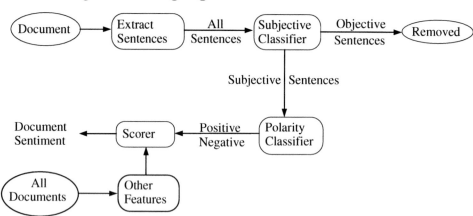

the sentiment scores of subjective sentences in isolation to evaluate the sentiment of a document, the relationship between documents can also be exploited to make more accurate predictions. We can expect a higher degree of similarity between a positive document and the set of all positive documents, than with the entire collection of documents.

Building and Evaluating the Subjectivity Classifier

We first need to build the two classifiers. In this example, we use movie review data to train the classifiers. The `Readme` files in the `data/training/polarity` and `data/training/subjectivity` directories contains information regarding the source of the training data. The training data for the polarity classifier is made up of 2000 reviews, a 1000 reviews per category. Each review is saved in a separate file. The subjectivity classifier is trained on a total of 10K sentences, 5K sentences per category. Notice, the subjectivity and polarity classifiers use different training units (see Table 9.5).

Both classifiers are binary classifiers and use the same Naïve Bayes method to assign a category. Consider the subjectivity classifier. We train the classifier using the set of objective and subjective sentences extracted from movie reviews. The 10K training sentences are divided into two sets of 5K sentences in two separate files. The

Table 9.5: Subjectivity and Polarity Classifiers

Classifier	Unit	Categories	Method
Subjectivity	Sentence	objective, subjective	Bayes
Polarity	Document	positive, negative	Bayes

plot and the *quote* files in the subjectivity training directory contains the objective and subjective sentences respectively. Listing 9.3 contains the code to build a model of the subjective category.

Listing 9.3: Building the Model for the Subjective Category

```
1  public class TrainSubjectivity {
2    File mSubjectivityDir = new File(
3      TRAINING_DIR + FS + "subjectivity");
4    String[] mCategories = new String[] {
5      "plot", "quote" };
6    DynamicLMClassifier mClassifier;
7
8    TrainSubjectivity() {
9      int nGram = 8;
10     mClassifier = DynamicLMClassifier.createNGramBoundary(
11       mCategories, nGram);
12   }
13
14   void run() throws ClassNotFoundException, IOException {
15     for (int i = 0; i < mCategories.length; ++i) {
16       File file = new File(mSubjectivityDir,
17         mCategories[i] + ".tok.gt9.5000");
18       String data = Files.readFromFile(file);
19       String[] sentences = data.split("\n");
20       int numTraining = (sentences.length * 9) / 10;
21       for (int j = 0; j < numTraining; ++j)
22         mClassifier.train(mCategories[i], sentences[j]);
23     }
24     FileOutputStream fileOut =
25       new FileOutputStream(mSubjectivityDir + FS
26         + "subjectivity_classifier");
27     ObjectOutputStream objOut =
28       new ObjectOutputStream(fileOut);
```

```
29        mClassifier.compileTo(objOut);
30        objOut.close();
31      }
32      public static void main(String[] args) {
33        new TrainSubjectivity().run();
34      }
35    }
```

The constructor of the TrainSubjectivity (line 8) class allocates a ngram language model that adds an extra character at the start and end of every training sequence. This ngram model is the subjectivity classifier that is trained and dumped to a file. The ngram size is set to eight characters and can be tweaked with higher or lower order ngrams for better performance. The file containing 5K objective training sentences is called plot.tok.gt9.5000 (line 16-17). The text of the file is split into individual sentences and passed to the train (line 22) method of the classifier. Notice, we use nine tenths of the 5K sentences per category to train the classifier and save the remaining 500 sentences to test the classifier. The code to test the classifier is shown in Listing 9.4.

Listing 9.4: Testing the Subjectivity Classifier with 1000 Sentences

```
1   public class TestSubjectivity {
2     File mSubjectivityDir =
3       new File(TRAINING_DIR + FS + "subjectivity");
4     String[] mCategories = new String[] { "plot", "quote" };
5     LMClassifier mClassifier;
6
7     TestSubjectivity() throws
8       FileNotFoundException, ClassNotFoundException {
9       String modelFile = TRAINING_DIR + FS + "subjectivity"
10        + FS + "subjectivity_classifier";
11      ObjectInputStream oi = new ObjectInputStream(
12        new FileInputStream(modelFile) );
13      mClassifier = (LMClassifier) oi.readObject();
14      oi.close();
15    }
16
17    void run() throws IOException {
18      int numCorrect = 0; int numIncorrect = 0;
19      for (int i = 0; i < mCategories.length; ++i) {
20        File file = new File(mSubjectivityDir, mCategories[i]
```

```
21        + ".tok.gt9.5000");
22      String data = Files.readFromFile(file);
23      String[] sentences = data.split("\n");
24      int numTraining = (sentences.length * 9) / 10;
25      for (int j = numTraining;j < sentences.length;++j){
26        Classification classification =
27          mClassifier.classify(sentences[j]);
28        if (classification.bestCategory().equals(
29            mCategories[i]) )
30          numCorrect++;
31        else numIncorrect++;
32      }
33    }
34  }
35  public static void main(String[] args) {
36    new TestSubjectivity().run();
37  }
38 }
```

The classifier file that was dumped in Listing 9.3 is first read into a classifier (line 13) object. Next, we use the last 500 sentences (lines 24-25) in each of the training files to test the classifier. The number of correct and incorrect classifications is tracked. A correct classification is noted, when subjective and objective sentences are assigned into the correct quote and plot categories respectively. The results of the test are shown in a confusion matrix in Table 9.6.

Table 9.6: A Confusion Matrix showing the Subjectivity Categorization Performance

		Assigned Category	
		Plot	Quote
Reference Category	Plot	461	39
	Quote	34	466

A total of 73 sentences were mis-categorized out of 1K test sentences, giving an accuracy of 0.93. Two examples of plot sentences that were mis-categorized as quotes is shown below.

She's not disappointed - Oliver turns out to be a nightmare.

355

> William Hundert , a retired " old-school " classics teacher is passionate about his subject .

The adjectives – *disappointed* and *passionate* are possible reasons that the classifier was unable to make a correct categorization. Adjectives found in plot statements that are also frequently found in quotes are sources of error. Consider the following two quotes that were mis-categorized as plot sentences.

> Elaborate special effects take center screen, so that the human story is pushed to one side .

> Green might want to hang onto that ski mask , as robbery may be the only way to pay for his next project.

The description of the human story in the first sentence is unique and is not found in any of the training sentences. The second sentence does not have any adjectives that could be used to identify a quote and is an example of sarcasm that is difficult to detect automatically. The sentiment of reviews that use humor and sarcasm are difficult to detect without some background knowledge.

Building and Evaluating the Polarity Classifier

The code to train and test the polarity classifier is very similar to the Listings 9.3 and 9.4 and is omitted for brevity. The primary difference between the two classifiers is that the entire text of a positive review is used to train the polarity classifier, unlike the subjectivity classifier that was trained on individual sentences. The classes TrainPolarity and TestPolarity contain the code to build and evaluate the polarity classifier respectively. Nine tenths of the 1K files per category are used to build the individual category models. The results from a test with a total of 200 files, 100 positive and 100 negative, gave an accuracy rate of 0.82. The reasons that a review was mis-categorized are not as easily identified as our earlier example with sentences.

Review files contain more text to analyze than the single sentences used in the subjectivity classifier, but the additional text may also be a source of *noise* that can mislead the classifier. It is interesting to note that the subjectivity classifier outperforms the polarity classifier despite the limited amount of training text. This leads to the observation that the presence of a few good discriminating features is sufficient to make an accurate classification.

A Sentiment Analyzer

We can assemble a sentiment analyzer using the subjectivity and polarity classifiers together with a sentence extractor. The following code returns the sentiment of the passed text string.

```
SentimentAnalyzer sa = new SentimentAnalyzer();
String text = "It was wonderful !";
System.out.println("The text \"" + text
  + "\" is " + sa.getSentiment(text) );


Generated Output:
The text "It was wonderful !" is pos
```

The constructor of the `SentimentAnalyzer` class reads both classifiers from files and creates separate instances of each classifier (not shown in the listing). The `getSentiment` method uses the `buildSentences` method from the `LingpipeTools` to class to extract the sentences. All subjective sentences are collected in a single text string, that is passed to the polarity classifier. The category returned by the polarity classifier is returned to the caller.

The use of two consecutive classifiers has an additional cost. The overall accuracy of the sentiment analyzer is the product of the individual classifier accuracies, which is less than the accuracy of both classifiers. Still, the sentiment analyzer has a baseline accuracy rate of 0.75 for a movie review test dataset. The accuracy of the classifier depends on whether the training set is appropriate for the domain and is large enough to build a representative model for each category.

The discussion till now has been limited to binary classifiers alone. Many sites like Amazon.com allow for multiple categories using a five star rating scheme. It is harder for an automatic categorizer to differentiate between a three and four star rating than between a one and five star rating. A simple solution is to assign multiple categories based on the ratio of the number of positive sentences to the total number of subjective sentences. The positive sentence percentage (PSP) value of a document can be viewed as the degree of positive sentiment expressed in the document. Documents that have a higher PSP value will be assigned more stars than documents with a low PSP value. In most cases, reviewers submit text that is not offensive, but on occasion, a reviewer may intentionally post hateful text. The next section will cover some of the issues in automatically detecting such messages.

9.3 Detecting Offensive Content

The automatic detection of hostile messages or flames is important for several reasons. An organization that supports an Intranet or a Web site is responsible for the content posted on its servers and in some cases may be liable, if a particular employee becomes the target of hostile messages.

A series of flames or a flame war is usually counter-productive. A large number of hostile messages are exchanged in a flame war and usually there is no winner in such a war. The after effects of a flame war leave an organization that may be divided into two camps. The administrator of a server has the responsibility of monitoring its contents in addition to the maintenance of the server. It can be time consuming for an administrator to manually scan message after message. The readers of material posted on a server may notify an administrator of a potentially hostile message. This detection method is dependent on the cooperation of the users of the server.

Automated techniques to detect flames will save the administrator time and possibly prevent a fruitless flame war. Most flame wars occur in public forums. However, hostile messages are also exchanged between individuals through email. In some cases, a sender may direct flames at an individual. The administrator of a mail server may not notice such messages and automatic detection can prevent the use of email to harass or to intimidate others.

9.3.1 Detection Methods

The easiest method to detect flames is to simply check for the presence of a word from a list of banned or obscene terms. However, this is not very effective since only about 12% of flames contained vulgarities [Spertus]. Further, all messages with vulgar expressions are not flames. A profanity associated with an individual that both the sender and recipient dislike would not be considered a flame. A list of banned words is usually not effective, since the authors of flame messages have many ways of generating hostile messages by intentionally mis-spelling banned words, but whose meaning is easily detected.

A study [Spertus] of hostile messages found that it was possible to characterize such messages using a set of specific features. These features were more likely to be found in flames than other messages. For example, it was found that sentences with the word *you* followed by a noun phrase were potential insults (*"you bozos"* or *"you people"*). The phrases *"you guys"* and *"you folks"* were less likely to be hostile descriptions.

Imperative statements are usually short sentences that are good indicators of sentiment. Examples of insulting imperative sentences include - *"Get over it"*, *"Get a life"*, *"Have your fun"*, and *"Get lost"*. On the other hand, imperative sentences can also be examples of positive sentiment. These types of sentences would include - *"Keep up the good work"* or *"Have a nice day"*.

The occurrence of a profanity in a sentence is very likely to be an insulting reference. The list of profanities to identify such sentences depends on the domain. The list of bad words includes verbs (*stink, suck*), nouns (*loser, idiot*), and adjectives (*bad, lousy*). Derogatory phrases include *"Slick Willy"* *"Dubya"*, *"liberal commies"*, and *"conservative fascists"*. Finally, the most useful rule to detect insulting sentences was the word get followed by words or phrases such as *life, lost, "with it"*, or *real* in a ten character window. Some of these sentences may be tagged as offensive by the rule for imperative statements.

The standard methods for text categorization cannot be used directly for problems like flame detection and are typically modified to use the unique features of flame messages. An implementation of a flame detector can be built based on the Naïve Bayes classifier we saw in Chapter 7. The classifier would use a custom Lucene `Analyzer` to tokenize text and extract the unique features of flames, to create a document representative. A training set of flame messages is also needed to build the classifier model. The detection of plagiarism is another type of specialized classification problem. The next section describes a plagiarism detector to classify a document into an *original* or *plagiarized* categories.

9.4 Plagiarism Detection

The view of owning the rights to original ideas and written text expressing opinions and facts is commonly accepted in many universities and organizations. Another author cannot directly copy and use text without giving the original author credit. In many cases, the original author's permission is also needed. Here, our definition of *plagiarism* is the act of claiming and using someone else's written work in a supposedly original document.

9.4.1 Forms of Plagiarism

The most obvious form of plagiarism is a document that has been copied word for word. A student given an assignment to write a paper can find a large number of sources on the Web for most topics. The most flagrant form of plagiarism is to simply cut and paste an entire document with no changes beyond the title and author. This type of plagiarism is easily detected, since the original and copied documents are almost identical. A series of phrases extracted from the copied document submitted to a search engine, will return a link to the original document. Further, a student who does not have a reputation as a writer, is unlikely to have written a document that could have been published in a well known journal or magazine. Automatic methods to detect plagiarism, can also easily identify documents that have a high degree of overlap.

A more difficult type of plagiarism is the collection of material from multiple sources, that is pasted together to create a paper. In this case, an automated plagiarism detector will not find a strong degree of overlap with any single document. The styles of pasted text may clash, if the types of sources are not uniform. It is possible to create a complete article by carefully assembling passages from multiple sources without attributing any of the sources. This takes more effort than the first form of plagiarism. Such a paper may not be considered plagiarized, provided a list of sources is included and the copied text is clearly identified.

The use of someone else's text or code is not necessarily wrong. Emails frequently contain quotes from other emails, research papers refer to work in previous papers, and collaborators build versions of documents and code that are very similar to each other. A commercial organization may charge for copies of digital content from a book, music, or software. These legitimate copies usually are distributed with many restrictions on usage and the creation of additional copies.

9.4.2 Methods to Detect Plagiarism

Earlier methods to prevent copying, used various security mechanisms to limit the number of copies with keys and passwords. These methods became cumbersome for legitimate users to make copies and share information. Instead methods to detect copied documents or code have become more popular than copy prevention techniques. The *signature* and *registration* methods are two ways of detecting copied documents. A digital signature is added at the end of the original document to identify the source. A signature may include a watermark or a checksum. The idea behind the use of a signature is to prevent the creation of copies that misrepresent the author or source of the document. Further, a signature is useful to detect identical copies of a document but is not suitable to identify partial overlaps. A determined plagiarizer can find ways to remove a signature and hack into a document.

The alternate registration method detects copies by comparing a test document with a large collection of copyrighted documents. There are at least two ways to detect a copied document. One, is to submit a number of queries to Web search engines using terms or phrases extracted from the text of the test document. The results of these queries are analyzed for overlap with a test document to check for plagiarism. Another method is to maintain a set of original documents, against which test documents are compared. We will build an implementation based on the use of a registration server to detect copied documents. A registration server is a repository of indexed copyrighted documents (see Figure 9.5).

Registration Based Plagiarism Detection

The copyrighted documents are scanned and indexed in the registration server. A chunker uses the plain text of the documents to build a list of tokens, ngrams, or any other type of text unit that will be used in the overlap computation. The chunker extracts text units that are more likely to overlap between the test and copyrighted document. A text unit could be as large as a paragraph or as small a character-based ngram. A number of identical paragraphs or sentences in the copyrighted and test documents is a strong indicator of plagiarism. We can also make comparisons with smaller text units such as individual words or ngrams.

Figure 9.5: A Registration Server to Detect Copied Documents

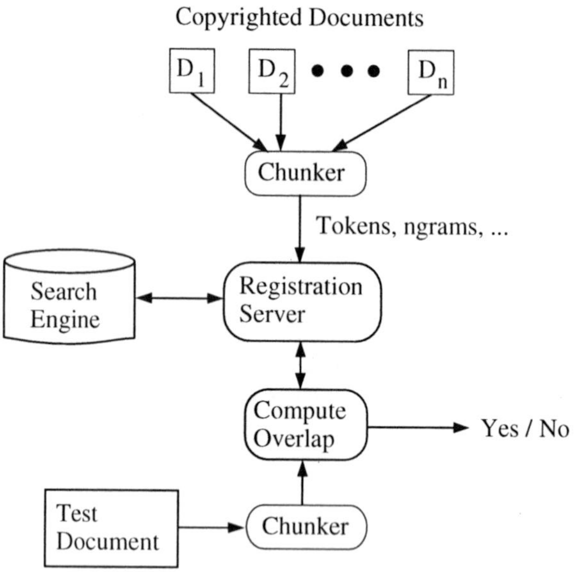

Sentence-based comparisons may not perform as well, since an overlap measure cannot detect minor changes to sentences. A word based comparison evaluates the degree of overlap at a finer grain and small changes to the text are not sufficient to make a major change in the overlap computation. A plagiarizer is unlikely to take the effort to make substantial changes to the text, since the primary aim is to minimize the work required to generate a document.

Notice, we use a search engine to find overlap, instead of a database or some other data structure. A registration server may store the contents of thousands or even millions of copyrighted documents. It would take a long time to individually compare a test document with every copyrighted document. A faster method is to use a search engine to find overlap, with a series of queries made up of the text chunks extracted from the test document. The results of the queries are tabulated and a score is computed for the top n documents that matched many of the generated queries.

9.4.3 Copy Detection using SCAM

SCAM [Shivakumar] is a copy detection mechanism for documents using a registration server. We follow the similar pattern of training a model followed by an evaluation to check if a document has been plagiarized or not. In this case, our model is the search engine of the registration server and the evaluation is a similarity measure between a test document and a set of indexed copyrighted documents. The cosine measure (see Section 6.2.2, Similarity Measures) is one measure to compare two documents. However, the cosine measure was designed to compare two documents for IR and is not the most appropriate to detect plagiarism.

The ideal similarity measure should return a high value, when the contents of the registered document are either a superset or a subset of a test document. The use of normalized weights in a cosine similarity computation tends to favor the smaller of the two compared documents. The cosine measure is also independent of the actual number of occurrences of a term in a document. Consider a document with the term a repeated k times and another document with three terms a, b, and c. The cosine similarity between the two documents is $\frac{1}{\sqrt{3}}$ or 0.58. The similarity is the same (0.58) regardless of the number (k) of occurrences of term a in the first document.

We define a new relative similarity measure like the cosine measure that has the properties to detect overlap between documents using the relative term frequency within a document. Two documents are said to be overlapping, when their relative similarity value exceeds a threshold. The relative measure is a custom similarity computation to detect overlap, irrespective of differences in document sizes. We first look for a set of words that occur in roughly the same number in both the registered and test documents. A word w_i is included in a set C if the following condition is true

$$\epsilon - \left(\frac{f_i(R)}{f_i(T)} + \frac{f_i(T)}{f_i(R)}\right) > 0 \qquad (9.2)$$

where ϵ is some constant greater than 2, $f_i(R)$ and $f_i(T)$ are the number of times w_i occurs in documents R and T. Notice, the expression in equation 9.2 will always be positive, if $f_i(R)$ and $f_i(T)$ are identical. The value of the subtrahend in the expression grows when the skew between the frequencies of w_i in the pair of documents is large. A large ϵ will expand the set of selected words C, leading to higher false positives. A lower ϵ reduces the ability to detect minor overlap, since the set of selected words may exclude words that occur in overlapping text chunks. Values of 2.5 and higher are reasonably good values for ϵ. Our similarity measure must be able to detect cases, where a test document is a subset and superset of a registered document. Therefore, we use an asymmetric subset measure $S(T, R)$.

$$S(T, R) = \frac{\sum_{w_i \in C} f_i(R) \times f_i(T)}{\sum_{i=1}^{N} f_i(T) \times f_i(T)} \tag{9.3}$$

This measure returns the degree to which document R overlaps document T. The subset measure normalizes the numerator with respect to the test document T alone. The numerator uses just the frequencies of words in the pair of documents from the set C. This modification returns a high value when T is a subset of R, unlike the cosine measure. The final relative similarity measure is defined as

$$similarity(T, R) = max[S(T, R), S(R, T)] \tag{9.4}$$

or the maximum of two asymmetric similarity computations. The $similarity(T, R)$ value is limited to the range 0 to 1. Consider the following example to compare the relative similarity measure with the cosine measure (see Table 9.7). We have one registered document and four test documents.

Table 9.7: Comparison of Cosine and Relative Similarity Measures for Four Test Documents

Doc	Contents	Cosine	Relative
Registered	It will work	-	-
Test 1	It will	0.82	0.99
Test 2	It will work	1.00	1.00
Test 3	Work Work Work	0.58	0.18
Test 4	It will work and may even return results	0.61	1.00

The similarity between the registered and each of the four test documents is compared using the cosine and relative similarity measures. The relative score of the first test document, that is a subset of the registered document, is 0.99. The second test document is identical to the registered document and has a similarity of 1.0 using both measures. The third test document with three occurrences of the word work, has cosine and relative similarity values of 0.58 and 0.18 respectively. The relative similarity reduces as the number of occurrences of work increases and will become zero, when the skew between word frequencies in the test and registered documents exceeds the ϵ value. The final fourth document is a superset of the registered document and has a value of 1.0, indicating a complete overlap. Test documents that are both supersets and subsets of the registered document have relative similarity scores close to 1.0. We will use the relative similarity measure in the following implementation to compare a test document with registered documents.

An Implementation based on SCAM

The `TrainPDetector` class in the `org.btest.ch9` package accepts a string parameter containing the name of a Lucene index directory. The text from the registered documents in the `plaintext` directory is tokenized and indexed. The code in `TrainPDetector` uses a character based **NgramAnalyzer** to create the text units that are stored in the Lucene index. We could have used any of the other **Analyzer**s that we covered in Chapter 2, but have selected an **NgramAnalyzer**, since it will work with multiple languages and is not dependent on finding word boundaries.

```
TrainPDetector trainPD =
  new TrainPDetector(PD_INDEX_DIR);
File mRegisteredDir = new File(
  TRAINING_DIR + FS + "registered" + FS + "plaintext");
trainPD.train(mRegisteredDir);
```

The `mRegisteredDir` is a directory that contains a list of copyrighted documents. The list of files are tokenized and indexed, one at a time, in the given index directory. We will have a Lucene index to search the copyrighted document using ngram queries, when the `train` method of the class `TrainPDetector` completes.

The `eval` method of `TestPDetector` class accepts the name of the test document and returns a list of files whose similarity with the test document exceeds a threshold. The documents with high scores above a threshold are registered documents that have a high degree of overlap with the test document.

```
TestPDetector testPD = new TestPDetector(PD_INDEX_DIR);
String testDoc = TESTING_DIR + FS + "plagiarized"
  + FS + "plaintext" + FS + "doc.txt";
ArrayList<String> files = testPD.eval(testDoc);
```

The constructor of the `TestPDetector` class uses the name of the Lucene index directory to create an `IndexSearcher` to submit queries. Next, the text from the passed file is tokenized into a set of character ngrams and a vector of ngrams with associated frequencies is created. We have used three character ngrams for our simple example in Table 9.7. Longer ngrams may be more suitable for large collections. A separate query is created for each unique ngram and submitted to the search engine. The list of hits from all queries is collapsed into a single list. The ngrams from the test document are compared with each of the hits using the relative similarity measure. The list of files with high similarity scores are flagged and returned to the caller.

9.4.4 Other Applications

We have looked at the detection of overlap between text documents alone. There are other types of media such as audio and video that can also be plagiarized. The use of character based ngrams may have some advantages in creating a multimedia plagiarism detector. The detection of code that has been copied has become important with the large volume of open source code that is freely available. Students can easily download programs and submit assignments that are substantially based on external code without acknowledging the original authors or mentioning any references.

The plagiarism detector that we created earlier will need to be modified to function as a duplicate code detector. It is quite simple to add large sections of comments to modify the original code and alter variable names using a few edit commands. A source code file will usually be pre-processed before being tokenized and indexed. The pre-processing will include the removal of all comments and the substitution of variable names with a generic name.

A programmer may take chunks of code from multiple sources and paste it together to create a new program. Plagiarism of this type is harder to detect, when there is no sign of high overlap with a single source. However, this type of copying also involves more effort on the part of the plagiarizer. We assume that most plagiarizers whose main aim is to minimize effort, will not take the trouble to create a sophisticated copy.

We can use this same method to detect near copies of HTML pages and even addresses. Web crawlers that visit many pages may download multiple pages with very similar content. These types of pages may be located on mirror sites and have different timestamps. The signatures of these pages will not be close, even though the differences between the text contents are minimal. The use of a relative overlap measure will find such pages. A company with a huge database of addresses may have several duplicate addresses that differ due to minor changes. The relative similarity measure with a small character based ngram may find addresses that are near duplicates.

9.5 Summary

This chapter began with the collection and tracking of news on the Web. Weather and news Web sites generate information on a daily basis, that is more easily monitored using automatic methods than manually downloading and analyzing individual Web pages. A company needs to monitor the sentiment of product reviews generated on the Web. A negative review from an influential site can affect the sales of a company's product. Automated methods to first isolate the subjective sentences followed by a polarity classification have been successful. Sentiment analysis has become a popular research topic with the widespread availability of information and the large number of sources on the Web.

An organization is responsible for the type of content stored on its servers. The automatic detection of offensive content before an incident is reported can limit a company's liability. Plagiarism has become relatively simple with the widespread access to online text and source code that can be easily copied and pasted.

Many of the solutions in this chapter were specialized text categorization applications. Documents were typically classified into one of two categories- subjective or objective, negative or positive, and copied or original. Standard classification methods could not be directly applied to these problems and we used some of the special features of these problems to create a custom classifier.

10 Future Directions in Search

Imagine a hand held device with voice recognition, a Q&A search engine, a one terabyte disk, and text to speech capability. This device would respond to a question posed in natural language and respond with a text or audio answer. An answer maybe a single fact, a set of sentences, or even a list of entities. This type of device would store all the digital files that someone could conceivably use, including messages, emails, Web pages, audio and video files, letters, and books. Information collected from the Web, an Intranet, and other sources would be stored in a single repository and accessed using an intelligent search tool, that would interpret questions and return possible answers instead of a list of hits. All types of information would be captured, indexed, and analyzed with press of a single *Cache* button.

The idea of capturing and storing personal information is not new. *Memex* (memory extender), a device conceived by Vannevar Bush in the 1940s, was a theoretical device to store all of one's books, records, and other communications on microfilm with links between related text. This information could theoretically be rapidly retrieved with minimal effort. Even though Vannevar Bush could not build such a device, his ideas led to the development of hypertext that was subsequently incorporated into the World Wide Web. But, merely capturing and storing large volumes of information is not sufficient.

Currently, it is possible to at least store all the information that any one person could read on a desktop PC. Managing and retrieving information continues to be harder than anticipated. Still, the invaluable computer-based Q&A as seen in the "*Star Trek*" TV series, will be a reality in the near future. This chapter deals with some of the current search applications and research based tools to build more user friendly ways of finding information.

10.1 Improving Search Engines

Most users of the Web are familiar with search engines and have become accustomed to the almost instant access to information. A list of hits is returned for practically any legitimate query. Unfortunately, this type of response is not usually found on an Intranet or desktop.

The low user satisfaction with Intranet search engines compared to Web-based search engines may not be entirely due to a poor search engine implementation. Information on an Intranet that is not well organized with tagged descriptions and appropriate titles, cannot be accurately indexed and made available in response to a relevant query. Other information located on sources like a laptop that are intermittently connected to the network may not be indexed. An Intranet crawler simply follows all possible links from an initial set and anything outside the Web graph will never be seen and indexed by the search engine. In general, you are more likely to get a larger number of results from a Web than an Intranet search engine. However, the precision of the results from a Web search engine is not always guaranteed. Clearly, automated solutions to capture and index information do have limitations

10.1.1 Adding Human Intelligence

Search engine developers have added features to include human intelligence along with the list of automatically generated hits. This hybrid approach may offer better results than the list of hits from a search engine based on purely automated methods. There are a few advantages to adding manually collected Web pages to the index.

A crawler that follows the `robots.txt` protocol may not visit pages that are authoritative sources and could be highly relevant for some queries. A human using a browser has no such restrictions and can recommend any page that is accessible through a browser. There are a large number of Web pages that can only be accessed through queries. Pages from these sites are dynamically generated in response to a query and a crawler cannot find such pages, since a static link to the dynamic page may not exist in a page. A human is also not fooled by a page whose rank has been manipulated by a large number of artificial links. Pages that use link or term spamming are unlikely to be seen in a hit list that contains manually verified pages.

The search engine ChaCha (`http://www.chacha.com`) goes one step further. It uses the help of human guides to assist in real time searches. The computer not only provides a list of hits, but also initiates a communication link between the searcher and a professional guide who has been selected based on expertise. A chat box gives the searcher an opportunity to provide real time relevance feedback and solicit the opinion of an expert. The use of many thousands of paid experts, who can be online at any given time may be sufficient to provide a more reliable and precise search service than an automated search engine. An expert can request online feedback and direct the searcher to the intended sources, or even suggest alternate queries that may be better suited for the search requirements. Automated methods to accomplish these tasks will almost always be of lower quality compared to the results from a human expert.

Mahalo (`http://www.mahalo.com`) is another human guided Web search engine. The hits for a query may contain useful links that are not available using a traditional automated Web search engine and is one of the main reasons to use these types of search engines The quality of the returned links for some areas of search such as shopping, health, and travel may be more precise. Some product vendors, who have optimized a site for a higher search engine rank, but are of poorer quality than another site, may be excluded from the list of hits. It is also easier for manual search engines like Mahalo or ChaCha to correct the results of a query. Pages that appear to be spam or are mainly advertisements are simply excluded from the list of results.

Some sites have content that has been manipulated exclusively to generate advertisement revenue. These sites are in most cases not useful, unless the advertisements are relevant to the searcher. A blog may include articles that have been cut and pasted from several sources, but essentially contains no useful information. A search engine crawler cannot easily detect such articles that have been put together by a human, simply to direct Web traffic. An article with no spelling mistakes and grammatical errors can be quickly assembled with a few queries on a search engine. The corrections to an automated search engine to fix this problem are not as simple, since an algorithm must be tuned to exclude spam articles and any corrections may introduce new errors, while removing other errors.

Search engines that add humans in the loop are based on the assumption that on the Web, more is not always better. Searchers are interested in locating a few good sources and the added value of crawling billions of pages is minimal, unless ranking has been implemented to weed out pages that are not useful.

10.1.2 Special Features

Search engine developers have long known that a core list of hits can be supplemented with more relevant information that is not accessible through a crawler or from an initial set of pages. For example, the results for a query that contains the name of a place could additionally include the results from a gazetteer. The information from a gazetteer may include the latitude, longitude, time zone, and any number of other facts related to the location. Added results are query sensitive and may include the results from multimedia search engines, blogs, and many other sources (see Figure 10.1).

Figure 10.1: Expanding the List of Hits with Other Queries

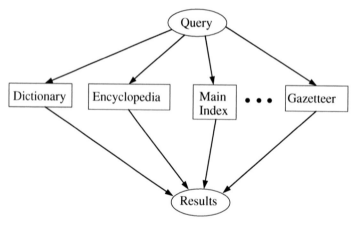

Searches outside the main index of the search engine are also called *vertical searches*. These search engines are specific to a particular domain like news, blogs, or weather. The term *federated search* has been used to describe the concurrent search of multiple indexes or databases. A federated search is more complex than it appears. There are several sub-tasks that need to be accomplished, before returning a list of results in a reasonable time. One, a query may need to be translated into the search engine specific syntax before submission. Two, the results from multiple queries must be merged before generating the list of hits that will be returned to the searcher. Three, all the results must be presented in a single screen.

The ranking algorithm of each vertical search engine is typically unique, since the indexed documents are from different domains. Consider a dictionary or gazetteer, any links between entries do not represent the distribution of authority and algorithms like PageRank are not useful here. Therefore, combining the results from different sources into a single list is non-trivial and an alternate solution is to simply list the results by vertical search type. A search can also be expanded by dropping or using more general terms and made more specific with the addition of new terms (see Figure 10.2). The core results are extracted from the main index of the search engine that contains the bulk of the indexed documents.

Figure 10.2: A Query Supplemented with the Results from Additional Sources

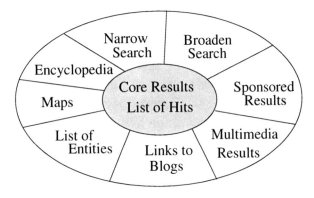

Currently, search engines like a9.com , ask.com, and Google provide results from multiple sources. For example, a query with the term *Baghdad* will return a window with the results from an encyclopedia search, the current time in *Baghdad*, a map of the city, the current weather, and other links. Consider a query - "*Iraq war*" for which the results are shown in Figure 10.3.

The left column contains additional queries that the searcher can submit to either expand or narrow the query. A more specific query adds new terms to the original query "*Iraq war*" and a more general query may drop the term *Iraq*. In addition to the standard list of hits in the center column, there are other hits from image,

Figure 10.3: Results for the Query "*Iraq war*"

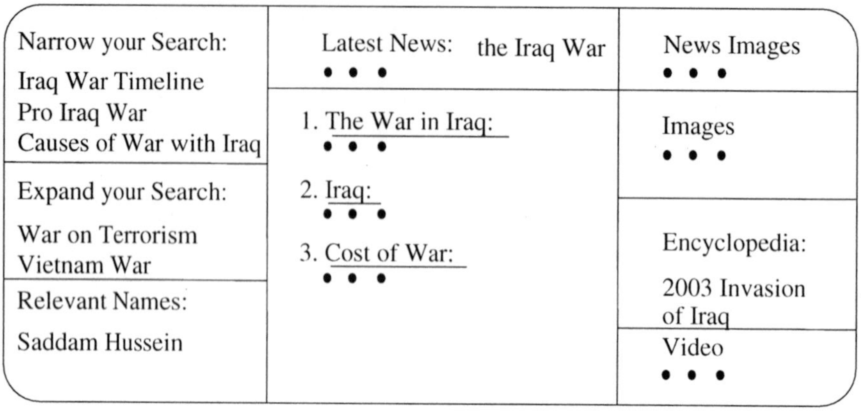

Narrow your Search: Iraq War Timeline Pro Iraq War Causes of War with Iraq	Latest News: the Iraq War • • •	News Images • • •
	1. The War in Iraq: • • •	Images • • •
Expand your Search: War on Terrorism Vietnam War	2. Iraq: • • •	Encyclopedia: 2003 Invasion of Iraq
Relevant Names: Saddam Hussein	3. Cost of War: • • •	Video • • •

video, and encyclopedia searches. The results from a blog search and a timeline are possible additions to the results.

There are substantial benefits to adding the results from multiple searches, despite the risk of overwhelming the user with too much information in a single screen. The Web is probably the most popular source for information on movies, electronic products, restaurants, the weather, the current news, and people. It is a challenge for a general purpose search engine to combine hits from multiple searches to present a coherent set of results. We can simplify this problem by separating the presentation of results following the query submission. A standard query submission protocol makes it easy to submit and fetch the results from multiple search engines.

10.1.3 OpenSearch

OpenSearch was developed by a9.com, an Amazon.com company, to make it simple to search multiple search engines using a set of formats. The results of a search engine query are returned in *RSS* or *Atom* (see section 9.1) formats, that include OpenSearch elements describing the list of hits. The response from a OpenSearch query is a XML file containing the list of results and other information describing the number of hits, hits per page, and the query. An OpenSearch client submits the query to multiple search engines and parses the returned XML files (see Figure 10.4).

Figure 10.4: Querying Multiple Search Engines using OpenSearch

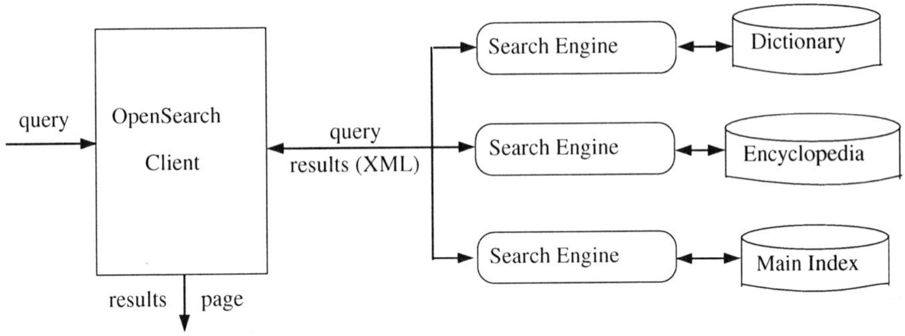

A client can submit queries to specialized search engines that support OpenSearch, collect the results, and generate a composite results page. Notice, an OpenSearch client could be written in any language such as Php, Perl, or Ruby, provided the language supported functions to send and receive data using the *http* protocol. We will consider the necessary changes to support OpenSearch on the client and server using Java Server Pages and the Lucene API respectively.

The servlet code (OpenSearch.java) in the package org.btext.web to support OpenSearch queries has been adopted from similar code in the Nutch (see section 8.4) project. This servlet code has been tested under the Tomcat servlet container alone. We begin by defining the sources for the specifications of the XML tags (see Listing 10.1). Two namespaces have been defined (lines 15-18). The first namespace uses the specifications for a basic OpenSearch client. These elements would include the totalResults, startIndex, and itemsPerPage. The second namespace includes the names of specific elements that have been adopted to customize the OpenSearch interface. Links to the sources of both specifications are included in the returned XML file. The CommonBean and DocumentBean objects (line 4) are parameters that have been populated with information relevant to the query and a list of document specific information respectively. Methods from these two classes are used to extract the results of the query.

Listing 10.1: Servlet Code to Support OpenSearch Queries

```
1   private void createOpenSearch(
2     HttpServletRequest request,
3     HttpServletResponse response,
4     CommonBean cbean, DocBean dbean)
5     throws ParserConfigurationException,
6       UnsupportedEncodingException, IOException {
7
8     DocumentBuilderFactory factory =
9       DocumentBuilderFactory.newInstance();
10    factory.setNamespaceAware(true);
11    org.w3c.dom.Document doc =
12      factory.newDocumentBuilder().newDocument();
13    Element rss = addNode(doc, doc, "rss");
14    addAttribute(doc, rss, "version", "2.0");
15    addAttribute(doc, rss, "xmlns:opensearch",
16      (String)NS_MAP.get("opensearch"));
17    addAttribute(doc, rss, "xmlns:mustru",
18      (String) NS_MAP.get("mustru"));
19    Element channel = addNode(doc, rss, "channel");
20    addNode(doc, channel, "title", "Mustru: "
21      + cbean.getQuery());
22    addNode(doc, channel, "description",
23      "Hits for query: " + cbean.getQuery());
24    String requestUrl =
25      request.getRequestURL().toString();
26    String base = requestUrl.substring(
27      0, requestUrl.lastIndexOf('/'));
28    String params = "&currentPage=" +
29      cbean.getCurrentPage() + "&type=SEARCH" +
30      "&startPage=" + cbean.getStartPage();
31    String encQuery = java.net.URLEncoder.encode(
32      cbean.getQuery(), "UTF-8");
33    addNode(doc, channel, "link", base + "/search.jsp"
34      + "?query=" + encQuery + params);
35    addNode(doc, channel, "opensearch",
36      "totalResults", "" + cbean.getNumHits());
37    addNode(doc, channel, "opensearch",
38      "startIndex", "" + cbean.getStart());
39    addNode(doc, channel, "opensearch",
40      "itemsPerPage", "" + cbean.getPageInc());
```

```
41    addNode(doc, channel, "mustru", "query",
42      cbean.getQuery() );
43    if ( cbean.getEnd() < cbean.getNumHits() ) {
44      // more hits to show
45      addNode(doc, channel, "mustru", "nextPage",
46        requestUrl +"?query=" + encQuery + params);
47    }
48
49    for (int i = 0; i < dbean.getDocuments().length; i++) {
50      Doc document = dbean.documents[i];
51      String title = document.getTitle();
52      String fileName = document.getFileName();
53      String encFileName =
54        java.net.URLEncoder.encode(fileName, "UTF-8");
55      String url = (document.getFileLocation().length() > 0)?
56        document.getFileLocation(): fileName;
57      String summary = document.getContents().toString();
58      if (title == null || title.equals("")) title = url;
59      Element item = addNode(doc, channel, "item");
60      addNode(doc, item, "title", title);
61      addNode(doc, item, "description", summary);
62      addNode(doc, item, "link", url);
63    }
64
65    // dump the DOM tree
66    DOMSource source = new DOMSource(doc);
67    TransformerFactory transFactory =
68      TransformerFactory.newInstance();
69    Transformer transformer =
70      transFactory.newTransformer();
71    transformer.setOutputProperty("indent", "yes");
72    StreamResult result = new StreamResult(
73      response.getOutputStream());
74    response.setContentType("text/xml");
75    transformer.transform(source, result);
76 }
```

We have used the Document Object Model (DOM) to build the XML document with a W3C API (line 11). An open search client can use either the DOM-based or the Simple API for XML (SAX) parsers to extract the results from the returned document. Following the description of the header, all the results are captured in the `channel` element (line 19). The first part of the file contains header information such as the total number of hits, the hits per page, the query, and the starting index of the results (lines 20-46). A link to the next page of results is included, if more hits can be shown. Finally, the list of hits are returned in a sequence of `item` elements (lines 56-62). Each `item` contains the title, description, and a link to the document.

The Java 2 Standard Edition includes several classes from the `javax.xml` package to build a DOM-based document. The `DOMSource` (line 66) object is the holder of the DOM tree that is eventually returned to the caller. The input to the constructor of the `DOMSource` object is the DOM-based document that was instantiated earlier and populated with the results of the query. The `StreamResult` (line 72) object is a holder for the transformed DOM-based object. A sample XML file returned from an OpenSearch query is shown in Listing 10.2.

Listing 10.2: A Sample XML File Returned from an OpenSearch Query

```
1   <?xml version="1.0" encoding="UTF-8"?>
2     <rss xmlns:mustru="http://localhost/spec/opensearchrss/1.0"
3     xmlns:opensearch="http://a9.com/-/spec/opensearchrss/1.0/"
4     version="2.0">
5     <channel>
6       <title>Mustru: text</title>
7       <description>Mustru search results for query: text
8       </description>
9       <link>
10         http://localhost:8080/btext/search.jsp?query=text&amp;
                currentPage=0
11      </link>
12      <opensearch:totalResults>4</opensearch:totalResults>
13      <opensearch:startIndex>0</opensearch:startIndex>
14      <opensearch:itemsPerPage>10</opensearch:itemsPerPage>
15      <mustru:query>text</mustru:query>
16      <mustru:showAllHits>
17        http://localhost:8080/btext/opensearch?query=text&amp...
18      </mustru:showAllHits>
19
20      <item>
21        <title>
22          Integration of Data Mining and Relational Databases
23        </title>
24        <description>Integration of Data Mining and Relational ...
```

```
25          </description>
26          <link>http://...</link>
27        </item>
28    . . . more items
29      </channel>
30    </rss>
```

The listing has been truncated for the sake of brevity. A single `item` out of the ten items has been shown. Each `item` has three attributes – a `title`, a `description`, and a `link` to the item's URL. A few changes still need to be made to the JSP pages that will display the link to the RSS feed. The `header.jsp` and `footer.jsp` files are modified with the following code.

```
<jsp:useBean id="cbean" type="org.btext.web.CommonBean"
  scope="request"/>
<%
  String encQ = java.net.URLEncoder.encode(
    cbean.getQuery(), "UTF-8");
  String rss = "./opensearch?type=SEARCH&q=" + encQ;
%>

<!-- Footer RSS Logo -->
<table bgcolor="3333ff" align="right">
<tr><td bgcolor="ff9900">
  <a href="<%=rss%>"><font color="ffffff"><b>RSS</b> </font></a>
</td></tr>
</table>
```

The passed query is first URL encoded and used to generate an rss URL. The link to the RSS feed is shown with a standard orange background and the letters *RSS* in the footer of the Web page. A meta search Web page would hide the links to specific search engines and simply display a single query box and the results from multiple queries.

10.1.4 Specialized Search Engines

Specialized search engines for medical, financial, and legal information can customize the results based on the domain. For example, a financial search engine can return more than a simple list of hits in response to a stock quote. The current stock price, a plot of the price over some period, news articles that mention the company, the current sentiment of the articles, list of names mentioned in the articles, and links to other financial information may be collected and returned in a single screen. A searcher still has to do some analysis to understand the text. Most search engines do not provide information showing how a company's stock price fluctuates in relationship to events, announcements, and the overall sentiment of articles that mention the company. This type of analysis is useful to detect articles that are intended to artificially boost the price of a stock with false information.

Automated methods to display trends are valuable, since it is difficult for a human to summarize a large volume of information. A plot showing a list of product announcements and the sentiment from product reviews for a company over a period of six months to a year is easier to compile automatically, than to build manually. This type of analysis can be done quickly on a computer and summarized graphically to simplify decision making. A key benefit of using computers to analyze information is the creation of new knowledge using captured information, that is either not apparent or very hard to accomplish manually. New knowledge includes direct and indirect links, summarizing information with a map or plot, and identifying trends. Consider a specialized metasearch engine to extract the sentiment and analyze the text of published documents following the announcement of a new product (see Figure 10.5).

Figure 10.5: A Metasearch Engine to Analyze Published Documents

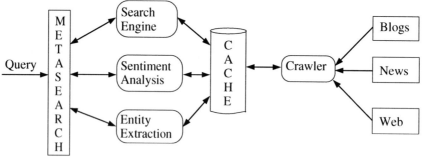

A crawler (see section 8.3) periodically collects information related to the product from blogs, news sites, and the Web. Dynamic information sources typically include RSS feeds from which a crawler can monitor published information. Collected

information is saved in a cache with a timestamp. The search engine function is implemented with an API like Lucene to create a searchable index from the contents of the cache. The sentiment (positive, negative, or neutral) is automatically extracted using a model (see section 9.2). Finally, the entity extraction function (see section 5.4) associates the occurrences of entities such as the names of people, places, or organizations with a particular document.

The metasearch function combines the results from each of these specific functions and returns a screen with a summary of results. For example, the summary may include a map showing the locations and frequency of occurrence of the product name in customer complaints. The overall sentiment of published articles can be shown in a plot over a time period. Finally, influential or significant publishers can be identified from a graph. This type of search is hard to accomplish with a Web search engine and new metasearch applications will combine content from several sources to generate novel or summarized information. The term *mashup* is used to describe this type of activity and is rapidly becoming popular, since there are many innovative applications that can be created from the numerous combinations of information sources. Most large information providers allow limited access to content using a published API.

Some commercial search engine providers include additional results to supplement the standard hit list. Figure 10.6 shows part of the results from a query for the largest city in Myanmar using two search engines - Exalead and Factiva, a Dow Jones company.

The standard hit list returned by both search engines is not shown in the figure. A set of ten or more hits with snippets of text containing the query terms and a link to the URL are returned in both search engines. The additional results from Factiva are shown in bar charts to quickly compare results by time, entity, or source. For example, there is a spike in the number of articles published in October 2007. Similarly, the company Chevron, is mentioned more often than other companies. Factiva also includes news clusters around themes that are popular in text of documents from the hit list. Exalead summarizes supplemental information in a textual format. A list of related terms followed by links to multimedia sources for the query are shown. Links to directories where additional information can be found is included. These are two examples of commercial organizations that use extracted information to generate results that may be more useful than a plain list of hits.

Figure 10.6: Supplemental Results from Two Search Engines, Factiva and Exalead
(*Reprinted with the permission of Exalead and Factiva – A Dow Jones Company*)

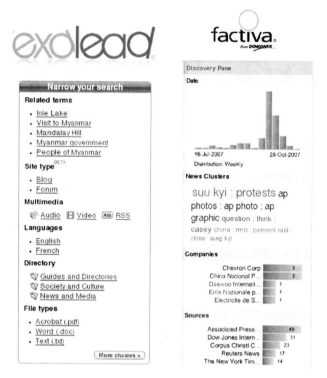

10.2 Using Collective Intelligence to Improve Search

Consider, the evaluation of a new Intranet search engine. Many gigabytes of text have been indexed and are now available to a large audience. The developers of the search engine may submit a few queries and verify that the results seem reasonable. A more thorough evaluation would involve tests with a much larger user group. The evaluation from a small test group may not be substantial enough and therefore insufficient to judge the precision of the new search engine. A more complete test would evaluate the results from thousands of queries and hundreds of users.

The first step in the evaluation of the search engine is to build a large number of test queries. The set of test queries would be carefully selected from the most likely popular queries. A small percentage of queries tend to be repeatedly submitted and optimizing the search engine for just these queries would improve the precision of the search engine with less effort than the use of all possible test queries. The results of the test queries are saved in a database for evaluation.

We now have all the information needed to run the evaluation. This type of problem was first encountered in computationally intensive jobs that required a long time to run on supercomputers. A huge problem was solved more efficiently, if many small sub-problems were distributed to a large number of processors, provided there was little or no communication needed to solve the individual sub-problems. In our search engine example, we can consider the manual evaluation of the results from a single query as one sub-problem that requires no communication. The final precision of the search engine is collectively computed from the manual evaluations of many thousands of test queries. Notice, there is no communication needed to solve each sub-problem and many sub-problems can be solved concurrently. The computer's role here is not to solve problems, but instead to facilitate the division of a large problem, distribute sub-problems, and collect the results.

Mechanical Turk from Amazon.com is a Web based system that manages the distribution of tasks and collection of results. A task is some chunk of work that a computer cannot currently solve as efficiently as a human. For example, the evaluation of a list of hits from a search engine is much easier for a human than a computer. A human has substantial background knowledge to quickly make an accurate relevance judgment that a computer is unable to perform. The function of the computer in Mechanical Turk is to coordinate the distribution and collection of tasks instead of the more typical problem solving role. Other types of problems that humans currently outperform computers include scanning images for an object, evaluating beauty, and judging the correctness of answers.

10.2.1 Tag-Based Search Engines

We look at a slightly different use of collaboration to improve the quality of search. Some resources without accompanying metadata, are hard to describe using automated methods. These types of resources would include audio, video, images, and Web pages. The publishers of these resources provide metadata in the form of tags (word descriptors). Metadata tags to describe Web pages have been in use since the early days of the Web. The huge number of Web pages and the increasing use of metadata tags to boost ranking on a search engine in a large information space has made the use of these tags on the Web, less effective than expected.

However, tags have been successfully used in a collaborative environment to improve the search of resources that cannot be precisely described using automatic methods. Consider a search engine for images. The automated method of tagging images builds an approximate description of images based on the neighboring and anchor text found in the source Web page. This method is reliable to some extent, but does not permit the publishers of these images to participate in the search process. The basic design for a tag-based search engine is shown in Figure 10.7.

Figure 10.7: Basic Design for a Tag-based Search

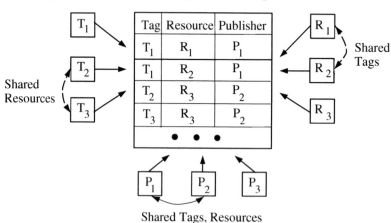

Three entities *tags*, *resources*, and *publishers*, participate in the search engine. A resource is described by one or more tags and the same tag can be used to describe more than one resource. A publisher submits the resource to the repository and selects the tags to describe the resource. For example, a photo of Mount Everest may be published with a set of tags that reveal the timestamp of the photo, location of the photographer, and other features. The manual description of such images will in almost all cases, be more precise than an automated description generated from an analysis of the image content alone. Typically, tags are the best representation for resources that can be summarized in one or two sentences.

At first, relying on a large group of unrelated collaborators with varying degrees of motivation and expertise appears to be an unlikely model of success. There are at least three possible sources of errors in the use of tags (see Figure 10.8) to build a better search engine. The first type of error is described in the false positive (*FP*) and false negative (*FN*) boxes that represent the use of the wrong tags and the absence of the correct tags respectively, to describe a resource.

Figure 10.8: Sources of Errors in the Tagging Model

		Resources					Meanings	
		Similar	Dissimilar				Institution	Depend
Tags	Similar	TP	FP		Words	Bank	✓	✓
	Dissimilar	FN	TN			Rely		✓

The second type of error is due to polysemy and synonymy. A word like *bank* has over 15 meanings (from WordNet) and a meaning can be expressed with more than one word. Queries with polysemous words like *bank*, will have lower precision than other types of queries with words that have a singular meaning. The recall of a query that uses just one synonym of a meaning will be lower, if a resource has not been tagged with all possible synonyms. A carefully selected tagging design can mitigate the effects of these types of errors. We will compare a few tagging methods in a collaborative environment.

Most tag-based search engines allow anyone to publish information. The group of publishers and taggers of resources are taken from the general population and therefore will have varying degrees of expertise. A few publishers may provide long detailed explanations of resources, while many others will be more succinct. This type of behavior is predicted by Zipf's law and was observed in a study of the usage of tags in Flickr [Marlow].

The absence of explicit links between resources makes it difficult to rank resources in response to a query. In Chapter 8, we covered the use of ranking algorithms like PageRank and Hubs & Authorities to find key sources of information based on the embedded hyperlink Web graph. Hyperlinks between resources represented the distribution of authority and Web pages with a large number of incoming links were ranked higher than other pages. We can still rank resources fairly precisely, despite the lack of explicit links. But, first we compare tag-based and Web search engines in Table 10.1.

Table 10.1: Differences between a Web and Tag-based Search Engine

Web	Tag-based
Publishers usually have no accounts	All publishers are registered and can establish social networks with other publishers
No control over the contents of Web pages	Can restrict tagging to a specific vocabulary and owned or shared resources alone
A Web page must have some text that can be indexed	Any type of resource including multimedia can be tagged
Term and link spam is a constant headache for administrators	Tag spam can quickly be identified and removed in a collaborative environment
Large Web search engines attempt to cover a broad range of topics	Specialized search engines to retrieve bookmarks, images, or audio can be focused to address a single domain or media
A large Web graph is exploited to find authority pages	Links are optionally created between publishers and implicit links between resources are defined based on shared tags

A tag-based search engine has a known set of publishers who may also be linked to each other based on common interests. Large Web search engines are not focused on any media or domain, while tag-based search engines are usually specialized and more focused to handle searches for media and resources that Web search engines are unable to retrieve with high precision. Spam is more easily controlled in a tag-based search engine. The vocabulary can be controlled or collaboratively monitored.

There are several design decisions that need to be made to produce a high performance tag-based search engine. These decisions ultimately result in an emergent behavior from the multitude of tags that are individually selected. There are three components in a tag-based search engine – agents, an environment, and rules to guide the behavior of agents. The agents represent the publishers who may follow rules that control the type of tags used and the set of resources that can be tagged. The environment is the search index of tags and resources that is constantly evolving as resources are published and tagged. The rules may restrict the tag vocabulary explicitly, suggest suitable tags based on synonyms or popular lingo, or permit an unrestricted set of tags. Further, a publisher may be allowed to tag owned resources, or a group's resources, or any indexed resource. Some tags will emerge as the popular tags that the community has selected to represent a particular type of resource.

This type of emergent behavior tends to occur naturally and is facilitated by features to share and select tags. Spam is less of an issue in a tag-based search engine provided design decisions are made to encourage the detection of spam and the creation of a strong community. A publisher who uses tags to manipulate ranking may be penalized by the community. Relevance feedback is collected in the form of votes to identify popular resources and in association, highly regarded publishers.

Current popular tags may be shown in a tag cloud (see Figure 1.4). The size of a tag is roughly proportional to its frequency in the index. We can view the tag cloud as equivalent to the current hot topics that may evolve over time. Tag-based search engines have become popular alternatives to the large Web search engine. The participation of the publisher in building a community-based search implies a stronger link to the tag-based search engine than an anonymous user submitting pages to the crawler of a Web search engine.

10.3 Question & Answer

We began this chapter with a futuristic handheld device that could answer questions stated in natural language. Such a device would store many gigabytes of indexed information that could be easily searched. Although, we can store and retrieve large volumes of information, we still need to read and extract answers from documents. The search engine API Lucene, that we covered in Chapters 3 and 4, is designed to retrieve documents that are relevant to a keyword-based query.

Some information needs can be stated in the form of a keyword-based query, but others are more easy to state in the form of a question. For example, it is easier to conceive of the question, *Who wrote Macbeth?* than the equivalent query, *Macbeth*

AND (wrote OR author). Nevertheless, some questions like, *What is Professor Smith's home page?* are succinctly stated in a query, *"Professor Smith" AND "home page".* Queries will continue to be appropriate for some types of information needs that can be simply stated with a set of nouns and adjectives. Later in this section, we will look at examples of questions that are hard to translate into queries.

10.3.1 Q&A Engine Design

First, we examine the basic design of a Q&A engine. Most Q&A engines use a search engine with pre-processing and post-processing functions before and after a search engine query (see Figure 10.9). This is a pipeline design that starts with a question and ends with an answer. The pre-processing function analyzes the question and prepares one or more queries that will be submitted to the search engine.

Figure 10.9: Basic Design for a Q&A Engine

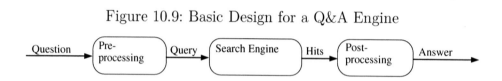

The post processing function extracts answers (text chunks) from the text of the list of hits and returns the top ranking answers. We have not shown the processing that occurs when a document is added to the search engine index. This processing can be performed apriori or when a question is submitted. In an interactive Q&A system, it is preferable to maximize offline processing in order to minimize the response time. Offline indexing would include functions such as POS tagging and entity extraction (see Chapter 5) that provide some meaning to the text. We can use both a search engine and a database to manage the storage of text and entities respectively.

Pre-Processing

The pre-processing function in Figure 10.9 is primarily a question categorization step to identify the type of question. There are infinite ways to ask questions and we look at a few of the most common question patterns. We can broadly categorize question into factoid and procedural questions (see Figure 10.10). The answer to a factoid question is a short phrase or even a single word. The answers to procedural questions, may consist of a sentence or a paragraph. Most of the early Q&A engines were designed to answer factoid questions. Answer to these questions were relatively easier to extract than to assemble a chunk of text to describe a procedure.

Figure 10.10: Categorization of a Question to Identify Answer Type

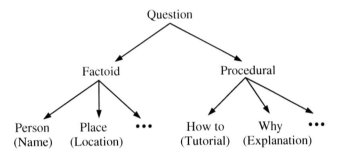

A generated query for a factoid question would use the question nouns, question adjectives, and the potential entity type that the answer should contain. For example, the answers to *who, where,* and *when* questions should contain person, place, and time entity types respectively. Table 10.2 lists a set of ten sample questions and types.

A precise hierarchical question classifier in Figure 10.10 is hard to implement due to the limited amount of text in a question and the absence of any standard format to state questions. In most of the questions in Table 10.2, the occurrence of question words (*Who, What, Where,* and *How*) do suggest the type of question. However, question words are also likely to be appear in procedural questions. Part of speech and question structure are additional features that can help in the classification.

Search Engine Query Generation

Once we have categorized a question, we need to generate a search engine query. For example, the query for the third question in Table 10.2 that is most likely to return a document containing the answer to the question, is - "*largest city*" AND *Myanmar.* The nouns and adjectives of the question are the best initial source of query keywords.

Table 10.2: Sample List of Questions and Types

Question	TypeType	Entity/Process
Who is Alvaro Uribe Velez	Factoid	Person
What plant can be used to treat blood pressure	Factoid	Thing
What is the largest city in Myanmar	Factoid	Place
Did A.Q. Khan visit North Korea in December 1994	Procedural	Reasoning
Does Iran have missiles that can reach Tel Aviv	Procedural	Reasoning
Is Sudan ending its war in Darfur	Procedural	Reasoning
How tall is Christina Aquilar	Factoid	Dimension
Where does moss grow	Factoid	Location
What is pink noise	Factoid	Definition
How do I remove rust	Procedural	Tutorial

A series of queries may be submitted when an insufficient number of hits are returned. For example, the earlier query may be generalized by dropping the term *largest* from the phrase *"largest city"*. Additional synonyms may be included with the boolean *OR* operator. A query can also be specialized by additional keywords that must appear in the document, to limit the number of hits.

Post-processing

This is the final step in the pipeline that begins with a question and ends with an answer. We assume that a relevant document that contains the answer has been found by the search engine. A passage extractor looks for a chunk of text that has the highest word, noun, verb, adjective, and word bigram overlap with the question.

10.3.2 **Performance**

The additional steps to answer a question increase the response time and lower the precision of a Q&A engine. Most Q&A engines have not achieved the same level of precision as search engines for several reasons. One, the use of a pipeline process design (Figure 10.9) will propagate errors that arise early in the pre-processing or search engine functions. These errors cannot be corrected in the post-processing step. Two, in a live system, the Q&A engine must deal with all types of questions that may have typographical errors and be stated in non-standard ways. For example, the statement – *My Megatron PC is broken*, does not indicate the type of information sought and possible answers.

The large collection of FAQs on the Web are a good source of question patterns and a system should be optimized to handle these types of questions. Like queries, the same questions are repeated in similar or identical forms and cached answers can improve the performance of a Q&A engine. Finally, the problems of synonymy and polysemy arise in Q&A engines as well. The best answer may not have the highest degree of word overlap. An answer may use synonyms and still be correct. The generated search engine queries must include synonyms to search for all possible answers.

TREC

The question and answering track of the annual Text Retrieval Conference(TREC) series held by the National Institute of Standards and Technology was one of the first systematic attempts to evaluate the performance of Q&A engines using a common document collection. A set of training questions and answers along with a document collection was provided to all participants. Text chunks from one or more documents in the collection contained the answers to all questions.

A Q&A system was evaluated based on the number of test (unseen) questions that were correctly answered. The top five answers for each question were considered and a score was assigned proportional to the rank. So, the top answer in the first hit would receive a score of 1.0, the second 0.5, the third 0.33, and so on. The answers returned by Q&A engines were manually corrected. Some answers were harder to judge than others. For example, a text chunk that contains the year *2004* is a valid answer for the question – *When was George W. Bush re-elected?*, but may originate in an irrelevant document that just happens to mention the year 2004. There are four possibilities when we consider the correctness of answers and documents (see Table 10.3).

Table 10.3: Judging the Correctness of an Answer

		Answer	
		Relevant	Irrelevant
Document	Relevant	Correct	Incorrect
	Irrelevant	Incorrect	Incorrect

The case of where both the document and answer belong to the same category (*relevant* or *irrelevant*) is easy to resolve. An answer that is relevant, but arises in an irrelevant document by coincidence should probably be judged incorrect. A Q&A engine deserves partial credit for finding a relevant document, but not the right answer. The TREC conference series have become quite popular and a number of academic, non-profit, and commercial organizations participate in the annual contests.

10.4 Summary

In this chapter, we looked at search applications that return more than just a list of hits. Some of these applications use the tools described in Chapter 5 to extract entities such as company and person names and in Chapter 6 to organize the results of a query into groups or clusters. The OpenSearch API that we covered can be used to build a metasearch application that combines the results from multiple queries. The use of results from many sources have become popular to create a mashup or a novel application.

A question and answer engine that can correctly answer all types of questions has not yet been developed. This problem is harder to solve due to the innumerable ways of asking question, the interpretation of questions, complex reasoning that may be needed to answer a question, the precise retrieval of relevant documents, and the extraction of answers.

A Software

The sample code used in this book can be downloaded from `http://mustru.sf.net`. You can use Ant (`http://ant.apache.org`) or the Eclipse platform (`http://www.eclipse.org`) to compile the Java code. The source code is organized by chapter with separate packages for database classes, utilities, and WordNet functions. All of the attached source code has been tested under the following versions and may or may not work with other versions of the software in Table A.1.

Table A.1: Versions of Software used in Sample Code		
Software	**Version**	**Description**
Lucene	2.3	Search Engine API
LingPipe	3.3	Natural Language Processing API
Gate	4.0	Framework for Text Processing
WordNet	3.0	Thesaurus / Dictionary
Berkeley DB	3.2	Berkeley Database from Oracle

Open source software is constantly under development and therefore there will be features in newer versions of some tools that will replace the ones mentioned in this book. However, an effort has been made to use functions that are not likely to become obsolete in the near future.

Lucene

You can download the latest version of Lucene from `http://lucene.apache.org`. It is supported by the Apache Software Foundation and released under the Apache Software License. Lucene has been ported to several other languages including Ruby, Perl, and Python. The code examples in this book use Java alone and some features that have been implemented in the Java version of Lucene may not be available in other ports.

LingPipe

LingPipe is distributed by a commercial organization *Alias-i*, under a range of licenses from a royalty-free to a paid license (`http://www.alias-i.com`). Like Lucene, Ling-Pipe is a set of Java libraries to build search and natural language applications. The API includes functions to build classifiers, extractors, and other search applications. There are a number of tutorials included in the documentation that describe more specific code details and domain specific issues such as the use of Medline text.

Gate

Gate is a General Architecture for Text Engineering, distributed by the University of Sheffield under the GNU General Public License (`http://www.gate.ac.uk`). A sample of the functions in the Gate API have been used to extract sentences, entities, and tokens from text.

WordNet

WordNet is a dictionary / thesaurus developed at the Princeton University distributed under an open source like license (`http://wordnet.princeton.edu`). The source data files of WordNet have been transformed to create database tables that can be searched using SQL. The `data/wordnet` directory of the source code distribution for the book contains these source data files.

Berkeley DB

The Berkeley DB is an embedded database distributed by Oracle Corporation under a dual license. The commercial license provides technical support and maintenance that is not included in the open source license. Appendix C includes more information on the use of the Berkeley DB.

Sample Code

The directory structure of the sample code included in the book is shown below in Table A.2. The source code for all the listings in the book can be found under the `src` directory. You can import this directory in *Eclipse* or use *Ant* to compile the code. All the jar files used in the sample code can be found in the `lib` directory.

Table A.2: Directory Structure of Sample Code	
Name	**Description**
bin /	Binary directory
bin/classes /	Binary files created from source code
data /	Data directory
data/bdb /	Berkeley DB for WordNet and search engine
data/bdb_test /	Berkeley DB to test database functions
data/config /	Configuration files
data/gate /	Gate source files
data/models /	Tagging and other model files
data/testing /	Data to test sentiment analysis, clustering and categorization
data/textfiles /	Sample plain text files
data/training /	Data to train models
data/wordnet /	Source files for WordNet database tables
docs /	Documentation directory
doc/api /	Java API documentation
lib /	Jar files used in sample code
src /	Source code

Most search engines use text filters to extract the text from formatted files. These formatted files may use proprietary or open formats to encode text. The open source Mustru project at `http://mustru.sf.net` includes several text filters to extract text from HTML, PDF, DOC, and OpenOffice.org files. The use of these text filters increases the coverage of a search engine.

Table A.3 is a cross reference of listings to the class names in the source code. The `data` directory contains files to train and test various functions described in the book. Note, the actual code is more verbose than the code shown in the listings of the book. A number of `import` and `try` / `catch` statements used in the code have not been shown in the listings for the sake of brevity.

Table A.3 Cross Reference of Listings and Sample Code Classes	
Listing	**Class Name with Prefix org.btext**
2.1	ch2.LuceneTokens
2.2	ch2.PorterAnalyzer
2.3	ch2.StandardBgramAnalyzer
2.4	ch2.LingpipeTokens
2.5	ch2.NgramAnalyzer
2.6	ch2.StandardBgramTokenizerFactory
2.7	ch2.GateTokens
2.8	ch2.GateAnalyzer
2.9	ch2.DocFilter
2.10	ch2.TestWord
2.11	ch2.WordNetExamples
3.1	ch3.CreatePDFIndex
3.2	ch3.ModifyPDFIndex
3.3	ch3.CreatePDFIndex
3.4	utils.IndexTools (indexRepair)
3.5	utils.IndexTools (dbRepair)
3.6	ch3.MemoryIndex
3.7	test.TestDateTools
4.1	ch4.SearchQuery
4.2	utils.SearchTools

Table A.3 Cross Reference of Listings and Sample Code Classes	
Listing	Class Name with Prefix org.btext
4.3	ch4.SearchSimilarity
4.4	ch4.SecurityFilter
LingPipe Spell Check Model	ch4.CreateTxtIndex
LingPipe Spell Check Search	ch4.SearchQuery
5.1	ch5.ExtractLingpipeSentences
5.2	ch5.ExtractGateSentences
5.3	ch5.ExtractLingpipePOS
5.4	utils.LingpipeTools
5.5	ch5.ExtractGatePOS
5.6	ch5.ExtractPhrases
5.7	ch5.ExtractLingpipePhrases
5.8	ch5.ExtractGateEntities
5.9	ch5.ExtractLingpipeChunk
6.1	ch6.TestCluster
7.1	ch7.TrainBClassifier
7.2	ch7.TestBClassifier
7.3	ch7.TestMClassifier
8.1	ch8.custom.jsp
9.1	ch9.news.xml
9.2	ch9.user.prof
9.3	ch9.TrainSubjectivity
9.4	ch9.TestSubjectivity
10.1	web.OpenSearch

Brown POS Tags

The Brown corpus was the first million word POS tagged corpus for English created in 1961. A set of over 200 POS tags were used to tag each of the million words (tokens). Table A.4 is a sample list of some of the popular POS tags. We implemented a POS tagger using LingPipe in Chapter 5 trained on the Brown corpus.

Table A.4: Sample List of Brown POS Tags		
Tag	**Description**	**Examples**
ABL	determiner/pronoun, pre-qualifier	quite, such, rather
ABN	determiner/pronoun, pre-quantifier	all, half, many, nary
AP	determiner/pronoun, post-determiner	many, other, next, more, last, former, little
AT	article	the, a
BE	verb "to be", infinitive or imperative	be
BEG	verb "to be", present participle or gerund	being
BEN	verb "to be", past participle	been
CC	conjunction, coordinating	and, or, but, plus, &, either, neither, nor
CD	numeral, cardinal	two, one, 1, four, 2, 1913, 71, 74 637, 1937
CD$	numeral, cardinal, genitive	1960's, 1961's, 404's
CS	conjunction, subordinating	that, as, after, whether, before, while, like
DOD	verb "to do", past tense	did, done
DT	determiner/pronoun, singular	this, each, another, that
DT$	determiner/pronoun, singular, genitive	another's
DTX	determiner, pronoun or double conjunction	neither, either, one
WRB	WH-adverb	however, when, where, why, whereby, wherever

	Table A.4: Sample List of Brown POS Tags	
Tag	Description	Examples
EX	existential there	there
HVD	verb "to have", past tense	had
HVG	verb "to have", present participle or gerund	having
HVN	verb "to have", past participle	had
IN	preposition	of, in, for, by, considering, to, on
JJ	adjective	ecent, over,-all, possible, hard-fought
JJ$	adjective, genitive	adjective, genitive
JJ+JJ	adjective, hyphenated pair	big,-large, long,-far
JJR	adjective, comparative	greater, older, further, earlier, later, freer
JJS	adjective, semantically superlative	top, chief, principal, northernmost, master
JJT	adjective, superlative	best, largest, coolest, calmest, latest, greatest
MD	modal auxillary	should, may, might, will, would, must
NN	noun, singular, common	failure, burden, court, fire, appointment
NN$	noun, singular, common, genitive	season's, world's, player's, night's, chapter's
NNS	noun, plural, common	irregularities, presentments, thanks, reports
NNS$	noun, plural, common, genitive	taxpayers' children's members' States' women's
WRB	WH-adverb	however, when, where, why, whereby, wherever

Table A.4: Sample List of Brown POS Tags		
Tag	**Description**	**Examples**
NP	noun, singular, proper	Fulton, Atlanta, September-October, Durwood
NP$	noun, singular, proper, genitive	Green's, Landis', Smith's, Carreon's
NPS	noun, plural, proper	Chases, Aderholds, Chapelles, Armisteads
NPS$	noun, plural, proper, genitive	Republicans', Orioles', Birds', Yanks', Redbirds'
NR	noun, singular, adverbial	Friday, home, Wednesday, Tuesday, Monday
NR$	noun, singular, adverbial, genitive	Saturday's, Monday's, yesterday's, tonight's
NRS	noun, plural, adverbial	Sundays, Mondays, Saturdays, Wednesdays
OD	numeral, ordinal	first, 13th, third, nineteenth, 2d, 61st, second
PN	pronoun, nominal	none, something, everything, one, anyone
PN$	pronoun, nominal, genitive	one's, someone's, anybody's, nobody's
PP$	determiner, possessive	our, its, his, their, my, your, her, out
PP$$	pronoun, possessive	ours, mine, his, hers, theirs, yours
PPL	pronoun, singular, reflexive	itself, himself, myself, yourself, herself
PPLS	pronoun, plural, reflexive	themselves, ourselves, yourselves
PPO	pronoun, personal, accusative	them, it, him, me, us, you, 'em, her
WRB	WH-adverb	however, when, where, why, whereby, wherever

Table A.4: Sample List of Brown POS Tags		
Tag	**Description**	**Examples**
RB	adverb	only, often, generally, also, nevertheless, upon
RP	adverb, particle	up, out, off, down, over, on, in, about
TO	infinitival to	to
UH	interjection	whee, hmpf, ah, oops, c'mon, 'mon
VBG	verb, present participle or gerund	modernizing, improving, purchasing
VBN	verb, past participle	conducted, charged, won, received, studied
VBZ	verb, present tense, 3rd person singular	deserves, believes, receives, takes, goes, expires
WDT	WH-determiner	which, what, whatever, whichever
WP$	WH-pronoun, genitive	whose, whosoever
WPO	WH-pronoun, accusative	whom, that, who
WPS	WH-pronoun, nominative	that, who, whoever, whosoever, what
WQL	WH-qualifier	however, how
WRB	WH-adverb	however, when, where, why, whereby, wherever

B Bayes Classification

The Naïve Bayes (NB) classifier is one of the most popular classifiers, that is relatively simple to implement and returns results whose accuracy is comparable to other classifiers. We have used this classifier in analyze sentiment, categorize text, and assign POS tags. In Chapter 9, we used two different NB classifiers to classify sentences into subjective and objective categories and categorize subjective sentences into positive, neutral, or negative sentences. In Chapter 7, we categorized documents into topics using a model created from a training set of documents. Finally, in Chapter 5, we assigned a POS tag to every word based on the context and prior samples.

We illustrate the use of the NB classifier with a simple example. Consider the problem of sentiment analysis. We have 100 reviews, of which 60 are negative (see Figure B.1). The word *bad* occurs in four reviews, three of which are negative.

Figure B.1: Occurrence of the Word bad and Negative Reviews

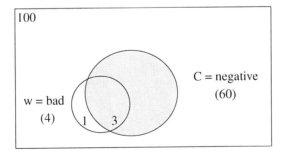

The probability of the word *bad* occurring in the set of 100 reviews is $p(w = bad) = (\frac{4}{100})$, the probability of a negative category is $p(C = negative) = (\frac{60}{100})$, and the probability of the occurrence of the word *bad* in a negative review $p(C =$

$negative \cap w = bad) = \left(\frac{3}{100}\right)$. The conditional probability of a negative category given the word *bad* is -

$$p(C = negative|w = bad) = \frac{p(C = negative \cap w = bad)}{p(w = bad)} = \frac{\left(\frac{3}{100}\right)}{\left(\frac{4}{100}\right)} \tag{B.1}$$

or 0.75. We can also state the conditional probability of the word *bad* given a negative category as -

$$p(w = bad|C = negative) = \frac{p(C = negative \cap w = bad)}{p(C = negative)} = \frac{\left(\frac{3}{100}\right)}{\left(\frac{60}{100}\right)} \tag{B.2}$$

or 0.05. The word *bad* is a single feature to identify a negative review. Consider other words such as *poor* and *downgrade* that are also more likely to be found in negative reviews. Good features for a category have high conditional probability values and can be combined to make a reasonably accurate prediction of a category given the occurrence of these words. We can state the conditional probability of a negative category given the occurrence of the set of negative words as

$$p(C = negative|w_1 = bad, \ldots w_n = downgrade) =$$

$$\frac{p(w_1 = bad, \ldots w_n = downgrade \cap C = negative)}{p(w_1 = bad, \ldots w_n = downgrade)} \tag{B.3}$$

or equivalently

$$\frac{p(w_1 = bad, \ldots w_n = downgrade|C = negative) \times p(C = negative)}{p(w_1 = bad, \ldots w_n = downgrade)} \tag{B.4}$$

The denominator is constant across both categories and since we are maximizing the probability per category we can drop the denominator from the equation. The probability $p(C = negative)$ can be estimated from the training set $\left(\frac{60}{100}\right)$. Finally, we make the assumption that the occurrence of the set of words (features) are independent and we can compute the conditional probability of a negative category given the occurrence of negative words as

$$p(w_1 = bad|C = negative) \times \dots p(w_n = downgrade|C = negative) \qquad \text{(B.5)}$$

The conditional probability for each word or feature is computed separately and combined in the calculation. In most cases, the independence assumption does not hold true. The accuracy of the NB classifier has been shown to be reasonable, despite the assumption of feature independence.

The conditional probability values for each word will be small in a large collection and the product of these probabilities may cause an underflow error. Therefore, typically the sum of the logs of the conditional probabilities is used instead of the product. The references below have more on probability and specifically Bayesian classification.

1. *Pattern Classification* by Richard O. Duda, Peter E. Hart, and David G. Stork, Wiley-Interscience, October 2000.

2. *Introduction to Probability* by Dimitri P. Bertsekas (Author), John N. Tsitsiklis, Athena Scientific, June 2002.

C The Berkeley DB

Open source databases such as MySQL, PostgreSQL, and Apache Derby are familiar to many developers. A lesser known but extremely popular database, the Berkeley DB is available on almost every Linux distribution. Components of the Linux, Apache, MySQL, Perl/PHP/Python (LAMP) stack used in many enterprise information systems depend on the Berkeley DB.

The current version of the Berkeley DB evolved from various Database Manager (Dbm) implementations in early versions of UNIX. Sleepycat software (acquired by Oracle in 2006) was formed in 1996 to provide commercial support and implement additional features. With an estimated 200 million copies deployed worldwide, the Berkeley DB is possibly the most popular open source database. It is available under a dual license.

The original version of Berkeley DB was written in C with bindings in many other languages. Berkeley DB has a limited set of features compared to a traditional relational database such as MySQL or Oracle. Often, a smaller set of database features may be sufficient for an application. In such cases, the additional unused features may add to higher maintenance costs, lower performance, and greater storage requirements.

Most Linux distributions include the two libraries - `libdb-*.*` and `libdb-cxx-*.*` (the * represents the version number) in the `/usr/lib` directory. These two libraries along with header files in `/usr/include` provide the C API for the Berkeley DB. This section will focus on the more recent Java Edition (JE) of the Berkeley DB that was introduced in response to demand for a purely Java implementation. Note, databases written using the C API cannot be read from the JE and vice versa. Following are the main features of the Berkeley DB, Java Edition -

- The data model provided is in the form of a persistent hash map and keys provide access to object data. The database is maintained on a file system with support for concurrent access and transactions.

- Access to data is NOT provided through SQL, instead Java method calls through an API return objects. The code to access data is embedded within an application and database calls are made similar to library function calls.

- Data is portable across platforms, i.e. different endian systems are transparent to the database application.

- The JE supports multi-threaded applications with record level locking

Other features include support for secondary indices, foreign keys, log file management, backup and restore utilities, and APIs to access the database using either the Java collections interface or Plain Old Java Objects.

Installation

Download the tar file for the recent version of Berkeley DB Java Edition. The size of version 3.0.12 is roughly 20 megabytes, which includes the source, test code, and documentation. The jar file (lib/je.jar) alone is about 1 megabyte and is the only file needed to use the JE. Once you have added the jar file to your classpath, you can begin using the JE classes and methods. The word *database* in the Berkeley DB context is equivalent to a table in a relational database. A collection of Berkeley databases is referred to as a *database environment*. It is merely a location on the file system where database information and log files are maintained.

Usage

To begin, instantiate an `Environment` object with two parameters - a `File` object pointing to the file system location where the database files will be maintained and an `EnvironmentConfig` object.

```
EnvironmentConfig econfig = new EnvironmentConfig();
econfig.setAllowCreate(true);
Environment env = new Environment(
  new File("/opt/bdb"), econfig);
```

The `EnvironmentConfig` class has setter methods to specify whether transactions will be used or if the databases are read only. Here, a new environment is permitted to be created, if it does not already exist. The application must have appropriate permissions to use the specified directory. Notice, there is no userid or password transmitted to a server to check for authentication. Instead, we rely on the underlying operating system read/write permissions assigned to the directory for the database environment.

Secondly, no space is allocated or formatted when an environment is created. The developer must specify a directory location that has sufficient space to hold the log files and the databases. You can create multiple environment handles for different directories in your file system. A database exception is thrown if you have insufficient permission to use the environment directory or if the directory does not exist. You can use the environment handle for administrative tasks to rename a database, remove a database, or fetch a list of database names that exist in the current environment.

Linux developers using the C version of the Berkeley DB will be familiar with the creation of an environment structure that is associated with a directory. While the C version offers multiple data access methods, JE uses the Btree method alone. The creation of a database associated with an environment is also similar. A set of predefined flags for the environment and database are used for configuration.

Create a Database

Next, we create a database handle. First a database configuration object is created and passed to the database constructor along with the name of the database.

```
DatabaseConfig dbconfig = new DatabaseConfig();
dbconfig.setAllowCreate(true);
Database db = env.openDatabase(
  null, dbname, dbconfig);
```

The `DatabaseConfig` class has setter methods to specify database specific options such as whether the database is read only or if duplicate keys should be allowed. The `openDatabase` method accepts three parameters - a transaction reference, the database name, and the database configuration object and returns a database handle. Create a transaction object if you need the atomicity of database operations using the `Transaction` class and `TransactionConfig` class. A null in the `openDatabase` method implies an auto-commit and may leave the database in an inconsistent state if you require either the success of a set of database operations or a failure when any one of the set of operations fails. The `dbname` parameter is a string representing the name of the database.

Recall, the database is the equivalent of a table in a relational database with some differences. A Berkeley DB is conceptually equivalent to a two column (key and data) table. We also do not specify the contents of the two columns in a schema. The column specifications are maintained external to the database.

Load a Database

We can populate the database using keys and objects. A key can be a `String` or any other type of object that identifies one or more records and a record contains a single object. Both the key and object are wrapped using `DatabaseEntry` class instances before storage in the database. There is no restriction that a single database contain objects of one particular class alone. However, maintenance will be simpler, if individual databases are created for objects of a particular class. Consider, the `Employee` and `EmployeeBinding` classes shown below, for brevity the constructor, headers, and getter/setter methods are not shown.

```
public class Employee {
   String name;
   double salary;
   long ssno;
   // add constructor and getter/setter methods
}

final class EmployeeBinding extends TupleBinding {
   public void objectToEntry (Object o, TupleOutput to) {
     Employee employee = (Employee) o;
     to.writeString( employee.getName() );
     to.writeLong( employee.getSsno() );
     to.writeDouble( employee.getSalary() );
   }
   public Object entryToObject (TupleInput ti) {
     Employee employee = new Employee();
```

```
    employee.setName(ti.readString() );
    employee.setSsno(ti.readLong() );
    employee.setSalary(ti.readDouble() );
    return (employee);
  }
}
```

Consider an *Employee* database that contains three columns - a *name*, *social security number*, and *salary*. Create an `Employee` class as shown above to generate `Employee` instances that will be stored in the database. The purpose of the `EmployeeBinding` class is to convert `Employee` objects to byte arrays and create `Employee` objects from byte arrays (see Figure C.1). Database methods work with byte arrays and are not aware of the type of objects being stored or retrieved.

Figure C.1: Store/Retrieve Objects in JE

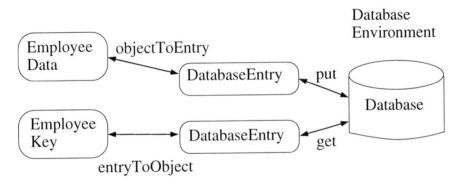

The `EmployeeBinding` class extends the abstract `TupleBinding` class and implements two methods - `objectToEntry` and `entryToObject`. Both methods are called indirectly through `EntryBinding` interface methods that accept `DatabaseEntry` objects. Inherited `TupleBinding` methods perform the conversion of `DatabaseEntry` objects to/from `TupleInput` and `TupleOutput` objects.

The first method `objectToEntry` accepts an object and a `TupleOutput` object and returns the `TupleOutput` object populated with fields from the passed object. The order in which the output object is populated is important when the object is fetched from the database. Notice, the `entryToObject` method reads the object data in the

411

same order that it was written to the database. We can store an `Employee` object in the database with its associated key as follows -

```
Employee employee = new Employee();
// populate the employee object
DatabaseEntry dbKey = new DatabaseEntry();
LongBinding.longToEntry(employee.getSsno(), dbKey);
DatabaseEntry dbValue = new DatabaseEntry();
EmployeeBinding binding = new EmployeeBinding();
binding.objectToEntry(employee, dbValue);
db.put(null, dbKey, dbValue);
```

The social security number of the employee is the key for the `Employee` object. Convert the number to a `DatabaseEntry` object using the `longToEntry` method of the `LongBinding` class. The `Employee` object is converted to a `DatabaseEntry` object using the `objectToEntry` method of the `EmployeeBinding` class.

The Database `put` method will store the `Employee` object and associate the object with the passed key. Since we are not using transactions, the first parameter is null. The `put` method returns an `OperationStatus` code that can be checked for success or failure of the operation. An error code will be returned if the operation was not successful. If an `Employee` object exists with the same key and the duplicates allowed flag is true, then the existing `Employee` object will be overwritten. Use the `putNoOverwrite` method to prevent an existing Employee object from being overwritten.

Retrieve an Object

You can use the same key to fetch the employee object as shown below. The database `get` method accepts the key and a blank uninitialized `DatabaseEntry` object, `dbValue` to fetch the matching employee object. The `LockMode` specifies how locks will be acquired during the read operation. The default `LockMode` allows for concurrent database read operations.

```
DatabaseEntry dbKey = new DatabaseEntry();
LongBinding.longToEntry(999999999, dbKey);
DatabaseEntry dbValue = new DatabaseEntry();
db.get(null, dbKey, dbValue, LockMode.DEFAULT);
EmployeeBinding binding = new EmployeeBinding();
```

```
Employee employee = binding.entryToObject(dbValue);
```

An `Employee` object is returned from the `entryToObject` method that is part of the `EmployeeBinding` class. Exception and error handling code has been omitted for the sake of brevity in the above examples.

Cursors

More than one object may match a key, if duplicates are allowed in a database. A single key typically fetches a single object, but with a cursor you can iterate over all objects in a database. A cursor can also be used to fetch objects with identical keys in a database that allows duplicates.

```
Cursor cursor = db.openCursor(null, null);
DatabaseEntry dbKey = new DatabaseEntry();
StringBinding.stringToEntry(key, dbKey);
DatabaseEntry dbValue = new DatabaseEntry();
OperationStatus ostat = cursor.getSearchKey(
dbKey, dbValue, LockMode.DEFAULT);
while (ostat == OperationStatus.SUCCESS) {
  // add the object in dbValue to a list
  dbValue = new DatabaseEntry();
  ostat = cursor.getNextDup(
    dbKey, dbValue, LockMode.DEFAULT);
}
cursor.close();
```

The `openCursor` method takes two parameters - a `transaction` and a `CursorConfig`. When the `CursorConfig` object is null, default parameters that are sufficient for most cases are used. The `getSearchKey` method of cursor finds the first matching object with the assigned key. The `getNextDup` method will iteratively fetch objects that contain the same key. Cursor search methods also accept partial keys. Set the search key to "Jo" to search for all employees whose names start with "Jo".

`Employee` objects are typically retrieved in lexical order unless a custom `Comparator` was created for the database. A custom `Comparator` implements the `Comparator` interface that contains a `compare` method which accepts two objects and returns an integer. The cursor must be closed after a list of objects have been fetched to avoid an exception, when the database is closed. Cursor methods can start at the first or last database object and traverse forwards or backwards. A `SecondaryCursor` class which works almost identically is used to browse a database with a secondary key.

Transactions

At first, the Berkeley DB appears to be a rudimentary persistent hash to fetch/store objects. But, there are many other features to handle transactions, manage memory allocation, optimize disk I/O, recovery mechanisms, locking methods for concurrency, and various administration tools.

Most databases offer transactions to maintain data integrity and protect the database from an application or system failure. The Berkeley DB has an optional transaction feature that can be turned on when the environment is opened. The default is an auto-commit which essentially commits after every modify database operation. A transaction enabled database allows you to group a set of database operations into a transaction and commit the collection of operations, only when all the operations have been completed.

Transactions implemented in the Berkeley DB offer the traditional Atomicity, Consistency, Isolation, and Durability (ACID) support. An application must explicitly specify transaction support with a transaction reference when the database environment and individual databases are opened. The committ or abort method should be called after the completion of the transaction. Applications that run in multiple threads must be coded for the possibility of deadlocks. This is true for non-transactional applications as well. The Berkeley DB offers methods with timers to limit the time a lock will be held and also an option to read uncommitted (dirty) data. When a lock times out, a deadlock exception is thrown and the application must release current resources and either restart or abort the transaction. Set a fixed number of tries before giving up a particular transaction.

A concurrent application with transactions must be written carefully to avoid deadlock and other timing problems. More information on transactions is included in the Transaction User Guide provided in the Berkeley DB documentation.

Administration

The maintenance of a schema that describes columns, tables, views, etc. is not present in the Berkeley DB. This is implicitly handled by the application itself. Two other administration tasks are backup and recovery of the database. For a backup operation, copy all files from the database environment to a safe storage location and similarly for a recovery operation restore files from the same location to the current database environment.

You can browse the database environment directory after storing a few objects. You should see database log files like `00000001.jdb` (an eight digit hex number followed by a `jdb` suffix) and a lock file `je.lck`. When one log file is full, a new log file with the next hex number is created. All writes are append only and existing log records are not modified or deleted. When an update or a delete operation is completed, the log record for the new object is appended to a log file. The old log record becomes obsolete and is marked for deletion. Note, the log files created by the JE are not compatible with log files generated with the C version of the Berkeley DB.

Performance

The log file design to maintain the database offers several advantages over a traditional relational database. There is no penalty in fetching and storing variable length objects since objects are not stored in fixed length pages. All writes to the database are performed sequentially and therefore the time for disk I/O should be minimal. Separate log and database files are not maintained, instead consolidated log files contain database information as well.

Each log file has a pre-configured limit of 10 megabytes that can be altered. Even with the default limit, a database can be scaled to many terabytes. Log files also have a `minUtilization` parameter that specifies minimum disk utilization percentage within a log file. The default is 50% which means that half the space allocated for the file will be vacant. This percentage can be increased up to 90% if few or no future database modifications are expected.

Index

Index

Bibliography

[Abiteboul]   http://www2003.org/cdrom/papers/refereed/p007/
p7-abiteboul.html, S. Abiteboul, M. Preda, G. Cobena, *Adaptive On-Line Page Importance Computation*, World Wide Web Conference, 2003.

[Atom]   http://www.ietf.org/html.charters/atompub-charter.html, The ATOM Protocol.

[Brill]   http://research.microsoft.com/~brill/, The Brill Tagger.

[Broder]   Broder at al., *Graph Structure in the Web*, Proceedings of the Ninth World Wide Web Conference, 2000.

[Brown]   Kucera H. and W. Nelson Francis W. N., Computational Analysis of Present-Day American English, Brown University Press, Providence, RI, 1967.

[Burstein]   Burstein, J. and Shemis M.D., *Automated Essay Scoring: A Cross-Disciplinary Perspective*, Lawrence Erlbaum, 2002.

[Carmi]   http://www.pnas.org/cgi/content/abstract/104/27/11150, Shai Carmi, Shlomo Havlin, Scott Kirkpatrick, Yuval Shavitt, and Eran Shir, *A model of Internet topology using k-shell decomposition*, Proceedings of the National Academy of Sciences of USA, June 2007.

[Cluster]   http://clusty.com, http://www.webclust.com, Cluster-based Web Search Engines.

[Digest]   http://java.sun.com/j2se/1.4.2/docs/api/java/security/
MessageDigest.html, Java classes to create a message digest.

[Donato]   http://delis.upb.de/specials/paris05/paper/ECCS05_Donato.
              pdf, Donato, D., Leonardi, S., Millozzi, S., and Tsaparas, P., *Mining*
              the inner structure of the Web graph, Proceedings of the Eighth
              International Workshop on the Web and Databases (WebDB). pp
              145–150, 2005.

[Federalist] http://www.foundingfathers.info/federalistpapers/, The Feder-
              alist Papers.

[GATE]   http://www.gate.ac.uk, General Architecture for Text Engineering,
              University of Sheffield, UK.

[Genetic]   http://www.geocomputation.org/2000/GC015/Gc015.htm,   Using
              Genetic Algorithms in Clustering Problems.

[Google]   http://desktop.google.com/linux/, Google's Desktop Search En-
              gine.

[Kmeans]   http://www-2.cs.cmu.edu/awm/tutorials/kmeans.html, K-Means
              Algorithm Tutorial.

[LDA]   http://en.wikipedia.org/wiki/Latent_Dirichlet_Allocation,
              The Latent Dirichlet Allocation Model.

[Lawrence]   S. Lawrence and C.L. Giles, *Accessibility of Information on the Web*,
              Nature, July 1999.

[Manning]   C.D. Manning and H. Schütze, *Foundations of Statistical Natural Lan-*
              guage Processing, MIT Press, Cambridge, MA, 1999.

[Mikheev]   A. Mikheev, *Periods, capitalized words, etc.*, Computational Linguistics,
              Volume 28, Issue 3 September 2002).

[Mime]   http://www.boutell.com/newfaq/definitions/mimetype.html,
              List of Mime Types.

428

[Marlow]   `http://www.danah.org/papers/Hypertext2006.pdf`, C. Marlow, Berkeley, M. Naaman, D. Boyd, M. Davis, *HT06, tagging paper, taxonomy, Flickr, academic article, to read*, Proceedings of the seventeenth conference on Hypertext and hypermedia table of contents, 2006.

[Omnifind]   `http://omnifind.ibm.yahoo.net/productinfo.php`, IBM's and Yahoo!'s Search Engine.

[Pajek]   `htpp://vlado.fmf.uni-lj.si/pub/networks/pajek/`, Pajek Network Analysis Tool.

[PangLee]   B. Pang and L. Lee, *A Sentimental Education: Sentiment Analysis Using Subjectivity Summarization Based on Minimum Cuts*, Proceedings of ACL, pp 271–278, 2004.

[Pdfbox]   `http://www.pdfbox.org/`, PDFBox Library to parse PDF files.

[Pierce]   John R. Pierce, *An Introduction to Information Theory*, Dover Publications, New York, 1980.

[Porter]   `http://www.tartarus.org/~martin/PorterStemmer/`, The Porter Stemming Algorithm.

[Querylog]   `http://www.clickz.com/showPage.html?page=3611296` Patricia Seybold Group Report, 2006.

[RSS]   `http://www.whatisrss.com/`, The RSS Protocol.

[Salton]   `http://www-faculty.cs.uiuc.edu/~kcchang/classes/cs511-recent/other_papers/p613-salton.pdf`, G. Salton, A. Wong, and C.S. Yang, *A Vector Space Model for Automatic Indexing*, Communications of the ACM, Vol.18, No.11, 1975.

[Shivakumar]   `http://citeseer.ist.psu.edu/shivakumar95scam.html`, N. Shivakumar and H'ector Garc'ia-Molina. *SCAM: A copy detection mechanism for digital documents.* Proceedings of the 2nd International Conference in Theory and Practice of Digital Libraries (DL'95), Austin, Texas, June 1995.

Bibliography

[Silverstein] http://www.cs.ucsb.edu/~almeroth/classes/tech-soc/
2005-Winter/papers/analysis.pdf, C. Silverstein, M. Henzinger, H. Marais, M. Moricz: *Analysis of a Very Large Web Search Engine Query Log,* ACM SIGIR Forum, Volume 33 , Issue 1, pp 6 - 12, Fall 1999.

[SpellError] http://en.wikipedia.org/wiki/Wikipedia:Lists_of_common_
misspellings, List of Common Spelling Errors.

[Spertus] http://people.mills.edu/spertus/Smokey/smokey.pdf, E. Spertus, *Smokey: Automatic Recognition of Hostile Messages,* Proceedings of Innovative Applications of Artificial Intelligence (IAAI), pp 1058 - 1065, 1997.

[Unicode] http://www.unicode.org, Unicode Standard.

[Viterbi] http://www.comp.leeds.ac.uk/roger/HiddenMarkovModels/html_
dev/viterbi_algorithm/s1_pg1.html, The Viterbi Algorithm.

[Wiebe] http://citeseer.ist.psu.edu/wiebe00learning.html, J. Wiebe, *Learning subjective adjectives from corpora,* Proceedings of the 17th National Conference on Artificial Intelligence, 2000.

Breinigsville, PA USA
31 October 2010
248379BV00003B/30/P